Wing-And-Wing; Or, Le Feu-Follet.
by J. Fenimore Cooper

WING-AND-WING;

OR,

LE FEU-FOLLET.

A TALE.

By J. FENIMORE COOPER.

"Know,
Without star or angel for their guide,
who worship God shall find him."
YOUNG.

COMPLETE IN ONE VOLUME.

NEW YORK:
PUBLISHED BY HURD AND HOUGHTON.
Cambridge: Riverside Press.
1871.

WING-AND-WING.

PREFACE.

THE question, of how much of the following legend is severely true, and how much fiction, is left in doubt, with the express intention, that such historians, as having nothing useful to do, may employ their time in drawing the lines for their own amusement.

As to the scene chosen for this tale, no apology is deemed necessary. To invent excuses for carrying a man, either physically or in the imagination, into a sea like the Mediterranean, and on a coast like that of Italy, would be an affectation of which we have no idea of being guilty. It is true—nay, it is probable—that we may render the execution unequal to the design, but there can be no great harm in nobly daring, except to him who is injured by his own failure. We hope that they who have ever beheld the scenes we have faintly and so imperfectly described, will pardon our defects, for the good we have intended them; and that those who have never been so fortunate, will find even our tame pictures so much superior to the realities they have elsewhere witnessed, as to fancy we have succeeded.

Of Raoul Yvard Ghita Caraccioli, and the Little Folly, we have no more to say than is to be found in the body of the work. As Sancho told the knight, they

3)

who gave us the facts connected with all three—w
class a vessel among animals—said they were so certain, that we might safely swear they were absolutely
true.   If we are in error, it is a misfortune we share
in common with honest Panza, and that, too, on a
subject about equal, in moment, to the one in which
he was misled.

After all, the world hears little, and knows less, of
the infinity of details that make up the sum of the
incidents of the sea.   Historians glean a few prominent circumstances, connected perhaps with battles,
treaties, shipwrecks, or chases, and the rest is left
a blank to the great bulk of the human race.   It has
been well said, that the life of every man, if simply
and clearly related, would be found to contain a fund
of useful and entertaining information ; and it is
equally true, that the day of every ship would furnish something of interest to relate, could the dry
records of the log-book be given in the graphic language of observation and capacity.   A ship, alone,
in the solitude of the ocean, is an object for reflection,
and a source of poetical, as well as of moral feeling ;
and as we seldom tire of writing about her, we have
more than a sympathetic desire, that they who do us
the honour to form a sort of literary *clientelle,* will
never tire of reading.

Our chief concern, on the present occasion, is on
the subject of the contrast we have attempted to
draw between profound belief and light-hearted infidelity   We think both pictures true to the periods

and the respective countries, and we have endeavoured to draw both with due relief, and totally without
exaggeration. That strong natural sympathies can
exist between those who are widely separated on such
a subject, every day's experience proves; and that
some are to be found in whom principle is stronger
than even the most insinuating and deceptive of all
our passions, we not only hope, but trustfully believe.
We have endeavoured to assign the higher and most
enduring quality to that portion of the race, in which
we are persuaded it is the most likely to be found.

This is the seventh sea-tale we have ventured to
offer to the public. When the first was written, our
friends confidently predicted its failure, on account
of the meagreness of the subject, as well as of its
disagreeable accompaniments. Not only did that pre-
diction prove untrue, as to our own humble effort,
but the public taste has lasted sufficiently long to
receive, from other quarters, a very respectable pro-
geny of that parent of this class of writing. We
only hope that, in the present instance, there may be
found a sufficient family resemblance, to allow of this
particular bantling to pass in the crowd, as one of a
numerous family.

LE FEU-FOLLET.

CHAPTER I.

" Filled with the face of heaven, which from afar,
Comes down upon the waters; all its hues,
From the rich sunset to the rising star,
Their magical variety diffuse :
And now they change ; a paler shadow strews
Its mantle o'er the mountains ; parting day
Dies like the dolphin, whom each pang imbues
With a new colour as it gasps away,
The last still loveliest, till — 'tis gone — and all is grey."
Childe Harold

THE charms of the Tyrrhenian Sea have been sung since
the days of Homer. That the Mediterranean, generally,
and its beautiful boundaries of Alps and Apennines, with its
deeply indented and irregular shores, forms the most delightful
region of the known earth, in all that relates to climate,
productions, and physical formation, will be readily enough
conceded by the traveller. The countries that border on
this midland water, with their promontories buttressing a
mimic ocean—their mountain-sides teeming with the pictu
resque of human life — their heights crowned with watch-
towers—their rocky shelves consecrated by hermitages, and
their unrivalled sheet dotted with sails, rigged, as it might be,
expressly to produce effect in a picture, form a sort of world
apart, that is replete with delights to all who have the happy
fortune to feel charms, which not only fascinate the beholder,
but which linger in the memories of the absent like visions
of a glorious past.

Our present business is with this fragment of a creation
that is so eminently beautiful, even in its worst aspects, but

which is so often marred by the passions of man, in its best.
While all admit how much nature has done for the Mediterranean, none will deny that, until quite recently, it has been
the scene of more ruthless violence, and of deeper personal
wrongs, perhaps, than any other portion of the globe. With
different races, more widely separated by destinies, than even
by origin, habits and religion, occupying its northern and
southern shores, the outwork, as it might be, of Christianity
and Mohammedanism, and of an antiquity that defies history,
the bosom of this blue expanse has mirrored more violence,
has witnessed more scenes of slaughter, and heard more
shouts of victory, between the days of Agamemnon and
Nelson, than all the rest of the dominions of Neptune together.
Nature and the passions have united to render it like the
human countenance, which conceals by its smiles and god-
like expression, the furnace that so often glows within the
heart, and the volcano that consumes our happiness. For
centuries, the Turk and the Moor rendered it unsafe for the
European to navigate these smiling coasts; and when the
barbarian's power temporarily ceased, it was merely to give
place to the struggles of those who drove him from the
arena by their larger resources.

The circumstances which rendered the period that occurred
between the years 1790 and 1815, the most eventful of
modern times, are familiar to all; though the incidents which
chequered that memorable quarter of a century, have already
passed into history. All the elements of strife that then
agitated the world, appear now to have subsided as completely as if they owed their existence to a remote age; and
living men recall the events of their youth, as they regard
the recorded incidents of other centuries. Then, each month
brought its defeat, or its victory; its account of a government overturned, or of a province conquered. The world
was agitated like men in a tumult. On that epoch the timid
look back with wonder; the young, with doubt; and the
restless, with envy.

The years 1798 and 1799 were two of the most memorable of this ever-memorable period; and to that stirring and
teeming season we must carry the mind of the reader, in
order to place it in the midst of the scenes it is our object to
portray.

Towards the close of a fine day in the month of August, a light fairy-like craft was fanning her way, before a gentle westerly air, into what is called the Canal of Piombino, steering easterly. The rigs of the Mediterranean are proverbial for their picturesque beauty and quaintness, embracing the xebeque, the felucca, the polacre, and the bombarda, or ketch; all unknown, or nearly so, to our own seas; and occasionally the lugger. The latter, a species of craft, however, much less common in the waters of Italy than in the Bay of Biscay and the British Channel, was the construction of the vessel in question; a circumstance that the mariners who eyed her from the shores of Elba, deemed indicative of mischief. A three-masted lugger, that spread a wide breadth of canvass, with a low, dark hull, relieved by a single and almost imperceptible line of red beneath her channels, and a waist so deep that nothing was visible above it but the hat of some mariner, taller than common, was considered a suspicious vessel, and not even a fisherman would have ventured out within reach of a shot, so long as her character was unknown. Privateers, or corsairs, as it was the fashion to term them, (and the name, with even its English signification, was often merited by their acts,) not unfrequently glided down that coast; and it was sometimes dangerous for those who belonged to friendly nations to meet them, in moments when the plunder that a relic of barbarism still legalizes, had failed.

The lugger was actually of about one hundred and fifty tons admeasurement; but her dark paint, and low hull, gave her an appearance of being much smaller than she really was; still, the spread of her canvass, as she came down before the wind wing-and-wing, as seamen term it, or with a sail fanning like the heavy pinions of a sea-fowl, on each side, betrayed her pursuits; and, as has been intimated, the mariners on the shore, who watched her movements, shook their heads in distrust, as they communed among themselves, in very indifferent Italian, concerning her destination and object. This observation, with its accompanying discourse, occurred on the rocky bluff above the town of Porto Ferrajo, in the Island of Elba, a spot that has since become so renowned as the capital of the mimic dominion of Napoleon. Indeed, the very dwelling which was subsequently used by

the fallen emperor as a palace, stood within a hundred yards
of the speakers, looking out towards the entrance of the
canal, and the mountains of Tuscany ; or rather, of the
little principality of Piombino, the system of merging the
smaller in the larger states of Europe not having yet been
brought into extensive operation. This house, a building
of the size of a better sort of country residence of our own,
was then, as now, occupied by the Florentine governor of
the Tuscan portion of the island.   It stands on the extremity
of a low rocky promontory that forms the western ramparts
of the deep extensive bay, on the side of which, ensconced
behind a very convenient curvature of the rocks, which here
incline westward in the form of a hook, lies the small port,
completely concealed from the sea, as if in dread of visits
like those which might be expected from craft resembling
the suspicious stranger. This little port, not as large in
itself as a modern dock in places like London or Liverpool,
was sufficiently protected against any probable dangers, by
suitable batteries ; and as for the elements, a vessel laid upon
a shelf in a closet would be scarcely more secure.   In this
domestic little basin, which, with the exception of a narrow
entrance was completely surrounded by buildings, lay a
few feluccas, that traded between the island and the adjacent main, and a solitary Austrian ship, which had come
from the head of the Adriatic, in quest of iron, as it was
pretended, but as much to assume the appearance of trade
with the Italian dependency, as with any other purpose.
    At the moment of which we are writing, however, but a
dozen living beings were visible in or about all these craft.
The intelligence that a strange lugger, resembling the one
described, was in the offing, had drawn nearly all the mariners ashore ; and most of the habitués of the port had followed them up the broad steps of the crooked streets which
led to the heights behind the town ; or to the rocky elevation that overlooks the sea from north-east to west.   The
approach of the lugger had produced some such effect on the
mariners of this unsophisticated and little-frequented port,
as that of the hawk is known to excite among the timid
tenants of the barn-yard.   The rig of the stranger, in itself
a suspicious circumstance, had been noted two hours before,
ny one or two old coasters, who habitually passed their idle

moments on the heights, examining the signs of the weather, and indulging in gossip; and their conjectures had drawn to the Porto Ferrajo mall some twenty men, who fancied themselves, or who actually were, *cognoscenti* in matters of the sea. When, however, the low, long, dark hull, which upheld such wide sheets of canvass, became fairly visible, the omens thickened, rumours spread, and hundreds collected on the spot, which, in Manhattanese parlance, would probably have been called a battery. Nor would the name have been altogether inappropriate, as a small battery was established there, and that, too, in a position which would easily throw a shot two-thirds of a league, into the offing; or about the distance that the stranger was now from the shore.

Tommaso Tonti was the oldest mariner of Elba, and luckily, being a sober, and usually a discreet man, he was the oracle of the island, in most things that related to the sea. As each citizen, wine-dealer, grocer, innkeeper, or worker in iron, came upon the height, he incontinently inquired for Tonti, or 'Maso, as he was generally called; and getting the bearings and distance of the grey-headed old seaman, he invariably made his way to his side, until a group of some two hundred men, women and children, had clustered near the person of the *pilota*, as the· faithful gather about a favourite expounder of the law, in moments of religious excitement. It was worthy of remark, too, with how much consideration this little crowd of gentle Italians treated their aged seaman, on this occasion; none bawling out their questions, and all using the greatest care not to get in front of his person, lest they might intercept his means of observation. Five or six old sailors, like himself, were close at his side : these, it is true, did not hesitate to speak as became their experience. But Tonti had obtained no small part of his reputation by exercising great moderation in delivering his oracles, and, perhaps, by seeming to know more than he actually revealed. He was reserved, therefore; and while his brethren of the sea ventured on sundry conflicting opinions concerning the character of the stranger, and a hundred idle conjectures had flown from mouth to mouth, among the landsmen and females, not a syllable that could commit the old man, had escaped his lips. He let the others talk at will; as for himself, it suited his habits, and possibly his difficulties in deciding, to main.a.n a grave and portentous silence.

We have spoken of females : as a matter of course, an event like this, in a town of some three or four thousand souls, would be likely to draw a due proportion of the gentler sex to the heights. Most of them contrived to get as near as possible to the aged seaman, in order to obtain the first intelligence, that it might be the sooner circulated ; but, it would seem, that among the younger of these, there was also a sort of oracle of their own, about whose person gathered a dozen of the prettiest girls ; either anxious to hear what Ghita might have to say in the premises, or, perhaps, influenced by the pride and modesty of their sex and condition, which taught them to maintain a little more reserve than was necessary to the less refined portion of their companions. In speaking of condition, however, the word must be understood with an exceedingly limited meaning. Porto Ferrajo had but two classes of society, the trades-people and the labourers ; although there were, perhaps, a dozen exceptions, in the persons of a few humble functionaries of the government, an avvacato, a medico, and a few priests. The governor of the island was a Tuscan of rank, but he seldom honoured the place with his presence, and his deputy was a professional man, a native of the town, whose original position was too well known to allow him to give himself airs on the spot where he was born. Ghita's companions, then, were daughters of shopkeepers, and persons of that class, who, having been taught to read, and occasionally going to Leghorn, beside being admitted by the deputy to the presence of his housekeeper, had got to regard themselves as a little elevated above the more vulgar curiosity of the less culti-vated girls of the port. Ghita herself, however, owed her ascendency to her qualities, rather than to the adventitious advantage of being a grocer's or an inkeeper's daughter, her origin being unknown to most of those around her, as indeed was her family name. She had been landed six weeks before, and left by one who passed for her father, at the inn of Cristoforo Dovi, as a boarder, and had acquired all her influence, as so many reach notoriety in our own simple society, by the distinction of having travelled ; aided, some-what, by her strong sense, great decision of character, per feet modesty and propriety of deportment, with a form which was singularly graceful and feminine, and a face, that, while it could scarcely be called beautiful, was, in the highest degree, winning and attractive. No one thought of asking her family name; and she never appeared to deem it necessary to mention it. Ghita was sufficient; it was familiar to every one; and, although there were two or three others of the same appellation, in Porto Ferrajo, this, by common consent, got to be *the* Ghita, within a week after she had landed.

Ghita, it was known, had travelled, for she had publicly reached Elba in a felucca, coming, as was said, from the Neapolitan states. If this were true, she was probably the only person of her sex in the town, who had ever seen Vesuvius, or planted her eyes on the wonders of a part of Italy that has a reputation second only to that of Rome. Of course, if any girl in Porto Ferrajo could imagine the character of the stranger, it must be Ghita; and it was on this supposition that she had unwittingly, and, if the truth must be owned, unwillingly, collected around her a *cliem lle* of at least a dozen girls of her own age, and apparently of her own class. The latter, however, felt no necessity for the reserve maintained by the curious who pressed near 'Maso; for, while they respected their guest and friend, and would rather listen to her surmises than those of any other person, they had such a prompting desire to hear their own voices, that not a minute escaped without a question, or a conjecture, both volubly and quite audibly expressed. The interjections, too, were somewhat numerous, as the guesses were crude and absurd. One said it was a vessel with despatches from Livorno, possibly with " His Eccellenza" on board; but she was reminded that Leghorn lay to the north, and not to the west. Another thought it was a cargo of priests, going from Corsica to Rome; but she was told that priests were not in sufficient favour, just then, in France, to get a vessel so obviously superior to the ordinary craft of the Mediterranean, to carry them about. While a third, more imaginative than either, ventured to doubt whether it was a vessel at all; deceptive appearances of this sort not being of rare occurrence, and usually taking the aspect of something out of the ordinary way.

" *Si*," said Annina, " but that would be a miracle, Maria

2

and why should we have a miracle, now that Lent and most of the holidays are past? *I* believe it is a real vessel."

The others laughed, and, after a good deal of eager chattering on the subject, it was quite generally admitted that the stranger was a *bonâ fide* craft, of some species or another, though all agreed she was not a felucca, a bombarda, or a sparanara. All this time Ghita was thoughtful and silent; quite as much so, indeed, as Tommaso himself, though from a very different motive. Notwithstanding all the gossip, and the many ludicrous opinions of her companions, her eyes scarcely turned an instant from the lugger, on which they seemed to be riveted by a sort of fascination. Had there been one, there, sufficiently unoccupied to observe this interesting girl, he might have been struck with the varying expression of a countenance that was teeming with sensibility, and which too often reflected the passing emotions of its mistress's mind. Now an expression of anxiety, and even of alarm, would have been detected by such an observer, if acute enough to separate these emotions, in the liveliness of sentiment, from the more vulgar feelings of her companions; and now, something like gleamings of delight and happiness flashed across her eloquent countenance. The colour came and went often; and there was an instant, during which the lugger varied her course, hauling to the wind, and then falling off again, like a dolphin at its sports, when the radiance of the pleasure that glowed about her soft blue eyes, rendered the girl perfectly beautiful. But none of these passing expressions were noted by the garrulous group around the stranger female, who was left very much to the indulgence of the impulses that gave them birth, unquestioned, and altogether unsuspected.

Although the cluster of girls had, with feminine sensitiveness, gathered a little apart from the general crowd, there were but a few yards between the spot where it stood, and that occupied by 'Maso; so that when the latter spoke, an attentive listener among the former might hear his words. This was an office that Tonti did not choose to undertake, however, until he was questioned by the podestà, Vito Viti, who now appeared on the hill in person, puffing like a whale that rises to breathe, from the vigour of his ascent.

"What dost thou make of her, good 'Maso?" demanded

the magistrate, after he had examined the stranger himself some time in silence, feeling authorized in virtue of his office, to question whom he pleased.

"Signore, it is a lugger;" was the brief, and, certainly, the accurate reply.

"Ay, a lugger; we all understand that, neighbour Tonti but what sort of a lugger? There are felucca-luggers, and polacre-luggers, and bombarda-luggers, and all sorts of luggers; which sort of lugger is this?"

"Signor Podestà, this is not the language of the port. We call a felucca, a felucca; a bombarda, a bombarda; a polacre, a polacre; and a lugger, a lugger. This is, therefore, a lugger."

'Maso spoke authoritatively, for he felt that he was now not out of his depth, and it was grateful to him to let the public know how much better he understood all these matters than a magistrate. On the other hand, the podestà was nettled, and disappointed into the bargain, for he really imagined he was drawing nice distinctions, much as it was his wont to do in legal proceedings; and it was his ambition to be thought to know something of every thing.

"Well, Tonti," answered Signor Viti, in a protecting manner, and with an affable smile, "as this is not an affair that is likely to go to the higher courts at Florence, your explanations may be taken as sufficient, and I have no wish to disturb them—a lugger, is a lugger."

"Si, Signore; that is just what we say in the port. A lugger, is a lugger."

"And yonder strange craft, you maintain, and at need are ready to swear, is a lugger?"

Now 'Maso seeing no necessity for any oath in the affair, and being always somewhat conscientious in such matters, whenever the custom-house officers did not hold the book, was a little startled at this suggestion, and he took another, and a long look at the stranger, before he answered.

"Si, Signore," he replied, after satisfying his mind once more, through his eyes, "I *will* swear that the stranger, yonder, is a lugger."

"And canst thou add, honest Tonti, of what nation? The *nation* is of as much moment, in these troubled times, as the *rig*"

"You say truly, Signor Podestâ; for if an Algerine, or a
Moor, or even a Frenchman, he will be an unwelcome visiter
in the Canal of Elba. There are many different signs about
him, that sometimes make me think he belongs to one people,
and then to another; and I crave your pardon, if I ask a
little leisure, to let him draw nearer, before I give a positive
opinion."

As this request was reasonable, no objection was raised.
The podestâ turned aside, and observing Ghita, who had
visited his niece, and of whose intelligence he entertained
a favourable opinion, he drew nearer to the girl, determined
to lose a moment in dignified trifling.

"Honest 'Maso, poor fellow, is sadly puzzled," he observed, smiling benevolently, as if in pity for the pilot's embarrassment; "he wishes to persuade us that the strange craft
yonder is a lugger, though he cannot, himself, say to what
country she belongs!"

"It is a lugger, Signore," returned the girl, drawing a long
breath, as if relieved by hearing the sound of her own voice.

"How! dost thou pretend to be so skilled in vessels, as
to distinguish these particulars at the distance of a league?"

"I do not think it a league, Signore—not more than half
a league; and the distance lessens fast, though the wind is
so light. As for knowing a lugger from a felucca, it is as
easy as to know a house from a church; or one of the
reverend padri, in the streets, from a mariner."

"Ay, so I would have told 'Maso on the spot, had the
obstinate old fellow been inclined to hear me. The distance is just about what you say; and nothing is easier than
to see that the stranger is a lugger. As to the nation?—"

"That may not be so easily told, Signore, unless the vessel show us her flag."

"By San Antonio! thou art right, child; and it is fitting
she should show us her flag. Nothing has a right to approach so near the port of his Imperial and Royal Highness,
that does not show its flag, thereby declaring its honest
purpose, and its nation. My friends, are the guns in the
battery loaded, as usual?"

The answer being in the affirmative, there was a hurried
consultation among some of the principal men in the crowd,
and then the podestâ walked towards the government-house

with an important air. In five minutes soldiers were seen in the batteries, and preparations were made for levelling an eighteen-pounder in the direction of the stranger. Most of the females turned aside, and stopped their ears, the battery being within a hundred yards of the spot where they stood; but Ghita, with a face that was pale, certainly, though with an eye that was steady, and without the least indications of fear, as respected herself, intensely watched every movement. When it was evident the artillerists were about to fire, anxiety induced her to break silence.

"They surely will not aim *at* the lugger!" she exclaimed. "*That* cannot be necessary, Signor Podestà, to make the stranger hoist his flag. Never have I seen *that* done in the south."

"You are unacquainted with our Tuscan bombardiers, Signorina," answered the magistrate, with a bland smile, and an exulting gesture. "It is well for Europe that the grand duchy is so small, since such troops might prove even more troublesome than the French!"

Ghita, however, paid no attention to this touch of provincial pride, but pressing her hands on her heart, she stood like a statue of suspense, while the men in the battery executed their duty. In a minute the match was applied, and the gun was discharged. Though all her companions uttered invocations to the saints, and other exclamations, and some even crouched to the earth in terror, Ghita, the most delicate of any, in appearance, and with more real sensibility than all united expressed in her face, stood firm and erect. The flash and the explosion evidently had no effect on her; not an artillerist among them was less unmoved in frame, at the report, than this slight girl. She even imitated the manner of the soldiers, by turning to watch the flight of the shot, though she clasped her hands as she did so, and appeared to await the result with trembling. The few seconds of suspense were soon past, when the ball was seen to strike the water fully a quarter of a mile astern of the lugger, and to skip along the placid sea for twice that distance further, when it sunk to the bottom by its own gravity.

"Santa Maria be praised!" murmured the girl, a smile half pleasure, half irony, lighting her face, as unconsciously

2 *   2

to herself she spoke, "these Tuscan artillerists are no fatal marksmen!"

"That was most dexterously done, bella Ghita!" exclaimed the magistrate, removing his two hands from his ears; "that was amazingly well aimed! Another such shot as far ahead, with a third fairly between the two, and the stranger will learn to respect the rights of Tuscany. What say'st thou now, honest 'Maso — will this lugger tell us her country, or will she further brave our power?"

"If wise, she will hoist her ensign; and yet I see no signs of preparation for such an act."

Sure enough, the stranger, though quite within effective range of shot from the heights, showed no disposition to gratify the curiosity, or to appease the apprehensions of those in the town. Two or three of her people were visible in her rigging, but even these did not hasten their work, or in any manner seem deranged at the salutation they had just received. After a few minutes, however, the lugger jibed her mainsail, and then hauled up a little, so as to look more towards the head-land, as if disposed to steer for the bay, by doubling the promontory. This movement caused the artillerists to suspend their own, and the lugger had fairly come within a mile of the cliffs, ere she lazily turned aside again, and shaped her course once more in the direction of the entrance of the Canal. This drew another shot, which effectually justified the magistrate's eulogy, for it certainly flew as much ahead of the stranger, as the first had flown astern.

"There, Signore," cried Ghita eagerly, as she turned to the magistrate, "they are about to hoist their ensign, for now they know your wishes. The soldiers surely will not fire again!"

"That would be in the teeth of the law of nations, Signorina, and a blot on Tuscan civilization. Ah! you perceive the artillerists are aware of what you say, and are putting aside their tools. Cospetto! 'tis a thousand pities, too, they couldn't fire the third shot, that you might see it strike the lugger; as yet, you have only beheld their preparations."

"It is enough, Signor Podestà," returned Ghita, smiling, for she could smile now that she saw the soldiers intended no further mischief; "we have all heard of your Elba gunners, and what I *have* seen convinces me of what they can do, when there is occasion. Look, Signore! the lugger is about to satisfy our curiosity."

Sure enough, the stranger saw fit to comply with the usages of nations. It has been said, already, that the lugger was coming down before the wind wing-and-wing, or with a sail expanded to the air on each side of her hull, a disposition of the canvass that gives to the felucca, and to the lugger in particular, the most picturesque of all their graceful attitudes. Unlike the narrow-headed sails that a want of hands has introduced among ourselves, these foreign, we might almost say classical mariners, send forth their long pointed yards aloft, confining the width below by the necessary limits of the sheet, making up for the difference in elevation, by the greater breadth of their canvass. The idea of the felucca's sails, in particular, would seem to have been literally taken from the wing of the large sea-fowl, the shape so nearly corresponding, that, with the canvass spread in the manner just mentioned, one of those light craft has a very close resemblance to the gull or the hawk, as it poises itself in the air, or is swooping down upon its prey. The lugger has less of the beauty that adorns a picture, perhaps, than the strictly latine rig; but it approaches so near it as to be always pleasing to the eye, and, in the particular evolution described, is scarcely less attractive. To the seaman, however, it brings with it an air of greater service, being a mode of carrying canvass that will buffet with the heaviest gales, or the roughest seas, while it appears so pleasant to the eye in the blandest airs, and smoothest water.

The lugger that was now beneath the heights of Elba had three masts, though sails were spread only on the two that were forward. The third mast was stepped on the taffrail; it was small, and carried a little sail, that, in English, is termed a jigger, its principal use being to press the bows of the craft up to the wind, when close hauled, and render her what is termed weatherly. On the present occasion, there could scarcely be said to be anything deserving the name of wind, though Ghita felt her cheek, which was warmed with he rich blood of her country, fanned by an air so gentle, that occasionally it blew aside tresses, that seemed to vie with the floss silk of her native land. Had the natural ringlets been less light, however, so gentle a respiration of the sea air could scarcely have disturbed them. But the lugger had her lightest duck spread — reserving the heavier canvass for the storms — and it opened like the folds of a balloon, even before these gentle impulses ; occasionally collapsing, it is true, as the ground-swell swung the yards to and fro, but, on the whole, standing out and receiving the air, as if guided more by volition than any mechanical power. The effect on the hull was almost magical ; for, notwithstanding the nearly imperceptible force of the propelling power, owing to the lightness and exquisite mould of the craft, it served to urge her through the water at the rate of some three or four knots in the hour ; or quite as fast as an ordinarily active man is apt to walk. Her motion was nearly unobservable to all on board, and might rather be termed gliding than sailing, the ripple under her cut-water not much exceeding that which is made by the finger, as it is moved swiftly through the element ; still the slightest variation of the helm changed her course, and this so easily and gracefully, as to render her deviations and inclinations like those of the duck. In her present situation, too, the jigger, which was brailed, and hung festooned from its light yard, ready for use, should occasion suddenly demand it, added singularly to the smart air which everything wore about this craft, giving her, in the seaman's eyes, that particularly knowing and suspicious look, which had awakened 'Maso's distrust.

The preparations to show the ensign, which had caught the quick and understanding glance of Ghita, and which had not escaped even the duller vision of the artillerists, were made at the outer end of this jigger-yard. A boy had appeared on the taffrail, and he was evidently clearing the ensign-halyards for that purpose. In half a minute, however, he disappeared, and then a flag rose steadily, and by a continued pull, to its station. At first the bunting hung suspended in a line, so as to evade all examination ; but, as if everything on board this light craft were on a scale as airy and buoyant as herself, the folds soon expanded, showing a white field, traversed at right angles with a red cross, and having a union of the same tint in its upper and inner corner

' *Inglese !*'' exclaimed 'Maso, infinitely aided in this conjecture by the sight of the stranger's ensign — " Si, Signore ; it is an Englishman ; I *thought* so, from the first, but as the lugger is not a common rig for vessels of that nation, I did not like to risk anything, by saying it."

" Well, honest Tommaso, it is a happiness to have a mariner as skilful as yourself, in these troublesome times, at one's elbow ! I do not know how else we should ever have found out the stranger's country. An Inglese ! Corpo di Bacco ! Who would have thought that a nation so maritime, and which lies so far off, would send so small a craft this vast distance ! Why, Ghita, it is a voyage from Elba to Livorno, and yet, I dare say, England is twenty times farther."

" Signore, I know little of England, but I have heard that it lies beyond our own sea. This is the flag of the country, however ; for *that* have I often beheld. Many ships of that nation come upon the coast, further south."

" Yes, it is a great country for mariners ; though they tell me it has neither wine nor oil. They are allies of the emperor, too, and deadly enemies of the French, who have done so much harm in upper Italy. That is something, Ghita, and every Italian should honour the flag. I fear this stranger does not intend to enter our harbour !"

" He steers as if he did not, certainly, Signor Podestà," said Ghita, sighing so gently that the respiration was audible only to herself. " Perhaps he is in search of some of the French, of which they say so many were seen, last year, going east."

" Ay, that was truly an enterprise !" answered the magistrate, gesticulating on a large scale, and opening his eyes by way of accompaniments. " General Bonaparte, he who had been playing the devil in the Milanese, and the states of the Pope, for the last two years, sailed, they sent us word, with two or three hundred ships, the saints, at first, knew whither. Some said, it was to destroy the holy sepulchre ; some, to overturn the Grand Turk ; and some thought, to seize the islands. There was a craft in here, the same week, which said he had got possession of the Island of Malta ; in which case we might look out for trouble in Elba. I had my suspicions, from the first !"

" All this I heard, at the time, Signore, and my uncle probably could tell you more—how we all felt at the tidings !" ,

" Well, that is all over now, and the French are in Egypt
Your uncle, Ghita, has gone upon the main, I hear ?" this
was said inquiringly, and it was intended to be said care
lessly ; but the podestâ could not prevent a glance of suspicion
from accompanying the question.

" Signore, I believe he has ; but I know little of his affairs.
The time has come, however, when I ought to expect him.
See, Eccellenza," a title that never failed to mollify the
magistrate, and turn his attention from others entirely to
himself, " the lugger really appears disposed to look into
your bay, if not actually to enter it !"

This sufficed to change the discourse. Nor was it said
altogether without reason ; the lugger, which by this time
had passed the western promontory, actually appearing disposed to do as Ghita conjectured. She had jibed her mainsail — brought both sheets of canvass on her larboard side,
and luffed a little, so as to cause her head to look towards
the opposite side of the bay, instead of standing in, as before,
in the direction of the canal. This change in the lugger's
course produced a general movement in the crowd, which
began to quit the heights, hastening to descend the terraced
streets, in order to reach the haven. 'Maso and the podestâ
led the van, in this descent ; and the girls, with Ghita in their
midst, followed with equal curiosity, but with eager steps.
By the time the throng was assembled on the quays, in the
streets, on the decks of feluccas, or at other points that
commanded the view, the stranger was seen gliding past, in
the centre of the wide and deep bay, with his jigger hauled
out, and his sheets aft, looking up nearly into the wind's eye,
if that could be called wind, which was still little more than
the sighing of the classical zephyr. His motion was necessarily slow, but it continued light, easy, and graceful. After
passing the entrance of the port a mile or more, he tacked
and looked up towards the haven. By this time, however,
he had got so near in to the western cliffs, that their lee deprived him of all air ; and after keeping his canvass open
half an hour in the little roads, it was all suddenly drawn to
the yards, and the lugger anchored.

CHAPTER II.

"His stock, a few French phrases, got by heart,
With much to learn, but nothing to impart;
The youth obedient to his sire's commands,
Sets off a wanderer into foreign lands."
COWPER.

IT was now nearly dark, and the crowd, having satisfied its idle curiosity, began slowly to disperse. The Signor Viti remained till the last, conceiving it to be his duty to be on the alert, in such troubled times ; but with all his bustling activity, it escaped his vigilance and means of observation to detect the circumstance that the stranger, who, while he steered into the bay with so much confidence, had contrived to bring up at a point where not a single gun from the batteries could be brought to bear on him ; while his own shot, had he been disposed to hostility, would have completely raked the little haven. But Vito Viti, though so enthusiastic an admirer of the art, was no gunner himself, and little liked to dwell on the effect of shot, except as it applied to others, and not at all to himself.

Of all the suspicious, apprehensive and curious, who had been collected in and about the port, since it was known the lugger intended to come into the bay, Ghita and 'Maso alone remained on watch, after the vessel anchored. A loud hail had been given by those entrusted with the execution of the quarantine laws, the great physical bug-bear and moral mystification of the Mediterranean ; and the questions put had been answered in a way to satisfy all scruples for the moment. The " From whence came ye ?" asked, how-ever, in an Italian idiom, had been answered by " Inghilterra, touching at Lisbon and Gibraltar," all regions beyond distrust, as to the plague, and all happening, at that moment, to give clean bills of health. But the name of the craft, her-self, had been given in a way to puzzle all the proficients in Saxon English that Porto Ferrajo could produce. It had been distinctly enough pronounced by some one on board, and at the request of the quarantine department, had been

three times slowly repeated, very much after the following
form ; viz. —

"*Come chiamate il vostro bastimento ?*"

"The Wing-And-Wing."

"*Come ?*"

"The Wing-And-Wing."

A long pause, during which the officials put their heads
together, first to compare the sounds of each with those of
his companions' ears, and then to inquire of one who professed to understand English, but whose knowledge was such
as is generally met with in a linguist of a little-frequented
port, the meaning of the term.

"Ving-y-ving!" growled this functionary, not a little
puzzled, "what ze devil **sort** of name is zat! Ask zem
again."

"*Come si chiama la vostra barca, Signori Inglesi ?*"
repeated he who hailed.

"*Diable !*" growled one back, in French, "she is called
ze Wing-And-Wing, 'Ala e Ala,'" giving a very literal
translation of the name, in Italian.

"*Ala e ala !*" repeated they of the quarantine, first looking at each other in surprise, and then laughing, though in
a perplexed and doubtful manner ; "Ving-y-Ving!"

This passed just as the lugger anchored, and the crowd
had begun to disperse. It caused some merriment, and it
was soon spread in the little town that a craft had just
arrived from Inghilterra, whose name, in the dialect of that
island, was "Ving-y-Ving ;" which meant "*Ala e ala*," in
Italian ; a cognomen that struck the listeners as sufficiently
absurd. In confirmation of the fact, however, the lugger
hoisted a small square flag, at the end of her main-yard, on
which were painted, or wrought, two large wings, as they
are sometimes delineated in heraldry, with the beak of a
galley between them ; giving the whole conceit something
very like the appearance that the human imagination has
assigned to those heavenly beings, cherubs. This emblem
seemed to satisfy the minds of the observers, who were too
much accustomed to the images of art, not to obtain some
tolerably distinct notions, in the end, of what "*Ala e ala*'
meant.

But 'Maso, as has been said, remained after the rest had

departed to their homes and their suppers, as did Ghita. The pilot, for such was Tonti's usual appellation, in consequence of his familiarity with the coast, and his being principally employed to direct the navigation of the different craft in which he served, kept his station on board a felucca to which he belonged, watching the movements of the lugger, while the girl had taken her stand on the quay, in a position that better became her sex, since it removed her from immediate contact with the rough spirits of the port, while it enabled her to see what occurred about the Wing-And-Wing. More than half an hour elapsed, however, before there were any signs of an intention to land ; but, by the time it was dark, a boat was ready, and it was seen making its way to the common stairs, where one or two of the regular officials were ready to receive it.

It is unnecessary to dwell on the forms of the pratique officers. These troublesome persons had their lanterns, and were vigilant in examining papers, as is customary ; but it would seem, the mariner in the boat had everything *en règle*, for he was soon suffered to land. At this instant Ghitá passed near the group, and took a close and keen survey of the stranger's form and face, her own person being so enveloped in a mantle, as to render a recognition of it difficult, if not impossible. The girl seemed satisfied with this scrutiny, for she immediately disappeared. Not so with 'Maso, who by this time had hurried round from the felucca, and was at the stairs in season to say a word to the stranger.

"Signore," said the pilot, "his Eccellenza, the podestâ, has bidden me say to you, that he expects the honour of your company, at his house, which stands so near us, hard by here, in the principal street, as will make it only a pleasure to go there ; I know he would be disappointed, if he failed of the happiness of seeing you."

"His Eccellenza is a man not to be disappointed," returned the stranger, in very good Italian, "and five minutes shall prove to him how eager I am to salute him ;" then turning to the crew of his boat, he ordered them to return on board the lugger, and not to fail to look out for the signal by which he might call them ashore.

'Maso, as he led the way to the dwelling of Vito Viti,

3

would fain ask a few questions, in the hope of appeasing
certain doubts that beset him.

"Since when, Signor Capitano," he inquired, "have you
English taken to sailing luggers? It is a novel rig for one
of your craft."

"Corpo di Bacco!" answered the other, laughing, "friend
of mine, if you can tell the precise day when brandy and laces
were first smuggled from France into my country I will
nswer your question. I think you have never navigated
as far north as the Bay of Biscay and our English Channel
or you would know that a Guernsey-man is better acquainted
with the rig of a lugger, than with that of a ship."

"Guernsey is a country I never heard of," answered
'Maso, simply; "is it like Holland—or more like Lisbon?"

"Very little of either. Guernsey is a country that was
once French, and where many of the people still speak the
French language, but of which the English have been masters this many an age. It is an island subject to King
George, but which is still half Gallic in names and usages.
This is the reason why we like the lugger better than the
cutter, which is a more English rig."

'Maso was silent, for, if true, the answer at once removed
many misgivings. He had seen so much about the strange
craft which struck him as French, that doubts of her character had obtruded; but, if her captain's account could only
be substantiated, there was an end of distrust. What could
be more natural than the circumstance that a vessel fitted
out in an island of French origin, should betray some of the
peculiarities of the people who built her?

The podestà was at home, in expectation of this visit, and
'Maso was first admitted to a private conference, leaving the
stranger in an outer room. During this brief conference,
the pilot communicated all he had to say — both his suspicions and the seeming solution of the difficulties; and then
he took his leave, after receiving the boon of a paul. Vito
Viti now joined his guest, but it was so dark, lights not
having yet been introduced, that neither could distinguish
the other's countenance.

"Signor Capitano," observed the magistrate, "the deputy-
governor is at his residence, on the hill, and he will expect

me to do him the favour to bring you thither, that he may do you the honours of the port."

This was said so civilly, and was, in itself, both so reasonable and so much in conformity with usage, that the other had not a word to say against it. Together, then, they left the house, and proceeded towards the government-dwelling —a building which has since become celebrated as having been the residence of a soldier who came so near subjugating Europe. Vito Viti was a short, pursy man, and he took his time to ascend the stairs-resembling street ; but his companion stepped from terrace to terrace with an ease and activity that, of themselves, would have declared him to be young, had not this been made apparent by his general bearing and his mien, as seen through the obscurity.

Andrea Barrofaldi, the vice-governatore, was a very different sort of person from his friend the podestà. Although little more acquainted with the world, by practice, the vice-governatore was deeply read in books ; owing his situation, in short, to the circumstance of his having written several clever works, of no great reputation, certainly, for genius, but which were useful in their way, and manifested scholarship. It is very seldom that a man of mere letters is qualified for public life ; and yet there is an affectation, in all governments, most especially in those which care so little for literature in general, as to render some professions of respect for it necessary to their own characters, of protecting it ; and thus it is, that among ourselves, where the laws are so indifferent to the *rights* and interests of men of this class as to subject them to costs and penalties, in the prosecution of their ordinary labours, that no other Christian nation dreams of exacting, we hear high-sounding pretensions to this species of liberality, although the system of rewards and punishments* that prevails, usually requires that its beneficiary

---

* So much is said in the journals of this country concerning the patronage the public bestows on letters, a patronage which is very much confined to buying such works as the reader wants, and not purchasing hose for which he feels no occasion, that it forcibly reminds one of the story of the Creole woman, who was descanting on the subject of ruling negroes, among some friends. " If you will gouverne nègres," she said, " you moost have système. I have système. Mon système à moi, is système of reward and poonishment." Then she turns to her negroes, and addresses them, desiring her friends to note the effect.

should first *rat*, in order to prove his adaptation to the du·
Andrea Barrofaldi, however, had thrown no political summe·
set, and had consequently been inducted into his present
office without even the sentimental profession of never having
asked for it.   The situation had been given to him by the
Fossombrone of his day, without a word having been said
in the journals of Tuscany of his doubts about accepting it,
  nd everything passed, as things are apt to pass when there
are true simplicity and good faith at the bottom, without
pretension or comment.   He had now been ten years in
office, and had got to be exceedingly expert in discharging all the ordinary functions of his post, which he certainly did with zeal and fidelity.   Still, he did not desert
his beloved books, and, quite àpropos of the matter about to
come before him, the Signor Barrofaldi had just finished a
severe, profound, and extensive course of study in geography.

The stranger was left in the ante-chamber, while Vito
Viti entered an inner room, and had a short communication
with his friend, the vice-governatore.   As soon as this was
ended. the former returned, and ushered his companion into
the presence of the substitute for a grand duke, if not for a
king.   As this was the sailor's first appearance within the
influence of a light sufficiently strong to enable the podestà
to examine his person, both he and Andrea Barrofaldi turned
their eyes on him with lively curiosity, the instant the rays
of a strong lamp enabled them to scrutinize his appearance.
Neither was disappointed, in one sense, at least ; the countenance, figure, and mien of the mariner much more than
equalling his expectations.

The stranger was a man of six-and-twenty, who stood five
feet ten in his stockings, and whose frame was the very
figure of activity, united to a muscle that gave very fair
indications of strength.   He was attired in an undress naval
uniform, which he wore with a smart air, that one who
understood these matters, more by means of experience, and

"*Mes amis*," she begins, " zo-morrow ze cane will be roipe, and you
moost moosh vork.   You know me — you know *mon* système — it is
système of reward and poonishment.   If you shall not vork, you *shall*
be flog ; zat is poonishment ; mais if you shall *very* moosh — *very*
moosh vork ; you shall *no* be flog — zat is ze reward !"

less by means of books, than Andrea Barrofaldi, would at once have detected did not belong to the manly simplicity of the English wardrobe. Nor were his features, in the slightest degree, those of one of the islanders, the outline being beautifully classical, more especially about the mouth and chin, while the cheeks were colourless, and the skin swarthy. His eye, too, was black as jet, and his cheek was half covered in whiskers of a hue dark as the raven's wing. His face, as a whole, was singularly beautiful — for handsome is a word not strong enough to express all the character that was conveyed by a conformation that might be supposed to have been copied from some antique medal, more especially when illuminated by a smile that, at times, rendered the whole countenance almost as bewitching as that of a lovely woman. There was nothing effeminate in the appearance of the young stranger, notwithstanding; his manly though sweet voice, well-knit frame, and firm look, affording every pledge of resolution and spirit.

Both the vice-governatore and the podestà were struck with the unusual personal advantages and smart air of the stranger, and each stood looking at him half-a-minute in silence, after the usual salutations had passed, and before the party was seated. Then, as the three took chairs, on a motion from Signor Barrofaldi, the latter opened the discourse.

"They tell me that we have the honour to receive into our little haven a vessel of Inghilterra, Signor Capitano," observed the vice-governatore, earnestly regarding the other through his spectacles as he spoke, and that, too, in a manner not altogether free from distrust.

"Signor Vice-governatore, such is the flag under which I have the honour to serve;" returned the mariner.

"You are an Inglese, yourself, I trust, Signor Capitano—what name shall I enter in my book, here?"

"Jaques Smeet," answered the other, betraying what might have proved two very fatal Shibboleths, in the ears of those who were practised in the finesse of our very unmusical language, by attempting to say "Jack Smith."

"Jaques Smeet!" repeated the vice-governatore — "that is, Giacomo, in our Italian —"

"No —no—Signore," hastily interrupted Captain Smeet.

3 *

" not Jaqueomo, but Jaques — Giovanni, turned into Jaques by the aid of a little salt water."

" Ah ! — I begin to understand you, Signore ; you English have this usage in your language, though *you* have softened the word a little, in mercy to our ears. But we Italians are not afraid of such sounds ; and I know the name. — 'Giac Smeet' — Il Capitano Giac Smeet — I have long suspected my English master of ignorance, for he was merely one of our Leghorn pilots, who has sailed in a bastimento de guerra of your country — he called your honourable name 'Smees,' Signore."

" He was very wrong, Signor Vice-governatore," answered the other, clearing his throat by a slight effort ; " we always call our family ' Smeet.' "

" And the name of your lugger, Signor Capitano Smeet ?" suspending his pen over the paper in expectation of the answer.

" Ze Ving-And-Ving ;" pronouncing the *w's* in a very different way from what they had been sounded in answering the hails.

" Ze Ving-y-Ving," repeated Signor Barrofaldi, writing the name in a manner to show it was not the first time he had heard it ; " ze Ving-y-Ving ; that is a poetical appellation, Signor Capitano ; may I presume to ask what it signifies ?"

" *Ala e ala*, in your Italian, *Mister* Vice-governatore. When a craft like mine has a sail spread on each side, resembling a bird, we say, in English, that she marches ' Ving-and-Ving.' "

Andrea Barrofaldi mused, in silence, near a minute. During this interval, he was thinking of the improbability of any but a bonâ fide Englishman's dreaming of giving a vessel an appellation so thoroughly idiomatic, and was fast mystifying himself, as so often happens by tyros in any particular branch of knowledge, by his own critical acumen. Then he half whispered a conjecture on the subject to Vito Viti, influenced quite as much by a desire to show his neighbour his own readiness in such matters, as by any other feeling. The podestà was less struck by the distinction than his superior, but, as became one of his limited means, he did not venture an objection.

"Signor Capitano," resumed Andrea Barrofaldi, "since when have you English adopted the rig of the lugger? It is an unusual craft for so great a naval nation, they tell me."

"Bah! I see how it is, Signor Vice-governatore — you suspect me of being a Frenchman, or a Spaniard, or something else than I claim to be. On this head, however, you may set your heart at rest, and put full faith in what I tell you. My name is Capitaine Jaques Smeet; my vessel is ze Ving-and-Ving; and my service that of the king of England."

"Is your craft, then, a king's vessel; or does she sail with the commission of a corsair?"

"Do I look like a corsair, Signor?" demanded le Capitaine Smeet, with an offended air; "I have reason to feel myself injured by so unworthy an imputation!"

"Your pardon, Signor Capitano Smees — but our duty is a very delicate one, on this unprotected island, in times as troubled as these in which we live. It has been stated to me, as coming from the most experienced pilot of our haven, that your lugger has not altogether the appearance of a vessel of the Inglese, while she has many that belong to the corsairs of France; and a prudent caution imposes on me the office of making certain of your nation. Once assured of that, it will be the delight of the Elbans to prove how much we honour and esteem our illustrious allies."

"This is so reasonable, and so much according to what I do myself, when I meet a stranger at sea," cried the captain, stretching forth both arms in a frank and inviting manner, "that none but a knave would object to it. Pursue your own course, Signor Vice-governatore, and satisfy all your scruples, in your own manner. How shall this be done — will you go on board ze Ving-and-Ving, and look for yourself — send this honourable magistrate, or shall I show you my commission? Here is the last, altogether at your service, and that of his Imperial Highness, the Grand Duke."

"I flatter myself with having sufficient knowledge of Inghilterra, Signor Capitano, though it be by means of books, to discover an impostor, could I believe you capable of appearing in so unworthy a character; and that, too, in a very brief conversation. We book-worms," added Andrea Barrofaldi, with a glance of triumph at his neighbour, for he

now expected to give the podestâ an illustration of the prac-
tical benefits of general learning, a subject that had ofter.
been discussed between them, " we book-worms can manage
these trifles in our own way ; and if you will consent tc
enter into a short dialogue on the subject of England, her
habits, language and laws, this question will be speedily put
at rest."

" You have me at command ; and nothing would delight
me more than to chat for a few minutes about that little
island.   It is not large, Signore, and is doubtless of little
worth ; but, as my country, it is much in my eyes."

" This is natural.   And now, Signor Capitano, added
Andrea, glancing at the podestâ, to make sure that he was
listening, " will you have the goodness to explain to me
what sort of a government this Inghilterra possesses —
whether monarchy, aristocracy or democracy ?"

" Peste !—that is not so easily answered.   There is a king,
and yet there are powerful lords ; and a democracy, too, that
sometimes gives trouble enough.   Your question might
puzzle a philosopher, Signor Vice-governatore."

" This may be true enough, neighbour Vito Viti, for the
constitution of Inghilterra is an instrument of many strings !
Your answer convinces me you have thought on the subject
of your government, Capitano, and I honour a reflecting
man, in all situations in life.   What is the religion of the
country ?"

" Corpo di Bacco ! that is harder to answer than all the
rest !   We have as many religions, in England, as we have
people.   It is true, the law says one thing, on this head, but
then the men, women and children say another.   Nothing
has troubled me more than this same matter of religion."

" Ah ! you sailors do not disquiet your souls with such
thoughts, if the truth must be said.   Well, we will be indulgent on this subject—though, out of doubt, you and all your
people are Luterani ?"

" Set us down as what you please," answered the captain.
with an ironical smile.   " Our fathers, at any rate, were
all good Catholics once.   But seamanship and the altar are
the best of friends, living quite independent of each other."

" That I will answer for.   It 4 much the same here, caro

Vito Viti, though our mariners do burn so many lamps, and offer up so many aves."

"Your pardon, Signor Vice-governatore," interrupted the Signor Smeet, with a little earnestness;" this is the great mistake of your seamen, in general. Did they pray less, and look to their duties more, their voyages would be shorter, and the profits more certain."

"Scandalous!" exclaimed the podestà, in hotter zeal than it was usual for him to betray —

"Nay, worthy Vito Viti, it is even so." interrupted the deputy, with a wave of the hand, that was as authoritative as the concession was liberal and indicative of a spirit enlightened by study; "the fact must be conceded. There is the fable of Hercules and the wagoner, to confirm it. Did our men first strive, and then pray, more would be done, than by first praying and then striving; — and now, Signor Capitano, a word on your language, of which I have some small knowledge, and which doubtless you speak like a native."

"Sairtain*lee*," answered the captain, with perfect self-composure, changing the form of speech from the Italian to the English with a readiness that proved how strong he felt himself on this point; "one cannot fail to speak ze tongue of his own mozair."

This was said without any confusion of manner, and with an accent that might very well mislead a foreigner, and it sounded imposing to the vice-governatore, who felt a secret consciousness that he could not have uttered such a sentence, to save his own life, without venturing out of his depth; therefore, he pursued the discourse in Italian.

"Your language, Signore," observed Andrea Barrofaldi, with warmth, "is no doubt a very noble one, for the language in which Shakspeare and Milton wrote cannot be else but, you will permit me to say that it has a uniformity of sound, with words of different letters, that I find as unreasonable as it is embarrassing, to a foreigner."

"I have heard such complaints before," answered the captain, not at all sorry to find the examination, which had proved so awkward to himself, likely to be transferred to a language about which he cared not at all, "and have little

3

to say in its defence. But, as an example of what you mean—"

" Why, Signore, here are several words that I have written on this bit of paper, which sound nearly alike, though, as you perceive, they are quite differently spelled. Bix, bax, box, bux, and bocks," continued Andrea, endeavouring to pronounce, " big," " bag," " bug," " bog," and " box," all of which, it seemed to him, had a very close family resemblance, in sound, though certainly spelled with different letters ; " these are words, Signore, that are enough to drive a foreigner to abandon your tongue in despair."

" Indeed they are ; and I often told the person who taught me the language—"

" How ; did you not learn your own tongue as we all get our native forms of speech, by ear, when a child ?" demanded the vice-governatore, his suspicions suddenly revived.

" Without question, Signore, but I speak of books, and of learning to read. When ' big,' ' bag,' ' bug,' ' bog,' and ' box,' " reading from the paper, in a steady voice, and a very tolerable pronunciation, " first came before me, I felt all the embarrassment of which you speak."

" And did you only pronounce these words when first taught to read them ?"

This question was an awkward one to answer ; but Vito Viti began to weary of a discourse in which he could take no part, and, most opportunely, he interposed an objection of his own.

" Signor Barrofaldi," he said, " stick to the lugger. All our motives of suspicion came from Tommaso Tonti, and all of his from the rig of Signor Smees' vessel. If the lugger can be explained, what do we care about bixy, buxy, boxy !"

The vice-governatore was not sorry to get creditably out of the difficulties of the language, and, smiling on his friend, he made a gentle bow of compliance. Then he reflected a moment, in order to plan another mode of proceeding, and pursued the inquiry.

" My neighbour Vito Viti is right," he said, " and we will stick to the lugger. Tommaso Tonti is a mariner of experience, and the oldest pilot of Elba. He tells us that the lugger is a craft much in use among the French, and not at all among the English. so far as he has ever witnessed."

" In that To.nmaso Tonti is no seaman. Many luggers are
.o be found among the English; though more, certainly,
among the French. But I have already given the Signor
Viti to understand that there is such an island as Guernsey,
which was once French, but which is now English, and that
accounts for the appearances he has observed. We are
Guernsey-men — the lugger is from Guernsey — and, no
doubt, we have a Guernsey look. This is being half French
I allow."

" That alters the matter, altogether. Neighbour Viti,
this is all true about the island, and about its habits and its
origin ; and if one could be as certain about the names,
why nothing more need be said. Are Giac Smees, and
Ving-y-Ving, Guernsey names ?"

" They are not particularly so," returned the sailor, with
difficulty refraining from laughing in the vice-governatore's
face ; " Jaques Smeet' being so English, that we are the
largest family, perhaps, in all Inghilterra. Half the nobles
of the island are called Smeet', and not a few are named
Jaques. But little Guernsey was conquered ; and our an-
cestors, who performed that office, brought their names with
them, Signore. As for Ving-And-Ving, it is *capital* English."

" I do not see, Vito, but this is reasonable. If the capitano, now, only had his commission with him, you and I
might go to bed in peace, and sleep till morning."

" Here, then, Signore, are your sleeping potions," continued the laughing sailor, drawing from his pocket several
papers. " These are my orders from the admiral ; and, as
they are not secret, you can cast your eyes over them.
This is my commission, Signor Vice-governatore — this is
the signature of the English minister of marine — and here
is my own, ' Jaques Smeet', as you see, and here is the
order to me, as a lieutenant, to take command of the Ving-
And-Ving."

All the orders and names were there, certainly, written in
a clear, fair hand, and in perfectly good English. The only
thing that one who understood the language perfectly would
have been apt to advert to, was the circumstance that the
words which the sailor pronounced " Jaques Smeet'," were
written, plainly enough, " Jack Smith" — an innovation on
the common practice, which, to own the truth, had proceeded

from his own obstinacy, and had been done in the very teeth
of the objections of the scribe who had forged the papers.
But Andrea was still too little of an English scholar to understand the blunder, and the Jack passed, with him, quite
as currently as would "John," "Edward," or any other
appellation. As to the Wing-And-Wing, all was right;
though, as the words were pointed out and pronounced by
both parties, one pertinaciously insisted on calling them
"Ving-And-Ving," and the other, "Ving-y-Ving." All this
evidence had a great tendency towards smoothing down
every difficulty, and 'Maso Tonti's objections were pretty
nearly forgotten by both the Italians, when the papers were
returned to, and pocketed again by, their proper owner.

"It was an improbable thing that an enemy, or a corsair,
would venture into this haven of ours, Vito Viti," said the
vice-governatore, in a self-approving manner; "for we have
a reputation for being vigilant, and for knowing our business,
as well as the authorities of Livorno, or Genova, or Napoli."

"And that too, Signore, with nothing in the world to gain
but hard knocks and a prison," added the Captain Sméet',
with one of his most winning smiles — a smile that even
softened the heart of the podestà, while it so far warmed that
of his superior, as to induce him to invite the stranger to
share his own frugal supper. The invitation was accepted
as frankly as it had been given, and, the table being ready
in an adjoining room, in a few minutes Il Capitano Smees
and Vito Viti were sharing the vice-governatore's evening
meal.

From this moment, if distrust existed any longer in the
breasts of the two functionaries of Porto Ferrajo, it was so
effectually smothered as to be known only to themselves.
The light fare of an Italian kitchen, and the light wines of
Tuscany, just served to strengthen the system, and enliven
the spirits; the conversation becoming general and lively,
as the business of the moment proceeded. At that day, tea
was known throughout southern Europe as an ingredient
only for the apothecary's keeping; nor was it often to be
found among his stores; and the *convives* used, as a substitute, large draughts of the pleasant mountain liquors of the
adjacent main, which produced an excitement scarcely
greater, while it may be questioned if it did as much injury

to the health. The stranger, however, both eat and drank sparingly, for while he affected to join cordially in the discourse and the business of *restoration*, he greatly desired to be at liberty to pursue his own designs.

Andrea Barrofaldi did not let so excellent an opportunity to show his acquirements to the podestà go by neglected. He talked much of England, its history, its religion, government, laws, climate, and industry; making frequent appeals to the Capitano Smees for the truth of his opinions. In most cases the parties agreed surprisingly, for the stranger started with a deliberate intention to assent to everything; but even this compliant temper had its embarrassments, since the vice-governatore so put his interrogatories as occasionally to give to acquiescence the appearance of dissent. The other floundered through his difficulties tolerably well, not withstanding; and so successful was he, in particular, in flat tering Andrea's self-love by expressions of astonishment that a foreigner should understand his own country so well — better, indeed, in many respects, than he understood it himself — and that he should be so familiar with its habits, institutions and geography, that, by the time the flask was emptied, the superior functionary whispered to his inferior, that the stranger manifested so much information and good sense, he should not be surprised if he turned out, in the long run, to be some secret agent of the British government, employed to make philosophical inquiries as to the trade and navigation of Italy, with a view to improve the business relations between the two countries.

" You are an admirer of nobility, and a devotee of aristocracy," added Andrea Barrofaldi, in pursuit of the subject then in hand; " if the truth were known, a scion of some noble house, yourself, Signore?"

" I? — Peste! — I hate an aristocrat, Signor Vice-governatore, as I do the devil!"

This was said just after the freest draught the stranger had taken, and with an unguarded warmth that he himself immediately regretted.

" This is extraordinary, in an Inglese! Ah — I see how it is — you are in the *opposizione*, and find it necessary to say this. It is most extraordinary, good Vito Viti, that these Inglese are divided into two political *castes*, that contradict

4

each other in everything. If one maintains that an object is white, the other side swears it is black ; and so *vice versâ.* Both parties profess to love their country better than any-thing else ; but the one that is out of power abuses even power itself, until it falls into its own hands."

" This is so much like Giorgio Grondi's course towards me, Signore, that I could almost swear he was one of these very opposizione ! I never approve of a thing that he does not condemn, or condemn, that he does not approve. Do you confess this much, Signor Capitano ?"

" Il vice-governatore knows us better than we know our-selves, I fear. There is too much truth in his account of our politics ; but, Signori," rising from his chair, " I now crave your permission to look at your town, and to return to my vessel. The darkness has come, and discipline must be observed."

As Andrea Barrofaldi had pretty well exhausted his stores of knowledge, no opposition was made ; and, returning his thanks, the stranger took his departure, leaving the two functionaries to discuss his appearance and character over the remainder of the flask.

CHAPTER III.

There 's Jonathan, that lucky lad,
Who knows it from the root, sir ; —
He sucks in all that 's to be had,
And always trades for boot, sir.
                    14,763d verse of Yankee Doodle.

Il Capitano Smeet' was not sorry to get out of the government-house — palazzo, as some of the simple people of Elba called the unambitious dwelling. He had been well badgered by the persevering erudition of the vice-governa-tore ; and, stored as he was with nautical anecdotes, and a olerable personal acquaintance with sundry sea-ports, for any expected occasion of this sort, he had never anticipated a conversation which would aspire as high as the institutions, religion and laws of his adopted country. Had the worthy Andrea heard the numberless maledictions, that the stranger muttered between his teeth, as he left the house, it would have shocked all his sensibilities, if it did not revive his suspicions.

It was now night; but a starry, calm, voluptuous evening such as are familiar to those who are acquainted with the Mediterranean and its shores. There was scarcely a breath of wind, though the cool air, that appeared to be a gentle respiration of the sea, induced a few idlers still to linger on the heights, where there was a considerable extent of land, that might serve for a promenade. Along this walk the mariner proceeded, undetermined, for the moment, what to do next. He had scarcely got into the open space, however before a female, with her form closely enveloped in a mantle brushed near him, anxiously gazing into his face. Her motions were too quick and sudden for him to obtain a look in return; but, perceiving that she held her way along the heights, beyond the spot most frequented by the idlers, he followed until she stopped.

" Ghita !" said the young man, in a tone of delight, when he had got near enough to the female to recognise a face and form she no longer attempted to conceal ; " this is being fortunate, indeed, and saves a vast deal of trouble. A thousand, thousand thanks, dearest Ghita, for this one act of kindness. I might have brought trouble on you, as well as on myself, in striving to find your residence."

" It is for that reason, Raoul, that I have ventured so much more than is becoming in my sex, to meet you. A thousand eyes, in this gossiping little town, are on your lugger, at this moment, and be certain they will also be on its captain, as soon as it is known he has landed. I fear you do not know for what you and your people are suspected, at this very instant !"

" For nothing discreditable, I hope, dear Ghita, if it be only not to dishonour your friends !"

" Many think, and say, you are Frenchmen, and that the English flag is only a disguise."

" If that be all, we must bear the infamy," answered Raoul Yvard, laughing. " Why, this is just what we are, to a man, a single American excepted ; who is an excellent fellow to make out British commissions, and help us to a little English when harder pushed than common ; and why should we be offended, if the good inhabitants of Porto Ferrajo take us for what we are !"

" Not offended, Raoul, but endangered. If the vice-governatore gets this notion, he will order the batteries to fire upon you, and will destroy you as an enemy."

" Not he, Ghita. He is too fond of le Capitaine Smeet', to do so cruel a thing ; and then he must shift all his guns, before they will hurt *le Feu-Follet*, where she lies. I never leave my little Jack-o'Lantern* within reach of an enemy's hand. Look here, Ghita ; you can see her through this opening in the houses — that dark spot on the bay, there — and you will perceive no gun from any battery in Porto Ferrajo can as much as frighten, much less harm her."

" I know her position, Raoul, and understood why you anchored in that spot. I knew, or thought I knew you, from the first moment you came in plain sight ; and so long as you remained outside, I was not sorry to look on so old a friend — nay, I will go farther, and say I rejoiced, for it seemed to me, you passed so near the island, just to let some, whom you knew to be on it, understand you had not forgotten them ; but when you came into the bay, I thought you mad !"

" Mad I should have been, dearest Ghita, had I lived longer without seeing you. What are these *misérables* of Elbans, that I should fear them ! They have no cruiser — only a few feluccas, all of which are not worth the trouble of burning. Let them but point a finger at us, and we will tow their Austrian polacre out into the bay, and burn her before their eyes. Le Feu-Follet deserves her name ; she is here, there, and everywhere, before her enemies suspect her."

" But her enemies suspect her now, and you cannot be too cautious. My heart was in my throat a dozen times, while the batteries were firing at you, this evening."

" And what harm did they ?—they cost the Grand Duke two cartridges, and two shot, without even changing the lugger's course ! You have seen too much of these things Ghita, to be alarmed by smoke and noise."

* The English of *Feu-Follet*.

"I have seen enough of these things, Raoul, to know that a heavy shot, fired from these heights, would have gone through your little Feu-Follet, and, coming out under water, would have sunk you to the bottom of the Mediterranean."

"We should have had our boats, then," answered Raoul Yvard, with an indifference that was not affected, for reckless daring was his vice, rather than his virtue; "besides, a shot must first hit, before it can harm, as the fish must be taken, before it can be cooked. But enough of this, Ghita; I get quite enough of shot, and ships, and sinkings, in everyday life, and, now I have at last found this blessed moment we will not throw away the opportunity by talking of such matters — "

"Nay, Raoul, I can think of nothing else, and therefore can talk of nothing else. Suppose the vice-governatore should suddenly take it into his head to send a party of soldiers to le Feu-Follet, with orders to seize her—what would then be your situation?"

"Let him; and I would send a boat's crew to his palazzo, here," the conversation was in French, which Ghita spoke fluently, though with an Italian accent, "and take him on a cruise after the English, and his beloved Austrians! Bah! — the idea will not cross his constitutional brain, and there is little use in talking about it. In the morning, I will send my prime minister, mon Barras, mon Carnot, mon Cambacérés, mon Ithuel Bolt, to converse with him on politics and religion."

"Religion," repeated Ghita, in a saddened tone; "the less you say on that holy subject, Raoul, the better I shall like it, and the better it will be for yourself, in the end. The state of your country makes your want of religion matter of regret, rather than of accusation, but it is none the less a dreadful evil."

"Well, then," resumed the sailor, who felt he had touched a dangerous ground, "we will talk of other things. Even supposing we are taken, what great evil have we to apprehend? We are honest corsairs, duly commissioned, and acting under the protection of the French Republic, one and undivided, and can but be made prisoners of war. That is a fortune which has once befallen me, and no greater calam

4 *

ity followed than my having to call myself le Capitaine
Smeet', and finding out the means of mystifying le vice-
governatori."

Ghita laughed, in spite of the fears she entertained, for
it was one of the most powerful of the agencies the sailor
employed in making others converts to his opinions, to cause
them to sympathize with his light-hearted gaiety, whether
it suited their natural temperaments or not. She knew that
Raoul had already been a prisoner in England two years,
where, as he often said himself, he staid just long enough to
acquire a very respectable acquaintance with the language,
if not with the institutions, manners, and religion, when he
made his escape, aided by the American, called Ithuel Bolt,
an impressed seaman of our own Republic, who fully entering into all the plans imagined by his more enterprising
friend and fellow-sufferer, had cheerfully enlisted in the
execution of his future schemes of revenge. States, like
powerful individuals in private life, usually feel themselves
too strong to allow any considerations of the direct consequences of departures from the right to influence their policy,
and a nation is apt to fancy its power of such a character,
as to despise all worldly amends, while its moral responsibility is divided among too many to make it a matter of much
moral concernment to its particular citizens. Nevertheless,
the truth will show that none are so low, but they may become dangerous to the highest ; and even powerful communities seldom fail to meet with their punishment for every
departure from justice. It would seem, indeed, that a principle pervades nature, which renders it impossible for man
to escape the consequences of his own evil deeds, even in
this life ; as if God had decreed the universal predominance
of truth, and the never-failing downfall of falsehood, from
the beginning ; the success of wrong being ever temporary,
while the triumph of the right is eternal. To apply these
consoling considerations to the matter more immediately
before us ; the practice of impressment, in its day, raised a
feeling among the seamen of other nations, as well as, in
fact, among those of Great Britain herself, that probably has
had as much effect in destroying the prestige of her nautical
invincibility, supported, as was that prestige by a vast
existing force, as any other one cause whatever .1 was

necessary, to witness the feeling of hatred and resentment that was raised by the practice of this despotic power, more especially among those who felt that their foreign birth ought at least to have assured them impunity from the abuse, in order fully to appreciate what might so readily become its consequences. Ithuel Bolt, the seaman just mentioned, was a proof, in a small way, of the harm that even an insignificant individual can effect, when his mind is fully and wholly bent on revenge. Ghita knew him well; and, although she little liked either his character or his appearance, she had often been obliged to smile at the narrative of the deceptions he practised on the English, and of the thousand low inventions he had devised to do them injury. She was not slow, now, to imagine that his agency had not been trifling in carrying on the present fraud.

"You do not openly call your lugger le Feu-Follet, Raoul;" she answered, after a minute's pause; "that would be a dangerous name to utter, even in Porto Ferrajo. It is not a week since I heard a mariner dwelling on her misdeeds, and the reasons that all good Italians have to detest her. It is fortunate the man is away, or he could not fail to know you."

"Of that I am not so certain, Ghita. We alter our paint often, and, at need, can alter our rig. You may be certain, however, that we hide our Jack-o'Lantern, and sail under another name. The lugger, now she is in the English service, is called the "Ving-And-Ving.""

"I heard the answer given to the hail from the shore, but it sounded different from this."

"Non — Ving-And-Ving. Ithuel answered for us, and you may be sure he can speak his own tongue. Ving-And-Ving is the word, and he pronounces it as I do."

"Ving-y-Ving!" repeated Ghita, in her pretty Italian tones, dropping naturally into the vice-governatore's fault of pronunciation—"it is an odd name, and I like it less than Feu-Follet."

"I wish, dearest Ghita, I could persuade you to like the name of Yvard," rejoined the young man, in a half-reproachful, half-tender manner, "and I should care nothing for any other. You accuse me of disrespect for priests; but no son could ever kneel to a father for his blessing, half so readily

or half so devoutly, as I could kneel with thee, before any
friar in Italy, to receive that nuptial benediction which I
have so often asked at your hand, but which you have so
constantly and so cruelly refused."

"I am afraid the name would not then be Feu-Follet, but
Ghita-Folie," said the girl, laughing, though she felt a bitter
pang at the heart, that cost her an effort to control ; — "no
more of this now, Raoul ; we may be observed, and watched;
it is necessary that we separate."

A hurried conversation, of more interest to the young
couple themselves, than it would prove to the reader, though
it might not have been wholly without the latter, but which
it would be premature to relate, now followed, when Ghita
left Raoul on the hill, insisting that she knew the town too
well to have any apprehensions about threading its narrow
and steep streets, at any hour, by herself. This much, in
sooth, must be said in favour of Andrea Barrofaldi's administration of justice ; he had made it safe for the gentle, the
feeble and the poor, equally, to move about the island by
day or by night ; it seldom happening that so great an enemy
to peace and tranquillity appeared among his simple depend-
ants, as was the fact at this precise moment.

In the mean time, there was not quite as much tranquillity
in Porto Ferrajo, as the profound silence which reigned in
the place might have induced a stranger to imagine. Tommaso Tonti was a man of influence, within his sphere, as
well as the vice-governatore ; and having parted from Vito
Viti, as has been related, he sought the little *clientelle* of
padroni and piloti, who were in the habit of listening to his
opinions as if they were oracles. The usual place of resort
of this set, after dark, was a certain house kept by a widow
of the name of Benedetta Galopo, the uses of which were
plainly enough indicated by a small bush that hung dangling
from a short pole, fastened above the door. If Benedetta
knew anything of the proverb. that "good wine needs no
bush," she had not sufficient faith in the contents of her own
casks, to trust their reputation ; for this bush of hers was as
regularly renewed, as its withering leaves required. Indeed,
it was a common remark, among her customers, that her
bush was always as fresh as her face, and that the latter
was one of the most comely that was to be met with on the

island; a circumstance that aided much indifferent wine, in finding a market. Benedetta bore a reasonably good name, nevertheless, though it was oftener felt, perhaps, than said, that she was a confirmed coquette. She tolerated 'Maso principally on two accounts; because, if he were old and unattractive in his own person, many of his followers were among the smartest seamen of the port, and because he not only drank his full proportion, but paid with punctuality. These inducements rendered the pilot always a welcome guest at La Santa Maria Degli Venti, as the house wa lled, though it had no other sign than the often-re . .. oush, already mentioned.

At the very moment, then, when Raoul Yvard and Ghita parted on the hill, 'Maso was seated in his usual place, at the table in Benedetta's upper room, the windows of which commanded as full a view of the lugger as the hour permitted; that craft being anchored about a cable's length distant, and, as a sailor might have expressed it, just abeam. On this occasion he had selected the upper room, and but three companions, because it was his wish that as few should enter into his counsels, as at all comported with the love of homage to his own experience. The party had been assembled a quarter of an hour, and there had been time to cause the tide to ebb materially in the flask, which it may be well to tell the reader at once, contained very little less than half a gallon of liquor, such as it was.

"I have told it all to the podestà," said 'Maso, with an important manner, as he put down his glass, after potation the second, which quite equalled potation the first, in quantity; "yes, I have told it all to Vito Viti, and no doubt he has told it to Il Signor Vice-governatore, who now knows as much about the whole matter as either of us four. Cospetto!—to think such a thing dare happen in a haven like Porto Ferrajo! Had it come to pass over on the other side of the island, at Porto Longone, one wouldn't think so much of it, or *they* are never much on the look-out; but, to take place here, in the very capital of Elba, I should as soon have expected it in Livorno!"

"But, 'Maso," put in Daniele Bruno, in the manner of one who was a little sceptical, "I have often seen the pavilion of the Inglese, and this is as much like that which all their frigates and corvettes wear, as one of our feluccas is like another. The flag, at least, is right."

"What signifies a flag, Daniele, when a French hand can hoist an English ensign as easily as the king of Inghilterra, himself? If that lugger was not built by the Francese, you were not built by an Italian father and mother. But, I should not think so much of the hull, for that may have been captured, as the English take many of their enemies on the high seas; but look at the rigging and sails—Santa Maria! I could go to the shop of the very sail-maker, in Marseilles, who made that foresail! His name is Pierre Benoit, and a very good workman he is, as all will allow who have had occasion to employ him."

This particularity greatly aided the argument; common minds being seldom above yielding to the circumstances which are so often made to corroborate imaginary facts. Tommaso Tonti, though so near the truth as to his main point —the character of the visiter—was singularly out as to the sail, notwithstanding; le Feu-Follet having been built, equipped, and manned at Nantes, and Pierre Benoit never having seen her or her foresail either; but, it mattered not, in the way of discussion and assertion, one sail-maker being as good as another, provided he was French.

"And have you mentioned this to the podestà?" inquired Benedetta, who stood with the empty flask in her hand, listening to the discourse; "I should think that sail would open his eyes."

"I cannot say I have; but then I told him so many other things, more to the point, that he cannot do less than believe this, when he hears it. Signor Viti promised to meet me here, after he has had a conversation with the vice-governatore; and we may now expect him every minute."

"Il Signor Podestà will be welcome," said Benedetta wiping off a spare table, and bustling round the room to make things look a little smarter than they ordinarily did; 'he may frequent grander wine-houses than this, but he will hardly find better liquor."

"Poverina!—Don't think that the podestà comes here on any such errand; he comes to meet *me*;" answered 'Maso, with an indulgent smile; "he takes his wine too often on the heights, to wish to come as low as this after a glass.

Friends of mine (*amigi mii*), there is wine up at that house,
that, when the oil is once out of the neck of the flask,* goes
down a man's throat as smoothly as if it were all oil itself!
I could drink a flask of it without once stopping to take
breath. It is that liquor which makes the nobles so light
and airy."

"I know the washy stuff," put in Benedetta, with more
warmth than she was used to betray to her customers;
"well may you call it smooth, a good spring running near
each of the wine-presses that have made it. I have seen
some of it that even oil would not float on!"

This assertion was a fair counterpoise to that of the sail
being about as true. But Benedetta had too much experi
ence in the inconstancy of men, not to be aware that if the
three or four customers who were present, should seriously
take up the notion that the island contained any better liquor
than that she habitually placed before them, her value might
be sensibly diminished, in their eyes. As became a woman who had to struggle singly with the world, too, her
native shrewdness taught her, that the best moment to refute
a calumny was to stop it as soon as it began to circulate,
and her answer was as warm in manner, as it was positive
in terms. This was an excellent opening for an animated
discussion, and one would have been very likely to occur,
had there not fortunately been steps heard without, that
induced 'Maso to expect the podestà. Sure enough, the door
opened, and Vito Viti appeared, followed, to the astonishment
of all the guests, and to the absolute awe of Benedetta, by
the vice-governatore himself.

The solution of this unexpected visit is very easily given.
After the departure of the Capitano Smees, Vito Viti returned
to the subject of 'Maso's suspicions, and by suggesting cer
tain little circumstances in the mariner's manner, that he had
noted during the interview, he so far succeeded in making
an impression on himself, that, in the end, his own distrust
revived, and with it that of the deputy-governor. Neither,
however, could be said to be more than uneasy, and the
podestà happening to mention his appointment with the pilot,
Andrea determined to accompany him, in order to recon-

---

* It is a practice of Tuscany, to put a few drops of oil in the neck
of each flask of the more delicate wines, to exclude the air

noitre the strange craft in person. Both the functionaries wore their cloaks, by no means an unusual thing in the cool night air of the coast, even in midsummer, which served them for all the disguise that circumstances required.

"Il Signor Vice-governatore!" almost gasped Benedetta, dusting a chair, and then the table, and disposing of the former near the latter by a sort of mechanical process, as if only one errand could ever bring a guest within her doors; "your eccellenza is most welcome; and it is an honour I could oftener ask. We are humble people, down here at the water side, but I hope we are just as good Christians as if we lived upon the hill."

"Doubt it not, worthy Bettina—"

"My name is Benedetta, at your eccellenza's command—Benedettina, if it please the vice-governatore; but not Bettina. We think much of our names, down here at the water side, eccellenza."

"Let it be so, then, good Benedetta, and I make no doubt you are excellent Christians. — A flask of your wine, if it be convenient."

The woman dropped a curtsy that was full of gratitude; and the glance of triumph that she cast at her other guests, may be said to have terminated the discussion that was about to commence, as the dignitaries appeared. It disposed of the question of the wine at once, and for ever silenced cavilling. If the vice-governatore could drink her liquor, what mariner would henceforth dare calumniate it?

"Eccellenza, with a thousand welcomes," Benedetta continued, as she placed the flask on the table, after having carefully removed the cotton and the oil with her own plump hand; this being one of half-a-dozen flasks of really sound, well-flavoured, Tuscan liquor, that she kept for especial occasions; as she well might, the cost being only a paul, or ten cents for near half a gallon; "Eccellenza, a million times welcome. This is an honour that don't befall the Santa Maria Degli Venti more than once in a century; and you, too, Signor Podestà, once before, only, have you ever had leisure to darken my poor door."

"We bachelors" — the podestà, as well as the vice-governor, belonged to the fraternity—"we bachelors are afraid to trust ourselves too often in the company of sprightly widows, like yourself, whose beauty has rather improved than less-ened, by a few years."

This brought a coquettish answer, during which time Andrea Barrofaldi, having first satisfied himself that the wine might be swallowed with impunity, was occupied in surveying the party of silent and humble mariners, who were seated at the other table. His object was to ascertain how far he might have committed himself, by appearing in such a place, when his visit could not well be attributed to more than one motive. 'Maso he knew, as the oldest pilot of the place; and he had also some knowledge of Daniele Bruno, but the three other seamen were strangers to him.

"Inquire if we are among friends, here, and worthy sub-jects of the Grand Duke, all;" observed Andrea to Vito Viti, in a low voice.

"Thou hearest, 'Maso," observed the podestà; "canst thou answer for all of thy companions?"

"Every one of them, Signore; this is Daniele Bruno, whose father was killed in a battle with the Algerines, and whose mother was the daughter of a mariner, as well known in Elba, as —"

"Never mind the particulars, Tommaso Tonti," interrupted the vice-governatore — "it is sufficient that thou knowest all thy companions to be honest men, and faithful servants of the *sovrano*. "You all know, most probably, the errand which has brought the Signor Viti and myself to this house, to-night?"

The men looked at each other, as the ill-instructed are apt to do, when it becomes necessary to answer a question that concerns many; assisting the workings of their minds, as it might be, with the aid of the senses; and then Daniele Bruno took on himself the office of spokesman.

"Signore, vostro eccellenza, we think we do," answered the man. "Our fellow, 'Maso here, has given us to under-stand that he suspects the Inglese that is anchored in the bay, to be no Inglese at all, but either a pirate or a French-man. The blessed Maria preserve us! but in these troubled times it does not make much difference which."

"I will not say as much as that, friend, for one would be an outcast among all people, while the other would have the rights which shield the servants of civilized nations;" re-

turned the scrupulous and just-minded functionary. "The
time was when His Imperial Majesty, the emperor, and his
illustrious brother, our sovereign, the Grand Duke, did not
allow that the republican government of France was a lawful government; but the fortune of war removed his scruples,
and a treaty of peace has allowed the contrary. Since the
late alliance, it is our duty to consider all Frenchmen as
enemies, though it by no means follows that we are to consider them as pirates."

"But their corsairs seize all our craft, Signore, and treat
their people as if they were no better than dogs: then, they
tell me that they are not Christians—no, not even Luterani, or heretics!"

"That religion does not flourish among them, is true,"
answered Andrea, who loved so well to discourse on such
subjects, that he would have stopped to reason on religion
or manners, with the beggar to whom he gave a pittance,
did he only meet with encouragement; "but it is not as bad
in France, on this important head, as it has been; and we
may hope that there will be further improvement, in due
time."

"But, Signor Vice-governatore," put in 'Maso, "these
people have treated the holy father, and his states, in a way
that one would not treat an Infidel or a Turk!"

"Ay, that is it, Signori," observed Benedetta — "a poor
woman cannot go to mass without having her mind disturbed
by the thoughts of the wrongs done the head of the church.
Had these things come from Luterani, it might have been
borne, but they say the Francese were once all good Catholics!"

"So were the Luterani, bella Benedetta, to their chief
schismatic and leader, the German monk himself."

This piece of information caused great surprise, even the
podestà himself turning an inquiring glance at his superior,
as much as to acknowledge his own wonder that a Protestant should ever have been anything but a Protestant — or
rather, a Lutheran, anything but a Lutheran — the word
Protestant being too significant to be in favour among those
who deny there were any just grounds for a protest at all.
That Luther had ever been a Romanist, was perfectly won-
derful, even in the eyes of Vito Viti.

"Signore, you would hardly mislead these honest people, in a matter as grave as this!" exclaimed the podestà.

"I do but tell you truth; and one of these days you shall hear the whole story, neighbour Viti. 'Tis worth an hour of leisure, to any man, and is very consoling and useful to a Christian. But who have you below, Benedetta — I hear steps on the stairs, and wish not to be seen."

The widow stepped promptly forward to meet her new guests, and to show them into a commoner room, below stairs, when her movement was anticipated by the door's opening, and a man's standing on the threshold. It was now too late to prevent the intrusion, and a little surprise at the appearance of the new-comer, held all mute and observant for a minute.

The person who had followed his ears, and thus reached the sanctum sanctorum of Benedetta, was no other than Ithuel Bolt, the American seaman, already named in the earlier part of this chapter. He was backed by a Genoese, who had come in the double capacity of interpreter and boon companion. That the reader may the better understand the character he has to deal with, however, it may be necessary to digress, by giving a short account of the history, appearance and peculiarities of the former individual.

Ithuel Bolt was a native of what, in this great Union, is called the granite state. Notwithstanding he was not absolutely made of the stone in question, there was an absence of the ordinary symptoms of natural feeling about him, that had induced many of his French acquaintances in particular to affirm that there was a good deal more of marble in his moral temperament, at least, than usually fell to the lot of human beings. He had the outline of a good frame, but it was miserably deficient in the filling up. The bone predominated; the sinews came next in consideration; nor was the man without a proper share of muscle; but this last was so disposed of as to present nothing but angles, whichever way he was viewed. Even his thumbs and fingers were nearer square than round, and his very neck, which was bare, though a black silk kerchief was tied loosely round the throat, had a sort of pentagon look about it, that defied all symmetry or grace. His stature was just six feet and an inch, when he straightened himself; as he did from time to

time, seemingly with a desire to relieve a very inveterate
stoop in his shoulders; though it was an inch or two less in
the position he most affected. His hair was dark, and his
skin had got several coats of confirmed brown on it, by exposure, though originally rather fair, while the features were
good, the forehead being broad and full, and the mouth
positively handsome. This singular countenance was illuminated by. two keen, restless, whitish eyes, that resembled,
not spots on the sun, but rather suns on a spot.

Ithuel had gone through all the ordinary vicissitudes of
an American life, beneath those pursuits which are commonly thought to be confined to the class of gentlemen. He
had been farmer's boy, printer's devil, schoolmaster, stage-
driver, and tin-pedlar, before he ever saw the sea. In the
way of what he called "chores," too, he had practised all
the known devices of rustic domestic economy; having
assisted even in the washing and house-cleaning, besides
having passed the evenings of an entire winter in making
brooms.

Ithuel had reached his thirtieth year before he dreamed
of going to sea. An accident, then, put preferment in this
form before his eyes, and he engaged as the mate of a small
coaster, on his very first voyage. Fortunately, the master
never found out his deficiencies, for Ithuel had a self-pos-
sessed, confident way with him, that prevented discovery,
until they were outside of the port from which they sailed,
when the former was knocked overboard by the main boom,
and drowned. Most men, so circumstanced, would have
returned, but Bolt never laid his hand to the plough and
looked back. Besides, one course was quite as easy to him
as another. Whatever he undertook he usually completed,
in some fashion or other, though it were often much better
had it never been attempted. Fortunately it was summer,
the wind was fair, and the crew wanted little ordering; and
as it was quite a matter of course to steer in the right direction,
until the schooner was carried safely into her proper port,
she arrived safely; her people swearing that the new mate
was the easiest and *cleverest* officer they had ever sailed
with.   And well they might, for Ithuel took care not to issue
an order, until he had heard it suggested in terms by one
of the hands, and then he never failed to repeat it, word for

word, as if it were a suggestion of his own. As for the reputation of "cleverest" officer, which he so easily obtained, it will be understood, of course, that the term was used in the provincial signification that is so common in the part of the world from which Ithuel came. He was "clever" in this sense, precisely in proportion as he was ignorant. His success, on this occasion, gained him friends, and he was immediately sent out again as the regular master of the craft, in which he had so unexpectedly received his promotion. He now threw all the duty on the mate; but so ready was he in acquiring, that, by the end of six months, he was a much better sailor than most Europeans would have made in three years. As the pitcher that goes too often to the well is finally broken, so did Ithuel meet with shipwreck, at last, in consequence of gross ignorance on the subject of navigation. This induced him to try a long voyage, in a more subordinate situation, until, in the course of time, he was impressed by the commander of an English frigate, who had lost so many of his men by the yellow fever, that he seized upon all he could lay his hands on, to supply their places, even Ithuel being acceptable in such a strait.

CHAPTER IV.

"The ship is here put in,
A Veronese; Michael Cassio,
Lieutenant to the warlike Moor Othello,
Is come on shore:—"

Othello.

THE glance which Ithuel cast around him was brief, but comprehensive. He saw that two of the party in the room were much superior to the other four, and that the last were common Mediterranean mariners. The position which Benedetta occupied in the household could not be mistaken, for she proclaimed herself its mistress by her very air; wheher it were in the upper or in the lower room.

"Vino," said Ithuel, with a flourish of the hand, to help

5 *

along his Italian, this and one or two more being the only
words of the language he ventured to use directly, or without calling in the assistance of his interpreter; "vino —
vino, vino, Signora."

"Si, si, si, Signore," answered Benedetta, laughing, and
this with her meaning eyes so keenly riveted on the person
of her new guest, as to make it very questionable whether
she were amused by anything but his appearance; "your
eccellenza shall be served; but whether at a paul, or a half-
paul the flask, depends on your own pleasure. We keep
wine at both prices, and," glancing towards the table of
Andrea Barrofaldi, "usually serve the first to signori of
rank and distinction."

"What does the woman say?" growled Ithuel to his
interpreter, a Genoese, who from having served several
years in the British navy, spoke English with a very tolerable facility — "you know what we want, and just tell her
to hand it over, and I will fork out her St. Paul, without
more words. What a desperate liking your folks have for
saints, Philip-o," for so Ithuel pronounced Filippo, the name
of his companion — "what a desperate liking your folks
have for saints, Philip-o, that they must even call their
money after them."

"It not so in America, Signor Bolto?" asked the Genoese,
after he had explained his wishes to Benedetta, in Italian;
"it no ze fashion in your country to honour ze saints?"

"Honour the saints!" repeated Ithuel, looking curiously
around him, as he took a seat at a third table, shoving aside
the glasses at the same time, and otherwise disposing of
every thing within reach of his hand, so as to suit his own
notions of order, and then leaning back on his chair until
the two ends of the uprights dug into the plaster behind him,
while the legs on which the fabric was poised cracked with
his weight; "honour the saints! we should be much more
like to dishonour them! What does any one want to honour
a saint for? A saint is but a human — a man like you and
me, after all the fuss you make about 'em. — Saints abound
n my country, if you'd believe people's account of themselves."

"Not quite so, Signor Bolto. You and me no great saint.
Italian honour saint because he holy and good."

By this time Ithuel had got his two feet on the round of his seat, his knees spread so as to occupy as much space as an unusual length of leg would permit, and his arms extended on the tops of two chairs, one on each side of him, in a way to resemble what is termed a spread eagle.

Andrea Barrofaldi regarded all this with wonder. It is true, he expected to meet with no great refinement in a wine-house like that of Benedetta's; but he was unaccustomed to see such nonchalance of manner in a man of the stranger's class; or, indeed, of any class; the Italian mariners present occupying their chairs in simple and respectful attitudes, as if each man had the wish to be as little obtrusive as possible. Still he let no sign of his surprise escape him, noting all that passed in a grave but attentive silence. Perhaps he saw traces of national peculiarities, if not of national history, in the circumstances.

"Honour saint because he holy and good!" said Ithuel, with a very ill-concealed disdain — "why, that is the very reason why we *don't* honour 'em. When you honour a holy man, mankind may consait you do it on that very account, and so fall into the notion you worship him, which would be idolatry, the awfullest of all sins, and the one to which every ra'al Christian gives the widest bairth. I would rayther worship this flask of wine, any day, than worship the best saint on your parson's books."

As Filippo was no casuist, but merely a believer, and Ithuel applied the end of the flask to his mouth, at that moment, from an old habit of drinking out of jugs and bottles, the Genoese made no answer; keeping his eyes on the flask, which, by the length of time it remained at the other's mouth, appeared to be in great danger of being exhausted; a matter of some moment to one of his own relish for the liquor.

"Do you call *this* wine!" exclaimed Ithuel, when he stopped, literally to take breath; "there isn't as much true granite in a gallon on't, as in a pint of our cider. I could swallow a butt, and then walk a plank as narrow as your religion, Philip-o!"

This was said, nevertheless, with a look of happiness which proved how much the inward man was consoled by what it had received, and a richness of expression about the handsome mouth, that denoted a sort of consciousness that it had been the channel of a most agreeable communication to the stomach. Sooth to say, Benedetta had brought up a flask at a paul, or at about four cents a bottle ; a flask of the very quality which she had put before the vice-governatore ; and this was a liquor that flowed so smoothly over the palate, and of a quality so really delicate, that Ithuel was by no means aware of the potency of the guest which he had admitted to his interior.

All this time the vice-governatore was making up his mind concerning the nation and character of the stranger. That he should mistake Bolt for an Englishman, was natural enough, and the fact had an influence in again unsettling his opinion as to the real flag under which the lugger sailed. Like most Italians of that day, he regarded all the families of the northern hordes as a species of barbarians ; an opinion that the air and deportment of Ithuel had no direct agency in changing ; for, while this singular being was not brawlingly rude and vulgar, like the coarser set of his own countrymen, with whom he had occasionally been brought in contact, he was so manifestly uncivilized, in many material points, as to put his claim to gentility much beyond a cavil, and that in a negative way.

"You are a Genoese?" said Andrea to Filippo, speaking with the authority of one who had a right to question.

"Signore, I am, at your eccellenza's orders, though in foreign service at this present moment."

"In what service, friend? I am in authority, here in Elba, and ask no more than is my duty."

"Eccellenza, I can well believe this," answered Filippo, rising and making a respectful salutation, and one, too, that was without any of the awkwardness of the same act in a more northern man, "as it is to be seen in your appearance. I am now in the service of the king of England."

Filippo said this steadily, though his eyes dropped to the floor, under the searching scrutiny they endured. The answer of the vice-governatore was delivered coolly, though it was much to the point.

"You are happy," he said, "in getting so honourable masters ; more especially as your own country has again fallen into the hands of the French. Every Italian heart must yearn for a government that has its existence and its motives on this side of the Alps."

"Signore, we are a republic to-day, and ever have been, you know."

"Ay — such as it is. But your companion speaks no talian — he is an Inglese?"

"No, Signore—an Americano : a sort of an Inglese, and yet no Inglese, after all. He loves England very little, if I can judge by his discourse."

"Un' Americano!" repeated Andrea Barrofaldi; "Americano!" exclaimed Vito Viti ; "Americano!" said each of the mariners in succession, all eyes turning with lively curiosity towards the subject of the discourse, who bore it all with appropriate steadiness and dignity. The reader is not to be surprised that an American was then regarded with curiosity, in a country like Italy ; for, two years later, when an American ship of war anchored suddenly before the town of Constantinople, and announced her nation, the authorities of the Sublime Porte were ignorant that such a country existed. It is true, Leghorn was beginning to be much frequented by American ships, in the year 1799 ; but even with these evidences before their eyes, the people of the very ports into which these traders entered, were accustomed to consider their crews a species of Englishmen, who managed to sail the vessels for the negroes at home.* In a word, two centuries and a half of national existence, and more than half a century of national independence, have not yet sufficed to teach all the inhabitants of the old world, that the great modern Republic is peopled by men of a European origin, and possessing white skins. Even of those who are aware of the fact, the larger proportion, perhaps, have obtained their information through works of a light character, similar to this of our own, rather than by the more legitimate course of regular study, and a knowledge of history.

"Si," repeated Ithuel, with emphasis, as soon as he heard

---

* As recently as 1828, the author of this book was at Leghorn. The Delaware, 80, had just left there ; and speaking of her appearance to a native of the place, who supposed the writer to be an Englishman, the latter observed — "Of course, her people were all blacks." "I thought so, too, signore, until I went on board the ship," was the answer; "but they are as white as you and I are."

his nationality thus alluded to, and found all eyes on himself —
" Si, oon Americano—I 'm not ashamed of my country ; and
if you 're any way partic'lar in such matters, I come from
New Hampshire—or, what we call the Granite State.   Tell
'em this, Philip-o, and let me know their idees, in answer."

Filippo translated this speech, as well as he could, as he
did the reply ; and it may as well be stated here, once for
all, that in the dialogue which succeeded, the instrumentality
of this interpreter was necessary that the parties might
understand each other.   The reader will, therefore, give
Filippo credit for this arrangement, although we shall furnish the different speeches very much as if the parties fully
comprehended what was said.

" *Uno stato di granito !*" repeated the vice-governatore,
looking at the podestâ with some doubt in the expression of
his countenance — " it must be a painful existence which
these poor people endure, to toil for their food in such a
region.   Ask him, good Filippo, if they have any wine in
his part of the world."

" Wine !"   echoed Ithuel ;   " tell the Signore that we
shouldn't call this stuff wine at all.   Nothing goes down our
throats that doesn't rasp like a file, and burn like a chip out
of Vesuvius.   I wish, now, we had a drink of New England
rum here, in order to show him the difference.   I despise
the man who thinks all his own things the best, just because
they 're his 'n ; but taste *is* taste, a'ter all, and there 's no
denying it."

" Perhaps the Signor Americano can give us an insight
into the religion of his country — or are the Americani pa-
gans ?   I do not remember, Vito, to have read anything of
the religion of that quarter of the world."

" Religion, too ! — well a question like this, now, would
make a stir among our folks in New Hampshire !   Look
here, Signore ; we don't call your ceremonies, and images,
and robes, and ringing of bells, and bowing and scraping, a
religion at all ; any more than we should call this smooth
iquor, wine."

Ithuel was more under the influence of this " smooth liquor"
than he was aware of, or he would not have been so loud in
the expression of his dissent ; as experience had taught him
the necessity of reserve on such subjects, in most Catholic

communities. But of all this the Signor Barrofaldi was ignorant, and he made his answer with the severity of a good Catholic, though it was with the temper of a gentleman.

" What the Americano calls our ceremonies, and images, and ringing of bells, are probably not understood by him," he said ; " since a country as little civilized as his own, cannot very well comprehend the mysteries of a profound and ancient religion."

" Civilized ! I calculate that it would *stump* this part of the world to produce such a civilization as our very youngest children are brought up on. But it 's of no use *talking*, and so we will *drink*."

Andrea perceiving, indeed, that there was not much use in *talking*, more especially as Filippo had been a good deal mystified by the word " *stump*," was now disposed to abandon the idea of a dissertation on " religion, manners and laws," to come at once to the matter that brought him into the present company.

" This Americano is also a servant of the English king, it would seem," he carelessly remarked : " I remember to have heard that there was a war between his country and that of the Inglesi, in which the French assisted the Americani to obtain a sort of a national independence. What that independence is, I do not know ; but it is probable that the people of the New World are still obliged to find mariners to serve in the navy of their former masters."

Ithuel's muscles twitched, and an expression of intense bitterness darkened his countenance. Then he smiled in a sort of derision, and gave vent to his feelings in words.

" Perhaps you 're right, Signore ; perhaps this is the ra'al truth of the matter ; for the British *do* take our people, just the same as if they had the best right in the world to 'em. A'ter all, we *may* be serving our masters ; and all we say and think at home, about independence, is just a flash in the pan ! Notwithstanding, some on us contrive, by hook or by crook, to take our revenge, when occasion offers ; and if I don't sarve Master John Bull an ill turn, whenever luck hrows a chance in my way, may I never see a bit of the old State again — granite or rotten wood."

This speech was not very closely translated, but enough was said to awaken curiosity in the vice-governatore, who

.hought it odd one who served among the English should entertain such feelings towards them. As for Ithuel, himself, he had not observed his usual caution; but, unknown to himself, the oily wine had more " granite" in it than he imagined, and then he seldom spoke of the abuse of impressment without losing more or less of his ordinary self-command.

" Ask the Americano when he first entered into the service of the king of Inghilterra," said Andrea, " and why he stays in it, if it is unpleasant to him, when so many opportunities of quitting it offer ?"

" I never entered," returned Ithuel, taking the word in its technical meaning; " they pressed me, as if I had been a dog they wanted to turn a spit, and kept me seven long years, fighting their accursed battles, and otherwise sarving their eends. I was over here, last year, at the mouth of the Nile, in that pretty bit of work—and off Cape St. Vincent, too—and in a dozen more of their battles, and sorely against my will, on every account. This was hard to be borne, but the hardest of it has not yet been said; nor do I know that I shall tell on 't at all."

" Anything the Americano may think proper to relate, will be listened to with pleasure."

Ithuel was a good deal undecided whether to go on, or not; but taking a fresh pull at the flask, it warmed his feelings to the sticking point.

" Why, it was adding insult to injury. It 's bad enough to injure a man, but when it comes to insulting him into the bargain, there must be but little grit in his natur', if it don't strike fire."

" And yet few are wronged who are not calumniated," observed the philosophical vice-governatore. " This is only too much the case with our Italy, worthy neighbour, Vito Viti."

" I calculate the English treat all mankind alike, whether it 's in Italy or Ameriky," for so Ithuel would pronounce this word, notwithstanding he had now been cruising in and near the Mediterranean several years; " but what I found hardest to be borne, was their running their rigs on me about my language and ways, which they were all the time laughing at as Yankee conversation and usages, while they pretended that the body out of which all on it come, was an

English body, and so they set it up to be shot at, by any of their inimies that might happen to be jogging along our road. Then, squire, it is generally consaited among us in Ameriky, that we speak much the best English a-going; and sure am I, that none on us call a 'hog,' an ''og,' an 'anchor,' a 'hanchor,' or a 'horse,' an ''orse.' What is thought of that matter in this part of the world, Signor Squire?"

"We are not critics in your language, but it is reasonable to suppose that the English speak their own tongue better than any other people. That much must be conceded to them, at least, Signor Bolto."

"I shall acknowledge no such advantage as belonging to them. I have not been to school for nothing, not I. The English call c-l-e-r-k, clark; and c-u-c-u-m-b-e-r, cowcumber; an a-n-g-e-l, aingel; and no reasoning can convince me that's right. I've got a string of words, of this sort, that they pronounce out of all reason, that's as long as a pair of leading-lines, or a ship's tiller-rope. You must know, Signor Squire, I kept school, in the early part of my life."

"*Non e possibile!*" exclaimed the vice-governatore, astonishment actually getting the better of his habitual good breeding; "you must mean, Signor Americano, that you gave lessons in the art of rigging and sailing luggers."

"You never was more mistaken, Signore. I taught, on the general system, all sorts of things in the edication way; and had one of my scholars made such a blunder as to say, 'clark,' or 'aingel,' or 'harth,' or 'cowcumber,' he wouldn't have heard the last of it, for that week, at least. But I despise an Englishman, from the very bottom of my soul; for heart isn't deep enough for my feelings."

Absurd as Ithuel's critical dissertations must appear to all who have any familiarity with real English, they were not greatly below many criticisms on the same subject that often illustrate the ephemeral literature of the country; and, in his last speech, he had made a provincial use of the word "despise," that is getting to be so common, as almost to supplant the true signification. By "despising," Ithuel meant that he "hated;" the passion, perhaps, of all others, the most removed from the feeling described by the word he had used, inasmuch as it is not easy to elevate those for

6

whom we have a contempt, to the level necessary to be hated.

"Notwithstanding, the Inglese are not a despicable people," answered Andrea, who was obliged to take the stranger literally, since he knew nothing of his provincial use of terms; "for a nation of the north, they have done marvellous things, of late years, especially on the ocean."

This was more than Ithuel could bear. All his personal wrongs, and sooth to say they had been of a most grievous nature, arose before his mind, incited and inflamed by national dislike; and he broke out in such an incoherent tirade of abuse, as completely set all Filippo's knowledge of English at fault, rendering a translation impossible. By this time, Ithuel had swallowed so much of the wine, a liquor which had far more body than he supposed, that he was ripe for mischief, and it was only his extreme violence that prevented him from betraying more, than, just at the moment, would have been prudent. The vice-governatore listened with attention, in the hope of catching something useful; but it all came to his ears a confused mass of incoherent vituperation, from which he could extract nothing. The scene, consequently, soon became unpleasant, and Andrea Barrofaldi took measures to put an end to it. Watching a favourable occasion to speak, he put in a word, as the excited Bolt paused an instant, to take breath.

"Signore," observed the vice-governatore, "all this may be very true; but as coming from one who serves the Inglese, to one who is the servant of their ally, the Grand Duke of Tuscany, it is quite as extraordinary as it is uncalled for; and we will talk of other things. This lugger, on board which you sail, is out of all question English, notwithstanding what you tell us of the nation."

"Ay, *she* is English," answered Ithuel, with a grim smile, "and a pretty boat she is. But then it is no fault of hers and what can't be cured must be endured. A Guernsey craft, and a desperate goer, when she wakes up and puts on her travelling boots."

"These mariners have a language of their own," remarked Andrea to Vito Viti, smiling as in consideration of Ithuel's nautical habits; "to you and me, the idea of a vessel's using boots, neighbour, seems ridiculous; but the seamen, in their imaginations, bestow all sorts of objects on them. It is curious to hear them converse, good Vito; and now I am dwelling here on our island, I have often thought of collecting a number of their images, in order to aid in illustrating the sort of literature that belongs to their calling. This idea of a lugger's putting on her boots, is quite heroic!"

Now Vito Viti, though an Italian with so musical a name, was no poet, but a man so very literal, withal, as to render him exceedingly matter of fact, in most of his notions. Accordingly, he saw no particular beauty in the idea of a vessel's wearing boots; and, though much accustomed to defer to the vice-governatore's superior knowledge, and more extensive reading, he had the courage, on this occasion, to put in an objection to the probability of the circumstance mentioned.

"Signor Vice-governatore," he replied, "all is not gold that glitters. "Fine words sometimes cover poor thoughts, and, I take it, this is an instance of what I mean. Long as I have lived in Porto Ferrajo, and that is now quite fifty years, seeing that I was born here, and have been off the island but four times in my life — and long, therefore, as I have lived here, I never saw a vessel in the harbour that wore boots, or even shoes."

"This is metaphorical, good Vito, and must be looked at in a poetical point of view. Homer speaks of goddesses holding shields before their favourite warriors; while Ariosto makes rats and asses hold discourse together, as if they were members of an academy. All this is merely the effect of imagination, Signore; and he who has the most, is the aptest at inventing circumstances, which, though not strictly true, are vastly agreeable."

"As for Homer and Ariosto, Signor Vice-governatore, I doubt if either ever saw a vessel with a boot on, or if either ever knew as much about craft, in general, as we who live here in Porto Ferrajo. Harkee, friend Filippo, just ask this Americano if, in his country, he ever saw vessels wear boots. Put the question plainly, and without any of your accursed poetry."

Filippo did as desired, leaving Ithuel to put his own construction on the object of the inquiry; all that had just passed being sealed to him, in consequence of its having been uttered in good Tuscan.

"Boots!" repeated the native of the granite State, looking round him drolly;* "perhaps not exactly the foot-part, and the soles, for they ought, in reason, to be under water; but every vessel that isn't coppered shows her boot-*top*—of *them*, I 'll swear I 've seen ten thousand, more or less."

This answer mystified the vice-governatore, and completely puzzled Vito Viti. The grave mariners at the other table, too, thought it odd, for in no other tongue is the language of the sea as poetical, or figurative, as in the English, and the term of *boot-top,* as applied to a vessel, was Greek to them, as well as to the other listeners. They conversed among themselves on the subject, while their two superiors were holding a secret conference on the other side of the room, giving the American time to rally his recollection, and remember the precise circumstances in which not only he himself, but all his shipmates, were placed. No one could be more wily and ingenious than this man, when on his guard, though the inextinguishable hatred with which he regarded England, and Englishmen, had come so near causing him to betray a secret which it was extremely important, at that moment, to conceal. At length a general silence prevailed, the different groups of speakers ceasing to converse, and all looking towards the vice-governatore, as if in expectation that he was about to suggest something that might give a turn to the discourse. Nor was this a mistake, for, after inquiring of Benedetta if she had a private room, he invited Ithuel and the interpreter to follow him into it, leading the way, attended by the podestà. As soon as these four were thus separated from the others, the door was closed, and the two Tuscans came at once to the point.

"Signor Americano," commenced the vice-governatore, "between those who understand each other, there is little need of many words. This is a language which is comprehended all over the world, and I put it before you in the plainest manner, that we may have no mistake."

"It is tolerable plain, sartain!" exclaimed Ithuel—"two— four—six—eight—ten—all good-looking gold pieces, that, in this part of the world you call *zecchini* — or sequins, as we name 'em, in English. What have I done, Signor Squire, or what am I to do for these twenty dollars? Name your tarms; this working in the dark is ag'in the grain of my natur'."

"You are to tell the *truth ;* we suspect the lugger of being French; and by putting the proof in our hands, you will make us your friends, and serve yourself."

Andrea Barrofaldi knew little of America and Americans, but he had imbibed the common European notion that money was the great deity worshipped in this hemisphere, and that all he had to do was to offer a bribe, in order to purchase a man of Ithuel's deportment and appearance. In his own island, ten sequins would buy almost any mariner of the port, to do any act short of positive legal criminality; and the idea that a barbarian of the west would refuse such a sum, in preference to selling his shipmates, never crossed his mind. Little, however, did the Italian understand the American. A greater knave than Ithuel, in his own way, it was not easy to find; but it shocked all his notions of personal dignity, self-respect, and republican virtue, to be thus unequivocally offered a bribe; and had the lugger not been so awkwardly circumstanced, he would have been apt to bring matters to a crisis, at once, by throwing the gold into the vice-governatore's face; although, knowing where it was to be found, he might have set about devising some means of cheating the owner out of it, at the very next instant. Boon or bribe, directly and unequivocally offered in the shape of money, as coming from the superior to the inferior, or from the corrupter to the corrupted, had he never taken; and it would have appeared, in his eyes, a species of degradation to receive the first, and of treason to his nationality, to accept the last, though he would lie, invent, manage and contrive, from morning till night, in order to transfer even copper from the pocket of his neighbour to his own, under the forms of opinion and usage. In a word, Ithuel, as relates to such things, is what is commonly called law-honest, with certain broad salvoes, in favour of smuggling of all sorts, in foreign countries (at home he never dreamed of such a thing), custom-house oaths, and legal trickery; and this is just the class of men apt to declaim the loudest against the roguery of the rest of mankind. Had here been a law giving half to the informer, he might not

have hesitated to betray the lugger, and all she contained
more especially in the way of regular business; but he had
long before determined that every Italian was a treacherous
rogue, and not at all to be trusted like an American rogue;
and then his indomitable dislike of England would have kept
him true in a case of much less complicated risk than this.
Commanding himself, however, and regarding the sequins
with natural longing, he answered with a simplicity of manner that both surprised and imposed on the vice-governatore.

"No—no—Signor Squire," he said; "in the first place,
I 've no secret to tell; and it would be a trickish thing to
touch your money, and not give you its worth in return;
and then the lugger is Guernsey built, and carries a good
King George's commission. In my part of the world, we
never take gold unless we sell something of equal valie.
Gifts and begging we look upon as mean and unbecoming,
and the next thing to going on to the town as a pauper;
though if I can sarve you lawfully, like, I 'm just as willing
to work for *your* money, as for that of any other man's.
I 've no preference for king's, in that partic'lar."

All this time Ithuel held out the sequins, with a show of
returning them, though in a very reluctant manner, leaving
Andrea, who comprehended his actions much better than
his words, to understand that he declined selling his secret.

"You can keep the money, friend," observed the vice-
governatore, "for when we give, in Italy, it is not our
practice to take the gift back again. In the morning, perhaps, you will remember something that it may be useful
for me to know."

"I 've no occasion for gifts, nor is it exactly accordin' to
the granite rule to accept 'em," answered Ithuel, a little
sharply. "Handsome conduct is handsome conduct; and
I call the fellow-creetur' that would oppress and overcome
another with a gift, little better than an English aristocrat.
Hand out the dollars in the way of trade, in as large
amounts as you will, and I 'll find the man, and that, too, in
the lugger, who will see you out in 't, to your heart's content. — Harkee, Philip-o; tell the gentleman, in an under-
tone, like, about the three kegs of tobacco we got out of
the Virginy ship, the day we made the north end of Corsica,
and perhaps that will satisfy him we are not his inimies.

here is no use in bawling it out, so that the woman can hear what you say, or the men who are drinking in the other room."

" Signor Ithuello," answered the Genoese, in English, " it will no do to let these gentlemen know anything of them kegs—one being the deputy-governor and the other a magistrate. The lugger will be seized for a smuggler, which will be the next thing to being seized for an enemy."

" Yet I 've a longing for them 'ere sequins, to tell you the truth, Philip-o ! I see no other means of getting at 'em except it be through them three kegs of tobacco."

" Why you don't take 'em, when the Signore put 'em into your very hand ? All you do is put him in your pocket, and say, ' Eccellenza, what you please to wish ?' "

" That isn't granite, man, but more in the natur' of you Italians. The most disgraceful thing on 'airth is a paupe"— so Ithuel pronounced " pauper" — "the next is a street beggar ; after him comes your chaps who take sixpences and shillin's, in the way of small gifts ; and last of all an Eng lishman. All these I despise ; but let this Signore say but the word, in the way of trade, and he 'll find me as ready and expairt as he can wish. I 'd defy the devil in a trade !"

Filippo shook his head, positively declining to do so foolish a thing as to mention a contraband article to those whose duty it would be to punish a violation of the revenue laws. In the meanwhile the sequins remained in the hands of Andrèa Barrofaldi, who seemed greatly at a loss to understand the character of the strange being whom chance had thus thrown in his way. The money was returned to his purse, but his distrust and doubts were by no means removed.

" Answer me one thing, Signor Bolto," asked the vice-governatore, after a minute of thought; " if you hate the English so much, why do you serve in their ships ? — why not quit them, on the first good occasion ? The land is as wide as the sea, and you must be often on it."

" I calculate, Signor Squire, you don't often study charts, or you wouldn't fall into such a consait. There 's twice as much water as solid ground, on this 'airth, to begin with ; as in reason there ought to be, seeing that an acre of good productive land is worth five or six of oceans ; and then you nave little knowledge of my character and prospects to ask such a question. I sarve the king of England to make him pay well for it. If you want to take an advantage of a man, first get him in debt; then you can work your will on him, in the most profitable and safe manner!"

All this was unintelligible to the vice-governatore, who, after a few more questions and answers, took a civil leave of the strangers, intimating to Benedetta that they were not to follow him back into the room he had just quitted.

As for Ithuel, the disappearance of the two gentlemen gave him no concern; but as he felt that it might be unsafe to drink any more wine, he threw down his reckoning, and strolled into the street, followed by his companion. Within an hour from that moment, the three kegs of tobacco were in the possession of a shop-keeper of the place, that brief interval sufficing to enable the man to make his bargain, and to deliver the articles, which was his real object on shore. This little smuggling transaction was carried on altogether without the knowledge of Raoul Yvard, who was to all intents and purposes the captain of his own lugger, and in whose character there were many traits of chivalrous honour, mixed up with habits and pursuits that would not seem to promise qualities so elevated. But this want of a propensity to turn a penny in his own way, was not the only distinguishing characteristic between the commander of the little craft, and the being he occasionally used as a mask to his true purposes.

CHAPTER V.

"The great contention of the sea and skies
Parted our fellowship: — But, hark! a sail."
Cassio.

WHATEVER may have been the result of the vice-governore s further inquiries and speculations, that night, they were not known. After consuming an hour in the lower part of the town, in and around the port, he and the podestà sought their homes and their pillows, leaving the lugger riding quietly at her anchor, in the spot where she was last presented to the reader's attention. If Raoul Yvard and Ghita had another interview, too, it was so secretly managed as to escape all observation, and can form no part of this narrative.

A Mediterranean morning, at midsummer, is one of those balmy and soothing periods of the day, that affect the mind as well as the body. Everywhere we have the mellow and advancing light that precedes the appearance of the sun — the shifting hues of the sky—that pearly softness that seems to have been invented to make us love the works of God's hand, and the warm glow of the brilliant sun; but, it is not everywhere that these fascinating changes occur, on a sea whose blue vies with the darkest depths of the void of space, beneath a climate that is as winning as the scenes it adorns, and amid mountains whose faces reflect every varying shade of light, with the truth and the poetry of nature. Such a morning as this last, was that which succeeded the night with which our tale opened, bringing with it the reviving movements of the port and town. Italy, as a whole, is remarkable for an appearance of quiet and repose, that are little known in the more bustling scenes of the greedier commerce of our own quarter of the world, or, indeed, in those of most of the northern nations of Europe. There is in her aspect, modes of living, and even in her habits of business, an air of decayed gentility, that is wanting to the ports, shops, and marts of the more vulgar parts of the world · as if conscious of having been so long the focus of human refinement, it was unbecoming, in these later days, to throw aside all traces of her history and power. Man, and the climate, too, seem in unison ; one meeting the cares of life with a *far niente* manner, that is singularly in accordance with the dreamy and soothing atmosphere he respires.

Just as day dawned, the fall of a billet of wood, on the deck of the Feu-Follet, gave the first intimation that any one was stirring in or near the haven. If there had been a watch on board that craft, throughout the night—and doubt-less such had been the case — it had been kept in so quiet and unobtrusive a manner, as to render it questionable to the jealous eyes which had been riveted on her from the shore, until long past midnight. Now, however, everything was in motion, and in less than five minutes after that billet

of wood had fallen from the hands of the cook, as he was
about to light his galley-fire, the tops of the hats and caps of
some fifty or sixty sailors were seen moving to and fro, just
above the upper edge of the bulwarks.　　Three minutes late,
and two men appeared near the knight-heads, each with his
arms folded, looking at the vessel's hawse, and taking a
survey of the state of the harbour, and of objects on the surrounding shore.

The two individuals who were standing in the conspicuous
position named, were Raoul Yvard, himself, and Ithuel Bolt.
Their conversation was in French, the part borne by the
last being most execrably pronounced, and paying little or
no attention to grammar; but, it is necessary that we should
render what was said by both into the vernacular, with the
peculiarities that belonged to the men.

" I see only the Austrian that is worth the trouble of a
movement," quietly observed Raoul, whose eye was scan-
ning the inner harbour, his own vessel lying two hundred
yards without it, it will be remembered—" and she is light,
and would scarce pay for sending her to Toulon.　These
feluccas would embarrass us, without affording much reward,
and then their loss would ruin the poor devils of owners, and
bring misery into many a family."

" Well, that's a new idee, for a privateer!" said Ithuel
sneeringly; " luck's luck, in these matters, and every man
must count on what war turns up.　I wish you'd read the
history of *our* revolution, and then you'd ha' seen that
liberty and equality are not to be had without some ups and
downs in fortin's and chances."

" The Austrian *might* do," added Raoul, who paid little
attention to his companion's remarks, " if he were a streak
or two lower in the water—but, after all, E-too-*ell*," for so
he pronounced the other's name — " I do not like a capture
that is made without any *éclat*, or spirit, in the attack and
defence."

" Well," — this word Ithuel invariably pronounced,
" wa-a-l" — " well, to my notion, the most profitable and
the most agreeable battles, are the shortest; and the pleasant-
est victories are them in which there's the most prize-money.
Howsever, as that brig is only an Austrian, I care little what
you may detairmine to do with her; was she English, I'd

head a boat myself, to go in and tow her out here, **expressly**
to have the satisfaction of burning her. English ships make
a cheerful fire !"

" And that would be a useless waste of property, and perhaps of blood, and would do no one any good, Etoo*ell.*"

" But it would do the accursed English *harm*, and that
counts for a something, in my reckoning. Nelson wasn't so
over-scrupulous, at the Nile, about burning your ships, Mr.
Rule—"

" *Tonnère !* why do you always bring in that *malheureux*
Nile ?—Is it not enough that we were beaten—disgraced—
destroyed—that a friend must tell us of it so often ?"

" You forget, Mr. Rule, that I was an *inimy, then ;*" returned Ithuel, with a grin and a grim smile. " If you 'll
take the trouble to examine my back, you 'll find on it the
marks of the lashes I got for just telling my captain that it
went ag'in the grain for me, a republican as I was by idee
and natur', to fight other republicans. He told me he would
first try the grain of my skin, and see how that would agree
with what he called my duty ; and I must own, he got the
best on 't ; I fit like a tiger ag'in you, rather than be flogged
twice the same day. Flogging on a sore back is an awful
argument !"

" And now has come the hour of revenge, *pauvre Etooell ;*
this time you are on the right side, and may fight with heart
and mind those you so much hate."

A long and gloomy silence followed, during which Raoul
turned his face aft, and stood looking at the movements of
the men, as they washed the decks, while Ithuel seated him
self on a knight-head, and, his chin resting on his hand, he
sat ruminating, in bitterness of spirit, like Milton's devil, in
some of his dire cogitations, on the atrocious wrong of
which he had really been the subject. Bodies of men are
proverbially heartless. They commit injustice without reflection, and vindicate their abuses without remorse. And yet
it may be doubtful if either a nation, or an individual, ever
tolerated, or was an accessary in, a wrong, that the act
sooner or later did not recoil on the offending party, through
that mysterious principle of right, which is implanted in the
nature of things, bringing forth its own results as the seed
produces its grain, and the tree its fruits ; a supervision of

holiness that it is usual to term (and rightly enough, when
we remember who created principles) the providence of God.
Let that people dread the future, who, in their collected
capacity, systematically encourage injustice of any sort;
since their own eventual demoralization will follow as a
necessary consequence, even though they escape punishment
in a more direct form.

We shall not stop to relate the moody musings of the
New-Hampshire man. Unnurtured, and, in many respects,
unprincipled as he was, he had his clear conceptions of the
injustice of which he had been one, among thousands of
other victims; and, at that moment, he would have held life
itself as a cheap sacrifice, could he have had his fill of revenge. Time and again, while a captive on board the
English ship in which he had been immured for years, had
he meditated the desperate expedient of blowing up the vessel; and had not the means been wanting, mercenary and
selfish as he ordinarily seemed, he was every way equal to
executing so dire a scheme, in order to put an end to the
lives of those who were the agents in wronging him, and his
own sufferings, together. The subject never recurred to his
mind, without momentarily changing the current of its
thoughts, and tinging all his feelings with an intensity of
bitterness that it was painful to bear. At length, sighing
heavily, he rose from the knight-head, and turned towards
the mouth of the bay, as if to conceal from Raoul the expression of his countenance. This act, however, was
scarcely done, ere he started, and an exclamation escaped
him, that induced his companion to turn quickly on his heel,
and face the sea. There, indeed, the growing light enabled
both to discover an object that could scarcely be other than
one of interest to men in their situation.

It has been said already, that the deep bay, on the side of
which stands the town of Porto Ferrajo, opens to the north,
looking in the direction of the headland of Piombino. On
the right of the bay, the land, high and broken, stretches
several miles ere it forms what is called the Canal, while on
the left, it terminates with the low bluff on which stands the
residence then occupied by Andrea Barrofaldi; and which
has since become so celebrated as the abode of one far
greater than the worthy vice-governatore. The haven lying

under these heights, on the left of the bay, and by the side of the town, it followed, as a matter of course, that the anchorage of the lugger was also in this quarter of the bay, commanding a clear view to the north, in the direction of the main land, as far as eye could reach. The width of the Canal, or of the passage between Elba and the Point of Piombino, may be some six or seven miles; and at the distance of less than one mile from the northern end of the former, stands a small rocky islet, which has since become known to the world as the spot on which Napoleon stationed a corporal's guard, by way of taking possession, when he found his whole empire dwindled to the sea-girt mountains in its vicinity. With the existence and position of this island, both Raoul and Ithuel were necessarily acquainted, for they had seen it and noted its situation the previous night, though it had escaped their notice that, from the place where the Feu-Follet had brought up, it was not visible. In their first look to seaward, that morning, which was ere the light had grown sufficiently strong to render the houses on the opposite side of the bay distinct, an object had been seen in this quarter, which had then been mistaken for the rock; but, by this time, the light was strong enough to show that it was a very different thing. In a word, that which both Raoul and Ithuel had fancied an islet, was neither more nor less than a ship.

The stranger's head was to the northward, and his motion, before a light southerly air, could not have exceeded a knot an hour. He had no other canvass spread than his three topsails and jib; though his courses were hanging in the brails. His black hull was just beginning to show its details;-and along the line of light-yellow, that enlivened his side, were visible the dark intervals of thirteen ports; a real gun frowning in each. Although the hammocks were not stowed, and the hammock-cloths had that empty and undressed-look which is so common to a man-of-war in the night, it was apparent that the ship had an upper-deck, with quarter-deck and forecastle batteries; or, in other words, that she was a frigate. As she had opened the town of Porto Ferrajo several minutes before she was herself seen from the Feu-Follet. an ensign was hanging from the end of her gaff

though there was not sufficient air to open its folds, in a way
to let the national character of the stranger be known.

"Peste!" exclaimed Raoul Yvard, as soon he had gazed
a minute at the stranger, in silence — "a pretty *cul de sac*
are we in, if that gentleman should happen to be an Englishman! What say you, Etooell; can *you* make out anything of that ensign—your eyes are the best in the lugger?"

"It is too much for any sight to detairmine, at this distance, and that before the sun is risen; but, by having a
glass ready, we shall soon know. Five minutes will bring
us the Great Luminary, as our minister used to call him."

Ithuel had descended from the bulwark, while speaking;
and he now went aft in quest of a glass, returning to his old
station, bringing two of the instruments; one of which he
handed to his commander, while he kept the other himself.
In another minute both had levelled their glasses at the
stranger, whom each surveyed attentively, for some time, in
profound silence.

"*Pardie!*" exclaimed Raoul, "that ensign is the tricolor, or my eyes are untrue to my own country. Let me
see, Etooell, what ship of forty-two, or forty-four, has the
republic on this coast?"

"Not *that*, Monsieur Yvard," answered Ithuel, with a
manner so changed, and an emphasis so marked, as at once
to draw his companion's attention from the frigate to his own
countenance; "not *that*, Monsieur Capitaing. It is not easy
for a bird to forget the cage in which he was shut up for
two years; if that is not the accursed Proserpine, I have
forgotten the cut of my own jib!"

"La Proserpine!" repeated Raoul, who was familiar with
his shipmate's adventures, and did not require to be told his
meaning; "if you are not mistaken, Etooell, le Feu-Follet
needs put her lantern under a shade. This is only a forty,
if I can count her ports."

"I care nothing for ports, or guns; it is the Proserpine;
and the only harm I wish her is, that she were at the bottom of the ocean. The Proserpine, thirty-six, Captain Cuffe
though Captain Flog would have been a better name for him.
Yes, the Proserpine, thirty six, Captain Cuffe, Heaven bless
her!"

" Bah ! — this vessel has forty-four guns—now I can see to count them ; I make twenty-two of a side."

" Ay, that 's just her measure — a thirty-six on the list, and by rate, and forty-four by count; twenty-six long eighteens below; twelve thirty-two's, carronades, on her quarter-deck ; and four more carronades, with two barkers, for'ard. She 'd just extinguish your Jack-o'Lantern, Monsieur Rule, at one broadside ; for what are ten twelve-pound carronades, and seventy men, to such a frigate ?"

" I am not madman enough, Etooell, to dream of fighting a frigate, or even a heavy sloop-of-war, with the force you have just mentioned ; but I have followed the sea too long to be alarmed before I am certain of my danger. La Railleuse is just such a ship as that."

" Hearken to reason, Monsieur Rule," answered Ithuel, earnestly ; " La Railleuse, nor no other French frigate, would show her colours to an enemy's port ; for it would be uselessly telling her errand. Now, an English ship might show a French ensign, for *she* always has it in her power to change it ; and then *she* might be benefited by the cheat. The Proserpine is French built, and has French legs, too, boots or no boots" — here Ithuel laughed a little, involuntarily, but his face instantly became serious again — "and I have heard she was a sister vessel of the other. So much for size and appearance ; but every shroud, and port, and sail, about yonder craft, is registered on my back in a way that no sponge will ever wash out."

" Sa-a-c-r-r-r-e," muttered Raoul between his teeth, " Etooell, if an Englishman, he may very well take it into his head to come in here, and perhaps anchor within half-a-cable's length of us ! What think you of that, *mon brave Américain ?*"

" That it may very well come to pass ; though one hardly sees, either, what is to bring a cruiser into such a place as this. Every one hasn't the curiosity of a Jack-o'Lantern."

" *Mais que diable allait-il faire dans cette galère !* — *Bien ;* we must take the weather as it comes ; sometimes a gale, and sometimes a calm. As he shows his own ensign so loyally, let us return the compliment, and show ours. Hoist the ensign there, aft."

' Which one, Monsieur ?" demanded an old demure-

looking quarter-master, who was charged with that duty
and who was never known to laugh; "the captain will
remember we came into port under the *drapeau* of Monsieur
Jean Bull."

"*Bien*—hoist the drapeau of Monsieur Jean Bull, again.
We must brazen it out, now we have put on the masque.
Monsieur Lieutenant, clap on the hawser, and run the lugger ahead, over her anchor, and see everything clear for
spreading our pocket-handkerchiefs. No one knows when
le Feu-Follet may have occasion to wipe her face. — Ah!—
now, Etooell, we can make out his broadside fairly, he is
heading more to the westward."

The two seamen levelled their glasses, and renewed their
examinations. Ithuel had a peculiarity that not only charac-
terized the man, but, which is so common among Americans
of his class, as, in a sense, to be national. On ordinary occasions he was talkative, and disposed to gossip; but, whenever
action and decision became necessary, he was thoughtful,
silent, and, though in a way of his own, even dignified. This
last fit was on him, and he waited for Raoul to lead the
conversation. The other, however, was disposed to be as
reserved as himself, for he quitted the knight-head, and took
refuge from the splashing of the water, used in washing the
decks, in his own cabin.

Two hours, though they brought the sun, with the activity
and hum of the morning, had made no great change in the
relative positions of things within and without the bay. The
people of le Feu-Follet had breakfasted, had got everything
on board their little craft in its proper place, and were moody,
observant and silent. One of the lessons that Ithuel had
succeeded in teaching his shipmates, was to impress on them
he necessity of commanding their voluble propensities, if
they would wish to pass for Englishmen. It is certain, more
words would have been uttered, in this little lugger, in one
hour, had her crew been indulged to the top of their bent,
than would have been uttered in an English first-rate, in
two; but the danger of using their own language, and the
English peculiarity of grumness, had been so thoroughly
taught them, that her people rather caricatured, than otherwise, *ce grand talent pour le silence*, that was thought to
distinguish their enemies. Ithuel, who had a waggery of his

own, smiled as he saw the seamen folding their arms, throwing discontent and surliness into their countenances, and pacing the deck singly, as if misanthropical and disdaining to converse, whenever a boat came alongside from the shore. Several of these visiters arrived, in the course of the two hours mentioned; but the sentinel at the gangway, who had his orders, repulsed every attempt to come on board, pretending not to understand French, when permission was asked in that language.

Raoul had a boat's crew of four, all of whom had acquired the English, like himself, in a prison-ship, and with these men he now prepared to land; for, as yet, he had made little progress in the business which brought him into his present awkward predicament, and he was not a man to abandon an object so dear to him, lightly. Finding himself in a dilemma, he was resolved to make an effort to reap, if possible, some advantage from his critical situation. Accordingly, after he had taken his coffee, and given his orders, the boat's crew was called, and he left the lugger's side. All this was done tranquilly, as if the appearance of the stranger in the offing gave no trouble to any in le Feu-Follet.

On this occasion, the boat pulled boldly into the little harbour, its officer touching the shore at the common landing. Nor were the men in any haste to return. They lounged about the quay, in waiting for their captain, cheapening fruits, chatting with the women, in such Italian as they could muster, and affecting to understand the French of the old sea-dogs that drew near them, all of whom knew more or less of that universal language, with difficulty. That they were the objects of suspicion, their captain had sufficiently warned them, and practice rendered them all good actors. The time they remained in waiting for Raoul, was consequently spent in eluding attempts to induce them to betray themselves, and in caricaturing Englishmen. Two of the four folded their arms, endeavoured to look surly, and paced the quay in silence, refusing even to unbend to the blandishments of the gentler sex, three or four of whom endeavoured to insinuate themselves into their confidence, by offerings of fruit and flowers.

"Amico," said Annunziate, one of the prettiest girls of

7 *

her class in Porto Ferrajo, and who had been expressly
employed by Vito Viti to perform this office, " here are figs
from the main-land. Will you please to eat a few, that
when you go back to Inghilterra, you may tell your countrymen how we poor Elbans live?"

" Bad fig" — sputtered Jacques, Raoul's cockswain, to
whom this offering was made, and speaking in broken English ; " better at 'ome. Pick up better in ze street of Ports-
mout' !"

" But, Signore, you need not look as if they would hurt
you, or bite you ; you can eat them, and, take my word for
it, you will find them as pleasant as the melons of Napoli."

" No melon good, but English melon. English melon
plenty as pomme de terres — bah !"

" Yes, Signore, as the melons of Napoli," continued Annunziate, who did not understand a syllable of the ungra-
cious answers she received ; " Signor Vito Viti, our *podestà*,
ordered me to offer these figs to the forestieri — the Inglesi,
who are in the bay—"

" God-dam," returned Jacques, in a quick, sententious
manner, that was intended to get rid of the fair tormentor,
and which, temporarily, at least, was not without its effect.

But, leaving the boat's crew to be badgered in this manner, until relief came, as will be hereafter related, we must
follow our hero in his way through the streets of the town.
Raoul, guided by an instinct, or having some special object
before his eyes, walked swiftly up the heights, ascending to
the promontory, so often mentioned. As he passed, every
eye was turned on him, for, by this time, the distrust in the
place was general ; and the sudden appearance of a frigate,
wearing a French ensign, before the port, had given rise to
apprehensions of a much more serious nature than any which
could possibly attend the arrival of a craft as light as the
lugger, by herself. Vito Viti had long before gone up the
street, to see the vice-governatore ; and eight or ten of the
principal men of the place had been summoned to a council,
including the two senior military dignitaries of the island.
The batteries, it was known, were manned ; and, although
it would have puzzled the acutest mind of Elba to give a
reason why the French should risk so unprofitable an attack,
as one on their principal port, long ere Raoul was seen

among them, such a result was not only dreaded, but, in a measure, anticipated with confidence. As a matter of course, then, every eye followed his movements, as he went with bounding steps up the narrow terraces of the steep street, and the least of his actions was subjected to the narrowest and most jealous scrutiny.

The heights were again thronged with spectators, of all ages and classes, and of both sexes. The mantles and flowing dresses of females prevailed as usual; for whatever is connected with curiosity, is certain to collect an undue proportion of a sex whose imaginations are so apt to get the start of their judgments. On a terrace, in front of the palace, as it was the custom to designate the dwelling of the governor, was the group of magnates, all of them paying the gravest attention to the smallest change in the direction of the ship, which had now become an object of general solicitude and apprehension. So intent, indeed, were they in gazing at this apprehended enemy, that Raoul stood in front of Andrea Barrofaldi, cap in hand, and bowing his salutation, before his approach was even anticipated. This sudden and unannounced arrival created great surprise, and some little confusion; one or two of the group turning away, instinctively, as it might be, to conceal the flushes that mounted to their cheeks, at being so unexpectedly confronted by the very man, whom, the minute before, they had been strongly denouncing.

" *Bon giorno*, Signor Vice-governatore," commenced Raoul, in his gay, easy and courteous manner, and certainly with an air that betrayed any feeling but those of apprehension and guilt; " we have a fine morning, on the land, here; and apparently a fine frigate, of the French republic, in the offing, yonder."

" We were conversing of that vessel, Signor Smees," answered Andrea, " as you approached. What, in your judgment, can induce a Frenchman to appear before our town, in so menacing a manner?"

" Cospetto! — you might as well ask me, Signore, what induces these republicans to do a thousand other out-of-the-way things. What has made them behead Louis XVI.? What has made them overrun half of your Italy, conquer Egypt, and drive the Austrians back upon their Danube?"

"To say nothing of their letting Nelsoni destroy them at Aboukir," added Vito Viti, with a grunt.

"True, Signore, or let Nelson, my gallant countryman, annihilate them near the mouth of the Nile. I did not consider it proper to boast of English glory, though that case, too, may very well be included. We have several men, in ze Ving-And-Ving, who were in that glorious battle, particularly our sailing-master, Etooell Bolt, who was on board Nelson's own ship, having been accidentally sent on service from the frigate to which he properly belonged, and carried off expressly to share, as it might be, in the glory of this famous battle."

"I have seen the Signore," drily remarked Andrea Barrofaldi — "*é uno Americano?*"

"An American!" exclaimed Raoul, starting a little in spite of his assumed indifference of manner; "why, yes, I believe Bolt *was* born in America — English America, you know, Signori, and that is much the same thing as having been born in England, herself. We look upon *ze Yankés*, as but a part of our own people, and take them into our service most cheerfully."

"So the Signor Ituello has given us reason to believe; he is seemingly a great lover of the English nation."

Raoul was uneasy, for he was entirely ignorant of all that had passed in the wine-house, and he thought he detected irony in the manner of the vice-governatore.

"Certainly, Signore," he answered, however, with unmoved steadiness; "certainly, Signore, the Americani adore Inghilterra; and well they may, considering all that great nation has done for them. But, Signor Vice-governatore, I have come to offer you the service of my lugger, should this Frenchman really intend mischief. We are small, it is true; and our guns are but light; nevertheless we may break the frigate's cabin-windows, while you are doing him still greater injury, from these heights. I trust you will assign ze Ving-And-Ving some honourable station, should you come to blows with the republicans."

"And what particular service would it be most agreeable to you to undertake, Signore," inquired the vice-governatore, with considerate courtesy; "we are no mariners, and must leave the choice to yourself. The colonello, here expects some firing, and has his artillerists already at their guns."

"The preparation of Porto Ferrajo is celebrated among the mariners of the Mediterranean, and, should the Frenchman venture within reach of your shot, I expect to see him unrigged faster than if he were in a dock-yard. As for ze teetl' Ving-And-Ving, in my opinion, while the frigate is easy with these batteries, it might be well for us to steer along the shore on the east side of the bay, until we can get outside of her, when we shall have the beggars between two fires. That was just what Nelson did at Aboukir, Signor Podestà, a battle you seem so much to admire."

"That would be a manœuvre worthy of a follower of Nelsoni, Signore," observed the colonel, "if the metal of your guns were heavier. With short pieces of twelve, however, you would hardly venture within reach of long pieces of eighteen; although the first should be manned by Inglese, and the last by Françese?"

"One never knows. At the Nile, one of our fifties laid the Orient, a three-decker, athwart-hawse, and did her lots of injury. The vaisseau, in fact, was blown up. Naval combats are decided on principles altogether different from engagements on the land, Signor Colonello."

"It must be so, truly," answered the soldier; "but what means this movement? you, as a seaman, may be able to tell us, Capitano."

This drew all eyes to the frigate again, where, indeed, were movements that indicated some important changes. As these movements have an intimate connexion with the incidents of the tale, it will be necessary to relate them in a manner to render them more intelligible to the reader.

The distance of the frigate from the town, might now have been five English miles. Of current there was none; and there being no tides in the Mediterranean, the ship would have lain perfectly stationary all the morning, but for a very light air from the southward. Before this air, however, she had moved to the westward about a couple of miles, until she had got the government-house nearly abeam. At the same time, she had been obliquely drawing nearer, which was the circumstance that produced the alarm. With the sun had arisen the wind, and a few minutes before the colo-

6

nel interrupted himself, in the manner related, the topsails
of the stranger had swelled, and he began to move through
the water at the rate of some four or five knots the hour.
The moment her people felt that they had complete command of their vessel, as if waiting only for that assurance,
they altered her course, and made sail.   Putting her helm
a-starboard, the ship came close by the wind, with her head
looking directly in for the promontory, while her tacks were
hauled on board, and her light canvass aloft was loosened
and spread to the breeze.   Almost at the same instant, for
everything seemed to be done at once, and as by instinct,
the French flag was lowered, another went up in its place,
and a gun was fired to leeward — a signal of amity.   As
this second emblem of nationality blew out, and opened to
the breeze, the glasses showed the white field and St. George's
cross of the noble old ensign of England.

An exclamation of surprise and delight escaped the spectators on the promontory, as their doubts and apprehensions
were thus dramatically relieved.   No one thought of Raoul
at that happy moment, though to him there was nothing of
new interest in the affair, with the exception of the apparent
intention of the stranger to enter the bay.   As le Feu-Follet
lay in plain view from the offing, he had his doubts, indeed,
whether the warlike appearance of that craft was not the
true reason of this sudden change in the frigate's course.
Still, lying as he did, in a port hostile to France, there was
a probability that he might yet escape without a very critical or close examination.

"Signor Smees, I felicitate you on this visit of a countryman," cried Andrea Barrofaldi, a pacific man by nature, and
certainly no warrior, and who felt too happy at the prospects
of passing a quiet day, to feel distrust at such a moment;
"I shall do you honour in my communications with Florence, for the spirit and willingness which you have shown
in the wish to aid us, on this trying occasion."

"Signor Vice-governatore, do not trouble yourself to
dwell on my poor services," answered Raoul, scarce caring
to conceal the smile that struggled about his handsome
mouth; "think rather of those of these gallant signori, who
greatly regret that an opportunity for gaining distinction
has been lost.   But here are signals that must be meant for

us —I hope my stupid fellows will be able to answer them, in my absence."

It was fortunate for le Feu-Follet, perhaps, that her commander was not on board, when the stranger, the Proserpine, the very ship that Ithuel so well knew, made her number. The mystification that was to follow was in much better hands, while conducted by the New-Hampshire man, than it could possibly be in his own. Ithuel answered promptly, though what, he did not know himself; but he took good care that the flags he showed should become so entangled, as not to be read by those in the frigate, while they had every appearance of being hoisted fearlessly, and in good faith.

CHAPTER VI.

"Are all prepared?"
"They are — nay more — embark'd; the latest boat
Waits but my chief—"
"My sword and my capote."
The Corsair.

WHAT success attended the artifice of Ithuel, it was impossible to tell, so far as the frigate was concerned; though the appearance of mutual intelligence between the two vessels, had a very favourable tendency towards removing suspicion from the lugger, among those on shore. It seemed so utterly improbable that a French corsair could answer the signals of an English frigate, that even Vito Viti felt compelled to acknowledge to the vice-governatore, in a whisper, that, so far, the circumstance was much in favour of the lugger's loyalty. Then the calm exterior of Raoul counted for something, more especially as he remained, apparently, an unconcerned observer of the rapid approach of the ship.

"We shall not have occasion to use your gallant offer, Signor Smees," said Andrea, kindly, as ne was about to retire into the house, with one or two of his counsellors, " but we thank you none the less. It is a happiness to be honoured with the visit of two cruisers of your great nation on the same day, and I hope you will so far favour me as to accompany your brother commander, when he shall do me the honour to pay the customary visit, since it would seem to be his serious intention to pay Porto Ferrajo the compliment of a call. Can you not guess at the name of the frigate?"

" Now I see she is a countryman, I think I can, Signore," answered Raoul, carelessly; " I take her to be la Proserpine, a French-built ship, a circumstance that first deceived me as to her character."

" And the noble cavaliere, her commander—you doubtless know his name and rank?"

" Oh! perfectly; he is the son of an old admiral, under whom I was educated, though we happen ourselves never to have met. Sir Brown is the name and title of the gentleman."

" Ah! that is a truly English rank, and name, too, as one might say. Often have I met that honourable appellation in Shakspeare, and other of your eminent authors. Miltoni has a Sir Brown, if I am not mistaken, Signore?"

" Several of them, Signor Vice-governatore," answered Raoul, without a moment's hesitation or the smallest remorse; though he had no idea whatever who Milton was; ' Milton, Shakspeare, Cicero, and all our great writers, often mention Signori of this family."

" Cicero!" repeated Andrea, in astonishment—" he was a Roman, and an ancient, Capitano, and died before Inghilterra was known to the civilized world."

Raoul perceived that he had reached too far, though he was not in absolute danger of losing his balance. Smiling, as in consideration of the other's provincial view of things, he rejoined, with an *à-plomb* that would have done credit to a politician, in an explanatory and half-apologetic tone.

" Quite true, Signor Vice-governatore, as respects him you mention," he said; " but not true as respects Sir Cicero, my illustrious compatriot. Let me see—I do not think it is yet a century since our Cicero died. He was born in Devonshire"—this was the county in which Raoul had been imprisoned—" and must have died in Dublin. Si— now I remember, it *was* in Dublin that this virtuous and distinguished author yielded up his breath."

To all this Andrea had nothing to say, for, half a century since, so great was the ignorance of civilized nations, as related to such things, that one might have engrafted a Homer on the literature of England, in particular, without much risk of having the imposition detected. Signor Barrofaldi was not pleased to find that the barbarians were seizing on the Italian names, it is true; but he was fain to set the circumstance down to those very traces of barbarism, which were the unavoidable fruits of their origin. As for supposing it possible that one who spoke with the ease and innocence of Raoul, was inventing as he went along, it was an idea he was himself much too unpractised to entertain; and the very first thing he did, on entering the palace, was to make a memorandum which might lead him, at a leisure moment, to inquire into the nature of the writings, and the general merits of Sir Cicero, the illustrious namesake of him of Rome. As soon as this little digression terminated, he entered the palace, after again expressing the hope that "Sir Smees" would not fail to accompany "Sir Brown," in the visit which the functionary fully expected to receive from the latter, in the course of the next hour or two. The company now began to disperse, and Raoul was soon left to his own meditations; which, just at that moment, were anything but agreeable.

The town of Porto Ferrajo is so shut in from the sea by the rock against which it is built, its fortifications, and the construction of its own little port, as to render the approach of a vessel invisible to its inhabitants, unless they choose to ascend to the heights, and the narrow promenade already mentioned. This circumstance had drawn a large crowd upon the hill, again; among which Raoul Yvard now threaded his way, wearing his sea cap, and his assumed naval uniform, in a smart, affected manner, for he was fully sensible of all the advantages he possessed on the score of personal appearance. His unsettled eye, however, wandered from one pretty face to another, in quest of Ghita, who alone was the object of his search, and the true cause of the awkward predicament in which he had brought not only himself,

8

but le Feu-Follet. In this manner, now thinking of her he sought, and then reverting to his situation in an enemy's port, he walked along the whole line of the cliff, scarce knowing whether to return, or to seek his boat, by doubling on the town, when he heard his own name pronounced in a sweet voice, which went directly to his heart. Turning on his heel, Ghita was within a few feet of him.

"Salute me distantly, and as a stranger," said the girl, in almost breathless haste, "and point to the different streets, as if inquiring your way through the town. This is the place where we met last evening; but, remember, it is no longer dark."

As Raoul complied with her desire, any distant spectator might well have fancied the meeting accidental, though he poured forth a flood of expressions of love and admiration.

"Enough, Raoul," said the girl blushing, and dropping her eyes, though no displeasure was visible on her serene and placid face, "another time I might indulge you. How much worse is your situation now, than it was last night! Then you had only the port to fear; now you have both the people of the port and this strange ship—an Inglese, as they tell me?"

"No doubt—la Proserpine, Etooell says, and he knows; you remember Etooell, dearest Ghita, the American who was with me at the tower—well, he has served in this very ship, and knows her to be la Proserpine, of forty-four." Raoul paused a moment; then he added, laughing in a way to surprise his companion—"Oui—la Proserpine, le Capitaine Sir Brown!"

"What you can find to amuse you in all this, Raoul, is more than I can discover. Sir Brown, or sir any-body-else, will send you again to those evil English prison-ships, of which you have so often told me; and there is surely nothing pleasant in *that* idea."

"Bah! my sweet Ghita, Sir Brown, or Sir White, or Sir Black, has not yet got me. I am not a child, to tumble into the fire because the leading-strings are off; and le Feu-Follet shines, or goes out, exactly as it suits her purposes. The frigate, ten to one, will just run close in, and take a near look, and then square away and go to Livorno, where there is much more to amuse her officers, than here, in Porto

Ferrajo. This Sir Brown has his Ghita, as well as Raoul Yvard."

"No, not a Ghita, I fear, Raoul," answered the girl smiling, spite of herself, while her colour almost insensibly deepened — "Livorno has few ignorant country girls, like me, who have been educated in a lone watch-tower on the coast."

"Ghita," answered Raoul, with feeling, "that poor lone watch-tower of thine, might well be envied by many a noble dame at Roma and at Napoli; for it has left thee innocent and pure — a gem that gay capitals seldom contain; or, if found there, not in its native beauty, which they sully by use."

"What know'st thou, Raoul, of Roma and Napoli, and of noble dames and rich gems?" asked the girl, smiling, the tenderness which had filled her heart at that moment betraying itself in her eyes.

"What do I know of such things, truly! why, I have been at both places, and have seen what I describe. I went to Roma on purpose to see the Holy Father, in order to make certain whether our French opinions of his character and infallibility were true, or not, before I set up in religion for myself."

"And thou *didst* find him holy and venerable, Raoul," interposed the girl, with earnestness and energy, for this was the great point of separation between them — "I *know* thou found'st him thus, and worthy to be the head of an ancient and true church. My eyes never beheld him; but this do I *know* to be true."

Raoul was aware that the laxity of his religious opinions, opinions that he may be said to have inherited from his country, as it then existed morally, alone prevented Ghita from casting aside all other ties, and following his fortunes, in weal and in woe. Still he was too frank and generous to deceive, while he had ever been too considerate to strive to unsettle her confiding and consoling faith. Her infirmity even, for so he deemed her notions to be, had a charm in his eyes; few men, however loose or sceptical in their own opinions on such matters, finding any pleasure in the contemplation of a female infidel; and he had never looked more fondly into her anxious but lovely face, than he did at this very instant, making his reply with a truth that bordered on magnanimity.

"*Thou* art my religion, Ghita!" he said; "in thee I worship purity, and holiness, and——"

"Nay — nay, Raoul, *do* not — refrain — if thou really lov'st me, utter not this frightful blasphemy; tell me, rather, if thou didst not find the holy father, as I describe him?"

"I found him a peaceful, venerable, and, I firmly believe, a *good* old man, Ghita; but *only* a man. No infallibility could I see about him; but a set of roguish cardinals, and other plotters of mischief, who were much better calculated to set Christians by the ears, than to lead them to Heaven, surrounded his chair."

"Say no more, Raoul — I will listen to no more of this. Thou knowest not these sainted men, and thy tongue is thine own enemy, without — hark! what means that?"

"'T is a gun from the frigate, and must be looked to; say, when and where do we meet again?"

"I know not, now. We have been too long, much too long, together, as it is; and must separate. Trust to me to provide the means of another meeting; at all events, *we* shall shortly be in our tower, again."

Ghita glided away as she ceased speaking, and soon disappeared in the town. As for Raoul, he was at a loss, for a moment, whether to follow or not; then he hastened to the terrace, in front of the government-house, again, in order to ascertain the meaning of the gun. The report had drawn others to the same place, and on reaching it, the young man found himself in another crowd.

By this time the Proserpine, for Ithuel was right as to the name of the stranger, had got within a league of the entrance of the bay, and had gone about, stretching over to its eastern shore, apparently with the intention to fetch fairly into it, on the next tack. The smoke of her gun was sailing off to leeward, in a little cloud, and signals were again flying at her main-royal-mast-head. All this was very intelligible to Raoul, it being evident, at a glance, that the frigate had reached in nearer both to look at the warlike lugger that she saw in the bay, and to communicate more clearly with her by signals. Ithuel's expedient had not sufficed; the vigilant Captain Cuffe, alias Sir Brown, who commanded the Proserpine, not being a man likely to be mystified by so stale a trick. Raoul scarcely breathed, as he watched the lugger, in anticipation of her course.

Ithuel certainly seemed in no hurry to commit himself, for the signal had now been flying on board the frigate several minutes, and yet no symptoms of any preparation for an answer could be discovered. At length the halyards moved, and then three fair, handsome flags rose to the end of le Feu-Follet's jigger-yard, a spar that was always kept aloft, in moderate weather. What the signal meant Raoul did not know, for though he was provided with signals by means of which to communicate with the vessels of war of his own nation, the Directory had not been able to supply him with those necessary to communicate with the enemy. Ithuel's ingenuity, however, had supplied the deficiency. While serving on board the Proserpine, the very ship that was now menacing the lugger, he had seen a meeting between her and a privateer English lugger, one of the two or three of that rig which sailed out of England, and his observant eye had noted the flags she had shown on the occasion. Now as privateersmen are not expected to be expert, or even very accurate, in the use of signals, he had ventured to show these very numbers, let it prove for better or worse. Had he been on the quarter-deck of the frigate, he would have ascertained through the benedictions bestowed by Captain Cuffe, that his *ruse* had so far succeeded as to cause that officer to attribute his unintelligible answer to ignorance, rather than to design. Nevertheless, the frigate did not seem disposed to alter her course; for, either influenced by a desire to anchor, or by a determination to take a still closer look at the lugger, she stood on, nearing the eastern side of the bay, at the rate of some six miles to the hour.

Raoul Yvard now thought it time to look to the safety of le Feu-Follet, in person. Previously to landing, he had given instructions as to what was to be done, in the event of the frigate's coming close in; but matters now seemed so very serious, that he hurried down the hill, overtaking Vito Viti, in his way, who was repairing to the harbour to give instructions to certain boatmen concerning the manner in which the quarantine laws were to be regarded, in an intercourse with a British frigate.

8 *

"You ought to be infinitely happy, at the prospect of meeting an honourable countryman, in this Sir Brown," observed the short-winded podestà, who usually put himself out of breath, both in ascending and descending the steep street, "for he really seems determined to anchor in our bay, Signor Smees."

"To tell you the truth, Signor Podesta, I wish I was half as well persuaded that it *is* Sir Brown, and la Proserpine, as I was an hour ago. I see symptoms of its being a republican, after all, and must have a care for ze Ving-And-Ving."

"The devil carry away all republicans, is my humble prayer, Signor Capitano; but I can hardly believe that so graceful and gracious-looking a frigate can possibly belong to such wretches."

"Ah! Signore, if that were all, I fear we should have to yield the palm to the French," answered Raoul, laughing; "for the best-looking craft in His Majesty's service are republican prizes. Even should this frigate turn out to be the Proserpine, herself, she can claim no better origin. But, I think the vice-governatore has not done well in deserting the batteries, since this stranger does not answer our signals as she should. The last communication has proved quite unintelligible to him."

Raoul was nearer to the truth than he imagined, perhaps, for certainly Ithuel's numbers had made nonsense, according to the signal-book of the Proserpine; but his confident manner had an effect on Vito Viti, who was duped by his seem ing earnestness, as well as by a circumstance, which, rightly considered, told as much against, as it did in favour of his companion.

"And what is to be done, Signore?" demanded the podestà, stopping short in the street.

"We must do as well as we can, under the circumstances. My duty is to look out for ze Ving-And-Ving, and yours to look out for the town. Should the stranger actually enter the bay, and bring his broadside to bear on this steep hill, there is not a chamber-window that will not open on the muzzles of his guns. You will grant me permission to haul into the inner harbour, where we shall be sheltered by the buildings from his shot, and then, perhaps, it will be wel enough to send my people into the nearest battery. I look for bloodshed and confusion, ere long."

All this was said with so much apparent sincerity, that it added to the podestà's mystification. Calling a neighbour to him, he sent the latter up the hill, with a message to Andrea Barrofaldi, and then he hurried down towards the port, it being much easier for him, just at that moment, to ascend, than to descend. Raoul kept at his side, and together they reached the water's edge.

The podestà was greatly addicted to giving utterance to any predominant opinion of the moment, being one of those persons who *feel* quite as much as they *think*. On the present occasion, he did not spare the frigate, for, having caught at the bait that his companion had so artfully thrown out to him, he was loud in the expression of his distrust. All the signalling and showing of colours, he now believed to be a republican trick; and precisely in proportion as he became resentful of the supposed fraud of the ship, was he disposed to confide blindly in the honesty of the lugger. This was a change of sentiment in the magistrate; and, as in the case of all sudden but late conversions, he was in a humour to compensate for his tardiness, by the excess of his zeal. In consequence of this disposition, the character and loquacity of the man, all aided by a few timely suggestions on the part of Raoul, in five minutes it came to be generally understood that the frigate was greatly to be distrusted, while the lugger was to rise in public favour exactly in the degree in which the other fell. This interposition of Vito Viti's was exceedingly à propos, so far as le Feu-Follet and her people were concerned, inasmuch as the examination of, and intercourse with, the boat's crew, had rather left the impression of their want of nationality, in a legal sense, than otherwise. In a word, had not the podestà so loudly and so actively proclaimed the contrary, Tommaso and his fellows were about to report their convictions that these men were all bonâ fide wolves in sheep's clothing—alias, Frenchmen.

"No, no—amici miei," said Vito Viti, bustling about on the narrow little quay, "all is not gold that glitters, of a certainty; and this frigate is probably no ally, but an enemy. A very different matter is it with ze Ving-y-Ving, and Il

Signor Smees — we may be said to know *him* — have seen his papers, and the vice-governatore and myself have examined him, as it might be, on the history and laws of his island, for England is an island, neighbours, as well as Elba - another reason for respect and amity — but we have gone over much of the literature and history of Inghilterra together, and find everything satisfactory and right; therefore are we bound to show the lugger protection and love."

"Most true, Signor Podestà," answered Raoul, from his boat; "and such being the case, I hasten to haul my vessel into the mouth of your basin, which I will defend against boats, or any attempt of these rascally republicans to land."

Waving his hand, the young sailor pulled quickly out of the crowded little port, followed by a hundred vivas. Raoul now saw that his orders had not been neglected. A small line had been run out from the lugger, and fastened to a ring in the inner end of the eastern side of the narrow haven, apparently with the intention of hauling the vessel into the harbour itself. He also perceived that the light anchor, or large kedge, by which le Feu-Follet rode, was under foot, as seamen term it; or that the cable was nearly " up and down." With a wave of the hand he communicated a new order, and then he saw that the men were raising the kedge from the bottom. By the time his foot touched the deck, indeed, the anchor was up and stowed, and nothing held the vessel but the line that had been run to the quay. Fifty pairs of hands were applied to this line, and the lugger advanced rapidly towards her place of shelter. But an artifice was practised to prevent her heading into the harbour's mouth, the line having been brought inboard abaft her larboard cat-head, a circumstance which necessarily gave her a sheer in the contrary direction, or to the eastward of the entrance. When the reader remembers that the scale on which the port had been constructed was small, the entrance scarce exceeding a hundred feet in width, he will better understand the situation of things. Seemingly to aid the movement, too, the jigger was set, and the wind being south, or directly aft, the lugger's motion was soon light and rapid. As the vessel drew nearer to the entrance, her people made a run with the line, and gave her a movement of some three or four knots to the hour, actually threatening to dash her bows against the pier-head. But Raoul Yvard contemplated no such blunder. At the proper moment, the line was cut, the helm was put a-port, the lugger's head sheered to starboard, and just as Vito Viti, who witnessed all without comprehending more than half that passed, was shouting his vivas, and animating all near him with his cries, the lugger glided past the end of the harbour, on its outside, however, instead of entering it. So completely was every one taken by surprise, by this evolution, that the first impression was of some mistake, accident, or blunder of the helmsman, and cries of regret followed, lest the frigate might have it in her power to profit by the mishap. The flapping of canvass, notwithstanding, showed that no time was lost, and presently le Feu-Follet shot by an opening between the warehouses, under all sail. At this critical instant, the frigate, which saw what passed, but which had been deceived, like all the rest, and supposed the lugger was hauling into the haven, tacked and came round with her head to the westward. But, intending to fetch well into the bay, she had stretched so far over towards the eastern shore, as, by this time, to be quite two miles distant; and as the lugger rounded the promontory close under its rocks, to avoid the shot of the batteries above, she left, in less than five minutes, her enemy that space directly astern. Nor was this all. It would have been dangerous to fire, as well as useless, on account of the range, since the lugger lay nearly in a line between her enemy's chase guns and the residence of the vice-governatore. It only remained, therefore, for the frigate to commence what is proverbially "a long chase," viz. a "stern chase."

All that has just been related may have occupied ten minutes; but the news reached Andrea Barrofaldi, and his counsellors, soon enough to allow them to appear on the promontory in time to see the Ving-y-Ving pass close under the cliffs beneath them, still keeping her English colours flying. Raoul was visible, trumpet in hand; but as the wind was light, his powerful voice sufficed to tell his story.

"Signori," he shouted, "I will lead the rascally republican away from your port, in chase; *that* will be the most effectual mode of doing you a service."

These words were heard, and understood, and a murmur

of applause followed, from some, while others thought the whole affair mysterious and questionable. There was no time to interpose, by acts, had such a course been contemplated, the lugger keeping too close in to be exposed to shot, and there being, as yet, no new preparations in the batteries, to meet an enemy. Then there were the doubts as to the proper party to assail, and all passed too rapidly to admit of consultation or preconcert. The movement of le Feu-Follet was so easy, as to partake of the character of instinct Her light sails were fully distended, though the breeze was far from fresh ; and, as she rose and fell on the long ground-swells, her wedge-like bows caused the water to ripple before them like a swift current meeting a sharp obstacle in the stream. It was only as she sunk into the water, in stemming a swell, that anything like foam could be seen under her fore-foot. A long line of swift-receding bubbles, however, marked her track, and she no sooner came abreast of any given group of spectators, than she was past it—resembling the progress of a porpoise, as he sports along a harbour.

Ten minutes after passing the palace, or the pitch of the promontory, the lugger opened another bay, one wider and almost as deep as that on which Porto Ferrajo stands, and here she took the breeze without the intervention of any neighbouring rocks, and her speed was essentially increased. Hitherto, her close proximity to the shore had partially becalmed her, though the air had drawn round the promontory, making nearly a fair wind of it ; but, now, the currents came fully on her beam, and with much more power. She hauled down her tacks, flattened in her sheets, luffed, and was soon out of sight, breasting up to windward of a point that formed the eastern extremity of the bay last mentioned.

All this time the Proserpine had not been idle. As soon as she discovered that the lugger was endeavouring to escape, her rigging was alive with men. Sail after sail was set, one white cloud succeeding another, until she was a sheet of canvass, from her trucks to her bulwarks. Her lofty sails taking the breeze above the adjacent coast, her progress was swift, for this particular frigate had the reputation of being one of the fastest vessels in the English marine.

It was just twenty minutes, by Andrea Barrofaldi's watch, after le Feu-Follet passed the spot where he stood, when the Proserpine came abreast of it. Her greater draught of water induced her to keep half a mile from the promontory, but she was so near as to allow a very good opportunity to examine her general construction and appearance, as she went by. The batteries were now manned, and a consultation was held on the propriety of punishing a republican for daring to come so near a Tuscan port. But there flew the respected and dreaded English ensign ; and it was still a matter of doubt whether the stranger were friend or enemy. Nothing about the ship showed apprehension, and yet she was clearly chasing a craft which, coming from a Tuscan harbour, an Englishman would be bound to consider entitled to his protection, rather than to his hostility. In a word, opinions were divided, and when that is the case, in matters of this nature, decision is obviously difficult. Then, if a Frenchman, she clearly attempted no injury to any on the island ; and those who possessed the power to commence a fire were fully aware how much the town lay exposed, and how little benefit might be expected from even a single broadside. The consequence was, that the few who were disposed to open on the frigate, like the two or three who had felt the same disposition towards the lugger, were restrained in their wishes, not only by the voice of superior authority, but by that of numbers.

In the meanwhile the Proserpine pressed on, and in ten minutes more she was not only out of the range, but beyond the reach of shot. As she opened the bay west of the town, le Feu-Follet was seen from her decks, fully a league ahead, close on a wind, the breeze hauling round the western end of the island, glancing through the water at a rate that rendered pursuit more than doubtful. Still the ship persevered, and in little more than an hour from the time she had crowded sail, she was up with the western extremity of the hills, though more than a mile to leeward. Here she met the fair southern breeze, uninfluenced by the land, as it came through the pass between Corsica and Elba, and got a clear view of the work before her. The studding-sails and royals had been taken in, twenty minutes earlier ; the bowlines were now all hauled, and the frigate was brought

close upon the wind. Still the chase was evidently hopeless, the little Feu-Follet having everything as much to her
mind, as if she had ordered the weather expressly to show
her powers. With her sheets flattened in until her canvass
stood like boards, her head looked fully a point to windward
of that of the ship, and, what was of equal importance, she
even went to windward of the point she looked at, while the
Proserpine, if anything, fell off a little, though but a very
little, from her own course. Under all these differences,
the lugger went through the water six feet to the frigate's
five, beating her in speed almost as much as she did in her
weatherly qualities.

The vessel to windward was not the first lugger, by fifty,
that Captain Cuffe had assisted in chasing, and he knew the
hopelessness of following such a craft, under circumstances
so directly adapted to its qualities. Then he was far from
certain that he was pursuing an enemy at all, whatever
distrust the signals may have excited, since she had clearly
come out of a friendly port. Bastia, too, lay within a few
hours' run, and there was the whole of the east coast of
Corsica, abounding with small bays and havens, in which a
vessel of that size might take refuge, if pressed. After convincing himself, therefore, by half-an-hour's further trial in
open sailing under the full force of the breeze, of the fruit
lessness of his effort, that experienced officer ordered the
Proserpine's helm put up, the yards squared, and he stood
to the northward, apparently shaping his course for Leghorn,
or the Gulf of Genoa. When the frigate made this change
in her course, the lugger, which had tacked some time previously, was just becoming shut in by the western end of
Elba, and she was soon lost to view entirely, with every
prospect of her weathering the island altogether, without
being obliged to go about again.

It was no more than natural that such a chase should
occasion some animation in a place as retired, and ordinarily
as dull, as Porto Ferrajo. Several of the young idlers of the
garrison obtained horses, and galloped up among the hills,
to watch the result ; the mountains being pretty well inter-
sected by bridle-paths, though totally without regular roads.
They who remained in the town, as a matter of course, were
not disposed to let so favourable a subject for discourse die

away immediately, for want of a disposition to gossip on it. Little else was talked of, that day, than the menaced attack of the republican frigate, and the escape of the lugger. Some, indeed, still doubted, for every question has its two sides, and there was just enough of dissent to render the discussions lively, and the arguments ingenious. Among the disputants, Vito Viti acted a prominent part. Having committed himself so openly by his " vivas," and his public remarks in the port, he felt it due to his own character to justify all he had said, and Raoul Yvard could not have desired a warmer advocate than he now had in the podestà. The worthy magistrate exaggerated the vice-governatore's knowledge of English, by way of leaving no deficiency in the necessary proofs of the lugger's national character. Nay, he even went so far as to affirm that he had comprehended a portion of the documents exhibited by the " Signor Smees," himself; and as to "ze Ving-y-Ving," any one acquainted in the least with the geography of the British Channel, would understand that she was precisely the sort of craft that the semi-Gallic inhabitants of Guernsey and Jersey would be apt to send forth to cruise against the altogether Gallic inhabitants of the adjacent main.

During all these discussions, there was one heart in Porto Ferrajo that was swelling with the conflicting emotions of gratitude, disappointment, joy and fear, though the tongue of its owner was silent. Of all of her sex in the place, Ghita alone had nothing to conjecture, no speculation to advance, no opinion to maintain, nor any wish to express. Still she listened eagerly, and it was not the least of her causes of satisfaction to find that her own hurried interviews with the handsome privateersman, had apparently escaped observation. At length her mind was fully lightened of its apprehensions, leaving nothing but tender regrets, by the return of the horsemen from the mountains. These persons reported that the upper sails of the frigate were just visible in the northern board, so far as they could judge even more distant than the island of Capraya, while the lugger had beaten up almost as far to windward as Pianosa, and then seemed disposed to stand over towards the coast of Corsica ; doubtless with an intention to molest the commerce of that hostile island

9   7

CHAPTER VII.

Ant. — " And, indeed, sir, there are cozeners abroad; therefore it
behoves men to be wary."
Clo. — " Fear not thou, man, thou shalt lose nothing here."
Ant. — " I hope so, sir; for I have about me many parcels of
change."

Winter's Tale.

Such was the state of things at Porto Ferrajo, at noon,
or about the hour when its inhabitants bethought them of
their mid-day meal. With most, the siesta followed, though
the sea air, with its invigorating coolness, rendered that
indulgence less necessary to these islanders, than to most
of their neighbours on the main. Then succeeded the reviving animation of the afternoon, and the return of the
zephyr, or the western breeze. So regular, indeed, are
these changes in the currents of the air, during the summer
months, that the mariner can rely, with safety, on meeting
a light breeze from the southward, throughout the morning,
a calm at noon — the siesta of the Mediterranean — and
the delightfully cool wind from the west, after three or
four o'clock; this last is again succeeded, at night, by a
breeze directly from the land. Weeks at a time have we
known this order of things to be uninterrupted; and when
the changes did occasionally occur, it was only in the slight
episodes of showers and thunder-storms, of which, however,
Italy has far fewer than our own coast.

Such, then, was the state of Porto Ferrajo, towards the
evening that succeeded this day of bustle and excitement.
The zephyr again prevailed, the idle once more issued
forth for their sun-set walk, and the gossips were collecting
to renew their conjectures, and to start some new point in
their already exhausted discussions, when a rumour spread
through the place, like fire communicated to a train, that
" ze Ving-y-Ving" was once more coming down on the
weather side of the island, precisely as she had approached
on the previous evening; with the confidence of a friend,
and the celerity of a bird. Years had passed since such a

tumult was awakened in the capital of Elba. Men, women and children, poured from the houses, and were seen climbing the streets, all hastening to the promenade, as if to satisfy themselves, with their own eyes, of the existence of some miracle. In vain did the infirm and aged call on the vigorous and more youthful, for the customary assistance; they were avoided like the cases of plague, and were left to hobble up the terraced street as best they might. Even mothers, after dragging them at their own sides till fearful of being too late, abandoned their young in the highway, certain of finding them rolled to the foot of the declivity, should they fail of scrambling to its summit. In short, it was a scene of confusion in which there was much to laugh at, something to awaken wonder, and not a little that was natural.

Ten minutes had not certainly elapsed, after the rumour reached the lower part of the town, ere two thousand persons were on the hill, including nearly all the principal personages of the place, 'Maso Tonti, Ghita, and the different characters known to the reader. So nearly did the scene of this evening resemble that of the past, the numbers of the throng on the hill and the greater interest excepted, that one who had been present at the former, might readily have fancied the latter merely its continuation. There, indeed, was the lugger, under her foresail and mainsail, with the jigger brailed, coming down wing-and-wing, and glancing along the glittering sea like the duck sailing towards her nest. This time, however, the English ensign was flying at the end of the jigger-yard, as if in triumph, and the little craft held her way nearer to the rocks, like one acquainted with the coast, and fearing no danger. There was a manner of established confidence in the way in which she trusted herself under the muzzles of guns that might have destroyed her in a very few minutes, and no one who saw her approach could very well believe that she was anything but a known, as well as a confirmed friend.

"Would any of the republican rascals, think you, Signor Andrea," asked Vito Viti, in triumph, "dare to come into Porto Ferrajo, in this style; knowing, too, as does this 'Sir Smees,' the sort of people he will have to deal with! Remember, Vice-governatore, that the man has actually been ashore among us, and would not be likely to run his head into the lion's mouth."

" Thou hast changed thine opinion greatly, neighbour Vito," answered the vice-governatore, somewhat drily, for he was far from being satisfied on the subject of Sir Cicero, and on those of certain other circumstances in English history and politics; " it better becomes magistrates to be cautious and wary."

" Well, if there be a more cautious and circumspect man in Elba than the poor podestâ of Porto Ferrajo, let him stand forth, o' God's name, and prove his deeds ! I do not esteem myself, Signor Vice-governatore, as the idlest, or as the most ignorant man in the Grand Duke's territories. There may be wiser, among whom I place your eccellenza ; but there is not a more loyal subject, or a more zealous friend of truth."

" I believe it, good Vito," returned Andrea, smiling kindly on his old associate, " and have ever so considered thy advice and services. Still, I wish I knew something of this Sir Cicero ; for, to be frank with thee, I have even foregone my siesta, in searching the books in quest of such a man."

" And do they not confirm every syllable the Signor Smees has said ?"

" So far from it, that I do not even find the name. It is true, several distinguished orators of that nation are styled *English* Ciceroes ; but then all people do this, by way of commendation."

" I do not know that, Signore — I do not know that — it may happen in our Italy ; but would it come to pass, think you, among remote and so lately barbarous nations as England, Germany and France ?"

" Thou forgettest, friend Viti," returned the vice-governatore, smiling now, in pity of his companion's ignorance and prejudices, as just before he had smiled in kindness, " that we Italians took the pains to civilize these people a thousand years ago, and that they have not gone backward all this time. But there can be no doubt that ' ze Ving-y-Ving' means to enter our bay again, and there stands the ' Signor Smees' examining us with a glass, as if he, too, contemplated another interview."

' It strikes me, Vice-governatore, that it would be a sin

next to heresy to doubt the character of those who so loyally put their trust in us. No republican would dare to anchor in the bay of Porto Ferrajo a second time. *Once*, it might possibly be done; but *twice?* — no, never, never."

"I do not know but you are right, Vito, and I am sure I hope so. Will you descend to the port, and see that the forms are complied with? Then glean such useful circumstances as you can."

The crowd was now in motion towards the lower part of the town, to meet the lugger; and at this suggestion the podestà hurried down, in the throng, to be in readiness to receive the "Signor Smees," as soon as he should land. It was thought more dignified and proper for the vice-governatore to remain, and await to hear the report of the supposed English officer, where he was. Ghita was one of the few, also, who remained on the heights, her heart now beating with renewed apprehensions of the dangers that her lover had again braved on her account, and now nearly overflowing with tenderness, as she admitted the agreeable conviction, that, had she not been in Porto Ferrajo, Raoul Yvard would never have incurred such risks.

Ghita delle Torri, or Ghita of the Towers, as the girl was ordinarily termed by those who knew her, from a circumstance in her situation that will appear as we advance in the tale, or Ghita Caraccioli, as was her real name, had been an orphan from infancy. She had imbibed a strength of character and a self-reliance, from her condition, that might otherwise have been wanting, in one so young, and of a native disposition so truly gentle. An aunt had impressed on her mind the lessons of female decorum; and her uncle, who had abandoned the world on account of a strong religious sentiment, had aided in making her deeply devout, and keenly conscientious. The truth of her character rendered her indisposed to the deception which Raoul was practising, while feminine weakness inclined her to forgive the offence, in the motive. She had shuddered again and again, as she remembered how deeply the young sailor was becoming involved in frauds,—and frauds, too, that might so easily terminate in violence and bloodshed; and then she had trembled under the influence of a gentler emotion, as she remembered that all these risks were run for her. Her

9 *

reason had long since admonished her that Raoul Yvard
and Ghita Caraccioli ought to be strangers to each other;
but her heart told a different story. The present was an
occasion suited to keeping these conflicting feelings keenly
alive, and, as has been said, when most of the others
hastened down towards the port to be present when the
Wing-And-Wing came in, she remained on the hill, brood-
ing over her own thoughts, much of the time bathed in tears.

But Raoul had no intention of trusting his Jack-o'-Lantern
where it might so readily be extinguished by the hand of
man. Instead of taking shelter against any new roving
republican who might come along, behind the buildings of
the port, as had been expected, he shot past the end of the
quay, and anchored within a few fathoms of the very spot
he had quitted that morning, merely dropping his kedge
under foot, as before. Then he stepped confidently into his
boat, and pulled for the landing.

"Eh. Signor Capitano," cried Vito Viti, as he met his
new protégé with an air of cordiality, as soon as the foot of
the latter touched the shore, "we looked for the pleasure
of receiving you into our bosom, as it were, here in the haven.
How ingeniously you led off that *sans culotte*, this morning!
Ah, the Inglese are the great nation of the ocean, Colombo
notwithstanding! The vice-governatore told me all about
your illustrious female admiral, Elisabetta, and the Spanish
armada; and there was Nelsoni; and now we have Smees!"

Raoul accepted these compliments, both national and personal, in a very gracious manner, squeezing the hand of the
podestà with suitable cordiality and condescension, acting
the great man as if accustomed to this sort of incense from
infancy. As became his public situation, as well as his
character, he proposed paying his duty immediately to the
superior authorities of the island.

"King George, my master," continued Raoul, as he and
Vito Viti walked from the quay towards the residence of
Andrea Barrofaldi, "is particularly pointed on this subject,
with us all, in his personal orders. 'Never enter a port of
one of my allies, Smeet,' he said, the very last time I took
leave of him, 'without immediately hastening with your
duty to the commandant of the place. You never lose any-

thing by being liberal of politeness ; and England is too polished a country to be outdone in these things, by even the Italians, the parents of modern civilization.' "

" You are happy in having such a sovrano, and still more so in being allowed to approach his sacred person."

" Oh ! as to the last, the navy is his pet ; he considers us captains, in particular, as his children. ' Never enter London, my dear Smeet,' he said to me, ' without coming to the palace, where you will always find a father'—you know he has one son among us who was lately a captain, as well as myself."

" San Stefano ! and he the child of a great king ! I did not know that, . confess, Signore."

" Why, it is a law, in England, that the king shall give at least one son to the marine. ' Yes,' said his Majesty, ' always be prompt in calling on the superior authorities, and remember me benevolently and affectionately to them, one and all, even down to the subordinate magistrates, who live in their intimacy."

Raoul delighted in playing the part he was now performing, but he was a little addicted to over-acting it. Like all exceedingly bold and decided geniuses, he was constantly striding across that step which separates the sublime from the ridiculous, and consequently ran no small hazard in the way of discovery. But with Vito Viti he incurred little risk on this score, provincial credulity and a love of the marvellous coming in aid of his general ignorance, to render him a safe depository of anything of this sort that the other might choose to advance. Vito Viti felt it to be an honour to converse with a man who, in his turn, had conversed with a king ; and as he puffed his way up the steep ascent again, he did not fail to express some of the feelings which were glowing in his breast.

" Is it not a happiness to serve such a prince ?" he exclaimed—" nay, to die for him !"

" The latter is a service I have not yet performed," answered Raoul, innocently, " but which may one day well happen. Do you not think, podestà, that he who lays down his life for his prince merits canonization ?"

" That would fill the calendar too soon, in these wars, Signor Smees , but I will concede you the generals and ad-

mirals, and other great personages. Si — a general or an
admiral who dies for his sovereign, does deserve to be made
a saint — this would leave these miserable French republicans, Signore, without hope or honour !"

"They are *canaille*, from the highest to the lowest, and
can reasonably expect nothing better. If they wish to be
canonized, let them restore the Bourbons, and put themselves
lawfully in the way of such a blessing. The chase of this
morning, Signor Vito Viti, must, at least, have amused the
town ?"

The podestà wanted but this opening to pour out a history
of his own emotions, sensations and raptures. He expatiated
in glowing terms on the service the lugger had rendered the
place by leading off the rascally republicans, showing that he
considered the manœuvre of passing the port, instead of
entering it, as one of the most remarkable of which he had
ever heard, or even read.

"I defied the vice-governatore to produce an example of
a finer professional inspiration in the whole range of history,
beginning with his Tacitus, and ending with your new English work on Roma. I doubt if the Elder Pliny, or Mark
Antony, or even Cæsar, ever did a finer thing, Signore; and
I am not a man addicted to extravagance, in compliments.
Had it been a fleet of vessels of three decks, instead of a
little lugger, Christendom would have rung with the glory
of the achievement !"

"Had it been but a frigate, my excellent friend, the manœuvre would have been unnecessary. Peste ! it is not a
single republican ship that can make a stout English frigate
skulk along the rocks, and fly like a thief at night."

"Ah, there is the vice-governatore walking on his terrace,
Sir Smees, and dying with impatience to greet you. We
will drop the subject, for another occasion, and a bottle of
good Florence liquor."

The reception which Andrea Barrofaldi gave Raoul, was
far less warm than that he received from the podestà, though
it was polite, and without any visible signs of distrust.

"I have come, Signor Vice-governatore," said the privateersman, "in compliance with positive orders from my
master, to pay my respects to you again, and to report my
arrival once more, in your bay, though the cruise made

since my last departure has not been so long as an East
India voyage."

" Short as it has been, we should have reason to regret
your absence, Signore, were it not for the admirable proofs
it has afforded us of your resources and seamanship," re-
urned Andrea with due complaisance. " To own the truth,
when I saw you depart, it was with the apprehension that we
should never enjoy this satisfaction again. But, like your
English Sir Cicero, the second coming may prove even mor
agreeable than the first."

Raoul laughed, and he even had the grace to blush a
little ; after which he appeared to reflect intensely on some
matter of moment. Smiles struggled round his handsome
mouth, and then he suddenly assumed an air of sailor-like
frankness, and disclosed his passing sensations in words.

" Signor Vice-governatore, I ask the favour of one moment's private conference ; Signor Vito Viti, give us leave
a single moment, if you please. I perceive, Signore," continued Raoul, as he and Andrea walked a little aside, " that
you have not easily forgotten my little fanfaronade about
our English Cicero. But what will you have ?—we sailors
are sent to sea children, and we know little of books. My
excellent father, Milord Smeet, had me put in a frigate when
I was only twelve, an age at which one knows very little
of Ciceros, or Dantes, or Corneilles, even, as you will
confess. Thus, when I found myself in the presence of a
gentleman whose reputation for learning has reached far
beyond the island he so admirably governs, a silly ambition
has led me into a folly that he finds it hard to forgive. If I
have talked of names of which I know nothing, it may be a
weakness, such as young men will fall into ; but surely it is
no heinous crime."

" You allow, Signore, that there has been no English Sir
Cicero ?"

" The truth compels me to say, I know nothing about it.
But it is hard for a very young man, and one, too, that feels
his deficiencies of education, to admit all this to a philosopher, on a first acquaintance. It becomes a different thing,
when natural modesty is encouraged by a familiar goodness
of heart ; and a day's acquaintance with the Signor Barrofaldi, is as much as a year with an ordinary man."

" If this be the case, Sir Smees, I can readily understand, and as willingly overlook what has passed," returned the vice-governatore, with a self-complacency that in nothing fell short of that which Vito Viti had so recently exhibited. " It must be painful, to a sensitive mind, to feel the deficiencies which unavoidably accompany the want of opportunities for study ; and I, at least, can now say how delightful it is to witness the ingenuousness which admits it. Then, if England has never possessed a Cicero, in name, doubtless she has had many in qualifications, after allowing for the halo which time ever throws around a reputation. Should your duty often call you this way, Signore, during this summer, it will add to the pleasure I experience in enjoying the advantage of your acquaintance, to be permitted, in some slight degree, to direct your reading to such works, as, with a mind like yours, will be certain to lead to profit and pleasure."

Raoul made a suitable acknowledgment for this offer, and from that moment the best understanding existed between the parties. The privateersman, who had received a much better education than he pretended to, and who was a consummate actor, as well as, on certain occasions, a practised flatterer, determined to be more cautious in future, sparing his literary conjectures, whatever liberties he might take with other subjects. And yet this reckless and daring mariner never flattered nor deceived Ghita in anything! With her he had been all sincerity, the influence he had obtained over the feelings of that pure-minded girl, being as much the result of the nature and real feeling he had manifested, as of his manly appearance and general powers of pleasing. It would have been, indeed, matter of interesting observation, for one curious in the study of human nature, to note how completely the girl's innocence and simplicity of character had extended itself over every act of the young man, that was any way connected with her, preventing his even feigning that religion which he certainly did not feel, and the want of which was the sole obstacle to the union he had now solicited for near a twelvemonth, and which, of all others, was the object by far the closest to his heart. With Andrea Barrofaldi, and Vito Viti, and most especially with the hated English, it was a very different thing, however ; and seldom was Raoul happier, than when he was employed in precisely such a scene of mystification as that in which he was at that moment engaged.

The vice-governatore having established relations so completely amicable with the 'Signor Smees,' could do no less than invite his guest to enter the palazzo, along with himself and the podestà. As it was yet too light for the sailor to seek an interview with Ghita, he cheerfully accepted the offer; making a careful examination of the whole of the northern margin of the sea, from his elevated position, however, before he crossed the threshold. This little delay, on Raoul's part, enabled the podestà to have a passing word with his friend unobserved.

"You have found 'Sir Smees,'" said Vito Viti, with earnestness, "all that your wisdom and prudence could desire, I trust? For my part, I consider him a most interesting youth; one destined, at some future time, to lead fleets, and dispose of the fortunes of nations."

"He is more amiable, and even better informed, than I had thought, neighbour Vito Viti. He gives up his Sir Cicero with a grace that causes one regret it was necessary; and, like yourself, I make no doubt of his becoming an illustrious admiral, in time. It is true, his father, 'Milordo Smees,' has not done justice to his education; but it is not too late, yet, to repair that evil. Go, desire him to enter; for I am impatient to draw his attention to certain works that may be useful to one in his line of life."

At this suggestion the podestà returned to the door, in order to usher the imaginary Guernsey-man into the residence. He found Raoul still standing on the entrance, examining the sea. There were two or three coasters, feluccas, as usual, stealing along the coast, in the Italian fashion, equally afraid of the barbarians of the south shore, and of the French of the north. All these would have been good prizes; but, to do the privateersman justice, he was little in the habit of molesting mariners of so low a class. There was one felucca, however, that was just rounding the promontory, coming in from the north; and with the people of this craft he determined to have some communication as soon as he returned to the port, with a view to ascertain if she had fallen in with the frigate. Just as he had come to

.his resolution, the podestâ joined him, and he was ushered into the house.

It is unnecessary to give the discourse which succeeded. It related more to literature and matters in general, than to anything connected with our tale, the worthy vice-governatore being disposed to reward the ingenuousness of the young sailor, by furnishing him as much instruction as the time and circumstances would allow. Raoul bore this very well, waiting patiently for the light to disappear, when he felt a perfect confidence of again meeting Ghita on the promenade. As he had discovered how much more safety there was in diffidence than in pretension, he found his task of deception comparatively easy; and by letting the vice-governatore have his own way, he not only succeeded in gaining that functionary over to a full belief in his assumed nationality, but in persuading him to believe the 'Signor Smees' a young man of even more erudition than he had at first supposed. By means as simple and natural as these, Raoul made more progress in the good graces of Andrea Barrofaldi, in the next two hours, than he could have done in a year, by setting up his own knowledge and reading as authority.

There is little doubt that the vice-governatore found this interview agreeable, from the time he was disposed to waste on it; and, it is certain, Raoul thought it some of the hardest duty in which he had ever been engaged. As for Vito Viti, he was edified, and he did not care to conceal it, giving frequent manifestations of his satisfaction, by expressions of delight; occasionally venturing a remark, as if expressly to betray his own ignorance.

"I have often known you great, vice-governatore," he cried, when Andrea had closed a dissertation on the earlier history of all the northern nations, which lasted fully half-an-hour, "but never so great as you are to-night! Signore, you have been most illustrious, this evening! Is it not so, Signor Smees? Could any professor of Pisa, or even of Padua, do more justice to a subject, than we have seen done to this to which we have been listening?"

"Signor Podestâ," added Raoul, "but one feeling has prevailed, in my mind, while attending to what has been said; and that has been deep regret that my profession has cut me off from all these rich stores of profound thought.

But it is permitted us to admire that even which we cannot imitate."

"Quite true, Signori," answered Andrea, with gentle benevolence, "but with dispositions like yours, Sir Smees, it is not so very difficult to imitate what we admire. I will write out a list of works, which I would recommend to your perusal; and, by touching at Livorno, or Napoli, you will obtain all the books at reasonable prices. You may expect to see the list on your breakfast-table to-morrow morning, as I shall not sleep until it is completed."

Raoul gladly seized upon this promise as a hint to depart, and he took his leave with suitable acknowledgments of gratitude and delight. When he got out of the palazzo however, he gave a long, low whistle, like a man who felt he had escaped from a scene in which persecution had been a little lightened by the ridiculous, and uttered a few curses on the nations of the north, for being so inconsiderate as to have histories so much longer and more elaborate than he conceived to be at all necessary. All this passed as he hastened along the promenade, which he found deserted, every human being having apparently left it. At length he thought he perceived a female form some distance ahead of him, and in a part of the walk that was never much frequented. Hastening towards it, his quick eye discerned the person of her he sought, evidently waiting for his approach.

"Raoul," exclaimed Ghita, reproachfully, "in what will these often-repeated risks finally end? When so fairly and cleverly out of the harbour of Porto Ferrajo, why did you not possess the prudence to remain there?"

"Thou know'st the reason, Ghita, and why ask this question? San Nettuno! was it not handsomely done; and is not this brave vice-governatore rarely mystified!—I sometimes think, Ghita, I have mistaken my vocation, which should have been that of a diplomate."

"And why a diplomate, in particular, Raoul — thou art too honest to deceive long, whatever thou may'st do on an occasion like this, and in a pressing emergency."

"Why?— but, no matter. This Andrea Barrofaldi, and this Vito Viti, will one day know why. And now to our business, Ghita, since le Feu-Follet cannot always decorate the bay of Porto Ferrajo."

10

" True," interrupted the girl, " and I have come for no
other purpose than to say as much myself. My dear uncle
has arrived, and he intends to sail for the Torri with the first
felucca."

" There!—this has done more to make me believe in a
Providence, than all the preaching of all the padri of Italy!
Here is the lugger to take the place of the felucca, and we
can sail this very night. My cabin shall be yours entirely
and with your uncle for a protector, no one can raise an
evil tongue against the step."

Ghita, to own the truth, expected this very offer, which,
agreeable as it was, her sense of propriety would certainly
have prevented her from accepting, but for one consideration : it might be made the means of getting Raoul out of
an enemy's port ; and, in so much, out of harm's way. This,
with one of her affectionate heart, was an object to which
she would have sacrificed appearances of even a graver
character. We do not wish the reader, however, to get a
false impression of this girl's habits and education. Although
the latter, in many particulars, was superior to that received
by most young women of her class in life, the former were
simple, and suited to her station, as well as to the usages of
her country. She had not been brought up with that severe
restraint which regulates the deportment of the young Italian
females of condition, perhaps, in a degree just as much too
severely, as it leaves the young American too little restrained ; but she had been taught all that decorum and
delicacy required, either for the beautiful or the safe ; and
her notions inculcated the inexpediency, if not the impro-
priety, of one in her situation taking a passage in a privateer
at all, and particularly so in one commanded by an avowed
lover. But, on the other hand, the distance between Porto
Ferrajo and the Towers, was only about fifty miles, and a
few hours would suffice to place her in safety beneath her
own roof; and, what was of more importance, in her view,
just then, Raoul in safety along with her. On all this had
she pondered, and she was consequently prepared with an
answer to the proposal that had just been made.

" If my uncle and myself could accept this generous offer
when would it be convenient for you to sail, Raoul ?" the

girl demanded; " we have now been absent longer than we intended, and longer than we ought."

" Within an hour, if there were any wind. But you see how it is, Ghita—the zephyr has done blowing, and it now seems as if every fan of Italy had gone to sleep. You can depend on our sailing the instant it shall be in our power. At need, we will use the sweeps."

" I will, then, see my uncle, and mention to him that there is a vessel about to sail, in which we had better embark. Is it not odd, Raoul, that he is profoundly ignorant of your being in the bay? He gets more and more lost to things around him every day, and I do believe he does not recollect that you command an enemy's vessel half the time."

" Let him trust to me; he shall never have occasion to know it, Ghita."

" We are assured of that, Raoul. The generous manner in which you interposed to save us from the corsair of the Algerines, which began our acquaintance, and for which we shall always have occasion to bless you, has made peace between you and *us*, for ever. But for your timely succour, last summer, my uncle and myself would now have been slaves with barbarians!"

" That is another thing that inclines me to believe in a Providence, Ghita! Little did I know, when rescuing you and your good kinsman from the boat of the Algerine, who I was saving. And yet, you see how all has come to pass, and that in serving you I have merely been serving myself."

· " Would that thou could'st learn to serve that God, who disposes of us all at his holy pleasure!" murmured Ghita, tears forcing themselves to her eyes, and a convulsive effort alone suppressing the deep emotion with which she uttered the words; " but we thank thee again and again, Raoul, as the instrument of his mercy, in the affair of the Algerine, and are willing to trust to thee now, and always. It will be easy to induce my uncle to embark; but, as he knows thy real character, when he chooses to recollect it, I hardly think it will do to say with *whom*. We must arrange an hour, and a place to meet, when I will see to his being there, and in readiness."

Raoul and Ghita next discussed the little details; a place of rendezvous without the town, a short distance below the

wine-house of Benedetta, being selected, in preference to
choosing one that would necessarily subject them to observation. This portion of the arrangements was soon settled,
and then Ghita thought it prudent to separate. In this proposal her companion acquiesced with a better grace than he
might have done, had he not the girl's assurance of meeting
him within an hour, in order that everything might be ready
for a start, with the first appearance of wind.

When left alone, Raoul bethought him that Ithuel and
Filippo were on shore, as usual; the New-Hampshire man
consenting to serve only on condition of being allowed to
land; a privilege he always abused by driving a contraband
trade, on occasions like the present. So great was the fellow's dexterity in such matters, that Raoul, who disdained
smuggling, while he thought himself compelled to wink at it
in others, had less apprehensions of his committing the lugger,
than he might have felt in the case of one less cunning.
But it was now necessary to get these two men off, or abandon them; and fortunately remembering the name of the
wine-house where they had taken their potations the previous
night, he repaired to it without delay, luckily finding Ithuel
and his interpreter deep in the discussion of another flask of
the favourite Tuscan beverage. 'Maso and his usual companions were present also, and there being nothing unusual
in the commander of an English ship of war's liking good
liquor, Raoul, to prevent suspicion, drew a chair, and asked
for his glass. By the conversation that followed, the young
privateersman felt satisfied that, though he might have succeeded in throwing dust into the eyes of the vice-governatore and the podestà, these experienced old seamen still
distrusted his character. It was so unusual a thing for a
French frigate, while it was so usual for an English frigate,
to be standing along the coast, near in, that these mariners,
who were familiar with all such matters, had joined this
circumstance to the suspicious signs about the lugger, and
were strongly disposed to believe the truth concerning both
vessels. To all this, however, Raoul was more indifferent
han he might have been, but for the arrangement to sail so
soon. He took his wine, therefore, with apparent indifference, and, in proper season, withdrew, carrying with him
Ithuel and the Genoese.

CHAPTER VIII.

"Within our bay, one stormy night,
The isle's men saw boats make for shore,
With here and there a dancing light
That flash'd on man and oar.
When hailed, the rowing stopp'd, and all was dark.
Ha! lantern work!—We'll home! They're playing shark."
                                                    DANA.

It was dark when Raoul quitted the government-house,
leaving Andrea Barrofaldi and Vito Viti, in the library of
the former. No sooner was the young seaman's back
turned, than the vice-governatore, who was in a humour to
display his acquirements, resumed a discussion that he had
found so agreeable to his self-esteem.

"It is easy to see, good Vito Viti, that this young Inglese
is a gentleman of noble birth, though not of a liberal education," he said; "doubtless, his father, Milordo Smees, has
a large family, and the usages of England are different from
those of Italy, in respect to birth-right. There, the eldest
son, alone, inherits the honours of the family, while the
cadets are put into the army and navy, to earn new distinctions. Nelsoni is the son of a priest, I hear—"

"Cospetto! of a padre! Signor Vice-governatore," inter
rupted the podestà—"it is most indecent to *own* it. A priest
must be possessed of the devil, himself, to *own* his issue;
though issue he may certainly have."

"There, again, good Vito, it is different with the Luterani
and us Catholics. The priests of England, you will please
to remember, marry, while ours do not."

"I should not like to be shrived by such a padre!—The
man would be certain to tell his wife all I confessed; and
the saints could only say what would be the end on't.
Porto Ferrajo would soon be too hot to hold an honest man—
ay, or even an honest woman, in the bargain."

"But the Luterani do not confess, and are never shrived
at all, you will remember."

10 *   8

" San Stefano!—How do they expect, then, ever to get
.o heaven?"

" I will not answer that they do, friend Vito—and we are
certain, that if they *have* such expectations, they must be
most treacherous to them.   But, talking of this Sir Smees,
you perceive in his air and manner, the finesse of the Anglo-
Saxon race; which is a people altogether distinct from the
ancient Gauls, both in history and characters.   Pietro
Giannone, in his *Storia Civile del Regno di Napoli*, speaks
of the Normans, who were a branch of these adventurers,
with great interest and particularity; and I think I can trace,
in this youth, some of the very peculiarities that are so admirably delineated in his well-told, but too free, writings.—
Well, Pietro; I was not speaking of thee, but of a namesake
of thine, of the family of Giannona, an historian of Naples,
of note and merit—what is thy will?"

This question was put to a servant, who entered at that
moment, holding in his hand a piece of paper, which he
desired to lay before his master.

" A cavaliere is without, Signor Andrea, who asks the
honour of an audience, and who sends in his name, as your
eccellenza will find it on this paper."

The vice-governatore took the slip of paper, and read
aloud; " Edward Griffin, tenente della marina Inglesa."

" Ah! here is an officer sent from ' ze Ving-y-Ving', with
some communication, friend Vito; it is fortunate you are
still here, to hear what he has to say.   Show the lieutenant
in, Pietro."

One who understood Englishmen better than Andrea
Barrofaldi, would have been satisfied, at a glance, that he
who now entered was really a native of that country.   He
was a young man of some two or three and twenty, of a
ruddy, round, good-natured face, wearing an undress coat
of the service to which he professed to belong, and whose
whole air and manner betrayed his profession, quite as much
as his country.   The salutations he uttered were in very
respectable Italian, familiarity with the language being the
precise reason why he had been selected for the errand on
which he had come.   After these salutations he put a piece
of parchment into Andrea's hand, remarking—

" If you read English, Signore, you will perceive y that commission I am the person I represent myself to be."

" Doubtless, Signor Tenente, you belong to ze Ving-y-Ving, and are a subordinate of Sir Smees?"

The young man looked surprised, and, at the same time, half disposed to laugh; though a sense of decorum suppressed the latter inclination.

" I belong to His Britannic Majesty's ship Proserpine Signore," he drily answered, " and know not what yo mean by the Ving-y-Ving. Captain Cuffe, of that ship, the frigate you saw off your harbour this morning, has sent me down in the felucca that got in this evening, to communicate intelligence concerning the lugger, which we chased to the southward about nine o'clock, but which, I see, is again snug at her anchor in this bay. Our ship was lying behind Capraya, when I left her, but will be here to take me off, and to hear the news, before daylight, should the wind ever blow again."

Andrea Barrofaldi and Vito Viti stared, and that, too, as if a messenger had come from the lower regions to summon them away for their misdeeds. Lieutenant Griffin spoke unusually good Italian, for a foreigner; and his manner of proceeding was so straight-forward and direct, as to carry with it every appearance of truth.

" You do not know what I mean by ze Ving-y-Ving?" demanded the vice-governatore, with emphasis.

" To be frank with you, I do not, Signore. Ving-y-Ving is not English; nor do I know that it is Italian."

Mr. Griffin lost a good deal of ground by this assertion, which implied a doubt of Andrea's knowledge of foreign tongues.

" You say, Signor Tenente, if I comprehend your meaning, that Ving-y-Ving is not English?"

" Indeed I do, sir; at least, no English that I have eve heard spoken, at sea or ashore; and we seamen have a language of our own."

" Will you, then, permit me to ask you what is the translation of *ala e ala ;* word for word."

The lieutenant paused a moment, and pondered. Then he laughed involuntarily, checking himself almost immediately with an air of respect and gravity.

"I believe I now understand you, Signor Vice-governatore," he said; "we have a sea-phrase something like thi., to describe a fore-and-aft vessel with her sails swinging off on both sides; but we call it wing-and-wing."

"Si, Signore — ving-y-ving. Such is the name of the lugger of your king, that now lies in our bay."

"Ah! we thought as much, Signori; the scoundrel has deceived you, as he has done a hundred before you, and will do to a hundred, again, unless we catch him to-night. The lugger is a celebrated French privateer, that we have six cruisers in chase of at this moment, our own ship included. She is called le Feu-Follet, which is not Wing-And-Wing, but Will-o'-the-Wisp, or Jack-o'-Lantern, in English; and which you, in Italian, would call *il Fuoco Fatuo*. Her commander is Raoul Yvard, than whom, there is not a greater desperado sailing out of France; though it is admitted that the fellow has some good — nay, some *noble* qualities."

At every word uttered by the lieutenant, a page of history was blotted out from the memory of his listener. The vice-governatore had heard the name of Raoul Yvard, and even that of le Feu-Follet, which the malignancy of a bitter war had blackened nearly to the hues of piracy. The thought that he had been the dupe of this corsair — nay, that he had actually been entertaining him with honours and hospitality, within an hour, was nearly too much for his philosophy. Men do not often submit to such humiliating sensations without a struggle; and before he would, or could, accord full credence to what was now told him, it was natural to oppose the objections that first offered.

"All this *must* be a mistake," observed the vice-governatore; "there are English, as well as French luggers; and this is one of the former. Her commander is a noble English gentleman, a son of Milordo Smees; and though his education has been, in a trifling degree, neglected, he shows his origin and national character in all he says and does. Ze Ving-y-Ving is commanded by Sir Smees, a young officer of merit, as you must have seen, yourself, Signore, by his evolutions this very morning. Surely, you have heard of Il Capitano Sir Smees, the son of Milordo Smees!"

"We do not deny that his escape, this morning, was a

clever thing, vice-governatore, for the fellow is a seaman, every inch of him; and he is as brave as a lion; but, then, he is as impudent as a beggar's dog. There is no Sir Smees, nor any Sir Any-Body else, in command of any of our lug-gers, anywhere. In the Mediterranean, we have no cruiser of this rig at all; and the two or three we have elsewhere, are commanded by old sea-dogs, who have been brought up in that sort of craft. As for Sirs, they are scarce out here, though the battle of the Nile has made a few of them, for the navy. Then you 'll not often meet with a nobleman's son in a clipper like this, for that sort of gentry generally go from a frigate's quarter-deck into a good sloop, as com-mander, and after a twelvemonth's work, or so, in the small one, into a fast frigate again, as a post-captain."

Much of this was gibberish to Andrea Barrofaldi, but Griffin being exclusively naval, he fancied every one ought to take the same interest as he did himself, in all these mat-ters. But, while the vice-governatore did not understand more than half of the other's meaning, that half sufficed to render him exceedingly uneasy. The natural manner of the lieutenant, too, carried conviction with it, while all the original impressions against the lugger were revived by his statements.

"What say you, Signor Vito Viti?" demanded Andrea; "you have been present at the interviews with Sir Smees."

"That we have been deceived by one of the most oily-tongued rogues that ever took in honest men, if we have been deceived at all, vice-governatore. Last evening, I would have believed this; but since the escape and return of the lugger, I could have sworn that we had an excellent friend and ally in our bay."

"You had your signals, Signor Tenente; and that is proof of amity and understanding."

"We made our number, when we saw the lugger with an English ensign set, for we did not suppose a Frenchman would be quietly lying in a Tuscan port; but the answer we got was nonsense; and then we remembered to have heard that this Raoul Yvard was in the habit of playing such tricks, all along the Italian coast. Once on the scent, we were not the men to be easily thrown off it. You saw the chase, and know the result."

"There must be some error in all this!   Would it not be
well, Signore, to see the commander of the lugger—or to go
on board of her, and satisfy yourself, with your own eyes,
of the truth or falsehood of your surmises?   Ten minutes
might clear up everything."

"Your pardon, Signor Vice-governatore; were I to trust
myself on board le Feu-Follet, I might remain a prisoner
until a peace was made; and I have yet two steps to gain,
before I can afford that risk.   Then, as to letting Yvard
know of my presence here, it would just give him the alarm,
and cause us to lose the bird, before we can spring the net.
My orders are positive, not to let any one but the authorities
of the island, know of my visit, or its object.   All we ask
of you is to detain the lugger until morning; then *we* will
see to it, that she will never trouble the Italian coast again "

"Nay, Signore, we have guns of our own, and could
easily dispose of so small a vessel, once assured of her being
an enemy," returned the vice-governatore, with a little pride
and loftiness of manner; " convince us of that fact, and
we'll sink the lugger at her anchors."

"That is just what we do not wish you to do, Signore,"
answered the lieutenant, with interest.   "From what passed
this morning, Captain Cuffe has thought it probable that
Monsieur Yvard, for some reason best known to himself,
would come back here, as soon as he was rid of us; or that,
finding himself on the south side of the island, he might put
into Porto Longone; and, had I not met him here, I was to
get a horse, and ride across to the latter place, and make
my arrangements there.   We wish, by all means, to get
possession of the lugger, which, in smooth water, is the
fastest craft in the Mediterranean, and would be of infinite
service to us.   We think the Proserpine would prove too
much for her, blowing fresh; but, in moderate weather, she
will go six feet to our five.   Now, if you open on her, she
will either escape or be sunk; for Raoul Yvard is not a man
to strike to a town.   All I ask is to be permitted to make
night-signals, for which I am prepared, as soon as the frigate
approaches, and that you will throw all the delays, by means
of forms and permits, in the way of the Frenchman's sailing,
until to-morrow morning.   We will answer for the rest."

"I should think there would be but little danger of the

lugger's departing in the night, Signor Tenente, her commander rather expressing an intention of passing several days with us; and it is this ease and confidence of his, which causes me to think he cannot be the person you take him for. Why should Raoul Yvard and le Feu-Follet come into Porto Ferrajo at all?"

"No one knows: it is the man's habit; and doubtless he has reasons for it. 'Tis said, he has even been in at Gibraltar; and it is certain, he has cut several valuable store-ships out of our convoys. There is an Austrian loading with iron, I perceive, in the harbour; probably he is waiting for her to fill up, and finds it easier to watch her at an anchor, than by lying outside."

"You naval gentlemen have ways known only to yourselves; and all this may be so; but it seems an enigma to me. Have you any other proofs of your own character, Signor Tenente, than the commission you have shown me? for Sir Smees, as I have been taught to call the commander of the lugger, has one too, that has an air of as much authenticity as this you have shown; and he wears quite as English-looking a uniform: how am I to judge between you?"

"That difficulty has been foreseen, Signor Vice-governatore, and I come well provided with the necessary proofs. I handed you my commission, as that is a document, which, if wanting, might throw a distrust on all other proofs. But, here is a communication from your superior, at Florence, recommending us to the kindness of the authorities of all the Tuscan ports; which you will readily understand. Captain Cuffe has furnished me with other proofs; which you can look over at your leisure."

Andrea Barrofaldi now set about a cautious and deliberate examination of all the papers shown him. They proved to be of a nature to remove every doubt; and it was not possible to distrust the party that presented them. This was a great deal towards convicting the Signor Smees of imposition, though both the vice-governatore and the podestà were of opinion that Captain Cuffe might yet be mistaken, as to the identity of the lugger.

"It is impossible, Signori," answered the lieutenant; We know every English cruiser in these seas, by name and description, at least, and most of them by sight. This is none ; and everything about her, particularly her sailing, betrays her real name. We hear there is a man in her who once belonged to our own ship, a certain Ithuel Bolt—"

"Cospetto !" exclaimed the podesta—"Then we must set down this Sir Smees, after all, for an arrant rogue ; for this is the very man we met at Benedetta's, the past night. An Americano, Signor Tenente, is he not ?"

"Why, the fellow *pretends* to be some such thing, answered the young man, colouring, for he was loth to confess the wrong that had been done the deserter ; "but half the British seamen one falls in with, now-a-days, call themselves Americans, in order to escape serving His Majesty. I rather think this rascal is a Cornish, or a Devonshire-man ; he has the twang and the nasal sing-song of that part of the island. If an American, however, we have a better right to him than the French ; speaking our language, and being descended from a common ancestry, and having a common character, it is quite unnatural for an American to serve any but the English."

"I did not know that, Vice-governatore ! — I thought the Americani a very inferior sort of people to us Europeans, generally ; and that they could scarcely claim to be our equals, in any sense."

"You are quite right, Signor Podestâ," said the lieutenant, briskly ; "they are all you think them ; and any one can see that at a glance. Degenerate Englishmen, we call them, in the service."

"And yet you take them, occasionally, Signor Tenente ; and, as I understand from this Ithuello, frequently contrary to their wishes, and by force," drily observed Andrea Barrofaldi.

"How can we help it, Signore ; the king has a right to ; and he has need of the services of all his own seamen ; and, in the hurry of impressing, we sometimes make a mistake. Then, these Yankees are so like our own people, that I would defy the devil himself to tell them apart."

The Vice-governatore thought there was something contradictory in all this ; and he subsequently said as much to his friend, the podestâ ; but the matter went no farther, at the moment, most probably because he ascertained that the young lieutenant was only using what might be termed a national argument; the English government constantly protesting that it was impossible to distinguish one people from the other, *quoad* this particular practice; while nothing was more offensive, to their eyes, in the abstract, than to maintain any affinity in appearance or characteristics.

The result of the discussion, notwithstanding, was to make the two Italians reluctant converts to the opinion of the Englishman, that the lugger was the dreaded and obnoxious Feu-Follet. Once convinced, however, shame, revenge and mortification, united with duty to quicken their exertions, and to render them willing assistants in executing the schemes of Captain Cuffe. It was, perhaps, fortunate for Raoul and his associates, that the English officers had so strong a desire, as Griffin expressed it, " to take the lugger alive;" else might she have been destroyed where she lay, by removing a gun or two from its proper embrasure, and planting them behind some natural ramparts among the rocks. The night was dark, it is true, but not so much so as to render a vessel sufficiently distinct, at the short distance at which le Feu-Follet lay; and a cannonade would have been abundantly certain.

When all parties were of a mind, as to the true character of the little craft in the bay, a consultation was had on the details of the course proper to be pursued. A window of the government-house, that looked towards the direction of Capraya, or that in which the Proserpine was expected to arrive, was assigned to Griffin. The young man took his station at it about midnight, in readiness to burn the blue-lights with which he was provided, the instant he should discern the signals of his ship. The position of this window was well adapted to the desired object, inasmuch as the lights could not be seen from the town, while they were plainly open to the sea. The same was essentially true as to the signals of the frigate, the heights interposing between her and the houses; and there being a still greater physical impossibility that anything lying in the bay, should discover an object at sea, on the northern side of the promontory.

In this manner, then, did hour after hour pass away, a light land-breeze blowing, but coming so directly into the bay, as to induce Raoul not to lift his kedge. Ghita, and

11

her uncle, Carlo Giuntotardi, had come off about ten; but there were still no signs of movement on board the lugger. To own the truth, Raoul was in no hurry to sail, for the longer his departure was protracted, the longer would he have the happiness of retaining the lovely girl on board; and the zephyr of the succeeding day would be almost certain to carry le Feu-Follet up to the island-like promontory of Monte Argentaro, the point where stood the watch-towers of which Carlo was the keeper, and in one of which he resided. Under the circumstances, therefore, it is not surprising that the rising of the land-breeze was overlooked, or at least disregarded; and that Raoul sat conversing with Ghita on deck, until long past midnight, ere he allowed her to seek her little cabin, where everything had been properly arranged for her reception. To own the truth, Raoul was so confident of having completely mystified all on shore, that he felt no apprehensions from that quarter; and, desirous of prolonging his present happiness as much as possible, he had very coolly determined not to sail until the southerly air of the morning should come; which, as usual, would just suffice to carry him well into the canal, when the zephyr would do the rest. Little did this hardy adventurer suspect what had occurred on shore, since he quitted it; nor was he at all aware that Tommaso Tonti was at watch in the harbour, ready to report the slightest indication, on the part of the lugger, of a wish to quit the bay.

But, while Raoul was so indifferent to the danger he ran, the feeling was quite the reverse with Ithuel Bolt. The Proserpine was the bane of this man's life; and he not only hated every stick, and every timber in her, but every officer and man who was attached to her——the king, whose colours she wore, and the nation whose interests she served. An active hatred is the most restless of all passions; and this feeling rendered Ithuel keenly alive to every chance which might still render the frigate dangerous to the lugger. He thought it probable the former would return in quest of her enemy; and, expressly with a view to this object, when he turned in, at nine, he left orders to be called at two, that he might be on the alert in season.

Ithuel was no sooner awoke, than he called two trusty men, whom he had prepared for the purpose, entered a light boat that was lying in readiness, on the offside of the lugger, and pulled with muffled oars towards the eastern part of the bay. When sufficiently distant from the town to escape observation, he changed his course, and proceeded directly out to sea. Half an hour sufficed to carry the boat as far as Ithuel deemed necessary, leaving him about a mile from the promontory, and so far to the westward, as to give him fair view of the window at which Griffin had taken post.

The first occurrence out of the ordinary course of things that struck the American, was the strong light of a lamp shining through an upper window of the government-house— not that at which the lieutenant was posted, but one above it—and which had been placed there expressly as an indication to the frigate, that Griffin had arrived, and was actively on duty. It was now two o'clock, or an hour or two before the appearance of light, and the breeze off the adjoining continent was sufficiently strong to force a good sailing vessel, whose canvass had been thickened by the damps of night, some four knots through the water; and as Capraya was less than thirty miles from Porto Ferrajo, abundant time had been given to the Proserpine to gain her offing; that ship having come from behind her cover, as soon as the sun had set, and the haze of evening settled upon the sea.

Ithuel, usually so loquacious and gossiping, in his moments of leisure, was silent and observant when he had anything serious on hand. His eye was still on the window in which the lamp was visible, the pure olive oil that was burning in it throwing out a clear, strong flame; when suddenly a blue light flashed beneath the place; and he got a momentary glimpse of the body of the man who held it, as he leaned forward from another window. The motion which now turned his head sea-ward, was instinctive; it was just in time to let him detect a light descending apparently into the water, like a falling star; but which, in fact, was merely a signal lantern of the Proserpine, coming rapidly down from the end of her gaff.

" Ah! d——n you," said Ithuel, grating his teeth, and shaking his fist in the direction of the spot where this transient gleam of brightness had disappeared — "I know you, and your old tricks, with your lanterns and night-signals. Here goes the answer."

As he said this, he touched a rocket, of which he had several in the boat, with the lighted end of the segar he had been smoking, and it went hissing up into the air; ascending so high as to be plainly visible from the deck of le Feu-Follet, before it exploded. Griffin saw this signal with wonder; the frigate noted it with embarrassment; for it was far to seaward of the lamp; and even 'Maso conceived it necessary to quit his station, in order to report the circumstance to the colonel, whom he was to call, in the event of any unusual occurrence. The common impression, however, among all these parties was, that a second cruiser had come through the canal, from the southward, in the course of the night, and that she wished to notify the Proserpine of her position, probably expecting to meet that ship off the island.

On board le Feu-Follet the effect was different. The land-breeze of Italy is a side-wind to vessels quitting the bay of Porto-Ferrajo; and two minutes after the rocket exploded, the lugger was gliding almost imperceptibly, and yet at the rate of a knot or two, under her jigger and jib, towards the outer side of the port, or along the very buildings past which she had brushed the previous day. This movement was made at the critical instant when 'Maso was off his watch; and the ordinary sentinels of the works had other duties to attend to. So light was this little vessel, that a breath of air set her in motion, and nothing was easier than to get three or four knots out of her in smooth water, especially when she opened the comparatively vast folds of her two principal luggs. This she did, when close under the citadel, or out of sight of the town, the sentinels above hearing the flaps of her canvass, without exactly understanding whence they came. At this instant Ithuel let off a second rocket, and the lugger showed a light on her starboard bow, so concealed, however, on all sides but one, as to be visible only in the direction of the boat. As this was done, she put her helm hard down, and hauled her fore-sheet over flat to windward. Five minutes later, Ithuel had reached her deck; and the boat was hauled in as if it had been inflated silk. Deceived by the second rocket, the Proserpine now made her number with regular signal lanterns, with the intention of obtaining that of the stranger; trusting that the promontory would conceal it from the vessels in the bay. This told Raoul the precise position of his enemy; and he was not sorry to see that he was already to the westward of her; a fact that permitted him to slip round the island again, so near in as to be completely concealed by the back-ground of cliffs. By the aid of an excellent night-glass, too, he was enabled to see the frigate, distant about a league, under everything that would draw, from her royals down, standing towards the mouth of the bay on the larboard tack; having made her calculations so accurately as to drop into windward of her port, with the customary breeze off the land. At this sight Raoul laughed, and ordered the mainsail taken in. Half-an-hour later, he directed the foresail to be brailed; brought his jigger-sheet in flat; put his helm hard down; and hauled the jib-sheet to windward.

As this last order was executed, day was just breaking over the mountains of Radicofani and Aquapendente. By this time le Feu-Follet lay about a league to the westward of the promontory, and abreast of the deep bay that has been already mentioned as being in that direction from the town. Of course she was far beyond the danger of missiles from the land. The night wind, however, had now failed, and there was every appearance that the morning would be calm. In this there was nothing extraordinary, at that season; the winds which prevailed from the south being usually short and light, unless accompanied by a gust. Just as the sun appeared, the south air came, it is true, but so lightly, as to render it barely possible to keep the little lugger in command, by heaving-to with her head to the south-west.

The Proserpine stood in until the day had advanced far enough to enable her look-outs to detect le Feu-Follet braving her, as it might be, in the western board, at the distance of about a league and a half, under her jib and jigger, as described. This sight produced a great commotion in the ship, even the watch below "tumbling up," to get another sight of a craft so renowned for evading the pursuit of all the English cruisers of those seas. A few minutes later, Griffin came off, chopfallen and disappointed. His first glance at the countenance of his superior, announced a coming storm; for the commander of a vessel of war is no more apt to be reasonable, under disappointment, than any other poten-

11 *

tate. Captain Cuffe had not seen fit to wait for his subordi
nate on deck; but as soon as it was ascertained that he was
coming off in a shore-boat, he retired to his cabin, leaving
orders with the first lieutenant, whose name was Winchester
to send Mr. Griffin below, as soon as he had reported him
self.

"Well, sir," commenced Cuffe, as soon as his lieutênan
came into the after-cabin, without offering him a seat —
"here *we* are; and out yonder, two or three leagues at sea
is the d——d Few-Folly!" for so most of the seamen of the
English service pronounced "Feu-Follet."

"I beg your pardon, Captain Cuffe," answered Griffin,
who found himself compelled to appear a delinquent, whatever might be the injustice of the situation; "it could not be
helped. We got in, in proper time; and I went to work with
the deputy-governor, and an old chap of a magistrate who
was with him, as soon as I could get up to the house of the
first. Yvard had been beforehand with me; and I had to
under-run about a hundred of his lying yarns, before I could
even enter the end of an idea of my own—"

"You speak Italian, sir, like a Neapolitan born; and I
depended on your doing everything as it should have been."

"Not so much like a Neapolitan, I hope, Captain Cuffe,
as like a Tuscan, or a Roman," returned Griffin, biting his
lip. "After an hour of pretty hard, and lawyer-like work,
and overhauling all the documents, I did succeed in convincing the two Elban gentry of my own character, and of
that of the lugger!"

"And while you were playing advocate, Master Raoul
Yvard coolly lifted his anchor, and walked out of the bay,
as if he were just stepping into his garden, to pick a nose-
gay for his sweetheart?"

"No, sir, nothing of the sort happened. As soon as I
had satisfied the Signor Barrofaldi, the vice-governatore—"

"Veechy-govern-the-tory. — D——n all veechys, and
d——n all the governatorys, too; do speak English, Griffin,
on board an English ship, if you please, even should your
Italian happen to be Tuscan. Call the fellow vice-governor
at once, if that be his rank."

"Well, sir, as soon as I had satisfied the vice-governo.
that the lugger was an enemy, and that we were frie.. ls,

everything went smoothly enough. He wanted to sink the lugger, as she lay at her anchor."

"And why the devil didn't he do it? Two or three heavy shot would have given her a stronger dose than she could bear."

"You know, Captain Cuffe, it has all along been your wish to take her alive. I thought it would tell so well for the ship, to have it to say she had *caught* le Feu-Follet, that I opposed the project. I know Mr. Winchester hopes to get her, as a reward for carrying her, himself."

"Ay, and that would make you first. Well, sir, even if you didn't sink her, it was no reason for letting her escape."

"We could not prevent it, Captain Cuffe. I had a look out set upon her—one of the very best men in Porto Ferrajo, as everybody will tell you, sir; and I made the signals of the lamp and the blue-lights, as agreed upon; and, the ship answering, I naturally thought all was as it should be, until—"

"And who burnt the rockets, off here, where we are at this moment? They deceived me, for I took them to be signals of their presence, from the Weasel or the Sparrow. When I saw those rockets, Griffin, I was just as certain of the Few-Folly, as I am now of having my own ship!"

"Yes, sir, those rockets did all the mischief; for, I have since learned, that, as soon as the first one was thrown, Master Yvard tripped his kedge, and went out of the bay as quietly as one goes out of a dining-room, when he don't wish to disturb the company."

"Ay, he took *French* leave, the b——y *sans culotte*," returned the captain, putting himself in a better humour with his own pun. "But did you *see* nothing of all this?"

"The first I knew of the matter, sir, was seeing the lugger gliding along under the rocks, so close in, that you might have jumped aboard her; and it was too late to stop her. Before those lazy *far nientes* could have pricked and primed, he was out of gun-shot."

"Lazy what?" demanded the captain.

"*Far nientes*, sir; which is a nickname we give these siesta-gentry, you know, Captain Cuffe."

"I know nothing about it, sir; and I'll thank you always to speak to me in English, Mr. Griffin. That is a language

which, I flatter myself, I understand; and it's quite good
enough for all my wants."

"Yes, sir, and for any man's wants. I'm sure, I am
sorry I can speak Italian, since it has led to this mistake."

"Poh—poh—Griffin, you mustn't lay everything to heart,
that comes wrong end foremost. Dine with me to-day, ant
we'll talk the matter over at leisure."

CHAPTER IX.

"Now in the fervid noon the smooth bright sea
Heaves slowly, for the wandering winds are dead
That stirr'd it into foam. The lonely ship
Rolls wearily, and idly flap the sails
Against the creaking masts. The lightest sound
Is lost not on the ear, and things minute
Attract the observant eye."

RICHARDSON.

THUS terminated the setting-down, like many others that
Captain Cuffe had resolved to give, but which usually ended
in a return to good-nature and reason. The steward was
told to set a plate for Mr. Griffin, among the other guests,
and then the commander of the frigate followed the lieutenant on deck. Here he found every officer in the ship, all
looking at le Feu-Follet with longing eyes, and most of them
admiring her appearance, as she lay on the mirror-like
Mediterranean, with the two light sails mentioned, just holding her stationary.

"A regular-built snake-in-the-grass!" growled the boatswain, Mr. Strand, who was taking a look at the lugger over
the hammock-cloths of the waist, as he stood on the heel of
a spare top-mast to do so; "I never put eyes on a scamp
that had a more d———n-my-eyes look!"

This was said in a sort of soliloquy, for Strand was not
exactly privileged to address a quarter-deck officer on such
an occasion, though several stood within hearing, and was
far too great a man to enlighten his subordinates with his

cogitations. It was overheard by Cuffe, however, who just at that instant stepped into the gangway to make an exami‑ nation for himself.

" It is a snake-*out*-of-the-grass, rather, Strand," observed the captain, for *he* could speak to whom he pleased, without presumption or degradation. " Had she stayed in port, now, she would have been *in* the grass, and we might have scotched her."

" Well, your honour, we can *English* her, as it is ; an 'hat 'll be quite as nat'ral, and quite as much to the purpose, as *Scotching* her, any day," answered Strand, who, being a native of London, had a magnificent sort of feeling towards all the dependencies of the empire, and to whom the word scotch, in that sense, was Greek, though he well understood what it meant, " to clap a Scotchman on a rope ;" " we are likely to have a flat calm all the morning, and our boats are in capital order ; and, then, nothing will be more agreeable to our gentlemen, than a row."

Strand was a grey-headed seaman, and he had served with Captain Cuffe when the latter was a midshipman, and had even commanded the top, of which the present boatswain had been the captain. He knew the " cut of the captain's jib" better than any other man in the Proserpine, and often succeeded with his suggestions, when Winchester and the other lieutenants failed. His superior now turned round, and looked him intently in the face, as if struck with the notion the other thus indirectly laid before him. This move‑ ment was noted ; and, at a sign secretly given by Winchester, the whole crew gave three hearty cheers ; Strand leading off, as soon as he caught the idea. This was the only manner in which the crew of a man-of-war can express their wishes to their commander ; it being always tolerated, in a navy, to hurrah, by way of showing the courage of a ship's company. Cuffe walked aft, in a thoughtful manner, and descended to his cabin again ; but a servant soon came up, tc say that the captain desired to see the first lieutenant.

" I do not half like this boat-service, in open day-light. Winchester," observed the senior, beckoning to the other to take a chair. " The least bungling may spoil it all ; and then it 's ten to one but your ship goes half-manned for a

9

twelvemonth, until you are driven to pressing from colliers and neutrals."

"But, we hope, sir, there 'll be no bungling in anything that the Proserpine undertakes. Nine times in ten, an English man-of-war succeeds, when she makes a bold dash in boats, against one of these picaroons. This lugger is so low in the water, too, that it will be like stepping from one cutter into another to get upon her decks; and then, sir, I suppose, you don't doubt what Englishmen will do?"

"Ay, Winchester, once on her deck, I make no doubt you 'd carry her; but it may not be so easy as you imagine, to get on her deck. Of all duty to a captain, this of sending off boats is the most unpleasant. He cannot go himself, and if anything unfortunate turns up, he never forgives himself. Now, it 's a very different thing with a fight in which all share alike; and the good or evil comes equally on all hands."

"Quite true, Captain Cuffe; and yet this is the only chance that the lieutenants have for getting ahead a little out of the regular course. I have heard, sir, that you were made commander, for cutting out some coasters, in the beginning of the war."

" You have not been misinformed; and a devil of a risk we all ran. Luck saved us—and that was all. One more fire from a cursed carronade, would have given a Flemish account of the whole party; for, once get a little under, and you suffer like game in a *batteau*." Captain Cuffe wished to say *battue*; but despising foreign languages, he generally made sad work with them, whenever he did condescend to resort to their terms, however familiar. " This Raoul Yvard is a devil incarnate, himself, at this boarding work; and is said to have taken off the head of a master's mate, of the Theseus, with one clip of his sword, when he retook that ship's prize, in the affair of last winter—that which happened off Alicant!"

" I 'll warrant you, sir, the master's mate was some slender-necked chap, that might better have been at home, craning at the girls, as they come out of a church-door. I should like to see Raoul Yvard, or any Frenchman who was ever born, take off *my* head at a single clip!"

" Well, Winchester, to be frank with you, I should *not*,

You are a good first; and that is an office in which a man usually wants all the head he has; and I'm not at all certain you have any to spare. I wonder if one could not hire a felucca, or something larger than a boat, in this place, by means of which we could play a trick upon this fellow, and effect our purpose quite as well as by going up to him in our open boats, bull-dog fashion?"

"No question of it at all, sir; Griffin says there are a dozen feluccas in port here, all afraid to budge an inch, in consequence of this chap's being in the offing. Now one of these trying to slip along shore might just serve as a bait for him, and then he would be famously hooked."

"I think I have it, Winchester. You understand; we have not yet been seen to communicate with the town; and luckily, our French colours have been flying all the morning. Our head, too, is in-shore; and we shall drift so far to the eastward, in a few minutes, as will shut in our hull, if not our upper sails, from the lugger, where she now lies. As soon as this is done, you shall be off, with forty picked men, for the shore. Engage a felucca, and come out, stealing along the rocks, as close as you can, as if distrusting *us*. In due time, we will chase you, in the boats; and then you must make for the lugger for protection, as fast as you can, when, betwixt ʌne two, I'll answer for it, you get this Master Yvard, by fair means or foul."

Winchester was delighted with the scheme; and in less than five minutes, orders were issued for the men to be detailed and armed. Then a conference was held, as to all the minor arrangements; when, the ship having become shut in from the lugger by the promontory, as expected, the boats departed. Half-an-hour later, or just as the Proserpine, after waring, had got near the point where the lugger would be again open, the boats returned, and were run up. Presently the two vessels were again in sight of each other, everything on board of each, remaining, apparently, *in statu quo* Thus far, certainly, the stratagem had been adroitly managed. To add to it, the batteries now fired ten or twelve guns at the frigate, taking very good care not to hit her; which the Proserpine returned, under the French ensign, having used the still greater precaution of drawing the shot. All this was done by an arrangement between Winchester

and Andrea Barrofaldi, and with the sole view to induce
Raoul Yvard to fancy that he was still believed to be an
Englishman, by the worthy vice-governatore, while the ship
in the offing was taken for an enemy.   A light air from
the southward, which lasted from eight to nine o'clock,
allowed the frigate to get somewhat more of an offing, the
while, placing her seemingly beyond the reach of danger.

During the prevalence of the light air mentioned, Raoul
Yvard did not see fit to stir tack or sheet, as it is termed
among   seamen. . Le Feu-Follet remained so stationary,
that, had she been set by compass, from any station on the
shore, her direction would not have varied a degree the
whole time.   But this hour of comparative breeze sufficed to
enable Winchester to get out of the harbour with la Divina
Providenza, the felucca he had hired, and to round the promontory, under the seeming protection of the guns by which
it was crowned ; coming in view of the lugger precisely as
the latter relieved her man at the helm for ten o'clock.
There were eight or nine men visible on the felucca's deck,
all dressed in the guise of Italians, with caps and striped
shirts of cotton.   Thirty-five men were concealed in the
hold.

Thus far everything was favourable to the wishes of Captain Cuffe and his followers.   The frigate was about a league
from the lugger, and half that distance from la Divina Providenza ; the latter had got fairly to sea, and was slowly
coming to a situation from which it might seem reasonable,
and a matter of course, for the Proserpine to send boats in
chase ; while the manner in which she gradually drew
nearer to the lugger, was not such as to excite distrust, or
to appear, in the least, designed.   The wind, too, had got to
be so light, as to favour the whole scheme.

It is not to be supposed that Raoul Yvard and his followers were unobservant of what was passing.   It is true, that
the latter wilfully protracted his departure, under the pretence that it was safer to have his enemy in sight, during
the day, knowing how easy it would be to elude him, in the
dark ; but, in reality, that he might prolong the pleasure of
having Ghita on board ; and it is also true, that he had
passed a delightful hour, that morning, in the cabin ; but,
then, his understanding eye noted the minutest fact that

occurred; and his orders were always ready to meet any emergency that might arise. Very different was the case with Ithuel. The Proserpine was his bane; and, even while eating his breakfast, which he took on the heel of the bowsprit, expressly with that intent, his eye was seldom a minute off the frigate, unless it was for the short period she was shut in by the land. It was impossible for any one in the lugger to say, whether her character was, or was not known in Porto Ferrajo; but the circumstance of the blue-lights burn in the government-house, itself, and witnessed by Ithuel, rendered the latter, to say the least, probable, and induced more caution than might otherwise have been shown. Still, there was no reason to suspect the character of the felucca; and the confident manner in which she came down towards the lugger, though considerably in-shore of her, gave reason to believe that *she*, at least, was ignorant that le Feu-Follet was an enemy.

"That felucca is the craft which lay near the landing," quietly observed Raoul, who had now come on the forecastle with a view to converse with Ithuel; "her name is la Divina Providenza; she is given to smuggling between Leghorn and Corsica, and is probably bound to the latter, at this moment. It is a bold step, too, to stand directly for her port, under such circumstances!"

"Leghorn is a free port," returned Ithuel; "and smuggling is not needed."

"Ay, free as to friends, but not free to come and go between enemies. No port is free, in that sense; it being treason for a craft to communicate with the foe, unless she happen to be le Feu-Follet," observed Raoul, laughing; "we *are* privileged, *mon brave!*"

"Corsica or Capraya, she'll reach neither, to-day, unless she find more wind. I do not understand why the man has sailed, with no more air than will serve to blow out a pocket-handkerchief."

"These little feluccas, like our little lugger, slip along even when there seems to be no wind at all. Then, he may be bound to Bastia; in which case he is wise in getting an offing before the zephyr sets in for the afternoon. Let him get a league or two out here, more to the northwest, and he can make a straight wake to Bastia, after his siesta is over."

12

"Ay, there go them greedy Englishmen a'rter him!" said Ithuel; "it's as I expected; let 'em see the chance of making a guinea, and they'll strive for it, though it be ag'in law, or ag'in natur'. Now, what have they to do with a Neapolitan felucca; England being a sworn friend of Naples?"

Raoul made no reply to this, but stood watching the movement in silence. The reader will readily enough understand that Ithuel's remark was elicited by the appearance of the boats, which, five in number, at that instant pulled off from the frigate's side, and proceeded steadily towards the felucca.

It may be necessary now to mention the relative positions of the parties, the hour, and the precise state of the weather with a view to give the reader clear ideas of the events that succeeded. Le Feu-Follet had not materially changed her place, since her jib-sheet was first hauled over. She still lay about a league, a little north-of-west, from the residence of Andrea Barrofaldi, and in plain view of it; a deep bay being south of her, and abeam. No alterations had been made in her canvass, or her helm; most of the first being still in the brails, and the latter down. As the head of the frigate had been kept to the westward, for the last hour, she had forged some distance in that direction, and was now quite as near the lugger as was the promontory, though near two miles off the land. Her courses were hauled up, on account of the lightness of the air; but all her upper-sails stood, and were carefully watched and trimmed, in order to make the most of the cats'-paws, or rather, of the breathings of the atmosphere, which occasionally caused the royals to swell outward. On the whole, she might be drawing nearer to the lugger, at the rate of about a knot in an hour. La Divina Providenza was just out of gun-shot from the frigate, and about a mile from the lugger, when the boats shoved off from the former, though quite near the land, just opening the bay so often named. The boats, of course, were pulling in a straight line from the vessel they had just left, towards that of which they were in pursuit.

As to the time, the day had advanced as far as eleven which is a portion of the twenty-four hours when the Mediterranean, in the summer months, is apt to be as smooth as a mirror, and as calm as if it never knew a tempest. Throughout the morning, there had been some irregularity in the currents of air; the southerly breeze, generally light, and frequently fickle, having been even more light and baffling than common. Still, as has been seen, there was sufficient air to force a vessel through the water; and, had Raoul been as diligent as the people of the two other crafts, he might, at that moment, have been off the western end of the island, and far out of harm's way. As it was, he had continued watching the result, but permitting all the other parties gradually to approach him.

It must be allowed, that the ruse of the felucca was well planned; and it now seemed about to be admirably executed. Had it not been for Ithuel's very positive knowledge of the ship—his entire certainty of her being his old prison, as he bitterly called her, it is not improbable that the lugger's crew might have been the dupe of so much well-acted ingenuity; and, as it was, opinions were greatly divided, Raoul, himself, being more than half disposed to fancy that his American ally, for once, was wrong, and that the ship in sight was actually what she professed to be — a cruiser of the republic.

Both Winchester, who was in la Divina Providenza, and Griffin, who commanded the boats, played their parts in perfection. They understood too well the character of the wily and practised foe with whom they had to deal, to neglect the smallest of the details of their well-concerted plan. Instead of heading towards the lugger as soon as the chase commenced, the felucca appeared disposed to enter the bay, and to find an anchorage under the protection of a small battery that had been planted, for this express purpose, near its head. But the distance was so great, as obviously to render such an experiment bootless; and, after looking in that direction a few minutes, the head of la Divina Providenza was laid off shore, and she made every possible effort to put herself under the cover of the lugger. All this was done in plain view of Raoul, whose glass was constantly at his eye, and who studied the smallest movement with jealous distrust. Winchester, fortunately for his purpose, was a dark-complexioned man, of moderate stature, and with bushy whiskers, such as a man-of-war's-man is apt to cultivate, on

a long cruise; and, in his red Phrygian cap, striped shirt
and white cotton trowsers, he looked the Italian as well as
could have been desired.   The men in sight, too, had been
selected for their appearance, several of them being actually
foreigners, born on the shores of the Mediterranean; it being
seldom, indeed, that the crew of an English, or an American
vessel of war, does not afford a representation of half the
maritime nations of the earth. These men exhibited a proper
degree of confusion and alarm, too; running to and fro, as
soon as the chase became lively; exerting themselves, but
doing it without order and concert.   At length, the wind
failing almost entirely, they got out two sweeps, and began
to pull lustily; the real, as well as the apparent desire being
to get as near as possible to the lugger.

"*Peste!*" exclaimed Raoul; "all this seems right —
what if the frigate should be French, after all.   These men
in the boats look like my brave compatriotes!"

"They are regular John Bulls," answered Ithuel, positively, "and the ship is the spiteful Proserpyne," for so
the New-Hampshire-man always called his old prison.   "As
for them French hats, and the way they have of rowing,
they act it all for a take-in.   Just let a six-pound shot in
among 'em, and see how they 'll throw off their French airs,
and take to their English schooling."

"I 'll not do that; for we might injure a friend.   What
are those fellows in the felucca about, now?"

"Why, they 've got a small gun — yes, it 's a twelve-
pound carronade, under the tarpaulin, for'rard of their fore-
mast, and they 're clearin' it away for sarvice.   We shall
have something doin' 'fore the end of the week!"

"Bien—it is as you say—and, voilà, they train the piece
on the boats!"

As this was said, the felucca was half concealed in smoke.
Then came the discharge of the gun.   The shot was seen
skipping along the water, at a safe distance from the leading
boat, certainly, and yet sufficiently near to make it pass for
indifferent gunnery.   This leading boat was the Proserpine's
launch, which carried a similar carronade on its grating,
forward, and not half-a-minute was suffered to pass, before
the fire was returned.   So steady were the men, and so
nicely were all the parts of this plot calculated, that the shot

came whistling through the air, in a direct line for the felucca, striking its mainyard about half-way between the mast and the peak of the sail, letting the former down by the run.

"Human natur'!" ejaculated Ithuel — "this is acting up to the contract, dollars and cents! Captain Rule, they shoot better in sport than when they're in downright airn est."

"This looks like real work," answered Raoul. "A man does not often shoot away the mainyard of his friend, on purpose."

As soon as the crews of the boats saw the end of the yard come down, they ceased rowing, and gave three hearty cheers, taking the signal from Griffin, who stood erect in the stern of the launch, to give it.

"Bah!"—cried Raoul—"these are English John Bulls, without a shadow of doubt. Who ever knew the men of the republic shout like so many Italian fantoccini, pulled by wires. Ah! Messieurs les Anglais, you have betrayed your secret by your infernal throats; now look to hear us tell the remainder of the story."

Ithuel rubbed his hands, with delight, perfectly satisfied that Raoul could no longer be deceived, though the fire between the felucca and the launch was kept up with spirit, the shooting being such as might have done credit to a *bonâ fide* conflict. All this time the sweeps of the felucca were plied, the boats advancing at least two feet to the chase's one. La Divina Providenza might now have been three hundred yards from the lugger; and the launch, the nearest of the pursuers, about the same distance astern of the felucca Ten minutes more would certainly bring the seeming combatants alongside of each other.

Raoul ordered the sweeps of le Feu-Follet to be run out and manned. At the same time, her guns, twelve-pound carronades, were cast loose, and primed. Of these she had four of a side, while the two sixes on her forecastle were prepared for similar service. When everything was ready, the twelve sweeps dropped into the water, as by a common instinct, and a powerful effort started the lugger ahead. Her jib and jigger were both brailed at that instant. A single minute sufficed to teach Winchester how hopeless

12 *

pursuit would be in the felucca, if not in the boats them
selves, should the lugger endeavour to escape in this manner;
it being quite practicable for her strong crew to force her
through the water, by means of her sweeps alone, from
three to three and a half knots in the hour.   But flight did
not appear to be her object ; for her head was laid towards
la Divina Providenza, as if, deceived by the artifice of the
English, she intended to prevent the capture of the felucca,
and to cover a friend.

Raoul, however, understood himself far better than this
supposition would give reason to suppose.   He swept the
lugger up in a line with la Divina Providenza and the boats,
in the first place, as the position in which she would be the
least likely to suffer from the fire of the latter ; well knowing
that whatever shot were thrown, were purposely sent so high
as to do no mischief; and, in the second place, that he
might bring his enemies in a single range from his own guns.
In the meanwhile, the felucca and the boats not only continued to use their carronades, but they commenced on both
sides a brisk fire of musketry ; the former being now distant
only a hundred yards from le Feu-Follet, exceedingly hard
pressed by her adversaries, so far as appearances were concerned.   There being no wind at all, at this juncture, the
little there had been having been entirely killed by the con-
cussions of the guns, the sea was getting to be fast covered
with smoke ; the felucca, in particular, showing more than
common of the wreathy canopy, over her decks, and about
her spars ; for, in truth, powder was burnt in considerable
quantities, in different parts of the vessel, with this express
object.   Ithuel observed, too, that in the midst of this confusion and cloud, the crew of la Divina Providenza was increasing in numbers, instead of diminishing by the combat,
four sweeps next being out, each manned by three men,
while near twenty more were shortly visible, running to and
fro, and shouting to each other in a language that was intended to be Italian, but which sounded much more, in his
practised ears, like bastard English.   The felucca was not
fifty yards distant, when this clamour became the loudest ;
and the crisis was near.   The cheers of the boats on the
other side of her, proclaimed the quick approach of Griffin
and his party ; the bows of la Divina Providenza having

beer laid, in a species of blind haste, directly in a lin which would carry her athwart-hawse of le Feu-Follet.

"*Mes enfans*,"—shouted Raoul—"*soyez calmes*—Fire!"

The whole of the five guns, loaded heavily with canister, were discharged into the smoke of la Divina Providenza The shrieks that succeeded, sufficiently proclaimed with what effect. A pause of solemn, wondering silence followed, on the part of the English; and then arose a manly shout as if, prepared for every contingency, they were resolved t brave the worst. The boats were next seen coming round the bows and stern of the felucca, dashing earnestly at their real enemy, while their two carronades returned the fire, this time loaded and aimed with deadly intent. But it was too late for success. As Griffin, in the launch, came out of ia Divina Providenza's smoke, he saw the lugger's sails all opened, and filled with a dying effort of the southerly air. So light, however, was le Feu-Follet, that a duck could hardly have sailed away more readily from the fowler, than this little craft shot ahead, clearing the smoke, and leaving her pursuers an additional hundred yards behind her. As the air seemed likely to stand long enough to place his party in extreme jeopardy, under the fire of the French, Winchester promptly ordered the boats to relinquish the pursuit, and to rally around the felucca. This command was reluctantly obeyed, when a moment was given to both sides for deliberation.

Le Feu-Follet had sustained no injury worth mentioning; but the English had not less than a dozen men slain or hurt. Among the latter was Winchester, himself; and as he saw that any success which followed would fall principally to the share of his subordinate, his wound greatly indisposed him to pursue any further a struggle that was nearly hopeless, as it was. Not so with Raoul Yvard, however. Perceiving that the frigate had taken the breeze, as well as himself, and that she was stealing along in the direction of the combatants, he determined to take an ample revenge for the audacity of the attempt, and then proceed on his voyage.

The lugger accordingly tacked, and passed to windward of the felucca, delivering a close and brisk fire as she approached. At first this fire was returned, but the opposition soon ceased; and when le Feu-Follet ranged up past her

adversary, a few yards to windward, it was seen that the
English had deserted her to a man, carrying off their
wounded. The boats were pulling through the smoke,
towards the bay, taking a direction opposite to that in which
the lugger's head was laid. It would have been easy for
the French to ware, and probably to have overtaken the
fugitives, sinking or capturing them to a man; but there was
a touch of high chivalry in the character of Raoul Yvard,
and he declared, that as the artifice had been ingeniously
planned, and daringly attempted, he would follow up his
success no farther. Perhaps the appearance of Ghita on
deck, imploring him to be merciful, had its influence; it is
certain that not another shot did he allow to be fired at the
enemy. Instead of pursuing her advantage, in this manner,
the lugger took in her after-sails, wore short round on her
heel, came to the wind to-leeward of the felucca, shivered all
forward, set her jigger again, and luffed up so near what
may be called the prize, that the two vessels came together
so gently as not to break an egg, as it is termed. A single
rope secured the felucca to the lugger, and Raoul, Ithuel,
and a few more, stepped on board the former.

The decks of la Divina Providenza were reeking with
blood; and grape and canister were sticking in handsful, in
different parts of the vessel. Three dead bodies were found
in her hold, but nothing having life was met with on board.
There was a tar-bucket filled at hand, and this was placed
beneath the hatch, covered with all the combustible materials
that could be laid hold of, and set on fire. So active were
the flames, at that dry season, that Raoul regretted he had
not taken the precaution to awaken them after he had removed his own vessel; but the southerly air continuing, he
was enabled to get to a safe distance before they actually
ascended the felucca's rigging, and seized upon her sails.

Ten minutes were thus lost, and they had sufficed to carry
the boats out of gun-shot, in-shore, and to bring the frigate
very nearly down within gun-shot from the south-east. But,
hauling aft all his sheets, Raoul soon took the lugger clear
of her flaming prize; and then she stood towards the west
end of Elba, going, as usual, in so light an air, three feet to
the frigate's two. The hour, however, was not favourable
to the continuance of the breeze, and in ten more minutes it

would have puzzled the keenest senses to have detected the slightest current of air over the surface of the sea. Such flickerings of the lamp, before it burnt entirely out, were common, and Raoul felt certain that there would be no more wind that day, until they got the zephyr. Accordingly, he directed all the sails to be hauled up, an awning to be spread over the quarter-deck, and permission was given to the people to attend to their own affairs. The frigate, too seemed to be aware that it was the moment for the siesta of vessels, as well as of men; for she clewed up her royals and top-gallant-sails, brailed her jib and spanker, hauled up her courses, and lay on the water as motionless as if sticking on a shoal. The two vessels were barely long-gun shot apart, and, under ordinary circumstances, the larger might have seen fit to attack the smaller in boats; but the lesson just given was a sufficient pledge to the French, against the renewal of any such attempt, and they scarcely paid their neighbour's prowess the compliment to watch him. Half-an-hour later, when Winchester got back to the ship, limping with a hurt in his leg, and with his people exhausted and mortified, it was found that the undertaking had cost the lives of seven good men, besides the temporary suspension of the services of fifteen more.

Captain Cuffe was aware that his enterprise had failed, as soon as he perceived the lugger under her canvass, playing around the felucca and the boats, held in perfect command. But, when he discovered the latter pulling for the shore, he was certain that they must have suffered, and he was prepared to learn a serious loss, though not one that bore so large a proportion to the whole numbers of the party sent on the expedition. Winchester he considerately declined questioning, while his wound was being dressed; but Griffin was summoned to his cabin, as soon as the boats were hoisted in and stowed.

"Well, Mr. Griffin, a d——d pretty scrape is this, into which you have led me, among you, with your wish to go boating about after luggers, and Raoul Yvards! What will the admiral say, when he comes to hear of twenty-two men's being laid on the shelf, and a felucca to be paid for, as a morning's amusement?"

'Really, Captain Cuffe, we did our best; but a man might

as well have attempted to put out Vesuvius with snow-balls, as to stand the canister of that infernal lugger! I don't think there was a square yard in the felucca that was not peppered. The men never behaved better; and down to the moment when we last cheered, I was as sure of le Feu-Follet, as I ever was of my own promotion."

" Ay, they needn't call her le Few-Folly any longer, the Great-Folly being a better name. What the devil did you cheer for at all, sir? did you ever know a Frenchman cheer, in your life? That very cheering was the cause of your being found out, before you had time to close. You should have shouted *vive la république*, as all their craft do, when we engage them. A regular English hurrah would split a Frenchman's throat."

" I believe we did make a mistake there, sir; but I never was in an action in which we did not cheer; and when it got to be warm—or to *seem* warm—I forgot myself, a little. But, we should have had her, sir, for all that, had it not been for one thing."

" And what is that, pray? You know, Griffin, I must have something plausible to tell the admiral; it will never do to have it published in the gazette that we were thrashed by our own hallooing."

" I was about to say, Captain Cuffe, that had not the lugger fired her first broadside just as she did, and had she given us time to get out of the range of her shot, we should have come in upon her before she could have loaded again, and carried her, in spite of the breeze that so much favoured her. Our having three men hurt in the launch, made some difference, too, and set as many oars catching crabs, at a most critical instant. Everything depends on chance, in these matters, you know, sir, and that was our bad luck."

" Umph!—It will never do to tell Nelson that.—'Everything was going well, my lord, until three of the launch's people went to work catching crabs with their oars, which threw the boat a-stern.'—No, no, *that* will never do for a gazette. Let me see, Griffin; after all, the lugger made off from you—you would have had her, had she not made sail, and stood to the southward and westward on a bowline?"

" Yes, sir, she certainly did *that*. Had she not made sail, as you say, nothing could have prevented our getting along-side."

"Well, then, she ran. Wind sprung up, enemy made sail—every attempt to get alongside unsuccessful.—Brave fellows, cheering and doing their utmost.—Not so bad an account, after all—but, how about that d——d felucca?—You see, she is burned to the water's edge, and will go down in a few minutes."

"Very true, Captain Cuffe, but not a Frenchman entered her, while we were there—"

"Yes, I now see how it was—threw all hands into the boats, in chase, the felucca being too unwieldy, and every effort to get alongside unsuccessful. He's a devil of a fellow, that Nelson & Bronte ; and I had rather hear the thunder of ten thousand tempests, than get one of his tempestuous letters. Well, I think I understand the affair, now, and shall speak of you all as you deserve. 'T was a gallant thing, though it failed. You deserved success, whatever may have caused you to lose it."

In this Captain Cuffe was nearer right than in anything, else he uttered on the occasion.

CHAPTER X.

"O! 'tis a thought sublime, that man can force
    A path upon the waste, can find a way
Where all is trackless, and compel the winds,
Those freest agents of Almighty power,
To lend their untamed wings, and bear him on
To distant climes."

                                            WARE.

THE situation of Ghita Caraccioli, on board the lugger was of the most unpleasant nature, during the fierce struggle we have related. Fortunately, for her, this struggle was very short, Raoul having kept her in profound ignorance of the approach of any danger, until the instant le Feu-Folle commenced her fire. It is true, she had heard the guns

between the felucca and the boats, but this she had been told
was an affair in which the privateer had no participation;
and the reports sounding distant, to one in the cabin, she
had been easily deceived. While the actual conflict was
going on, she was on her knees, at the side of her uncle;
and the moment it ceased, she appeared on deck, and interposed to save the fugitives, in the manner related.

Now, however, the scene was entirely changed. The
lugger had escaped all damage, worthy of notice; her decks
had not been stained with blood; and her success had been
as·complete as could be desired. In addition to these advantages, the result removed all apprehension from the only
source of danger that Raoul thought could exist, as between
his own vessel and the frigate; or a boat-attack in a calm;
for men who had just been so roughly handled in an enterprise so well concealed, would not be likely to renew the
attempt while they still smarted under the influence of the
late repulse. Affairs of this sort exact all the discipline and
resolution that a well-regulated service can afford; and are
not to be thought of under the temporary demoralization of
defeat. All in the lugger, therefore, considered this collision
with the Proserpine at an end, for the moment at least.

Ghita had dined, for the day had now turned some time,
and the girl had come on deck to escape the confinement of
a very small cabin, leaving her uncle to enjoy his customary
siesta. She was seated under the awning of the quarter-
deck, using her needle, as was her wont, at that hour, on
the heights of Argentaro. Raoul had placed himself on a
gun-slide, near her, and Ithuel was busy within a few feet
of them, dissecting a spy-glass, with a view to clean its
lenses.

"I suppose, the most excellent Andrea Barrofaldi will
sing a Te Deum for his escape from our fangs," suddenly
exclaimed Raoul, laughing. "*Pardie !* he is a great historian, and every way fit to write an account of this great
victory, which Monsieur l'Anglais, là bas, is about to send
to his government !"

"And you, Raoul, have you no occasion for a Te Deum,
after your escape?" demanded Ghita, gently, and yet with
emphasis. "Is there no God for you to thank, as well as
for the vice-governatore?"

"*Peste!*—our French deity is little thought of, just now, Ghita. Republics, as you know, have no great faith in religion—is it not so, mon brave Américan? Tell-us, Etooell; have you any religion in America?"

As Ithuel had often heard Raoul's opinions on this subject, and knew the prevailing state of France, in this particular, he neither felt nor expressed any surprise at the question. Still, the idea ran counter to all his own notions and prejudices, he having been early taught to respect religion, even when he was most serving the devil. In a word, Ithuel was one of those descendants of Puritanism, who, "Godward," as it is termed, was quite unexceptionable, so far as his theory extended; but who, "manward" was, "as the Scribes and Pharisees." Nevertheless, as he expressed it himself, "he always stood up for religion;" a fact that his English companions had commented on in jokes; maintaining that he even "stood up" when the rest of the ship's company were on their knees.

"I'm a little afraid, Monsieur Rule," he answered, "that in France you have entered the rope of republicanism at the wrong eend. In Ameriky, we even put religion before dollars; and if that isn't convincing, I'll give it up. Now, I do wish you could see a Sunday once in the Granite State, Signorina Ghita, that you might get some notion what our western religion ra'ally is."

"All real religion—all real devotion to God, is, or ought to be, the same, Signor Ithuello, whether in the east or in the west. A Christian, is a Christian; let him live and die where he may."

"That's not exactly platform, I fancy. Why, Lord bless ye, young lady—*your* religion, now, is no more like *mine*, than my religion is like that of the Archbishop of Canterbury's, or Monsieur Rule's, here!"

"La mienne!" exclaimed Raoul — "I pretend to none, mon brave; there can be no likeness to nothing."

Ghita's glance was kind, rather than reproachful; but it was profoundly sorrowful.

"In what can our religion differ," she asked, "if we are both Christians? Americans, or Italians, it is all the same."

"That comes of knowing nothing about Ameriky," said Ithuel, filled with the conceit of his own opinion of himself

13   10

and of the part of the world from which he came.   "In the first place, you have a Pope, and cardinals, and bishops, and all such things, in your religion ; while we have none."

"Certainly, there is the Holy Father, and there are cardinals ; but they are not my religion," answered Ghita, looking surprised.   "Bishops, it is true, are appointed of God, and form part of his church ; and the bishop of Rome is the ead of the church on earth—but nothing more."

"Nothing more !—Don't you worship images, and take off and put on garments at your prayers, and kneel down in a make-believe, profane way ; and don't you turn everything into vain ceremonies ?"

Had Ithuel been engaged, body and soul, in maintaining one of the propositions of the Oxford Tracts' controversy, he could not have uttered these words with greater zeal, or with a more self-righteous emotion.   His mind was stored with the most vulgar accusations of an exceedingly vulgar set of sectarian distinctions ; and he fancied it a high proof of Protestant perfection, to hold all the discarded usages in abhorrence.   On the other hand, Ghita listened with surprise ; for, to her, the estimation in which the rites of the Romish church were held by the great bulk of Protestants, was a profound secret.   The idea of worshipping an image, never crossed her innocent mind ; and although she often knelt before her own little ivory crucifix, she had never supposed any could be so ignorant as to confound the mere material representation of the sacrifice it was meant to pourtray, with the divine expiation itself.

"It is decent to use proper vestments, at the altar," sne replied ; "and its servants ought not to be clad like other men.   We know it is the heart, the soul, that must be touched, to find favour with God ; but this does not make the outward semblance of respect that we show even to each c'her, the less necessary.   As to worshipping images—that would be idolatry ; and as bad as the poor heathens, themselves."

Ithuel looked mystified ; for he never doubted, in the least, that the worshipping of images was a material part of Catholic devotion ; and, as for the pope and the cardinals, he deemed them all as indispensable to the creed of this church ; as he fancied it important, in his own, that the priests should not wear gowns; and that the edifices in which they worshipped, should have square-topped windows. Absurd as all this may seem, to-day, and wicked as it will probably appear a century hence, it formed, and forms, no small part of sectarian belief; and entered into the animosities and jealousies of those who seem to think it necessary to quarrel for the love of God. Could we but look back at our own changes of opinion, it would render us less confident of the justice of our sentiments; and, most of all, one would think that the American, who has lived long enough to witness the summersets that have been thrown in the practices and creeds of most of the more modern sects of his own country, within the last quarter of a century, would come to have something like a suitable respect for the more stable and venerable divisions of the Christian world.

"Proper vestments!" repeated Ithuel, with contempt; "what vestments are wanting, in the eyes of the Supreme Being? No; if I *must* have religion — and I know it's necessary and whullsum', let it be a pure, *naked* religion, that will stand to reason. Is not that your way of thinking, Monsieur Rule?"

"*Ma foi, oui.* Reason before all things, Ghita; and, most of all, reason in religion."

"Ah! Raoul, this it is which misleads and betrays you," returned the girl, earnestly. "Faith, and a meek dependence, is what makes a proper state of feeling; and yet you demand a reason of Him who created the universe, and breathed into you the breath of life!"

"Are we not reasoning creatures, Ghita," returned Raoul, gently, and yet with a sincerity and truth, for the circumstances, that rendered even his scepticism piquant and respectable; "and is it unreasonable to expect us to act up to our natures? Can I worship a God I do not understand?"

"Couldst thou worship one thou *didst?* He would cease to be a deity, and would become one of ourselves, were his nature and attributes brought down to the level of our comprehensions. Did one of thy followers come on this quarterdeck, and insist on hearing all thine own motives for the orders given in this little felucca, how readily wouldst thou drive him back, as mutinous and insolent; and yet thou wouldst question the God of the universe, and pry into his mysteries !"

Raoul was mute, while Ithuel stared. It was so seldom that Ghita lost her exceeding gentleness of manner, that the flush of her cheek, the severe earnestness of her eyes, the mpassioned modulations of her voice, and the emphasis with which she spoke on this occasion, produced a sort of awe, hat prevented the discourse from proceeding further. The girl, herself, was so much excited, that, after sitting for a minute with her hands before her face, the tears were seen forcing their way through her fingers. She then arose, and darted into the cabin. Raoul was too observant of the rules of propriety to think of following; but he sat moody and lost in thought, until Ithuel drew his attention to himself.

"Gals will be gals," said that refined and philosophical observer of the human family, " and nothing touches their natur's sooner than a little religious excitement. I dare say, if it wasn't for images, and cardinals, and bishops, and such creatur's, the Italians (Ithuel always pronounced this word *Eye*talians) would make a very good sort of Christians."

But Raoul was in no humour to converse; and as the hour had now arrived when the zephyr was to be expected, he rose, ordered the awning taken in, and prepared to make himself master of the state of things around him. There lay the frigate, taking her siesta, like all near ; her three topsails standing, but every other sail that was loose, hanging in festoons, waiting for the breeze. Notwithstanding her careless appearance, so closely had she been tended, for the last few hours, however, and so sedulously had even the smallest breath of air been improved, that Raoul started with surprise, when he found how much nearer she was than when he had last looked at her. The whole trick was apparent to him, at a glance ; and he was compelled to acknowledge his own remissness, when he perceived that he lay within the reach of the shot of this powerful foe ; though still so distant as to render her aim a little uncertain ; more especially should a sea get up. The felucca had burnt to the water's edge ; but, owing to the smoothness of the water her wreck still floated, and was slowly setting into the bay there being a slight current in that direction, where she now lay. The town was basking in the afternoon's sun, though hid from view, and the whole island of Elba had the appearance of being asleep.

"What a siesta!" said Raoul, to Ithuel, as both stood on the heel of the bowsprit, looking curiously at the scene: "sea, land, mountains, bourgeois and mariners all dozing. *Bien;* there is life, yonder at the west, and we must get farther from *votre Proserpine.* Call the hands, Monsieur Lieutenant. Let us get out our sweeps, and put the head of le Feu-Follet the other way. Peste! the lugger is so sharp, and has such a trick of going exactly where she looks, that I am afraid she has been crawling up towards her enemy, as the child creeps into the fire that burns its fingers."

All hands were soon in motion on board le Feu-Follet, the sweeps were on the point of being handled, when the jigger fluttered, and the first puff of the expected western breeze swept along the surface of the waters. To the seamen, it was like inhaling oxygen gas. Every appearance of drowsiness deserted the people of both vessels, and every one was instantly busy in making sail. Raoul had a proof into what dangerous proximity to the frigate he had got, by the sound of the calls on board her; and the stillness of the sea was yet so great, that the creaking of her fore-yard was actually audible to him, as the English rounded in their braces briskly, while laying their fore-top-sail aback.

At that moment a second respiration of the atmosphere gave birth to the breeze. Raoul whistled for the wind, and the lugger moved ahead, gliding towards the frigate. But, in half a minute, she had gathered sufficient way, her helm was put down, and she came round as easily and as gracefully as the bird turns on his wing. Not so with the heavier frigate. She had hauled in her starboard head-braces, and had to get the foretopsail aback, and to pay well off with her head to leeward, in order to swing her yards and fill her sails, while le Feu-Follet was slipping through the water, going seemingly into the wind's eye. By this single evolution, the lugger gained more than a cable's-length on her enemy, and five minutes more would have put her beyond all immediate danger. But, Captain Cuffe knew this, as well as his competitor, and had made his preparations accordingly. Keeping his head-yards aback, he knocked his

13 *

ship round off, until her broadside bore on the lugger, when he let fly every gun of his starboard batteries, the utmost care having been taken to make the shot tell. Twenty-two heavy round-shot coming in at once upon a little craft, like le Feu-Follet, was a fearful visitation; and, the boldest held their breath for a time, as the iron whirlwind whistled past them. Fortunately, the lugger was not hulled; but a grave amount of mischief was done aloft. The jigger-mast was cut in two, and flew upward like a pipe-stem. A serious wound was given to the mainmast below the hounds, and the yard itself was shivered in the slings. No less than six shot plunged through both luggs, leaving holes in the canvass that made it resemble a beggar's shirt, and the jib-stay was cut in two half-way between the mast-head and the end of the bowsprit. No one was hurt; and, yet, for a moment, every one looked as if destruction had suddenly lighted on the lugger. Then it was that Raoul came out, in his true colours. He knew he could not spare a stitch of canvass just at that moment, but, that on the next ten minutes depended every thing. Nothing was taken in, therefore, to secure spars and sails, but all was left to stand, trusting to the lightness of the breeze, which usually commenced very moderately. Hands were immediately set to work, to get up a new stay; a new main-yard and sail were got along, and every thing was prepared for hoisting both, as soon as it could be ascertained that the mast would bear them. Nearly similar preparations were made forward, as the shortest way of getting rid of the torn fore-sail; for these, it was the intention to unbend and bend, the yard being sound.

Luckily, Captain Cuffe determined to lose no more time with his guns, but swinging his head-yards, the frigate came sweeping up to the wind, and in three minutes every thing was trimmed for the utmost. All this time, le Feu-Follet had not stood still. Her canvass fluttered, but it held on, and even the spars kept their places, though so much injured. In a word, the wind was not yet strong enough to tear the one, or to carry away the other. It was an advantage, too, that these casualties, particularly the loss of her jigger, rendered le Feu-Follet less weatherly than she would otherwise have been, since by keeping the frigate directly in her wake, she was less exposed to the chase-guns, than she would have been a little on either bow. Of this truth, Raoul was soon persuaded, the Proserpine beginning to work both her bow-guns, as soon as she came to the wind, though neither exactly bore; the shot of one ranging a little to windward, and the other about as much on the other side. By these shot, too, the young Frenchman soon had the satisfaction of seeing that, notwithstanding her injuries, the lugger was drawing ahead;—a fact of which the English became so sensible themselves, that they soon ceased firing

So far, things went better than Raoul had reason, at first, to hope, though he well knew that the crisis was yet to come. The westerly wind often blew fresh at that period of the day, and should it now increase he would require all his canvass to get clear of a ship with the known qualities of the vessel in chase. How much longer his mast or his main-yard would stand he did not know, but as he was fast gaining, he determined to make hay while the sun shone, and get far enough ahead, if possible, before the breeze grew fresh, to enable him to shift his sails and fish his spars, without being again brought within the reach of visiters as rude as those who had so lately come hurtling into his thin hamper. The proper precautions were not neglected, in the meantime. Men were sent aloft to do what they could, under the circumstances, with the two spars; and the strain was a little relieved by keeping the lugger as much away, as might be done without enabling the frigate to set her studding sails.

There is always something so exciting in a chase, that seamen never fail to wish for more wind; forgetful that the power which increases their own speed, may also increase the speed of the other party, and that too in an undue proportion. It would have been more favourable to le Feu-Follet to have had less wind than even now blew, since her relative rate of sailing was greater in light than in strong breezes. Raoul knew, from Ithuel's statements, that the Proserpine was an exceedingly fast ship, more especially when it blew fresh; and yet it did not appear to him that his lugger got along with sufficient speed, though his enemy would be certain to follow at a rate of sailing in a just proportion to his own, did there come more wind.

The wish of the young privateersman, however, was soon

gratified. The wind freshened materially, and by the time
the two vessels opened the Canal of Corsica, as the passage
between that island and Elba is called, the frigate was
obliged to take in her royals, and two or three of those light
and lofty staysails, which it was then the custom for ships
to carry. At first, Raoul had thought he might fetch into
Bastia, which lies due-west of the southern end of Elba;
but though the wind drew a little down through the canal, it
soon blew too fresh to allow any formation of the land materially to alter its current. The zephyr, as the afternoon's
summer breeze of southern Italy, in particular, was termed
by the ancients, is seldom a due-west wind, there generally being a little northing in it, as seamen say; and, as one
gets farther up the coast, this same wind ordinarily comes
round the head of Corsica, blowing from nearly west-north-
west. This would have enabled the lugger to lay her course
for a deep bay on which lies the town of Biguglia, could she
have been jammed up on a wind, as might usually have been
done; but, a few minutes of experiment convinced Raoul
that he must be more tender on his wounded spars, and keep
off for the mouth of the Golo. This was a river of some
size into which it was possible for a vessel of a light draught
to enter; and, as there stood a small battery near the anchorage, he determined to seek shelter in that haven, in order to
repair his damages. His calculations were made accordingly, and, taking the snow-clad peaks in the neighbourhood
of Corte as his land-marks, he ordered the lugger to be
steered in the proper direction.

On board the Proserpine, there was scarcely less interest felt
in the result, than on board le Feu-Follet. If the people of
the frigate had nothing to apprehend, they had something to
revenge; in addition to the anticipated credit of having captured the boldest privateer that sailed out of France. For
a short time, as the ship came up with the west end of Elba,
it was a serious question whether she would be able to weather it, the lugger having gone past, within a cable's-length
of the cliffs, on the very verge of the breakers, and much
closer in than the frigate would dare to follow. But the last
had taken the breeze farther off the land than the first, and
might possibly fetch past the promontory, on the tack she
was then steering. To have gone about, would have been

to abandon the chase, as it would have carried the ship off, due north, while le Feu-Follet was gliding down to the southward and westward, at the rate of seven knots. The distance across the canal is only about thirty miles, and there would not have been time to recover the lost ground.

This uncertainty made a most feverish moment on board the Proserpine, as she came up fast towards the headland. All depended on getting by without tacking. The appearances were favourable for deep water, close in ; but there is always the danger of rocks to be dreaded, near mountainous coasts. The promontory, too, was comparatively low ; and this was rather an indication that it ought not to be approached too closely. Winchester was in his berth, just beginning to feel the smart of his wound ; but Griffin was at the captain's elbow, both he and the third lieutenant, entering keenly into all their commander's wishes and anxieties.

"There she goes, into the very breakers !" exclaimed Cuffe, as they watched le Feu-Follet, in her attempt to pass the promontory ; "Monsieur Yvard must be determined to cast away his craft, rather than be taken. It will be touch and go with him."

"I think not, Captain Cuffe," answered Griffin ; "the coast is bold, hereabouts, and even the Proserpine would find sufficient water, there, where the lugger now is. I hope we shall not be obliged to tack, sir."

"Ay, this is very well for an irresponsible—but, when it got to a court, and punishment, I fear that all the last would fall on my shoulders, should his Majesty's ship happen to lay her bones along-shore, here. No, no, Griffin ; we must go a clear cable's-length to windward of *that*, or I go about though Raoul Yvard were never taken."

"There, he fetches-up, by George!" cried Yelverton, the youngest lieutenant ; and, for a moment, it was, in truth, believed in the frigate, that le Feu-Follet, as a breaker actually curled directly under her lee, was aground. But this notion lasted a moment only, the little lugger continuing her course as swiftly as before ; and, a minute or two later, keeping a little away, to ease her spars, having been jammed up as close as possible, previously, in order to weather the extreme end of what was thought to be the dangerous point. The frigate was fully two miles a-stern ; and, instead of

losing anything of her vantage-ground, she was kept so near
the wind, as to be occasionally touching. This was the more
safe, inasmuch as the sea was perfectly smooth, and the
vessel made no lee-way. Still the frigate looked, as it is
termed, barely up to the point it was deemed indispensable
to weather; and as ships rarely "do" better than they "look,"
it became a question of serious doubt, on board the Proserpine, as she came up with the headland, whether she could
clear it.

"I am afraid, Captain Cuffe, we shall never clear it with
a good-enough berth, sir," observed the fidgeting Griffin; "it
seems, to me, the ship sets unaccountably to leeward, to-
day!"

"She never behaved better, Griffin. I am really in hopes
there is a slight current off-shore, here; if anything, we
actually open the highlands of Corsica, by this promontory.
You see that the wreck of la Divina Providenza is sweeping
round the bay, and is coming out to windward, again."

"*That* may serve us, indeed! All ready in the chains,
sir!—shall we make a cast of the lead?"

Cuffe assented, and the lead was hove. At this moment
the ship was going eight knots, and the man reported no
bottom, with fifteen fathoms of line out. This was well;
and two or three subsequent casts confirmed it. Orders
were now given to drag every bowline, swig-off on every
brace, and flatten-in all the sheets. Even the halyards
were touched, in order that the sails might stand like boards.
The trying moment was near; five minutes must decide
the matter.

"Let her shake a little Mr. Yelverton, and eat into the
wind," said Cuffe, addressing the officer of the watch; "we
must do all we can here; for, when abreast of the breakers,
everything must be a rap-full, to keep the ship under quick
command. There—meet her with the helm, and give her a
good full."

This experiment was repeated twice, and each time the
frigate gained her length to windward, though she necessarily lost more than three times that distance in her velocity.
At length, the trial came, and a profound silence, one in
which nervousness and anxiety were blended with hope,
reigned in the vessel. The eyes of all turned from the sails

to the breakers, from the breakers to the sails; and from both to the wake of the ship.

At such moments the voice of the lead's-man prevails over all other sounds. His warning cry is listened to with breathless attention, when the songs of a siren would be unheard. Cast after cast was made, as the ship drove on, and the answer to Cuffe's questions, was uniformly, " no bottom, sir, with fifteen fathoms out ;" but, just at this instant, arose the regular song from the weather main-chains, of " by the mark seven !" This came so suddenly on the Captain's ear, that he sprang upon the taffrail, where he could command a full view of all he wanted to see ; and then he called out, in a stentorian voice :

" Heave again, sir !—be brisk, my lad !—be brisk !"

" Be-e-e–ther-r-r–dee-e-e-eep six !" followed almost as soon as the Captain's voice had ceased.

" Ready-about !" shouted Cuffe. " See all clear, gentlemen.—Move lively, men ; move lively."

" And–a-a-eh half-ef-four—"

" Stand by !—What the devil are you at, sir, on that forecastle ?—Are you ready, forward ?"

" All ready, sir—"

" Down with your helm—hard down, at once—"

" Be-e-e–ther-r-r–dee-e-e-p nine—"

" Meet her ! — up with your helm. — Haul down your sheets, forward—brail the spanker—let go all the bowlines, aft.—So—well, there, well.—She flew round like a top ; but, by Jove, we 've caught her, gentlemen.—Drag your bowlines, again.—What 's the news from the chains ?"

" No bottom, sir, with fifteen fathoms out—and as good a cast, too, sir, as we 've had to-day."

" So—you 're rap full—don't fall off— very well dyce" (*Anglice*, thus)—" keep her as you are.—Well, by the Lord, Griffin, that *was* a shave ; half-four was getting to be squally, in a quarter of the world where a rock makes nothing of pouting its lips fifteen or twenty feet at a time at a mariner. We are past it all, however, and here is the land, trending away to the southward, like a man in a consumption, fairly under our lee. A dozen Raoul Yvards wouldn't lead me into such a d——d scrape, again !"

" The danger that is over, is no longer a danger at all,

sir," answered Griffin, laughing. "Don't you think, Captain Cuffe, we might ease her about half a point? that would be just her play; and the lugger keeps off a little, I rather suspect, to ease her mainmast. I'm certain I saw chips fly from it, when we dosed her with them two-and-twenty pills."

"Perhaps you're right, Griffin.—Ease her, with the helm, a little, Mr. Yelverton. If Master Yvard stands on his present course an hour longer, Biguglia will be too far to-windward for him; and, as for Bastia, that has been out of the question, from the first. There is a river, called Golo, into which he might run; and that, I rather think, is his aim. Four hours, however, will let us into the secret."

And four intensely interesting hours were those which succeeded. The wind was a cap-full; a good, fresh, westerly breeze, which seemed to have started out of the oven-like heat of a week of intensely hot weather that had preceded it, and to have collected the force of two or three zephyrs into one. It was not a gale, at all, nor did it induce either party to think of reefing; for, no trifle would have done that, under the circumstances; but it caused the Proserpine to furl her fore and mizzen-top-gallant-sails, and put Raoul in better humour with the loss of his jigger. When fairly round the headland, and, at a moment when he fancied the frigate would be compelled to tack, the latter had seized an opportunity to get in his foresail, to unbend it, and to bend and set a new one; an operation that took just four minutes, by the watch. He would have tried the same experiment with the other lugg, but the mast was scarce worth the risk, and he thought the holes might act as reefs, and thus diminish the strain. In these four hours, owing to the disadvantage under which le Feu-Follet laboured, there was not a difference of half a knot in the distance run by the two vessels, though each passed over more than thirty miles of water. During this time they had been drawing rapidly nearer to the coast of Corsica, the mountains of which, ragged and crowned with nearly eternal snows, had been glittering in the afternoon's sun, before them; though they lay many a long league inland. But the formation of the coast, itself, had now become plain, and Raoul, an hour before the sun disappeared, had noted his landmarks, by

which to make for the river he intended to enter. The
eastern coast of Corsica is as deficient in bays and harbours,
as its western is affluent with them; and this Golo, for which
the lugger was shaping her course, would never have been
thought of, as a place of shelter, under ordinary circumstances. But, Raoul had once anchored in its mouth, and
he deemed it the very spot in which to elude his enemy. It
had shoals off its embouchure; and these, he rightly enough
fancied, would induce Captain Cuffe to be wary.

As the evening approached, the wind began to decrease in
force, and then the people of the lugger lost all their apprehensions. The spars had all stood, and Raoul no longer
hesitated about trusting his wounded mainmast with a new
yard and sail. Both were got up, and the repairs were immediately commenced. The superiority of the lugger, in
sailing, was now so great, as to put it out of all question
that she was not to be overtaken in the chase; and Raoul, at
one time, actually thought of turning up along the land, and
going into Bastia, where he might even provide himself with
a new mainmast, at need. But this idea, on reflection, he
abandoned, as too hazardous; and he continued on, in the
direction of the mouth of the Golo.

Throughout the day the Proserpine had shown no colours,
except for the short period when her boats were engaged,
and while she herself was firing at the lugger. The same
was the fact with le Feu-Follet, though Raoul had run up
the tri-colour, as he opened on the felucca, and he kept it
flying as long as there was any appearance of hostilities.
As the two vessels drew in near to the land, several coasters
were seen beating up against the westerly wind, or running
down before it, all of which, however, seemed so much to distrust the appearance of the lugger, as to avoid her as far as
was possible. This was a matter of indifference to our
hero, who knew that they were all probably countrymen;
or, at least, smugglers, who would scarcely reward him for
the trouble, had he the time to bring them to, and capture
them. Corsica was then, again, in the hands of the French,
the temporary and imperfect possession of the English having terminated three or four years earlier; and Raoul felt
certain of a welcome anywhere in the island, and of protection wherever it could be offered. Such was the state of

14

things, when, just as the lugger was preparing to entei among the shoals, the Proserpine unexpectedly tacked, and seemed to bestow all her attention on the coasters of which three or four were so near that two fell into her hands almost without an effort to escape.

It appeared to Raoul, and those with him in his little craft that the English seized these insignificant vessels solely with a wish for vengeance, since it was not usual for ships of the force of the Proserpine to turn aside to molest the poor fishermen and coasters. A few execrations followed, quite as a matter of course, but the intricacy of the channel and the necessity of having all his eyes about him, soon drove every other thought from the mind of the dashing privateersman, but such as were connected with the care and safety of his own vessel.

Just as the sun set le Feu-Follet anchored. She had chosen a berth sufficiently within the shallow water to be safe from the guns of the frigate, though scarcely within the river. The latter the depth of the stream hardly permitted, though there was all the shelter that the season and weather required. The Proserpine manifested no intention to give up her pursuit; for she, too, came off the outlet, and brought up with one of her bowers, about two miles to-seaward of the lugger. She seemed to have changed her mind as to the coasters, having let both proceed, after a short detention; though, it falling calm, neither was enabled to get any material distance from her, until the land breeze should rise In these positions, the belligerents prepared to pass the night, each party taking the customary precautions as to his ground tackle, and each clearing up the decks and going through the common routine of duty, as regularly as if he lay in a riendly port.

CHAPTER XI.

"The human mind, that lofty thing,
  The palace and the throne,
Where reason sits, a scepter'd king,
  And breathes his judgment tone;
Oh! who with silent step shall trace
The borders of that haunted place,
  Nor in his weakness own,
That mystery and marvel bind
That lofty thing — the human mind.

ANONYMOUS.

It is unnecessary to dwell on the glories of the Mediterranean. They are familiar to every traveller, and books have, again and again, laid them before the imaginations of readers of all countries and ages. Still, there are lights and shades peculiar to every picture, and this of ours has some of its own that merit a passing notice. A sunset, in midsummer, can add to the graces of almost any scene. Such was the hour when Raoul anchored; and Ghita, who had come on deck, now that the chase was over, and the danger was thought to be past, fancied she had never seen her own Italy, or the blue Mediterranean, more lovely.

The shadows of the mountains were cast far upon the sea, long ere the sun had actually gone down, throwing the witchery of eventide over the whole of the eastern coast, some time before it came to grace its western. Corsica and Sardinia resemble vast fragments of the Alps, which have fallen into the sea by some accident of nature, where they stand in sight of their native beds, resembling, as it might be, out-posts to those great walls of Europe. Their mountains have the same formations, the same white peaks, for no small portion of the year at least, and their sides the same mysterious and riven aspect. In addition, however, to their other charms, they have one that is wanting in most of Switzerland, though traces of it are to be found in Savoy and on the southern side of the Alps; they have that strange admixture of the soft and the severe, of the sublime and beautiful, that so peculiarly characterize the witchery of

Italian nature. Such was now the aspect of all visible from
the deck of le Feu-Follet. The sea, with its dark-blue tint,
was losing every trace of the western wind, and was becoming glassy and tranquil; the mountains on the other side
were solemn and grand, just showing their ragged outlines
along a sky glowing with "the pomp that shuts the day;"
while the nearer valleys and narrow plains were mysterious,
yet soft, under the deep shadows they cast. Pianosa lay
nearly opposite, distant some twenty miles, rising out of the
water like a beacon; Elba was visible to the north-east, a
gloomy confused pile of mountain at that hour; and Ghita,
once or twice thought she could trace on the coast of the main,
the dim outline of her own hill, Monte Argentaro; though
the distance, some sixty or seventy miles, rendered this
improbable. Outside, too, lay the frigate, riding on the glassy
surface of the sea, her sails furled, her yards squared, every
thing about her cared for and in its place, until she formed
a faultless picture of nautical symmetry and naval propriety.
There are all sorts of men in a marine, as well as in civil
life; these taking things as they come, content to perform
their duties in the most quiet manner, while others again
have some such liking for their vessels as the dandy has for
his own person, and are never happy unless embellishing
them. The truth, in this, as in most other matters, lies in a
medium; the officer who thinks too much of the appearance
of his vessel, seldom having mind enough to bestow due attention on the great objects for which she was constructed,
and is sailed; while, on the other hand, he who is altogether
indifferent to these appearances is usually thinking of things
foreign to his duty and his profession; if, indeed, he thinks
at all. Cuffe was near the just medium, inclining a little too
much, perhaps, to the naval dandy. The Proserpine, thanks
to the builders of Toulon, was thought to be the handsomest
model then afloat in the Mediterranean, and like an established beauty, all who belonged to her were fond of deco-
rating her, and of showing her fine proportions to advantage.
As she now lay, at single anchor, just out of gun-shot from
his own berth, Raoul could not avoid gazing at her with
envy, and a bitter feeling passed through his mind, when
he recalled the chances of fortune and of birth, which deprived him of the hope of ever rising to the command of

such a frigate, but which doomed him, seemingly, to the fate of a privateersman for life.

Nature had intended Raoul Yvard for a much higher destiny than that which apparently awaited his career. He had come into active life with none of the advantages that accompany the accidents of birth, and, at a moment, in the history of his great nation when its morals, and its religious sentiments, had become unsettled by the violent reaction which was throwing off the abuses of centuries. They who imagine, however, that France, as a whole, was guilty of the gross excesses that disfigured her struggles for liberty, know little of the great mass of moral feeling that endured through all the abominations of the times ; and mistake the crimes of a few desperate leaders, and the exaggerations of misguided impulses, for a radical and universal depravity. The France of the Reign of Terror, even, has little more to answer for than the compliance which makes bodies of men the instruments of the enthusiastic, the designing, and the active—our own country often tolerating error, that differs only in the degree, under the same blind submission to combinations and impulses ; this very degree, too, depending more on the accidents of history and natural causes, than any agencies which are to be imputed to the one party, as a fault, or, to the other, as a merit. It was with Raoul, as it had been with his country—each was the creature of circumstances ; and if the man had some of the faults, he had also most of the merits of his nation and his age. The looseness on the subject of religion, which was his principal defect in the eyes of Ghita, but which could scarcely fail to be a material one, with a girl educated and disposed as was the case with our heroine, was the error of the day, and with Raoul it was, at least, sincere ; a circumstance that rendered him, with one so truly pious as the gentle being he loved, the subject of a holy interest, which, in itself, almost rivalled the natural tenderness of her sex, in behalf of the object of her affections.

While the short engagement with the boats lasted, and during the few minutes he was under the fire of the frigate, Raoul had been himself ; the excitement of actual war always nerving him to deeds worthy of his command, and the high name he had acquired ; but, throughout the remainder of the

day, he had felt little disposed to strife.   The chase, once
assured that his spars were likely to stand, gave him little
concern ; and now that he was at anchor within the shallow
water, he felt much as the traveller who has found a comfortable inn, after the fatigue of a hard day's ride.   When
Ithuel suggested the possibility of a night-attack, in boats,
he laughingly reminded the American that " the burnt child
dreads the fire," and gave himself no great concern in the
matter.   Still, no proper precaution was neglected.   Raoul
was in the habit of exacting much of his men, in moments
of necessity ; but, at all other times, he was as indulgent as
a kind father, among obedient and respectful children. This
quality, and the never-varying constancy and coolness that
he displayed in danger, was the secret of his great influence
with them ; every seaman under his orders feeling certain,
that no severe duty was required at his hands, without a
corresponding necessity for it.

On the present occasion, when the people of le Feu-Follet
had supped, they were indulged in their customary dance ;
and the romantic songs of Provence were heard on the forecastle.   A light-hearted gaiety prevailed, that wanted only
the presence of woman, to make the scene resemble the
evening amusement of some hamlet on the coast.   Nor was
the sex absent in the sentiment of the hour, or wholly so in
person.   The songs were full of chivalrous gallantry, and
Ghita listened, equally touched and amused.   She sat on
the taffrail, with her uncle standing at her side, while Raoul
paced the quarter-deck, stopping, in his turn, to utter some
thought, or wish, to ears that were always attentive.   At
length the song and the dance ended, and all but the few
who were ordered to remain on watch, descended to their
hammocks.   The change was as sudden, as it was striking.
The solemn, breathing stillness of a star-lit night succeeded
to the light laugh, melodious song, and spirited merriment
of a set of men, whose constitutional gaiety seemed to be
restrained by a species of native refinement, that is unknown
to the mariners of other regions, and who, unnurtured as
they might be deemed, in some respects, seldom or never
offended against the proprieties ; as is so common with the
mariners of the boasted Anglo-Saxon race.   By this time
the cool air from the mountains began to descend, and float-

ng over the heated sea, it formed a light land-bree ., that
blew in an exactly contrary direction to that, which, about
the same hour, came off from the adjacent continent. There
was no moon; but the night could not be called dark.
Myriads of stars gleamed out from the fathomless firmament,
filling the atmosphere with a light that served to render
objects sufficiently distinct; while it left them clad in a semi-
obscurity that suited the witchery of the scene and the hour.
Raoul felt the influence of all these circumstances in an
unusual degree. It disposed him to more sobriety of thought
than always attended his leisure moments, and he took a
seat on the taffrail, near Ghita, while her uncle went below,
to his knees and his prayers.

Every foot-fall in the lugger had now ceased. Ithuel
was posted on a knight-head, where he sat watching his old
enemy, the Proserpine; the proximity of that ship not allowing him to sleep. Two experienced seamen, who alone
formed the regular anchor-watch, as it is termed, were
stationed apart, in order to prevent conversation; one on the
starboard cat-head, and the other in the main rigging; both
keeping vigilant ward over the tranquil sea, and the different
objects that floated on its placid bosom. In that retired spot,
these objects were necessarily few, embracing the frigate,
the lugger, and three coasters; the latter of which had all
been boarded before the night set in, by the Proserpine, and,
after short detentions, dismissed. One of these coasters lay
about half-way between the two hostile vessels, at anchor,
having come-to, after making some fruitless efforts to get
to the northward, by means of the expiring west-wind.
Although the light land-breeze would now have sufficed to
carry her a knot or two through the water, she preferred
maintaining her position, and giving her people a good
night's rest, to getting under-way. The situation of this
felucca, and the circumstance that she had been boarded by
the frigate, rendered her an object of some distrust with
Raoul, through the early part of the evening, and he had
ordered a vigilant eye to be kept on her; but nothing had
been discovered to confirm these suspicions. The movements of her people—the manner in which she brought-up—
the quiet that prevailed on board her, and even the lubberly
disposition of her spars and rigging, went to satisfy Raoul

hat she had no man-of-war's men on board her. Still, as she lay less than a mile outside of the lugger, though now dead to leeward all that distance, she was to be watched, and one of the seamen, he in the rigging, rarely had his eyes off her, a minute at a time. The second coaster was a little to the southward of the frigate, under her canvass, hauling in for the land; doubtless with a view to get as much as possible of the breeze from the mountains; and standing slowly to the south. She had been set by compass, an hour before, and all that time had altered her bearings but half a point, though not a league off—a proof how light she had the wind. The third coaster, a small felucca, too, was to the northward; but, ever since the land-breeze, if breeze it could be called, had come, she had been busy turning slowly up to windward; and seemed disposed either to cross the shoals, closer in than the spot where the lugger lay, or to enter the Golo. Her shadowy outline was visible, though drawn against the land, moving slowly athwart the lugger's hawse, perhaps half-a-mile in-shore of her. As there was a current setting out of the river, and all the vessels rode with their heads to the island, Ithuel occasionally turned his head to watch her progress; which was so slow, however, as to produce very little change.

After looking around him several minutes, in silence, Raoul turned his face upward, and gazed at the stars.

"You probably do not know, Ghita," he said, "the use those stars may be, and are, to us mariners. By their aid, we are enabled to tell where we are, in the midst of the broadest oceans—to know the points of the compass; and so feel at home even when furthest removed from it. The seaman must go far south of the equator, at least, ere he can reach a spot where he does not see the same stars that he beheld from the door of his father's house."

"That is a new thought, to me," answered Ghita, quickly, her tender nature, at once, struck with the feeling and poetry of such an idea; "that is a new thought, to me, Raoul and I wonder you never mentioned it before. It is a great thing to be able to carry home and familiar objects with you, when so distant from those you love."

"Did you never hear that overs have chosen an hour

and a star, by gazing at which they might commune together, though separated by oceans and countries?"

"That is a question you might put to yourself, Raoul
all I have ever heard of lovers, and love, having come from
your own lips."

"Well, then, I tell it you; and hope that we shall not
part, again, without selecting *our* star, and *our* hour—if,
indeed, we ever part more. Though I have forgotten to tell
you this, Ghita, it is because you are never absent from my
thoughts—no star is necessary to recall Monte Argentaro
and the Towers."

If we should say Ghita was not pleased with this, it would
be to raise her above an amiable and a natural weakness.
Raoul's protestations never fell dead on her heart; and few
things were sweeter, to her ear, than his words, as they
declared his devotedness and passion. The frankness with
which he admitted his delinquencies, and most especially the
want of that very religious sentiment which was of so much
value in the eyes of his mistress, gave an additional weight
to his language, when he affirmed his love. Notwithstanding Ghita blushed, as she now listened, she did not smile;
she rather appeared sad. For near a minute she made no
reply; and when she did answer, it was in a low voice, like
one who felt and thought intensely.

"Those stars may well have a higher office," she said.
"Look at them, Raoul;—count them we cannot, for they
seem to start out of the depths of heaven, one after another,
as the eye rests upon the space, until they mock our efforts
at calculation. We see they are there in thousands, and
may well believe they are in myriads. Now, thou hast been
taught, else couldst thou never be a navigator, that those
stars are worlds, like our own, or suns, with worlds sailing
around them; how is it possible to see and know this, without
believing in a God, and feeling the insignificance of our
being?"

"I do not deny that there is a power to govern all this,
Ghita—but I maintain that it is a principle; not a being, in
our shape and form; and that it is the reason of things,
rather than a deity."

"Who has said that God is a being, in our shape and

form, Raoul? None know that—none *can* know it; none *say* it, who reverence and worship him as they ought!"

"Do not your priests say that man has been created in his image? and is not this creating him in his form and likeness?"

"Nay, not so, dear Raoul, but in the image of his spirit —that man hath a soul which partakes, though in a small degree, of the imperishable essence of God; and thus far doth he exist in his image. More than this, none have presumed to say. But what a being, to be the master of all those bright worlds!"

"Ghita, thou know'st my way of thinking, on these matters; and thou also know'st that I would not wound thy gentle spirit by a single word that could grieve thee."

"Nay, Raoul, it is *not* thy way of *thinking*, but thy fashion of *talking*, that makes the difference between us. No one, who *thinks*, can ever doubt the existence of a being superior to all of earth, and of the universe; and who is Creator and Master of all."

"Of a *principle*, if thou wilt, Ghita; but of a *being*, I ask for the proof. That a mighty principle exists, to set all these planets in motion — to create all these stars, and to plant all these suns, in space, I never doubted; it would be to question a fact which stands, day and night, before my eyes; but to suppose a *being* capable of producing all these things, is to believe in beings I never saw."

"And why not as well suppose that it is a being that does all this, Raoul, as to suppose it what you call a principle?"

"Because I see principles, beyond my understanding, at work all around me: in yonder heavy frigate, groaning under her load of artillery, which floats on this thin water, in the trees, of the land that lies so near us; in the animals, which are born, and die; the fishes, the birds, and the human beings. But I see no being—know no being, that i. able to do all this."

"That is because thou know'st not God! He is the creator of the principles of which thou speak'st, and is greater than thy principles, themselves."

"It is easy to say this, Ghita—but hard to prove. I take the acorn, and put it in the ground; in due time it comes up plant, in the course of years, it becomes a tree. Now, all this depends on a certain mysterious principle, which is unknown to me, but which I am sure exists, for I can cause it, myself, to produce its fruits, by merely opening the earth and laying the seed in its bosom. Nay, I can do more—so well do I understand this principle, to a certain extent, at least, that, by choosing the season and the soil, I can hasten or retard the growth of the plant, and, in a manner, fashion the tree."

"True, Raoul, *to a certain extent* thou canst; and it is precisely because thou hast been created after the image of God. The little resemblance thou enjoyest to that Mighty being, enables thee to do this much more than the beasts of the field : wert thou his equal, thou couldst create that principle of which thou speakest, and which, in thy blindness, thou mistakest for its master."

This was said with more feeling than Ghita had ever before manifested, in their frequent discourses on this subject, and with a solemnity of tone that startled her listener. Ghita had no philosophy, in the common acceptation of the term, while Raoul fancied he had much, under the limitations of a deficient education ; and yet the strong religious sentiment of the girl so quickened her faculties, that he had often been made to wonder why she had seemingly the best of the argument, on a subject in which he flattered himself with being so strong.

"I rather think, Ghita, we scarcely understand each other," answered Raoul. "I pretend not to see any more than is permitted to man ; or, rather, more than his powers can comprehend ; but this proves nothing, as the elephant understands more than the horse, and the horse more than the fish. There is a principle which pervades everything, which we call Nature ; and this it is which has produced these whirling worlds, and all the mysteries of creation. One of its laws is, that nothing it produces shall comprehend its secrets."

"You have only to fancy your principle a spirit, a being with mind, Raoul, to have the Christian God. Why not believe in him, as easily as you believe in your unknown principle, as you call it ? You know that you exist—that you can build a lugger—can reason on the sun and stars, so as to find your way across the widest ocean, by means

of your mind ; and why not suppose that some superior being
exists, who can do even more than this? Your principles
can be thwarted, even by yourself—the seed can be deprived
of its power to grow—the tree destroyed ; and, if principles
can thus be destroyed, some accident may one day destroy
creation, by destroying its principle. I fear to speak to
you of revelation, Raoul, for I know you mock it!"

"Not when it comes from *thy* lips, dearest. I may not
believe, but I never *mock* at what thou utterest and reve-
rencest."

"I could thank thee for this, Raoul, but I feel it would be
taking to myself a homage that ought to be paid elsewhere.
But, here is my guitar, and I am sorry to say that the hymn
to the Virgin has not been sung on board this lugger to-
night ; thou canst not think how sweet is a hymn sung upon
the waters. I heard the crew that is anchored towards the
frigate, singing that hymn, while thy men were at their light
Provençal songs, in praise of woman's beauty ; instead of
joining in praise of their Creator."

"Thou mean'st to sing thy hymn, Ghita, else the guitar
would not have been mentioned?"

"Raoul, I do. I have ever found thy soul the softest, after
holy music. Who knows, but the mercy of God may one
day touch it, through the notes of this very hymn!"

Ghita paused a moment, and then her light fingers passed
over the strings of her guitar, in a solemn symphony ; after
which came the sweet strains of "Ave Maria," in a voice
and melody that might, in sooth, have touched a heart of
stone. Ghita, a Neapolitan by birth, had all her country's
love for music ; and she had caught some of the science that
seems to pervade nations, in that part of the world. Nature
had endowed her with one of the most touching voices of her
sex ; one less powerful, than mellow and sweet ; and she never
used it, in a religious office, without its becoming tremulous
and eloquent with feeling. While she was now singing this
well-known hymn, a holy hope pervaded her moral system,
that, in some miraculous manner, she might become the
agent of turning Raoul to the love and worship of God ; and
the feeling communicated itself to her execution. Never
before had she sung so well ; as a proof of which, Ithuel left
his knight-head, and came aft, to listen, while the two French

mariners on watch, temporarily forgot their duty, in entranced attention.

"If anything could make me a believer, Ghita," murmured Raoul, when the last strain had died on the lips of his beloved, "it would be to listen to thy melody! What now, Monsieur Etooell! are you, too, a lover of holy music?"

"This is rare singing, Captain Rule; but we have different business on hand. If you will step to the other end of the lugger, you can take a look at the craft that has been crawling along, in-shore of us, for the last three hours—there is something about her that is unnat'ra.; she seems to be dropping down nearer to us, while she has no motion through the water. The last circumstance I hold to be unnat'ral with a vessel that has all sail set, and in this breeze."

Raoul pressed the hand of Ghita, and whispered her to go below, as he was fearful the air of the night might injure her. He then went forward, where he could command as good a view of the felucca, in-shore, as the obscurity of the hour permitted; and he felt a little uneasiness, when he found how near she had got to the lugger. When he last noted her position, this vessel was quite half-a-mile distant, and appeared to be crossing the bows of le Feu-Follet, with sufficient wind to have carried her a mile ahead, in the interval; yet could he not perceive that she had advanced as far, in that direction, as she had drifted down upon the lugger the while.

"Have you been examining her long?" he demanded of the New-Hampshire-man.

"Ever since she has seemed to stand still; which is now some twenty minutes. She is dull, I suppose, for she has been several hours getting along a league; and there is now air enough for such a craft to go three knots to the hour. Her coming down upon us is easily accounted for, there being a considerable current out of this river, as you may see by the ripple at our own cut-water; but I find nothing to keep her from going ahead, at the same time. I set her by the light you see, here, in the wake of the nearest mountain at least a quarter of an hour since, and she has not advanced five times her own length, since."

"'T is nothing but a Corsican coaster, after all, Etooell: I hardly think the English would risk our canister, again

15

for the pleasure of being beaten off, in another attempt to board !"

" They 're a spiteful set, aboard the frigate ; and the Lord only knows ! See, here is a good heavy night-air, and that felucca is not a cable's-length from us ; set her by the jib-stay, and judge for yourself, how slowly she goes ahead ! *That* it is, which non-plushes *me* !"

Raoul did as the other desired, and, after a short trial, he found that the coaster had no perceptible motion ahead, while, it was certain, she was drifting down with the current, directly athwart the lugger's hawse. This fact satisfied him that she must have drags astern ; a circumstance that, at once, denoted a hostile intention. The enemy was probably on board the felucca, in force ; and it was incumbent on him to make immediate preparations for defence.

Still, Raoul was reluctant to disturb his people. Like all firm and cool men, he was averse to the parade of a false alarm ; and it seemed so improbable that the lesson of the morning was so soon forgotten, that he could hardly per suade himself to believe his senses. Then the men had been very hard at work, throughout the day ; and most of them were sleeping the sleep of the weary. On the other hand, every minute brought the coaster nearer, and increased the danger, should the enemy be really in possession of her. Under all the circumstances, he determined, first, to hail ; knowing that his crew could be got up in a minute, and that they slept with arms at their sides, under an apprehension that a boat attack might possibly be attempted, in the course of the night.

" Felucca, ahoy !" called out the captain of le Feu-Follet, the other craft being too near to render any great effort of the voice necessary ; " What felucca is that ? and why have you so great a drift ?"

" La Bella Corsienne !" was the answer, in a patois, half French, half Italian, as Raoul expected, if all were right. ' We are bound into la Padulella ; and wish to keep in with the land, to hold the breeze the longer. We are no great sailer, at the best, and have a drift, because we are, just now, in the strength of the current."

' " At this rate, you will come athwart my hawse.—You know I am armed, and cannot suffer that !"

" Ah, Signore, we are friends of the republic, and would not harm you, if we could. We hope you will not injure poor mariners, like us. We will keep away, if you please, and pass you under your stern—"

This proposition was made so suddenly, and so unexpectedly, that Raoul had not time to object; and, had he been disposed to do so, the execution was too prompt to allow him the means. The felucca fell broad off, and came down almost in a direct line for the lugger's bows, before the wind and current; moving fast enough, now, to satisfy all Ithuel's scruples.

"Call all hands to repel boarders!" cried Raoul, springing aft to the capstan, and seizing his own arms — "Come up lively, *mes enfans!*—here is treachery!"

These words were hardly uttered before Raoul was back on the heel of the bowsprit, and the most active of his men— some five or six, at most—began to show themselves on deck. In that brief space, the felucca had got within eighty yards, when, to the surprise of all in the lugger, she luffed into the wind, again, and drifted down, until it was apparent that she was foul of the lugger's cable, her stern swinging round directly on the latter's starboard bow. At that instant, or just as the two vessels came in actual contact, and Raoul's men were thronging around him, to meet the expected attack, the sounds of oars, pulled for life or death, were heard, and flames burst upward from the open hatch of the coaster. Then a boat was dimly seen gliding away, in a line with the hull, by the glowing light.

" Un brûlot!—un brûlot!—a fireship!" exclaimed twenty voices together, the horror that mingled in the cries proclaiming the extent of a danger which is, perhaps, the most terrific that seamen can encounter.

But the voice of Raoul Yvard was not among them The moment his eye caught the first glimpse of the flames he disappeared from the bowsprit. He might have been absent about twenty seconds. Then he was seen on the taffrail of the felucca, with a spare shank-painter, which had been lying on the forecastle, on his shoulder.

" Antoine!—François!—Grégoire!"—he called out, in a voice of thunder,—" follow me!—the rest, clear away the cable, and bend a hawser to the better end!"

The people of le Feu-Follet were trained to order and implicit obedience. By this time, too, the lieutenants were among them; and the men set about doing as they had been directed. Raoul, himself, passed into the felucca, followed by the three men he had selected by name. The adventurers had no difficulty, as yet, in escaping the flames, though, by this time, they were pouring upward from the hatch in a torrent. As Raoul suspected, his cable had been grappled; and, seizing the rope, he tightened it to a severe strain, securing the in-board part. Then he passed down to the cable, himself, directing his companions to hand him the rope-end of the shank-painter, which he fastened to the cable by a jamming hitch. This took half-a-minute; in half-a-minute more, he was on the felucca's forecastle, again. Here the chain was easily passed through a hawse-hole; and a knot tied, with a marlinespike passed through its centre. To pass the fire, on the return, was now a serious matter; but it was done without injury, Raoul driving his companions before him. No sooner did his foot reach the bows of le Feu-Follet, again, than he shouted—

"Veer away!—pay out cable, men, if you would save our beautiful lugger from destruction!"

Nor was there a moment to spare. The lugger took the cable that was given her, fast enough, under the pressure of the current, and helped by the breeze; but at first the fire-vessel, already a sheet of flame, her decks having been saturated with tar, seemed disposed to accompany her. To the delight of all in the lugger, however, the stern of the felucca was presently seen to separate from their own bows; and a sheer having been given to le Feu-Follet, by means of the helm, in a few seconds even her bowsprit and jib had cleared the danger. The felucca rode stationary, while the lugger dropped astern, fathom after fathom, until she lay more than a hundred yards distant from the fiery mass. As a matter of course, while the cable was paid out, the portion to which the lanyard, or rope part of the shank-painter was fastened, dropped into the water, while the felucca rode by the chain.

These events occupied less than five minutes; and all had been done with a steadiness and promptitude that seemed more like instinct, than reason. Raoul's voice was not heard, except in the few orders mentioned; and when, by the glaring light, which illuminated all in the lugger and the adjacent water to some distance, nearly to the brightness of noon-day, he saw Ghita gazing at the spectacle in awed admiration and terror, he went to her, and spoke as if the whole were merely a brilliant spectacle, devised for their amusement.

"Our girandola is second only to that of St. Peter's," he said, smiling. "'T was a narrow escape, love; but, thanks to thy God, if thou wilt it shall be so, we have received no narm."

"And you have been the agent of his goodness, Raoul; I have witnessed all, from this spot. The call to the men brought me on deck; and, Oh! how I trembled, as I saw you on the flaming mass!"

"It has been cunningly planned, on the part of Messieurs les Anglais; but it has signally failed. That coaster has a cargo of tar, and naval stores, on board; and, capturing her, this evening, they have thought to extinguish our lantern by the brighter and fiercer flame of their own. But, le Feu-Follet will shine again, when their fire is dead!"

"Is there, then, no danger that the brûlot will yet come down upon us—she is fearfully near!"

"Not sufficiently so to do us harm; more especially as our sails are damp with dew. Here she cannot come, so long as our cable stands; and, as that is under water, where she lies, it cannot burn. In half-an-hour there will be little of her left; and we will enjoy the bonfire, while it lasts."

And, now the fear of danger was past, it was a sight truly to be enjoyed. Every anxious and curious face in the lugger was to be seen, under that brilliant light, turned toward he glowing mass, as the sun-flower follows the great source of heat, in his track athwart the heavens; while the spars, sails, guns, and even the smallest object on board the lugger, started out of the obscurity of night, into the brightness of such an illumination, as if composing parts of some brilliant scenic display. But so fierce a flame soon exhausted itself. Ere long, the felucca's masts fell, and with them a pyramid of fire. Then the glowing deck tumbled in; and finally, timber after timber, and plank after plank fell, until the conflagration, in a great measure, extinguished itself in

15 *

the water on which it floated. An hour after the flames appeared, little remained but the embers which were glowing in the hold of the wreck.

CHAPTER XII.

"A justice of the peace, for the time being,
They bow to, but may turn him out, next year;
They reverence their priest, but, disagreeing,
In price or creed, dismiss him without fear;
They have a natural talent for foreseeing
And knowing all things; — and should Park appear
From his long tour in Africa, to show
The Niger's source, they'd meet him with — We know."
HALLECK.

RAOUL was not mistaken as to the manner in which they were obtained, and the means employed by his enemies. The frigate had found one of the feluccas loaded with naval stores, including some ten or fifteen barrels of tar; and it instantly struck Griffin, who was burning to revenge the defeat of the morning, that the prize might be converted into a fire-vessel. As the second lieutenant volunteered to carry her in, always a desperate service, Cuffe gave his consent. Nothing could have been better managed than the whole duty connected with this exploit, including the manner in which our hero saved his vessel from destruction. The frigate kept between her prize and the lugger, to conceal the fact that a boat remained on board the former; and, when all was ready, the felucca was apparently permitted to proceed on her voyage. The other two prizes were allowed to go free, also, as cloaks to the whole affair. Griffin, as has been seen, kept standing in for the land; his object being to get up stream from the lugger, and as near her as possible. When he found himself almost as far ahead as was desirable, drags were used, to keep the craft stationary; and, in this manner, she drifted down on her intended victim, as has been already described. But for the sagacity and uneasiness of Ithuel, the plan would altogether have escaped detection ; and, but for the coolness, courage, and resources of Raoul, it would infallibly have succeeded, notwithstanding the suspicions that had been excited.

Cuffe, and the people on deck, watched the whole affair with the deepest interest. They were barely able to see the sails of the felucca, by means of a night-glass, as she was dropping down on the lugger ; and Yelverton had just exclaimed that the two vessels were foul of each other, when the flames broke out. As a matter of course, at that distance, both craft seemed on fire ; and when le Feu-Follet had dropped a hundred yards nearer to the frigate, leaving the felucca blazing, the two were so exactly in a line, as to bring them together, as seen from the former's decks. The English expected, every moment, to hear the explosion of the lugger's magazine ; but, as it did not happen, they came to the conclusion it had been drowned. As for Griffin, he pulled in-shore, both to avoid the fire of le Feu-Follet, in passing her broadside, and in the hope of intercepting Raoul, while endeavouring to escape in a boat. He even went to a landing in the river, quite a league from the anchorage, and waited there until long past midnight, when, finding the night beginning to cloud over, and the obscurity to increase, he returned to the frigate, giving the smouldering wreck a wide berth, for fear of accidents.

Such, then, was the state of things, when Captain Cuffe appeared on deck, just as the day began to dawn, on the following morning. He had given orders to be called at that hour, and was now all impatience to get a view of the sea, more particularly in-shore. At length the curtain began slowly to rise, and his view extended farther and farther towards the river, until all was visible, even to the very land Not a craft of any sort was in sight. Even the wreck had disappeared ; though this was subsequently discovered in the surf ; having drifted out with the current, until it struck an eddy, which carried it in again, when it was finally stranded. No vestige of le Feu-Follet, however, was to be seen. Not even a tent on the shore, a wandering boat, a drifting spar, or a rag of a sail ! All had disappeared, no doubt, in the conflagration. As Cuffe went below, he walked with a more erect mien than he had done since the affair of the pre

vious morning ; and as he opened his writing-desk, it was
with the manner of one entirely satisfied with himself, and
his own exertions.   Still, a generous regret mingled with
his triumph.   It was a great thing to have destroyed the
most pernicious privateer that sailed out of France ; and yet
it was a melancholy fate to befall seventy or eighty human
beings—to perish like so many curling caterpillars, destroyed by fire.   Nevertheless, the thing was done ; and it
must be reported to the authorities above him.   The following letter was consequently written to the commanding
officer in that sea, viz :

His Majesty's Ship, Proserpine, off the mouth of the Golo,
Island of Corsica, July 23, 1799.

My Lord—I have the satisfaction of reporting, for the
information of my Lords Commissioners of the Admiralty,
the destruction of the Republican privateer, the le Few-Folly,
commanded by the notorious Raoul Yvard, on the night of
the 22d inst.   The circumstances attending this important
success, are as follows.   Understanding that the celebrated
picaroon had been on the Neapolitan and Roman coasts,
doing much mischief, I took His Majesty's ship close in,
following up the peninsula, with the land in sight, until we
got through the Canal of Elba, early on the morning of the
21st.   On opening Porto Ferrajo bay, we saw a lugger
lying at anchor off the town, with English colours flying.
As this was a friendly port, we could not suppose the craft
to be the le Few-Folly ; but, determined to make sure, we
beat in, signalling the stranger, until he took advantage of
our stretching well over to the eastward, to slip round the
rocks, and get off to-windward.   We followed, for a short
distance, and then ran over under the lee of Capraya, where
we remained until the morning of the 22d, when we again
went off the town.   We found the lugger in the offing ; and
being now well satisfied of her character, and it falling calm,
I sent the boats after her, under Messrs. Winchester and
Griffin, the first and second of this ship.   After a sharp
skirmish, in which we sustained some loss, though that of
the Republicans was evidently much greater, Monsieur
Yvard succeeded in effecting his escape, in consequence of a
breeze's suddenly springing up.   Sail was now made on the
ship, and we chased the lugger into the mouth of the Golo.

Having fortunately captured a felucca, with a quantity of tar, and other combustible materials on board, as we drew in with the land, I determined to make a fire-ship of her, and to destroy the enemy by that mode; he having anchored within the shoals, beyond the reach of shot.   Mr. Winchester, the first, having been wounded in the boat-affair, I entrusted the execution of this duty to Mr. Griffin, who handsomely volunteered, and by whom it was effectually discharged, about ten last evening, in the coolest and most officer-like manner.   I enclose this gentleman's report of the affair, and beg leave to recommend him to the favour of my Lords Commissioners.   With Mr. Winchester's good conduct, under a sharp fire, in the morning, the service has also every reason to be satisfied.   I hope this valuable officer will soon be able to return to duty.

Permit me to congratulate you, my lord, on the complete destruction of this most pernicious cruiser of the enemy.   So effectual has it been, that not a spar, or a fragment of wreck, remains.   We have reason to think every soul on board perished; and though this fearful loss of human life is to be deeply deplored, it has been made in the service of good government and religion.   The lugger was filled with loose women; our people hearing them singing their philosophical and irreligious songs, as they approached with the fire-vessel. I shall search the coast for any rafts that may be drifting about, and then proceed to Leghorn for fresh provisions.

I have the honour to be, my lord,

Your lordship's most obedient servant,
RICHARD CUFFE

To Rear Admiral the Right Hon. Lord Nelson,
Duke of Bronte, &c., &c., &c.

Cuffe read this report over twice; then he sent for Griffin to whom he read it aloud, glancing his eye meaningly at his subordinate, when he came to the part where he spoke of the young man's good conduct.

"So much for that d——d Jack-o'-Lantern, Griffin. fancy it will lead no one else on a wild-goose chase."

"I trust not, sir.   Will you allow me to suggest a slight alteration in the spelling of the lugger's name, Captain Cuffe; the clerk can make it, when he writes out the letter fairly."

12

" Ay—I dare say, it is different from what *we* would have
it ; French spelling being no great matter, in general.　Put
it as you please ; though Nelson has as great a contempt
for their boasted philosophy and learning, as I have myself.
I fancy you will find all the English spelt right.　How do
you write their confounded gibberish ?"

" Feu-Follet, sir, pronouncing the last part of it fol-*lay ;*
not fol-*ly*.　I was thinking of asking leave, Captain Cuffe,
to take one of the cutters, and pull up to the lugger's anchorage, and see if anything can be found of her wreck.　The
ship will hardly get under-way until the westerly wind
comes."

" No, probably not.　I will order my gig manned, and
we 'll go together.　Poor Winchester must keep house
awhile ; so there is no use in asking him.　I saw no necessity for putting Nelson into a passion, by saying anything
about the exact amount of our loss, in that boat scrape,
Griffin."

" I agree with you, sir, that it is best as it is.—' Some loss'
covers every thing—it means, ' more or less.' "

" That was just my notion.—I dare say, there may have
been twenty women in the lugger ?"

" I can't answer for the number, sir ; but I heard female
singing, as we got near, in the fire-ship ; and think it likely
there may have been that number.　The lugger was full-
manned ; for they were like bees swarming on her forecastle,
when we were dropping foul.　I saw Raoul Yvard, by the
light of the fire, as plainly as I now see you ; and might
have picked him off with a musket ; but that would hardly
have been honourable."

To this Cuffe assented, and then he led the way on deck,
having previously ordered the boats manned.　The two
officers proceeded to the spot where they supposed the Feu-
Follet had been anchored, and rowed round, for near an
hour, endeavouring to find some traces of her wreck on the
bottom.　Griffin suggested that, when the magazine was
drowned, in the hurry and confusion of the moment, the cock
may have been left open—a circumstance that might very
well have carried down the bottom of so small a vessel, in
two or three hours ; more especially after her hull had
burnt to the water's edge.　The next thing was to find this

bottom, by no means a hopeless task, as the waters of the Mediterranean are usually so clear, that the eye can pene trate several fathoms, even off the mouth of the Golo; a stream that brought more or less débris from the mountains. It is scarcely necessary to say, that the search was not rewarded with success, the Feu-Follet being, just at that time, snug at anchor at Bastia, where her people had already taken out her wounded mainmast, with a view to step a new one in its place. At that very moment, Carlo Giuntotardi his niece, and Raoul Yvard, were walking up the principal street of the town, the place standing on a hill, like Porto Ferrajo, perfectly at their ease, as regards fire-ships, English frigates, and the dangers of the seas. But all this was a profound mystery to Cuffe and his companions, who had long been in the habit of putting the most favourable con structions on the results of their professional undertakings, and, certainly, not altogether without reason ; and who nothing doubted that le Feu-Follet had, to use their own language, " laid her bones somewhere along-shore, here."

After two or three hours passed in a fruitless search, Cuffe determined to return to his ship. He was a keen sportsman, and had brought a fowling-piece with him, in his gig, with a half-formed design of landing, and whiling away the time, until the westerly wind came, among some marshes that he saw near the shore ; but had been persuaded, by Griffin, not to venture.

" There must be woodcock in that wet ground, Griffin," he said, as he reluctantly yielded a little in his intention , " and Winchester would fancy a bird, exceedingly, in a day or two. I never was hit, in my life, that I did not feel a desire for game, after the fever was gone. Snipe, too, must ive on the banks of that stream. Snipe are coming in season, now, Griffin ?"

" It 's more likely, sir, that some of the privateersmen have got ashore on planks, and empty casks, and are prowl ing about in the weeds, watching our boats. Three or four of them would be too much for you, Captain Cuffe, as the scoundrels all carry knives as long as ships' cutlasses."

" I suppose your notion may be true ; and I shall have to give it up. Pull back to the frigate, Davy, and we 'll be off after some more of these French ragamuffins."

This settled the matter.   In half-an-hour, the boats were
swinging at the Proserpine's quarters ; and three hours
later, the ship was under her canvass, standing slowly off
the land.   That day, however, the zephyr was exceedingly
light, and the sun set, just as the ship got the small island
of 'Pianosa abeam ; when the air came from the northward,
and the ship's head was laid in to the eastward ; the course
lying between the land just mentioned, and that of Elba.
All night the Proserpine was slowly fanning her way along
the south side of the latter island, when, getting the southerly
air again, in the morning, she reappeared in the Canal of
Piombino, as the day advanced, precisely as she had done
before, when first introduced to the acquaintance of the
reader.   Cuffe had given orders to be called, as usual, when
the light was about to return ; it being a practice with him,
in that active and pregnant war, to be on deck at such moments, in order to ascertain, with his own eyes, what the
fortunes of the night had brought within his reach.

   " Well, Mr. Griffin," he said, as soon as he had received
the salutation of the officer of the watch, " you have had a
still night of it.   Yonder is the Point of Piombino, I see ; and
here we have got Elba, and this little rocky island, again,
on our larboard hand.   One day is surprisingly like another,
about these times, for us mariners, in particular."

   " Do you really think so, Captain Cuffe ?—Now, to my
notion, this day hasn't had its equal on the Proserpine's log,
since we got hold of l'Epervier, and her convoy.   You forget, sir, that we destroyed le Feu-Follet, last night !"

   " Ay — that is something — especially for *you*, Griffin.
Well, Nelson will hear of it by mail, as soon as we can get
into Leghorn ; which will be immediately after I have had
an opportunity of communicating with these people in Porto
Ferrajo.   After all that has passed, the least we can do is to
let your veechy-govern-the-tories know of our success."

   " Sail, ho !" shouted the look-out, on the foretopsail-yard.

   The two officers turned, and gazed around them, in every
direction, when the captain made the customary demand of
' Where-away ?"

   " Here, sir, close aboard of us, on our larboard hand, and
on our weather quarter."

   " On our weather quarter !—D——n me, if that *can* be

true, Griffin. There is nothing but the island, there.—The fellow cannot have mistaken this little island for the hull of a ship !"

" If he has, sir," answered Griffin, laughing, " it must be for a twenty-decker. That is Ben Brown, aloft ; and he is as good a look-out as we have in the ship."

" Do you see her, sir ?" demanded Ben Brown, looking over his shoulder, to put the question.

" Not a bit of her," cried Cuffe. " You must be dream ing, fellow.—What does she look like !"

" There, this small island shuts her in, from the deck, sir. She is a lugger ; and looks as much like the one we burnt last night, sir, as one of our cat-heads is like t'other."

" A lugger !" exclaimed Cuffe. " What, another of the blackguards ! By Jove ! I 'll go aloft, and take a look for myself. It 's ten to one that I see her from the maintop."

In three minutes more, Captain Cuffe was in the top in question ; having passed through the lubber-hole, as every sensible man does, in a frigate, more especially when she stands up for want of wind. That was an age in which promotion was rapid ; there being few grey-bearded lieuten-ants, then, in the English marine ; and even admirals were not wanting who had not cut all their wisdom-teeth. Cuffe, consequently, was still a young man ; and it cost him no great effort to get up his ship's ratlins, in the manner named. Once in the top, he had all his eyes about him. For quite a minute, he stood motionless, gazing in the direction that had been pointed out by Ben Brown. All this time Griffin stood on the quarter-deck, looking quite as intently at his superior, as the latter gazed at the strange sail. Then Cuffe deigned to cast a glance literally beneath him, in order to appease the curiosity, which, he well understood, it was so natural for the officer of the watch to feel. Griffin did not dare to ask his *captain* what he saw ; but he looked a volume of questions on the interesting subject.

" A sister corsair, by Jupiter Ammon !" cried Cuffe ; " a *twin* sister, too ; for they *are* as much alike as one cat-head 's like another. More, by Jove, if I am any judge."

" What will you have us do, Captain Cuffe ?" inquired the lieutenant. " We are now going to leeward, all the while.

16

I don't know, sir, that there is positively a current here but——"

"Very well, sir—very well—haul up on the larboard tack, as soon as possible, and get the larboard batteries clear. We may have to cripple the chap, in order to get hold of him."

As this was said, Cuffe descended through the same lubber-hole, and soon appeared on deck. The ship, now, became a scene of activity and bustle. All hands were called, and the guns were cleared away, by some, while others braced the yards, according to the new line of sailing.

The reader would be greatly aided, in understanding what is to follow, could he, perchance, cast a look at a map of the coast of Italy. He will there see that the eastern side of the Island of Elba, runs in a nearly north and south direction, Piombino lying off about north-north-east, from its northern extremity. Near this northern extremity, lies the little rocky islet, so often mentioned, or the spot which Napoleon, fifteen years later, selected as the advanced redoubt of his insular empire. Of course, the Proserpine was on one side of this islet, and the strange lugger on the other. The first had got so far through the Canal, as to be able to haul close upon the wind, on the larboard tack, and yet to clear the islet; while the last was just far enough to windward, or sufficiently to the southward, to be shut out from view, from the frigate's decks, by the intervening rocks. As the distance from the islet to the island did not much exceed a hundred or two yards, Captain Cuffe hoped to enclose his chase between himself and the land, never dreaming that the stranger would think of standing through so narrow and rocky a pass. He did not know his man, however, who was Raoul Yvard; and who had come this way, from Bastia, in the hope of escaping any further collision with his formidable foe. He had seen the frigate's lofty sails, above the rock, as soon as it was light; and being under no hallucination, on the subject of *her* existence, he knew her at a glance. His first order was to haul everything as flat as possible; and his great desire was, to get from under the lee of the mountains of Elba, into this very pass, through which the wind drew with more force, than it blew anywhere, near by.

As the Proserpine was quite a league off, in the Canal, le

Feu-Follet, which sailed so much the fastest, in light winds, had abundance of time to effect her object. Instead of avoiding the narrow pass between the two islands, Raoul glided boldly into it; and, by keeping vigilant eyes on his fore-yard, to apprize him of danger, he succeeded in making two stretches, in the strait itself, coming out to the southward, on the starboard tack, handsomely clearing the end of the islet, at the very instant the frigate appeared on the other side of the pass. The lugger had now an easy task of it; for she had only to watch her enemy, and tack in season, to deep the islet between them; since the English did not dare to carry so large a ship through so narrow an opening. This advantage Raoul did not overlook, and Cuffe had gone about twice, closing, each time, nearer and nearer to the islet before he was satisfied that his guns would be of no service, until he could, at least, weather the intervening object; after which they would most probably be useless, in so light a wind, by the distance between them and their enemy.

"Never mind, Mr. Griffin; let this scamp go," said the captain, when he made this material discovery; "it is pretty well to have cleared the seas of one of them.—Besides, we do not know that this *is* an enemy, at all. He showed no colours, and seems to have just come out of Porto Ferrajo, a friendly haven."

"Raoul Yvard did *that*, sir, not once, but twice," muttered Yelverton, who, from the circumstance that he had not been employed in the different attempts on le Feu-Follet, was one of the very few dissentients in the ship, touching her fate. "These twins *are* exceedingly alike; especially *Pomp*, as the American negro said of his twin children."

This remark passed unheeded; for so deep was the delusion, in the ship, touching the destruction of the privateer, it would have been as hopeless an attempt, to try to persuade her officers and people, generally, that le Feu-Follet was not burned, as it would be to induce a "great nation" to believe it had any of the weaknesses and foibles that confessedly beset smaller communities The Proserpine was put about, again; and, setting her ensign, she stood into the bay of Porto Ferrajo; anchoring quite near the place that Raoul had selected for the same purpose, on two previous occasions. The gig was lowered, and Cuffe, accompanied by Griffin, as an interpreter, landed, to pay the usual visit of ceremony to the authorities.

The wind being so light, several hours were necessary to effect all these changes ; and, by the time the two officers were ascending the terraced street, the day had advanced sufficiently to render the visit suitable, as to time. Cuffe appearing in full uniform, with epaulettes and sword, his approach attracted notice ; and Vito Viti had hurried off to apprize his friend of the honour he was about to receive. The vice-governatore was not taken by surprise, therefore, but had some little time to prepare his excuses, for being the dupe of a fraud, as impudent as that which Raoul Yvard had so successfully practised on him. The reception was dignified, though courteous ; and it had none the less of ceremony, from the circumstance that all which was said by the respective colloquists, had to be translated, before it could be understood. This circumstance rendered the few first minutes of the interview a little constrained ; but each party having something on his mind, of which it was his desire to be relieved, natural feeling soon got the better of forms.

"I ought to explain to you, Sir Cuffe, the manner in which a recent event occurred in our bay, here," observed the vice-governatore ; "since, without such explanation, you might be apt to consider us neglectful of our duties, and unworthy of the trust which the Grand Duke reposes in us. I allude, as you will at once understand, to the circumstance that le Feu-Follet has twice been lying peaceably under the guns of our batteries, while her commander, and, indeed, some of her crew, have been hospitably entertained on shore."

"Such things must occur, in times like these, Mr. Veechy-Governatory ; and we seamen set them down to the luck of war," Cuffe answered, graciously, being much too magnanimous, under his own success, to think of judging others too harshly. "It might not be so easy to deceive a man-of-war's-man, like myself ; but, I dare say, Veechy-Governatory, had it been anything relating to the administration of your little island, here, even Monsieur Yvard would have found you too much for him ?"

The reader will perceive that Cuffe had got a new way

of pronouncing the appellation of the Elban functionary; a circumstance that was owing to the desire we all have, when addressing foreigners, to speak in their own language, rather than in our own. The worthy captain had no more precise ideas of what a *vice*-governor means, than the American people, just now, seem to possess of the signification of *vice*-president; but, as he had discovered that the word was pronounced " veechy," in Italian, he was quite willing to give it its true sound; albeit, a smile struggled round the mouth of Griffin, while he listened.

" You do me no more than justice, Signor Kooffe, or Sir Kooffe, as, I presume, I ought to address you," answered the functionary; " for, in matters touching our duties on shore, here, we are by no means as ignorant, as on matters touching your honourable calling. This Raoul Yvard presented himself, to me, in the character of a British officer, one I esteem and respect; having audaciously assumed the name of a family of high condition, and of great power, I believe, among your people—"

" Ah—the Barone!" exclaimed Cuffe; who, having discovered by his intercourse with the southern Italians that this word meant a " rascal," as well as a " baron," was fond of using it, on suitable occasions. " Pray, Veechy-Governatory, what name did he assume? Ca'endish, or Howard, or Seymour, or some of those great nobs, Griffin, I'll engage. I wonder that he spared Nelson !"

" No, Signore, he took the family appellation of another illustrious race. The republican corsair presented himself before me as a Sir Smees—the son of a certain Milordo Smees."

" Smees—Smees—Smees !—I've no recollection of any such name, in the peerage. It can't be Seymour that the Veechy means !—*That* is a great name, certainly; and some of them have been in the service; it is possible this barone may have had the impudence to hail for a Seymour !"

" I rather think not, Captain Cuffe. 'Smees' is very much as an Italian would pronounce 'Smith,' as, you know, the French call it 'Smeet.' It will turn out that this Mr. Raoul has seized upon the first English name he fell in with, as a man overboard clutches at a spar adrift, or a life-buoy; and that happened to be ' Smith.' "

16 *

"Who the devil ever heard of a my lord Smith! A pretty sort of aristocracy we should have, Griffin, if it were made up of such fellows!"

"Why, sir, the *name* can make no great difference; the deeds and the antiquity forming the essentials."

"And he assumed a title to—*Sir* Smees!—I dare say, he was ready to swear His Majesty made him a Knight Banneret, under the royal ensign, and on the deck of his own ship; as was done with some of the old admirals. The veechy, however, has forgotten a part of the story, as it must have been Sir *John*, or Sir *Thomas* Smees, at least."

"No, sir; that is the way with the French and the Italians who do not understand our manner of using Christian names with titles; as in our Sir Edwards, and Lord Harrys, and Lady Bettys."

"Blast the French! I can believe anything of *them*, though I should have thought that these *Italians* knew better. However, it may be well to give the veechy a hint of what we have been saying, or it may seem rude—and, hearkee, Griffin, while you *are* about it, rub him down a little touching books, and that sort of thing; for the surgeon tells me, he has heard of him, in Leghorn, as a regular leaf cutter."

The lieutenant did as ordered, throwing in an allusion to Andrea's reputation for learning, that, under the circumstances, was not ill-timed; and which, as it was well-enough expressed, was exceedingly grateful to his listener, just at that awkward moment.

"My claims to literature are but small, Signore," answered Andrea, with humility, "as I beg you will inform Sir Kooffe; but they were sufficient to detect certain assumptions of this corsair; a circumstance that came very near bringing about an exposure, at a most critical moment. He had the audacity, Signore, to wish to persuade *me*, that there was a certain English orator of the same name, and of equal merit of him of Roma and Pompeii—one Sir Cicero!"

"The Barone!" again exclaimed Cuffe, when this new offence of Raoul's was explained to him. "I believe the rascal was up to anything. But there is an end of him, now, with all his Sir Smees, and Sir Ciceroes, into the bargain. Just let the veechy into the secret of the fellow's fate, Griffin."

Griffin then related to the vice-governatore the manner in which it was supposed that le Feu-Follet, Raoul Yvard, and all his associates, had been consumed, like caterpillars on a tree. Andréa Barrofaldi listened, with a proper degree of horror expressed in his countenance; but Vito Viti heard the tale with signs of indifference and incredulity that he did not care to conceal. Nevertheless, Griffin persevered, until he had even given an account of the manner in which he and Cuffe examined the lugger's anchorage, in the bootless attempt to discover the wreck.

To all this, the two functionaries listened with profound attention, and a lively surprise. After looking at each other several times, and exchanging significant gestures, Andrea assumed the office of explaining.

"There is some extraordinary mistake in this, Signor Tenente," he said; "for Raoul Yvard still lives. He passed this promontory just as day dawned, in his lugger, this very morning!"

"Ay, he has got that notion from having seen the fellow we fell in with off the harbour, here," answered Cuffe, when this speech was translated to him; "and I don't wonder at it, for the two vessels were surprisingly alike. But the Barone, that we saw burned with our own eyes, Griffin, can never float again. I say Barone; for, in my opinion, the Few-Folly was just as much of a rascal, as her commander, and all who sailed in her."

Griffin explained this; but it met with no favour from the two Italians.

"Not so, Signor Tenente—not so," returned the vice-governatore; "the lugger that passed, this morning, we *know* to be le Feu-Follet, inasmuch as she took one of our own feluccas, in the course of the night, coming from Livorno, and Raoul Yvard permitted her to come in, as he said to her padrone, on account of the civil treatment he had received, while lying in our port. Nay, he even carried his presumption so far, as to send me, by means of the same man, the compliments of 'Sir Smees,' and his hopes of being able, some day to make his acknowledgments in person."

The English Captain received this intelligence, as might be expected; and, unpleasant as it was, after putting various questions to the vice-governatore, and receiving the answers, he was obliged, unwillingly enough, to believe it all. He had brought his official report in his pocket; and, as the conversation proceeded, he covertly tore it into fragments, so small, that even a Mahommedan would reject them, as not large enough to write the word " Allah" on.

" It's d——h lucky, Griffin, that letter didn't get to Leghorn, this morning," he said, after a long pause. " Nelson would have Brontéd me, famously, had he got it! Yet, I never believed half as devoutly in the twenty-nine articles, as—"

" I believe there are *thirty*-nine of them, Captain Cuffe," modestly put in Griffin.

" Well, *thirty*-nine, if you will—what signifies ten, more or less, in such matters? A man is ordered to believe them *all*, if there were a hundred.—But I never believed in *them*, as devoutly, as I believed in the destruction of that infernal picaroon. My faith is unsettled, for life!"

Griffin offered a few words of condolence, but he was also too much mortified to be very able to administer consolation. Andrea Barrofaldi, understanding the state of the case, now interposed with his courtesies, and the two officers were invited to share his bachelor's breakfast. What followed, in consequence of this visit, and the communications to which it gave rise, will appear in the course of the narrative.

CHAPTER XIII.

" If ever you have looked on better days,
  If ever been where bells have knolled to church;
  If ever sat at any good man's feast !
  If ever from your eyelids wiped a tear,
  And know what 'tis to pity, and be pitied,
  Let gentleness my strong enforcement be."
  SHAKSPEARE.

IT is now necessary to advance the time, and to transfer
the scene of our tale to another, but not a distant part of the
same sea. Let the reader fancy himself standing at the
mouth of a large bay, of some sixteen or eighteen miles
in diameter, in nearly every direction; though the shores
must be indented, with advancing promontories, and receding
curvatures, while the depth of the whole might possibly a little
exceed the greatest width. He will then occupy the spot at
which we wish to present to him one of the fairest panoramas
of earth. On his right stands a high, rocky island, of dark
tufa, rendered gay, amid all its magnificent formations, by
smiling vineyards and teeming villages, and interesting bv
ruins that commemorate events as remote as the Cæsars.
A narrow passage of the blue Mediterranean separates this
island from a bold cape on the main, whence follows a succession of picturesque, village-clad heights and valleys,
relieved by scenery equally bold and soft, and adorned by
the monkish habitations called in the language of the country, Camaldolis, until we reach a small city which stands on
a plain that rises above the water between one and two hundred feet, on a base of tufa, and the houses of which extend
to the very verge of the dizzy cliffs that limit its extent on
the north. The plain, itself, is like a hive, with its dwellings
and scenes of life, while the heights behind it teem with cot-
tages and the signs of human labour. Quitting this smiling
part of the coast, we reach a point, always following the
circuit of the bay, where the hills or heights tower into
ragged mountains, which stretch their pointed peaks up-
vards to some six or seven thousand feet towards the

clouds, having sides now wild with precipices and ravines, now picturesque with shooting-towers, hamlets, monasteries and bridle-paths; and bases dotted, or rather lined, with towns and villages. Here the mountain formation quits the margin of the bay, following the coast southward, or running into the interior of the country; and the shore, sweeping round to the north and west, offers a glimpse into a back-ground of broad plain, ere it meets a high, insulated, conical mountain, which properly forms the head of the coast in-dentation. The human eye never beheld a more affluent scene of houses, cities, villages, vineyards and country resi-dences, than was presented by the broad breast of this isolated mountain; passing which, a wider view is obtained of the rich plain that seems to lie behind it, bounded, as it is, by a wall of a distant and mysterious-looking, yet bold range of the Apennines. Returning to the shore, which now begins to incline more westwardly, we come to another swell of tufa, which has all the characteristic fertility and abrupt-ness of that peculiar formation, a vast and populous town of near half a million of souls being seated, in nearly equal parts, on the limits of the plain and along the margin of the water, or on the hill-sides, climbing to their summits. From this point, the northern side of the bay is a confused mass of villages, villas, ruins, palaces and vines, until we reach its extremity; a low promontory, like its opposite neigh-bour. A small island comes next, a sort of natural sentinel; then the coast sweeps northward, into another and a smaller bay, rich, to satiety, with relics of the past, terminating at a point, some miles farther seaward, with a high, reddish, sandy bluff, which almost claims to be a mountain. After this we see two more islands, lying westward, one of which is flat, fertile, and more populous, as is said, than any other part of Europe of the same extent; while the other is a glorious combination of pointed mountains, thronged towns, fertile valleys, castles, country-houses, and the wrecks of long-dormant volcanoes, thrown together in a grand, yet winning confusion. If the reader will, to this description, add a shore that has scarce a foot that is not interesting with some lore of the past, extending from yesterday into the darkest recesses of history, give life to the water-view with a fleet of little latine-rigged craft, rendered more picturesque by an occasional ship, dot the bay with countless boats of fisher men, and send up a wreath of smoke from the summit of the cone-like mountain that forms the head of the bay, he will get an outline of all that strikes the eye, as the stranger approaches Naples from the sea.

The zephyr was again blowing, and the daily fleet of sparanaras, or undecked feluccas, that passes every morning, at this season, from the south shore to the capital, and returns at this hour, was stretching out from under Vesuvius; some looking up as high as Massa; others heading towards Sorrento, or Vico, or Persano, and many keeping more before the wind, towards Castel a Mare, or the landings in that neighbourhood. The breeze was getting to be so fresh, that the fishermen were beginning to pull in towards the land, breaking up their lines, which, in some places, had extended nearly a league, and this, too, with the boats lying within speaking distance of each other. The head of the bay, indeed, was alive with craft, moving in different directions, while a large fleet of English, Russians, Neapolitans, and Turks, composed of two-deckers, frigates and sloops, lay at their anchors, in front of the town. On board of one of the largest of the former, was flying the flag of a rear-admiral at the mizzen, the symbol of the commander's rank. A corvette, alone, was under-way. She had left the anchorage an hour before, and, with studding-sails on her starboard side, was stretching diagonally across the glorious bay, apparently heading towards the passage between Capri and the Point of Campanella, bound to Sicily. This ship might easily have weathered the island; but her commander, an easy sort of person, chose to make a fair wind of it from the start, and he thought, by hugging the coast, he might possibly benefit by the land-breeze, during the night, trusting to the zephyr that was then blowing, to carry him across the Gulf of Salerno. A frigate, too, shot out of the fleet, under her staysails, as soon as the westerly wind made, but, she had dropped an anchor under-foot, and seemed to wait some preparation, or orders, before taking her departure; her captain being, at that moment, on board the flag-ship, on duty with the rear-admiral. This was the Proserpine thirty six, Captain Cuffe, a vessel and an officer that are already both acquaintances of the reader. About an hour before he present scene opens, Captain Cuffe, in fact, had been called on board the Foudroyant, by signal, where he had found a small, sallow-looking, slightly-built man, with his right arm wanting, pacing the deck of the fore-cabin, impatient for his appearance.

"Well, Cuffe," said this uninviting-looking personage twitching the stump of the maimed arm, "I see you are ou of the flock; are you all ready for sailing?"

"We have one boat ashore, after letters, my lord; as soon as she comes off, we shall lift our anchor, which is only under-foot."

"Very well—I have sent the Ringdove to the southward, on the same errand, and I see she is half-a-league from the anchorage, on her way, already. This Mr. Griffin appears to be a fine young man—I like his account of the way he handled his fire-ship; though the French scoundrel did con trive to escape! After all, this Royl E—E— how do you pronounce the fellow's name, Cuffe?—I never can make anything out of their gibberish—"

"Why, to own the truth, Sir Horatio—I beg pardon—my lord—there is something in the English grain of my feelings that would prevent my ever learning French, had I been born and brought up in Paris. There is too much Saxon in me, to swallow words that half the time have no meaning."

"I like you all the better, for that, Cuffe," answered the admiral, smiling, a change that converted a countenance that was almost ugly, when in a state of rest, into one that was almost handsome—a peculiarity that is by no means of rare occurrence, when a strong will gives the expression to the features, and the heart, at bottom, is really sound. "An Englishman has no business with any Gallic tendencies. This young Mr. Griffin seems to have spirit; and I look upon it, always, as a good sign, when a young man *volunteers* for a desperate thing of this sort—but, he tells me, he is only second; where was your first, all the while?"

"Why, my lord, he got a little hurt in the brush of the morning; and I would not let him go, as a matter of course. His name is Winchester; I think you must remember him, as junior of the Captain, at the affair off St. Vincent. Miller*

---

* Ralph Willet Miller, the officer who commanded the ship to which Nelson shifted his pennant, at the battle of Cape St. Vincent. This

had a good opinion of him; and, when I went from the Arrow to the Proserpine, he got him sent as my second. The death of poor Drury made him first, in the natural way."

"I have some recollection of him, Cuffe.—That was a brilliant day, and all its events should be impressed on my mind. You tell me, Mr. Griffin fairly grappled the lugger's cable?"

"Of that there can be no manner of doubt.—I saw the two vessels foul of each other, with my night-glass — and, seemingly, both were on fire—as plainly as I ever saw Vesuvius, in a dark night."

"And yet this Few-Folly has escaped!—Poor Griffin has run a desperate risk, for little purpose."

"He has, indeed, my lord."

Here, Nelson, who had been pacing the cabin with quick steps, while Cuffe stood, respectfully declining the gesture to be seated, at the table in its centre, suddenly stopped, and looked the Captain steadily in the face. The expression of his countenance was now mild and earnest, and the pause which preceded his words, gave the latter solemnity and weight.

"The day will come, Cuffe," he said, "when this young man will rejoice that his design on these picaroons, Frenchmen as they are, failed. Yes, from the bottom of his heart, will he be glad."

'My lord!"

"I know you think this strange, Captain Cuffe; but no man sleeps the sounder for having burnt or blown up a hundred of his fellow-creatures, like so many widows at a suttee.—But we are not the less to commend those who did what was certainly their duty."

"Am I to understand, Lord Nelson, that the Proserpine is *not* to destroy the Few-Folly, at every hazard, should we again have the luck to fall in with her?"

"By no means, sir. Our orders are to burn, sink and

gentleman was an American, and a native Manhattanese; his near relatives, of the same name, still residing in New York. It is believed that he got the name of *Willet* from the first English mayor; a gentleman from whom are descended many of the old families of the lower part of the state; more particulary those on Long-Island.

destroy. Such is England's policy, in this desperate war, and it must be carried out. You know what we are contending for, as well as I do; and it is a struggle that is not to be carried on with courtesies; still, one would not wish to see a glorious and sacred cause tarnished by inhumanity. Men that fall in fair, manly combat, are to be envied rather than pitied, since it is only paying the great debt of nature little sooner than might otherwise have happened; but here is something revolting to humanity, in burning up our fellow-creatures, as one would burn rags, after the plague. Nevertheless, this lugger must be had, at any price; for English commerce and English power are not to be cut up and braved, in this audacious manner, with impunity. The career of these French tigers must be stopped, at every sacrifice, Captain Cuffe."

"I know that, my lord; and I like a republican as little as you can do; or His Majesty, himself, for that matter; and, I take it, *he* has as little relish for the animal as flesh and blood can give."

"I know you do, Cuffe—I'm *sure* you do; and I esteem you all the more for it. It is a part of an Englishman's religion, in times like these, to hate a Frenchman. I went across the Channel, after the peace of '83, to learn their language, but had so little sympathy with them, even in peaceable times, as never to be able to make out to write a letter in it, or even to ask intelligibly for the necessaries of life."

"If you can ask for anything, it far surpasses my efforts; I never can tell head from stern, in their dialect."

"It is an infernal jargon, Cuffe, and has got to be so confused by their academies, and false philosophy, and infidelity, that they will shortly be at a loss to understand it themselves. What sort of names they give their ships, for instance, now they have beheaded their king, and denounced their God!—Who ever heard of christening a craft, as you tell me this lugger is named, the 'Few-Folly?'—I believe I've got the picaroon's title right?"

"Quite right—Griffin *pronounces* it so, though he has got to be a little queerish, in his own English, by using so much French and Italian. The young man's father was a consul; and he has half-a-dozen foreign lingos stowed away in his brain. He pronounces Folly, something broadish—like Fol*lay*, I believe — but it means all the same thing. Folly is folly, pronounce it as you will."

Nelson continued to pace his cabin, working the stump of his arm, and smiling half-bitterly; half in a sort of irony that inclined him to be in a good-humour with himself.

"Do you remember the ship, Cuffe, we had that sharp brush with, off Toulon, in old Agamemnon?" he said, after making a turn or two, in silence? "I mean the dismasted eighty-four, that was in tow of the frigate, and which we peppered until their Gallic soup had some taste to it! Now, do you happen to know *her* real name, in good honest Eng-lish?"

"I do not, my lord. I remember, they said she was called the Ça Ira; and I always supposed that it was the name of some old Greek or Roman—or, perhaps, of one of their new-fangled republican saints."

"They!—D——n 'em, they 've *got* no saints, to name my good fellow, since they cashiered all the old ones! There *is* something respectable in the names of a *Spanish* fleet; and one feels that he is flogging gentlemen, at least, while he is at work on them. No, sir, Ça Ira means, neither more nor less, than 'That 'll Do;' and, I fancy, Cuffe, they thought of their own name more than once, while the old Greek was hanging on their quarter, smashing their cabin-windows for them! A pretty sound it would have been, had we got her, and put her into our own service—His Majesty's ship 'That 'll Do,' 84, Captain Cuffe!"

"I certainly should have petitioned my Lords Commissioners to change her name."

"You would have done quite right.—A man might as well sail in a man-of-war called the 'Enough.' Then, there was the three-decker, that helped her out of the scrape, the Sans-Culottes, as the French call her;—I suppose, you know what *that* means?"

"Not I, my lord; to own the truth, I 'm no scholar; and am entirely without ambition, in that way. 'Sans,' I suppose, is the French for 'saint;' but who 'Culottes' was, I 've not the least notion."

Nelson smiled, and the turn the conversation had taken appeared to give him secret satisfaction. If the truth were

known, something lay heavily on his mind; and, with one
of his strong impulses, his feelings disposed him to rush
from one extreme to the other, as is often the case, with men
who are controlled by such masters; more especially, if their
general disposition is to the right.

"You 're wrong, this time, my dear Cuffe," he said; "for
'sans,' means 'without,' in French, and 'culottes,' means
breeches.' Think of naming a three-decker, the 'Without
Breeches!' I do not see how any respectable flag-officer
can mention such names, in his despatches, without a feeling
of awkwardness, that must come near to capsizing all his
philosophy. The line was formed by the Republic's ship,
the 'That 'll Do,' leading, supported by the 'Without
Breeches,' as her second astern!—Ha! Cuffe—D——e, sir,
if I 'd serve in a marine, that had such names to the ships!
It 's a thousand times worse, than all those saints, the Span-
iards tack on to their vessels—like a line of boats, towing a
ship up to her moorings!"

Here the conversation was interrupted by the appearance
of a midshipman, who came down to say that a man and a
woman, from the shore, wished to see the rear-admiral, on
pressing business.

"Let them come down, sir," answered Nelson; "I 've a
hard life of it, Cuffe; there is not a washerwoman, or a shop-
keeper, in Naples, who does not treat me exactly as if I
were a podestâ, and it were my duty to hear all the con-
tentions about lost clothes, and mislaid goods. His Majesty
must appoint a Lord Chief Justice of the Steerage, to administer the law, for the benefit of the young gentlemen, or he 'll
soon get no officer to serve, with a flag at his mast-head."

"Surely, my lord, the captains can take this weight off
your shoulders!"

"Ay, there are men, in the fleet, that *can*, and there are
men who *do;* but there are men who do *not*. But here
comes the plaintiff, I suppose——you shall hear the case, and
act as a puisne judge, in the matter."

This was said as the cabin-door opened, and the expected
guests entered. They were, a man turned of fifty, and a
girl of nineteen. The former was a person of plain exterior,
abstracted air, and downcast look; but the latter had all
the expression, beauty, nature, and grace of mien, that so

singularly marked the deportment and countenance of Ghita Caraccioli. In a word, the two visiters were Carlo Giunto-tardi, and his gentle niece. Nelson was struck with the modesty of mien and loveliness of the latter, and he courte-ously invited her to be seated, though he and Cuffe both continued standing. A few efforts at making himself under-stood, however, soon satisfied this renowned admiral that he had need of an interpreter, his guests speaking no English, and his own Italian being too imperfect to carry on anything like a connected conversation. He hesitated an instant, and then went to the door of the inner cabin, an apartment in which voices had occasionally been heard, the whole time, one of the speakers being evidently a female. Here he stood, leaning against the bulkhead, as if in doubt; and then he uttered his wishes.

"I must ask a service of you, which I would not think of doing in any ordinary case," he said, with a gentleness of voice and manner that showed he addressed one who had habitual influence over him. "I want an interpreter, between myself and the second handsomest woman in the kingdom of Naples ; and I know no one so fit for the office, as the first."

"With all my heart, dear Nelson," answered a full, rich, female voice from within. "Sir William is busied in his antiquities ; and I was really getting to be ennuiéed, for want of an occupation. I suppose you have the wrongs of some injured lady to redress, in your capacity of Lord High Chan-cellor of the Fleet."

"I am yet ignorant of the nature of the complaint ; but it is not unlikely it will turn out to be something like that which you suspect. Even in such a case, no better inter-cessor can be required, than one who is so much superior to the frailties and weaknesses of her sex, in general."

The lady who now made her appearance from the inner cabin, though strikingly handsome, had not that in her appearance which would justify the implied eulogium of the British admiral's last speech. There was an appearance of art and worldliness, in the expression of her countenance, that was only so much the more striking, when placed in obvious contrast to the ingenuous nature and calm purity that shone in every lineament of the face of Ghita. One

17 *

might very well have passed for an image of the goddess
Circe; while the other would have made no bad model for
a vestal, could the latter have borne the moral impression
of the sublime and heart-searching truths that are inculcated
by the real oracles of God. Then the lady was a woman
in the meridian of her charms, aided by all the cunning of
the toilet, and a taste that was piquant and peculiar, if not
pure; while the other stood in her simple, dark Neapolitan
boddice, and a head that had no other ornament than its own
silken tresses; a style of dress, however, that set off her
faultless form, and winning countenance, more than could
have been done by any of the devices of the mantua-maker
or the milliner. The lady betrayed a little surprise, and,
perhaps, a shade of uneasiness, as her glance first fell on
Ghita; but, much too good an actress to be disconcerted
easily, she smiled, and immediately recovered her ease.

" Is *this* the being, Nelson, who comes with *such* a petition?" she demanded, with a touch of natural, womanly
sensibility, in her voice;—" and that poor old man, I dare
say, is the heart-stricken father."

" As to the errand, you will remember, I know nothing,
as yet; and pledge myself to nothing."

" Captain Cuffe, I hope I have the pleasure to see you
well.—Sir William joins the admiral, in hoping you will
make one of our little family party to-day, at dinner, and—"

" And what says the mistress—not of the house, but of
the *ship?*" put in Nelson, whose eyes had scarce turned an
instant from the face of the siren, since she entered the
fore-cabin.

" That she —always disclaiming the title, honourable
though it be—that she unites with all the rest, in inviting
Captain Cuffe to honour us with his company. Nelson tells
me you were one of his old Agamemnons, as he calls you
all, aged and young, men and boys, little and big; and I
love even the sound of the name. What a glorious title for
a ship—Agamemnon!—A Greek, led on by a true English
heart!"

" Ay, it *is* somewhat better than ' That 'll Do,' and the
other affair, Ha! Cuffe!" returned the admiral, smiling, and
glancing at his subordinate—" But, all this time, we are

iguorant of the errand of this honest-looking Italian, and his exceedingly innocent-looking companion."

"Well, then, in this matter, gentlemen, I am only to be regarded as a mere mouth-piece," put in the lady—"an echo, to repeat what reaches my ear, though it be an Irish echo, which repeats in a different tongue from that in which the sounds first reach it. Put your questions, my lord; they shall be faithfully rendered, with all the answers that may be given. I only hope Captain Cuffe will come out of this affair, as innocent as he now looks."

The two gentlemen smiled; but the trifling could not disturb its subject, as he was profoundly ignorant of the existence of the two strangers, five minutes before; while the boldness of the allusions, rather suited the freedom of a ship, and the habits of the part of the world in which they happened to be.

"We will first inquire the name of this worthy man, if you will condescend to ask it," observed Nelson, to his fair friend.

"Carlo Giuntotardi, noble lady—once a poor scholar, in Napoli, here, and now a keeper of the prince's watch-towers, on the heights of Argentaro," was the quiet, but respectful answer of the man, who, like his niece, had declined taking a seat, a circumstance that left the whole party standing; "Carlo Giuntotardi, illustrious lady."

"A very good name, Signore, and one of which you have no need to be ashamed. And thine?" turning to the girl.

"Ghita Caraccioli, Eccellenza; the sister's daughter of this honest tower-keeper of the prince."

Had a bomb exploded over the Foudroyant, Nelson certainly would not have been as much startled; while the lady's beautiful face assumed a look of dark resentment, not unmingled with fear. Even Cuffe understood enough of the sounds to catch the name, and he advanced a step, with lively curiosity, and an anxious concern expressed on his ruddy face. But these emotions soon subsided, the lady first regaining her self-possession, though Nelson paced the cabin five or six times, working the stump of his arm, before he even looked up, again.

"I was about to ask if there *never* is to be an end of these annoyances." observed the lady, in English; "but there must

be some mistake in this. The house of Caraccioli is one of the
most illustrious of Italy, and can scarcely have any of this
class, who feel an interest in him of whom we are thinking.
I will, therefore, inquire further into this matter. Signorina,"
—changing the language to Italian, and speaking with severity, like one who questioned what she heard—" Carac
cioli is a noble name ; and is not often borne by the daughter
of any prince's tower-keepers !"

Ghita trembled, and she looked abashed. But she was
sustained by too high a principle, and was too innocent,
herself, to stand long rebuked, in the presence of guilt ; and,
as the flush, which resembled that which so often passes over
her native skies, at even, left her countenance, she raised
her eyes to the dark-looking face of the lady, and gave her
answer.

" I know what your Eccellenza means," she said, " and
feel its justice. Still, it is cruel to the child, not to bear the
name of her parent. My father was called Caraccioli ; and
he left me his name as my sole inheritance. What may
have been *his* right to it, let my uncle say."

" Speak, then, Signor Giuntotardi. First, give us the
history of this *name ;* then tell us what has brought you
here."

" Noble lady, my sister, as pious and innocent a woman
as ever lived in Italy, and now, blessed in heaven, married
Don Francesco Caraccioli, the son of Don Francesco of that
illustrious family, who now stands condemned to death, for
having led the fleet against the king ; and Ghita, here, is
the only fruit of the union. It is true, that the church did
not authorize the connection which brought my niece's
father into being ; but the noble admiral never hesitated to
acknowledge his son, and he gave him his name, until love
bound him in wedlock with a poor scholar's sister. Then
indeed, his father turned his face from him ; and death soon
removed both husband and wife from the reach of all earthly
displeasure. This is our simple story, noble and illustrious
signora ; and the reason why my poor niece, here, bears a
name as great as that of Caraccioli."

" You mean us to understand, Signor Giuntotardi, that
your niece is the grand-daughter of Don Francesco Caraccioli, through a natural son of that unfortunate admiral ?"

"Such is the fact, Signora. As *my* sister was honestly married, I could do no less than bring up her daughter to bear a name that her father was permitted to bear before her."

"Such things are common; and require no apology. One question more, before I explain to the English admiral what you have said.—Does Prince Caraccioli know of the existence of this grand-daughter?"

"Eccellenza, I fear not. Her parents died so soon—I loved the child so well—and there was so little hope that one illustrious as he, would wish to acknowledge a connection through the holy church, with persons humble as we, that I have never done more to make my niece known, than to let her bear the same name as her father."

The lady seemed relieved, by this; and she now briefly explained to Nelson, the substance of what the other had said.

"It may be," she added, "they are here on that errand concerning which we have, already, heard so much, and so uselessly; but I rather think not, from this account; for what interest *can* they feel in one who is absolutely a stranger to them. It may be some idle conceit, however, connected with this same affair. What is your wish, Ghita? —This is Don Horatio Nelsoni, the illustrious English admiral, of whom you have heard so much."

"Eccellenza, I am sure of it," answered Ghita, earnestly; "my good uncle, here, has told you who we are; and you may well guess our business. We came from St. Agata, on the other side of the bay, only this morning, and heard from a relation in the town, that Don Francesco had been seized, that very hour. Since, we are told, that he has been condemned to die, for treason against the king; and that, by officers who met in this very ship. Some even say, signora that he is to meet his fate ere the sun set!"

"If this should be so, what reason is it that thou shoulds' give thyself concern?"

"Eccellenza, he was my father's father; and though I never saw him, I know that the same blood runs in our veins. When this is so, there should be the same feelings in our hearts."

"This is well. Ghita in appearance, at least; but thou

canst hardly feel much for one thou never saw'st, and who
has even refused to own thee for a child.   Thou art young,
too, and of a sex that should ever be cautious ; it is unwise
for men, even, to meddle with politics, in these troubled
times."

"Signora, it is not politics that brings me here, but nature,
and duty, and pious love for my father's father."

"What wouldst thou say, then?" answered the lady, im-
patiently ; "remember, thou occupiest one whose time is
precious, and of high importance to entire nations."

"Eccellenza, I believe it ; and will try to be brief. I wish
to beg my grandfather's life, of this illustrious stranger.
They tell me, the king will refuse him nothing ; and he has
only to ask it of Don Ferdinando, to obtain it."

Many would have thought the matured charms of the
lady superior to the innocent-looking beauty of the girl ; but
no one could have come to such an opinion, who saw them
both, at that moment.   While Ghita's face was radiant with
a holy hope, and the pious earnestness which urged her on,
a dark expression lowered about the countenance of the
English beauty, that deprived it of one of its greatest attrac-
tions, by depriving it of the softness and gentleness of her
sex.   Had there not been observers of what passed, it is
probable the girl would have been abruptly repulsed ; but
management formed no small part of the character of this
woman ; and she controlled her feelings, in order to effect
her purposes.

"This admiral is not a Neapolitan, but an Englishman,"
she answered ; "and can have no concern with the justice
of your king.   He would scarcely think it decent, to interfere with the execution of the laws of Naples."

"Signora, it is always decent to interfere to save life ;
nay, it is more—it is merciful, in the eyes of God."

"What canst thou know of this!   A conceit that thou
hast the blood of the Caraccioli, has made thee forget thy
sex and condition, and placed a romantic notion of duty
before thine eyes."

"No, signora, it is not so.   For eighteen years have I
been taught that the unfortunate admiral was my grandfather, but, as it has been his pleasure to wish not to see
me, never have I felt the desire to intrude on his time

Before this morning, never has the thought that I have the blood of the Caraccioli, crossed my mind; unless it was to mourn for the sin of my grandmother; and even now, it has come to cause me to mourn for the cruel fate that threatens the days of her partner in guilt."

"Thou art bold, to speak thus of thy parents, girl; and they, too, of the noble and great!"

This was said with a flushed brow, and still more lowering look; for, haply, there were incidents in the past life of that lady, which made the simple language of a severe morality, alike offensive to her ears and her recollections.

"It is not I, Eccellenza, but God, that speaketh thus. The crime, too, is another reason why this great admiral should use his influence to save a sinner from so hurried an end. Death is terrible to all, but to those who trust, with heart and soul, to the mediation of the Son of God; but it is doubly so, when it comes suddenly, and unlooked for. It is true, Don Francesco is aged; but have you not remarked, signora, that it is these very aged who become hardened to their state, and live on, as if never to die? — I mean those aged, who suffer youth to pass, as if the pleasures of life are never to have an end."

"Thou art too young to set up for a reformer of the world, girl; and forgettest that this is the ship of one of the greatest officers of Europe, and that he has many demands on his time. Thou canst now go; I will repeat what thou hast said."

"I have another request to ask, Eccellenza—permission to see Don Francesco; that I may, at least, receive his blessing."

"He is not in this ship. Thou wilt find him on board the Minerva frigate; no doubt, he will not be denied. Stop— these few lines will aid thy request. Addio, signorina."

"And may I carry hope with me, Eccellenza?—Think how sweet life is to those who have passed their days, so long, in affluence and honour. It would be like a messenger from heaven, for a grandchild to bring but a ray of hope."

"I authorize none. The matter is in the hands of the Neapolitan authorities; and we English cannot meddle. Go, now, both of you—the illustrious admiral has business of importance, that presses."

Ghita turned, and slowly and sorrowfully she left the cabin. At its very door, she met the English lieutenant, who was in charge of the unhappy prisoner, coming with a last request that he might not be suspended like a thief, but might, at least, die the death of a soldier. It would exceed the limits set to our tale, were we to dwell on the conversation which ensued; but every intelligent reader knows that the application failed.

CHAPTER XIV.

"Like other tyrants, Death delights to smite
What smitten most proclaims the pride of power,
And arbitrary nod."
                                              YOUNG.

It is probable that Nelson never knew, precisely, what passed between Ghita and the lady mentioned in the last Chapter. At all events, like every other application that was made to the English admiral, in connection with this sad affair, that of Ghita produced no results. Even the mode of execution was unchanged; an indecent haste accompanying the whole transaction; as in the equally celebrated trial and death of the unfortunate Duc d'Enghien. Cuffe remained to dine with the commander in chief, while Carlo Giuntotardi and his niece got into their boat, and took their way, through the crowded roadstead, towards the Neapolitan frigate, that now formed the prison of the unfortunate Caraccioli.

A request, at the gangway, was all that was necessary, to procure an admission on board the ship. As soon as the Signor Giuntotardi reached the quarter-deck, he let his errand be known, and a messenger was sent below, to ascertain if the prisoner would see two visiters; the name of the uncle being alone given. Francesco Caraccioli, of the Princes Caraccioli, or, as he was more commonly called, in English, Prince Caraccioli, was now a man approaching seventy; and being a member of one of the most illustrious nouses of Lower Italy, he had long been trusted in employments of high dignity and command. On his offence—its apology—the indecent haste of his trial and execution, and the irregularity of the whole proceedings, it is now unnecessary to dwell; they have all passed into history, and are familiarly known to the world. That very morning had he been seized, and sent on board the Foudroyant;—in the cabin of that vessel had a court of his own countrymen convened; and there had he been hastily condemned to death The hour of doom was near; and he was already in the ship where the execution was to take place.

The messenger of Carlo Giuntotardi found this unfortunate man with his confessor; by whom he had just been shrived. He heard the request with cold indifference, but granted it on the instant, under the impression that it came from some dependent of his family, or estates, who had a last favour to ask, or an act of justice to see performed.

"Remain here, father, I beseech you," said the prisoner, perceiving that the priest was about to retire; "it is some contadino, or some tradesman, whose claims have been over-looked. I am happy that he has come; for one would wish to stand acquitted of injustice, before he dies. Let them come in, my friend."

A sign was given, with these words, the door of the cabin was opened, and Ghita, with her uncle, entered. A pause of quite a minute followed, during which the parties regarded each other in silence; the prisoner endeavouring, in vain, to recall the countenances of his guests, and the girl trembling, equally with grief and apprehension. Then the last advanced to the feet of the condemned man, knelt, bowed her head, and said—

"Grandfather, your blessing, on the child of your only son."

"Grandfather!—Son!—and his child!" repeated Don Francesco. "I *had* a son, to my shame and contrition be it now confessed; but he has long been dead. I never knew that he left a child."

"This is his daughter, Signore," replied Carlo Giuntotardi; "her mother was my sister. You thought us, then, too humble to be received into so illustrious a connection

18

and we have never wished to bring ourselves before your
eyes, until we thought our presence might be welcome."

"And thou comest now, good man, to claim affinity with
a condemned criminal !"

"Not so, grandfather," answered a meek voice, at his
feet ; " it is your son's daughter, that craves a blessing from
her dying parent. The boon shall be well requited, in
prayers for your soul."

"Holy father ! I deserve not this ! Here has this tender
plant lived, neglected in the shade, until it raises its timid
head to offer its fragrance in the hour of death ! I deserve
not this !"

"Son, if heaven offered no mercies, until they are merited,
hopeless, truly, would be the lot of man. But we must not
admit illusions, at such a moment. Thou art not a husband,
Don Francesco ; hadst thou ever a son ?"

"That, among other sins, have I long since confessed ;
and, as it has been deeply repented of, I trust it is forgiven.
I had a son—a youth who bore my name, even ; though he
never dwelt in my palace ; until a hasty and indiscreet marriage, banished him from my presence. I ever intended
to pardon him, and to make provision for his wants ; but
death came too soon, to both husband and wife, to grant the
time. This much I *did* know ; and it grieved me that it
was so ; but, of his child, never, before this instant, have I
heard ! 'T is a sweet countenance, father ; it seems the very
abode of truth !"

"Why should we deceive you, grandfather," rejoined
Ghita, stretching her arms upward, as if yearning for an
embrace ; " most of all, at a time like this ? We come not
for honours, or riches, or your great name ; we come simply
to crave a blessing, and to let you know that a child of your
own blood will be left on earth, to thy aves, in behalf of
your soul !"

"Holy priest, there can be no deception, here !—This
dear child even looks like her wronged grandmother ; and
my heart tells me she is mine. I know not whether to consider this discovery a good or an evil, at this late hour ;
coming, as it does, to a dying man !"

"Grandfather, your blessing. Bless Ghita, once, that I
may hear the sound of a parent's benediction."

' Bless thee!—bless thee, daughter!" exclaimed the admiral, bending over the weeping girl, to do the act she solicited, and then, raising her to his arms, and embracing her tenderly; "this *must* be my child—I feel that she is no other."

"Eccellenza," said Carlo, "she is the daughter of your son, Don Francesco, and of my sister, Ghita Giuntotardi, born in lawful wedlock. I would not deceive any—least of all, a dying man."

"I have no estates to bequeath—no honours to transmit—no name to boast of. Better the offspring of the lazzaroni, than a child of Francesco Caraccioli, at this moment."

"Grandfather, we think not of this—care not for this. I have come only to ask the blessing you have bestowed, and to offer the prayers of believers, though we are so lowly. More than this we ask not—wish not—seek not. Our poverty is familiar to us, and we heed it not. Riches would but distress us, and we care not for them."

"I remember, holy father, that one great reason of displeasure at my son's marriage, was distrust of the motive of the family which received him; and yet, here, have these honest people suffered me to live on unmolested in prosperity, while they now first claim the affinity, in my disgrace and ignominy! I have not been accustomed to meet with wishes and hearts like these!"

"You did not know us, grandfather," said Ghita, simply, her face nearly buried in the old man's bosom. "We have long prayed for you, and reverenced you, and thought of you as a parent, whose face was turned from us in anger; but we never sought your gold and honours."

"Gold and honours!" repeated the admiral, gently placing his grand-daughter in a chair. "These are things of the past, for me. My estates are sequestered—my name disgraced, and, an hour hence, I shall have suffered an ignominious death. No selfish views *can* have brought these good people, father, to claim affinity with me, at a moment like this."

"It comes from the goodness of God, son. By letting you feel the consolation of this filial love, and by awakening in your own bosom the spark of parental affection, he foreshadows the fruits of his own mercy and tenderness, to the

erring but penitent.   Acknowledge his bounty, in your soul
it may bring a blessing on your last moment."

"Holy priest, I hope I do.—But what says this?—"

Don Francesco took a note from the hand of a servant,
and read its contents eagerly; the world, and its feelings,
having too much hold on his heart, to be plucked cut in an
instant.   Indeed, so sudden had been his arrest, trial and
conviction, that it is not surprising the priest found in him a
divided spirit, even at an instant like that.   His countenance
fell; and he passed a hand before his eyes, as if to conceal a
weakness that was unbecoming.

"They have denied my request, father," he said; "and
I must die like a felon—"

"The Son of God suffered on the cross, suspended between two thieves."

"I believe there is far less, in these opinions, than we are
accustomed to think—yet it is cruel for one who has filled
so high employments—a prince—a Caraccioli, to die like a
lazzarone!"

"Grandfather—"

"Did you speak, child? I wonder not that this indignity
should fill thee with horror."

"It is not *that*, grandfather," resumed Ghita, shaking off
her doubts, and looking up with flushed cheeks, and a face
radiant with holy feelings—"Oh! it is not *that*. If my
life could save thine, gladly would I give it up for such a
purpose; but, do not—do not—at this awful moment, mistake the shadow for the substance.   What matters it how
death is met, when it opens the gates of heaven?   Pain, I
am sure, *you* cannot fear;—even I, weak and feeble girl
that I am, can despise *that*;—what other honour can there
be, in the hour of death, than to be thought worthy of the
mercy and care of God?   Caraccioli or lazzarone—prince
or beggar—it will matter not, two hours hence; and let me
reverently beg of you, to humble your thoughts to the level
which becomes all sinners."

"Thou say'st thou art my grand-child, Ghita—the daugh
ter of my son Francesco?"

"Signore, I am, as all tell me—as my heart tells me—
and as I believe."

"And thou look'st upon these opinions as unworthy—

unsuited, if thou lik'st that better—to this solemn moment, and considerest the *manner* of a death, as matter of indifference, even to a soldier?"

" When placed in comparison with his hopes of heaven—when viewed through his own demerits, and the merits of his Saviour, grandfather."

" And wilt thou, then, just entering on the stage of life, with the world before thee, and all that its future can offer, accompany me to the scaffold; let it be known to the mocking crowd, that thou derivest thy being through the felon, and art not ashamed to own him for a parent?"

" I will, grandfather—this have I come to do," answered Ghita, steadily. " But do not ask me to look upon thy sufferings! All that can be done to lessen, by sharing thy disgrace, if disgrace it be, will I most gladly do; though I dread to see thy aged form in pain!"

" And this wilt thou do for one thou never beheld'st, until this hour?—one thou canst hardly have been taught to consider just to thyself?"

"If I have never seen thee before this visit, grandfather, I have loved thee, and prayed for thee, from infancy. My excellent uncle early taught me this lesson in duty; but he never taught me to hate thee, or any one. My own father is taken away; and that which he would have been to thee, this day, will I endeavour to be for him. The world is nought to me; and it will console thee to think that one is near, whose heart weeps for thee, and whose soul is lost in prayers, for thy eternal pardon."

" And this being, father, is made known to me, an hour before I die! God punishes me sufficiently for the wrong I 've done her, in letting me thus know her worth, when it is too late to profit by it. No, Ghita—blessed child, such a sacrifice shall not be asked of thee. Take this cross—it was my mother's; worn on her bosom, and has long been worn on mine—keep it as a memorial of thy unhappy parent, and pray for me; but, quit this terrible ship, and do not grieve thy gentle spirit with a scene that is so unfit for thy sex and years. Bless thee — bless thee, my child. Would to heaven I had earlier known thee—but even this glimpse of thy worth, has lightened my heart. Thou find'st me, here, a poor condemned criminal; unable to provide for

18 *　　　　　　14

thy future wants—nay, I *can* yet do a little for thee, too.
This bag contains gold. It has been sent to me by a relative, thinking it might be of service, in averting the punish
ment that awaits me. For that purpose, it is now useless;
with thy simple habits, however, it will render thy life easy,
and above care."

Ghita, with streaming eyes, steadily put aside the gold,
though she pressed the cross to her bosom, kissing it fervently,
again and again.

" Not that—not that, grandfather," she said; " I want it
not—wish it not. This is enough; and this will I keep to
my own last moment. I will quit the ship, too; but not the
place. I see many boats collecting, and mine shall be among
them; my prayers shall go up to God for thee, now thou
art living; and, daily, after thou art dead. There needs no
gold, grandfather, to purchase a daughter's prayers."

Don Francesco regarded the zealous and lovely girl with
intense feeling; then he folded her to his heart, once more,
blessing her audibly, again and again. While thus employed,
the Foudroyant's bell struck once, and then those of all the
surrounding ships, English and Neapolitan, repeated the
stroke. This Caraccioli, a seaman himself, well knew
denoted that the time was half-past four; five being the hour
named for his execution. He felt it necessary, therefore,
to dismiss his new-found relative, that he might pass a few
more minutes alone with his confessor. The parting was
solemn, but tender; and as Ghita left the cabin, her condemned grandfather felt, as he would, had he taken leave,
for ever, of one whom he had long loved, and whose virtues
had been a solace to him from the hour of his birth.

The deck of the Minerva presented a sorrowful scene.
Although the prisoner had been condemned by a court of
Neapolitan officers, the trial was had under the British
ensign; and the feeling of the public was with the prisoner.
There existed no necessity for the hurry in which everything
had been done; for no immediate danger pressed; and an
example would have been more impressive, had there been
less of the appearance of a desire for personal vengeance,
and more of the calm deliberation of justice, in the affair
Ghita's connexion with the prisoner could not be even suspected; but, as it was known that she had been in the cabin,

and believed that she felt an interest in the condemned, the officers manifested an interest in her wishes, and too evident emotions.   An immense throng of boats had assembled around the ship; for, hasty as had been the proceedings, the tidings that Francesco Caraccioli was to be hanged for treason, spread like wild-fire; and scarce a craft, of proper size, was left within the mole, so eager was the desire to witness that which was to occur.   Either in the confusion, or bribed by money, the man who had brought off Carlo Giuntotardi and his niece, was no longer to be found; and the means of quitting the ship seemed, momentarily, to be lost.

"Here is a boat, close to our gangway," said the officer of the deck, who had kindly interested himself in behalf of so interesting a girl, "with a single man in it; a few grani would induce him to put you ashore."

The fellow in the boat was of the class of the lazzaroni, wearing a clean cotton shirt, a Phrygian cap, and cotton trowsers, that terminated at the knees; leaving his muscular arms and legs entirely bare; models for the statuary, in their neatness, vigour and proportions.   The feet, alone, formed an exception to the ordinary attire, for they were cased in a pair of quaint canvass shoes, that were ornamented a little like the moccasins of the American Indian.   Carlo caught the eye of this man, who appeared to be eagerly watching the frigate's gangway, for a fare, and, holding up a small piece of silver, in a moment the light boat was at the foot of the accommodation-ladder.   Ghita now descended; and, as soon as her uncle and she were seated, the skiff, for it was little more, whirled away from the ship's side, though two or three more, who had also been left by recreant boat-men, for better fares, called out to him to receive them, also.

"We had best go alone, even though it cost us a heavier price," quietly observed Carlo, to his niece, as he noted this occurrence.   "Pull us a short distance from the ship, friend; —here, where there are fewer boats; and thou shalt meet with a fair reward.   We have an interest in this solemn scene, and could wish not to be observed."

"I know that well, Signor Carlo," answered the boat-man; "and will see that you are not molested."

Ghita uttered a faint exclamation, and, looking up, first

saw that the feigned lazzarone was no other than Raoul
Yvard.   As her uncle was too unobservant, in general, to
detect his disguise, he made a sign for her to command herself, and continued rowing, as if nothing had occurred.

"Be at ease, Ghita," said Carlo; "it is not yet the time,
and we have twenty good minutes, for our aves."

Ghita, however, was far from being at ease.   She felt all
the risks that the young man now ran, and she felt that it
was on her account, solely, that he incurred them.   Even
the solemn feeling of the hour, and the occasion, was disturbed by his presence; and she wished he were away, on
more accounts than one.   Here he was, nevertheless, and in
the midst of enemies; and it would not have been in nature,
for one of her years and sex, and, most of all, of her feelings,
not to indulge in a sentiment of tender gratitude towards
him, who had, as it were, thrust his head into the very lion's
mouth, to do her a service.   Between Raoul and Ghita, there
had been no reserves, on the subject of parentage; and the
former understood why his mistress was here, as well as the
motive that brought her.   As for the last, she glanced timidly
around her, fearful that the lugger, too, had been brought
into the throng of ships that crowded the anchorage.   Fo.
this, however, Raoul was much too wary, nothing resemblin,
his little craft being visible.

The reader will have understood that many vessels of wa
English, Russian, Turkish and Neapolitan, were now an
chored in the bay.   As the French still held the Castle of
St. Elmo, or the citadel that crowns the heights, that, in thei
turn, crown the town, the shipping did not lay quite as clos
to the mole as usual, lest a shot from the enemy above migh
do them injury; but they were sufficiently near to permit al.
the idle and curious of Naples, who had the hearts and th
means, to pull off and become spectators of the sad scen
that was about to occur.   As the hour drew near, boat afte
boat arrived, until the Minerva was surrounded with spect
tors, many of whom belonged even to the higher classes o
society.

The distance between the Neapolitan frigate, and the shi
of the English rear-admiral, was not great; and everythin,
that occurred on board the former, and which was not actu
ally hidden by the sides and bulwarks of the vessel itsel

was easily to be seen from the decks of the latter. Still, the Foudroyant lay a little without the circle of boats; and in that direction Raoul had pulled, to avoid the throng, resting on his oars, when about a third of a cable's-length from the British admiral's stern. Here it was determined to wait for the awful signal, and its fatal consequences. The brief interval was passed, by Ghita, in telling her beads, while Carlo joined in the prayers, with the devotion of a zealot. It is scarcely necessary to say, that all this Raoul witnessed without faith, though it would be doing injustice to his nature, as well as to his love for Ghita, to say he did so without sympathy.

A solemn and expecting silence reigned in all the neighbouring ships. The afternoon was calm and sultry, the zephyr ceasing to blow, earlier than common, as if unwilling to disturb the melancholy scene, even with its murmurs. On board the Minerva, no sign of life—scarcely of death—was seen; though a single whip was visible, rigged to the foreyard-arm, one end being led in-board, while the other ran along the yard, passed through a leading-block, in its quarter, and descended to the deck. There was a platform fitted, on two of the guns, beneath this expressive, but simple arrangement; but, as it was in-board, it was necessarily concealed from all but those who were on the Minerva's decks. With these preparations Raoul was familiar, and his understanding eye saw the particular rope that was so soon to deprive Ghita of her grandfather; though it was lost to her and her uncle, among the maze of rigging by which it was surrounded.

There might have been ten minutes passed, in this solemn stillness, during which the crowd of boats continued to collect; and the crews of the different ships were permitted to take such positions, as enabled them to become spectators of a scene that it was hoped might prove admonitory. It is part of the etiquette of a vessel of war to make her people keep close; it being deemed one sign of a well-ordered ship, to let as few men be seen as possible, except on those occasions when duty requires them to show themselves. This rigid rule, however, was momentarily lost sight of, and the teeming masses that floated around La Minerva, gave up their thousands, like bees clustering about their hives. I

was in the midst of such signs of expectation, that the cal.
of the boatswain was heard piping the side, on board the
Foudroyant, and four side-boys lay over on the accommodation-ladder, a mark of honour never paid to one of a rank
less than that of a captain. Raoul's boat was within fifty
yards of that very gangway, and he turned his head in idle
curiosity, to see who might descend into the gig that was
lying at the foot of the long flight of steps. A stranger, with
two epaulettes, came first, showing the way to two civilians,
and a sea-lieutenant ; when all descended in a line, and
entered the boat. The next instant, the oars fell, and the
gig whirled round under the Foudroyant's stern, and came
glancing up towards his own skiff. Four or five of the
strong man-of-war jerks, sufficed to send the long, narrow
boat as far as was desired, when the men ceased rowing,
their little craft losing her way within ten feet of the skiff
occupied by our party. Then it was that Raoul, to his
surprise, discovered that the two civilians were no other than
Andrea Barrofaldi, and Vito Viti, who had accompanied
Cuffe and Griffin, their companions in the gig, on a cruise ;
of which the express object was to capture himself and his
vessel.

Another man would have been alarmed, at finding himself
in such close vicinity to his enemies ; but Raoul Yvard was
amused, rather than rendered uneasy, by the circumstance.
He had faith in his disguise ; and he was much too familiar
with incidents of this sort, not to retain his self-command
and composure. Of course, he knew nothing of the persons
of the two Englishmen ; but, perfectly aware of the presence
of the Proserpine, he guessed at their identity, and very
correctly imagined the circumstances that brought companions, so ill-assorted, together. He had taken no precautions to disguise his face ; and the red Phrygian cap which
he wore, in common with thousands on that bay, left every
feature and lineament fully exposed. With Ghita, however,
the case was different. She was far better known to the
two Elbans, as indeed was the person of her uncle, than he
was himself; but both had veiled their faces in prayer.

"I do not half like this business, Griffin," observed the
captain, as his gig entirely lost its way ; "and wish, with al
my heart, we had nothing to do with it. I knew this old

Caraccioli; and a very good sort of man he was; and, as to
treason, it is not easy to say who is, and who is not a traitor,
in times like these, in such a nation as this.—Ha!—I believe
my soul, this is the same old man, and the same pretty girl,
that came to see Nelson, half-an-hour ago, about this very
execution?"

"What could *they* have to do with Prince Caraccioli, or
his treason, sir?—The old chap looks bookish; but he is not
a priest; and, as to the girl, she is trim-built enough; I fancy
the face is no great matter, however, or she would not take
so much pains to hide it."

Raoul muttered a "sacr-r-re," between his teeth, but he
succeeded in suppressing all outward expression of feeling.
Cuffe, on the contrary, saw no other motive for unusual discretion, beyond the presence of his boat's crew, before whom,
however, he was accustomed to less reserve, than with his
people in general.

"If she be the same as the one we had in the cabin," he
answered, "there is no necessity for a veil; for a prettier
or a more modest-looking girl, is not often fallen in with.
What she wanted, exactly, is more than I can tell you, as
she spoke Italian, altogether; and 'miladi' had the interview
pretty much to herself. But her good looks seem to have
taken with this old bachelor, the justice of the peace, who
eyes her as if he had an inclination to open his mind to the
beauty. Ask him, in Italian, Griffin, what mare's nest he
has run foul of, now."

"You seem to have found something to look at, beside the
Minerva, Signor Podestà," observed Griffin, in an under-
tone; "I hope it is not Venus."

"Cospetto!" grunted Vito Viti, nudging his neighbour
the vice-governatore, and nodding towards the other boat
"if that be not little Ghita, who came into our island like a
comet, and went out of it—to what shall I liken her sudden
and extraordinary disappearance, Signor Andrea?—"

"To that of le Feu-Follet, or ze Ving-y-Ving," put in
Griffin; who, now he had got the two functionaries fairly
afloat, spared none of the jokes that come so easy and natural
to a man-of-war's man. "*She* went out, too, in an 'extraordinary disappearance,' and perhaps the lady and the lugger
went out together."

Vito Viti muttered an answer; for, by this time, he had discovered that he was a very different personage, on board the Proserpine, from what the other had appeared to consider him, while in his native island. He might have expressed himself aloud, indeed; but, at that instant, a column of smoke glanced out of the bow part of the Minerva—a yellow flag was shown aloft—and then came the report of the signal-gun.

It has been said that vessels of war, of four differen nations, were, at that time, lying in the Bay of Naples. Nelson had come in, but a short time previously, with seventeen ships of the line; and he found several more of his countrymen lying there. This large force had been assembled to repel an expected attack on the Island of Minorca; and it was still kept together in an uncertainty of the future movements of the enemy. A Russian force had come out of the Black Sea, to act against the French, bringing with it a squadron of the Grand Signor; thus presenting to the world the singular spectacle of the followers of Luther, devotees of the Greek church, and disciples of Mahomet, uniting in defence of " our rights, our firesides, and our altars!" To these vessels must be added a small squadron of ships of the country; making a mixed force of four different ensigns, that was to witness the melancholy scene we are about to relate.

The yellow flag, and the signal-gun, brought everything, in the shape of duty, to a stand-still, in all the fleets. The hoarse commands ceased—the boatswains, and their mates, laid aside their calls, and the echoing midshipmen no longer found orders to repeat. The seamen gathered to the sides of their respective vessels—every part glistened with expectant eyes—the booms resembled clusters of bees, suspended from the boughs of a forest—and the knight-heads, taffrails gangways, and stretchers of the rigging, were garnished with those whose bright buttons, glazed hats, epaulettes, and dark-blue dresses, denoted to belong to the privileged classes of a ship. Notwithstanding all this curiosity, nothing like the feeling which is apt to be manifested, at an exhibition of merited punishment, was visible in a single countenance. An expression resembling a sombre gloom, appeared to have settled on all those grim warriors of the deep; English,

Russian, Neapolitan or Turk, apparently reserving all his sympathies for the sufferer, rather than for the majesty of justice. Still, no murmur arose—no sign of resistance was made—no look of remonstrance given. The unseen mantle of authority covered all; and these masses of discontented men submitted, as we bow to what is believed to be the fiat of fate. The deep-seated and unresisting habit of discipline, suppressed complaint; but there was a general conviction that some act was about to be committed, that, it were better for humanity and justice, should not be done; or, if done at all, that it needed more of form, greater deliberation, and a fairer trial, to be so done as to obtain the commendation of men. The Turks, alone, showed apathy; though all showed submission. These subjects of destiny looked on coldly: though even among them, a low rumour had passed, that a malign influence prevailed in the fleet; and that a great and proud spirit had gotten to be mastered by the passion that so often deprives heroes of their self-command and independence.

Ghita ceased her prayers, as the report of the gun broke rudely on her ears, and, with streaming eyes, she even dared to look towards the frigate. Raoul, and all the rest, bent their gaze in the same direction. The sailors, among them, saw the rope at the fore-yard-arm move, and then heads rose slowly above the hammock-cloths; when the prisoner and his attendant priest were visible even to their feet. The unfortunate Caraccioli, as has been said, had nearly numbered his threescore and ten years, in the regular course of nature; and his bare head now showed the traces of time. He wore no coat; and his arms were bound behind his back, at the elbows, leaving just motion enough to the hands, to aid him in the slighter offices about his own person. His neck was bare, and the fatal cord was tightened sufficiently around it, to prevent accidents, constantly admonishing its victim of its revolting office.

A low murmur arose among the people in the boats, as this spectacle presented itself to their eyes; and many bowed their faces in prayer. The condemned man caught a ray of consolation from this expression of sympathy; and he looked around him, an instant, with something like a return of those feelings of the world, which it had been his effort

19

and his desire totally to eradicate, since he had taken leave
of Ghita, and learned that his last request — that of
changing his mode of punishment—had been denied.   That
was a fearful moment, for one like Don Francesco Caraccioli, who had passed a long life in the midst of the scene
that surrounded him—illustrious by birth, affluent, honoured
for his services, and accustomed to respect and deference.
Never had the glorious panorama of the bay, appeared more
lovely than it did at that instant, when he was about to quit
it for ever, and this by means of a violent and disgraceful
death.   From the purple mountains—the cerulean void above
him—the blue waters over which he seemed already to be
suspended—and the basking shores, rich in their towns,
villas and vines, his eye turned toward the world of ships,
each alive with its masses of living men.   A glance of
melancholy reproach was cast upon the little flag that was
just waving at the mizzen-mast-head of the Foudroyant;
and then it fell on the carpet of faces beneath, that seemed
fairly to change the surface of the smooth sea, into an arena
of human countenances.   His look was steady, though his
soul was in a tumult.   Ghita was recognized by her companion, and by her dress.   He moved towards the edge of
his narrow scaffolding, endeavoured to stretch forth his arms,
and blessed her, again, aloud.   The poor girl dropped on
her knees, in the bottom of the boat, bowed her head, and in
that humble attitude did she remain, until all was over; not
daring once to look upward, again.

" Son," said the priest, " this is a moment when the earth,
and its feelings, must be forgotten."

" I know it, father," answered the old man, his voice
trembling with emotion, for his sensations were too powerful,
too sublime, even, for the degrading passion of fear—" but
never before did this fair piece of the creation seem so lovely
in my eyes, as now, when I am about to quit it for the last
time."

" Look beyond this scene, into the long vista of eternity,
son; there thou wilt behold that, which mocks at all human,
all earthly means, to equal.   I fear that our time is but
short—hast thou aught yet to say, in the flesh ?"

" Let it be known, holy priest, that in my dying moment
I prayed for Nelson, and for all who have been active in

bringing me to this end. It is easy for the fortunate, and the untempted, to condemn ; but he is wiser, as he is safer, who puts more reliance on the goodness of God, than on his own merits."

A ray of satisfaction gleamed athwart the pale countenance of the priest—a sincerely pious man, or fear of personal consequences might have kept aloof from such a scene— and he closed his eyes, while he expressed his gratitude to God, in the secret recesses of his own spirit. Then he turned to the prince, and spoke cheeringly.

" Son," he said, " if thou quittest life with a due dependence on the Son of God, and in this temper towards thy fellow-creatures, of all this living throng, thou art he who is most to be envied! Address thy soul in prayer, once more, to Him, whom thou feelest can alone serve thee."

Caraccioli, aided by the priest, knelt on the scaffold ; for the rope hung loose enough to permit that act of humiliation, and the other bent at his side.

" I wish to God, Nelson had nothing to do with this !" muttered Cuffe, as he turned away his face, inadvertently bending his eyes on the Foudroyant, nearly under the stern of which ship, his gig lay. There, in the stern-walk, stood the lady, already mentioned in this Chapter, a keen spectator of the awful scene. No one, but a maid, was near her, however, the men of her companionship not being of moods stern enough to be at her side. Cuffe turned away from this sight, in still stronger disgust ; and just at that moment, a common cry arose from the boats. Looking round, he was just in time to see the unfortunate Caraccioli dragged from his knees, by the neck, until he rose, by a steady, man-of-war pull, to the end of the yard ; leaving his companion alone on the scaffold, still lost in prayer. There was a horrible minute, of the struggles between life and death, when the body, so late the tenement of an immortal spirit, hung, like one of the jewel-blocks of the ship, dangling passively at the end of the spar, as insensible as the wood which sustained it.

CHAPTER XV.

"Sleep, sleep, thou sad one, on the sea!
  The wash of waters lulls thee, now;
  His arm no more will pillow thee,
    Thy hand upon his brow.
He is not near, to hurt thee, or to save:
  The ground is his — the sea must be thy grave."
                  DANA.

A LONG summer's evening did the body of Francesco Caraccioli hang suspended at the yard-arm of the Minerva; a revolting spectacle to his countrymen, and to most of the strangers who had been the witnesses of his end. Then was it lowered into a boat, its feet loaded with double-headed shot, and it was carried out a league, or more, into the bay, and cast into the sea. The revolting manner in which it rose to the surface, and confronted its destroyers, a fortnight later, has passed into history; and, to this day, forms one of the marvels related by the ignorant and wonder-loving of that region.*   As for Ghita, she disappeared, no one knew how; Vito Viti, and his companions, being too much absorbed with the scene, to note the tender and considerate manner in which Raoul rowed her off from a spectacle that could but be replete with horrors, to one so situated. Cuffe, himself, stood but a few minutes longer; but he directed his boat's crew to pull alongside of the Proserpine. In half-an-hour after the execution took place, this frigate was aweigh; and then she was seen standing out of the bay, before a light air,

---

* Singular as was this occurrence, and painful as it must have proved to the parties to the execution, it is one of the simplest consequences of natural causes. All animal matter swells, in water, previously to turning corrupt. A body that has become of twice its natural size, in this manner, as a matter of course, displaces twice the usual quantity of water; the *weight* of the mass remaining the same. Most human frames floating, in their natural state, so long as the lungs are inflated with air, it follows that one in this condition would bring up with it, as much weight, in iron, as made the difference between its own gravity, and that of the water it displaced. The upright attitude of Caraccioli, was owing to the shot attached to the feet; of which, it is also probable, one or two had become loosened.

covered with canvass, from her truck to her hammock-
cloths. Leaving her, for the moment, we will return to the
party in the skiff.

Neither Carlo Giuntotardi, nor Ghita Caraccioli—for so
we must continue to call the girl, albeit the name is much
too illustrious to be borne by one of her humble condition in
life—but, neither of these two had any other design, in thus
seeking out the unfortunate admiral, than to perform what
each believed to be a duty. As soon as the fate of Caraccioli was decided, both were willing to return to their old
position in life; not that they felt ashamed to avow their
connection with the dead; but because they were quite de-
void of any of that worldly ambition, which renders rank
and fortune necessary to happiness.

When he left the crowd of boats, Raoul pulled towards
the rocks which bound the shores of the bay, near the gardens of Portici. This was a point sufficiently removed from
the common anchorage, to be safe from observation; and
yet so near, as to be reached in considerably less than a.
hour. As the light boat proceeded, Ghita gradually regained
her composure. She dried her eyes, and looked around her
inquiringly, as if wondering whither their companion was
taking them.

"I will not ask you, Raoul, why you are here, at a moment like this, and whence you have come," she said; "but
I may ask whither you are now carrying us? Our home
is at St. Agata, on the heights above Sorrento, and on the
other side of the bay. We come there, annually, to pass
a month with my mother's sister; who asks this much of
our love."

"If I did not know all this, Ghita, I would not, and could
not be here. I have visited the cottage of your aunt, this
day; followed you to Naples; heard of the admiral's trial
and sentence; understood how it would affect your feelings;
traced you on board the English admiral's ship, and was in
waiting, as you found me; having first contrived to send
away the man who took you off. All this has come about
as naturally, as the feeling which has induced me to venture,
again, into the lion's mouth."

"The pitcher that goes often to the well, Raoul, gets
broken at last," said Ghita, a little reproachfully, though it

19 *

surpassed her power to prevent the tones of tenderness from mingling with her words.

"You know all, Ghita. After months of perseverance, and a love such as man seldom felt before, you deliberately and coldly refused to be my wife;—nay, you have deserted Monte Argentaro, purposely to get rid of my importunities; for there I could go with the lugger, at any moment; and have come here, upon this bay, crowded with the English, and other enemies of France, fancying that I would not dare to venture hither.—Well, you see with what success; for neither Nelson, nor his two-deckers, can keep Raoul Yvard from the woman he loves, let him be as victorious and skilful as he may!"

The sailor had ceased rowing, to give vent to his feelings in this speech, neither of the two colloquists regarding the presence of Carlo Giuntotardi, any more than if he had been a part of themselves. This indifference to the fact that a third person was a listener, proceeded from habit, the worthy scholar and religionist being usually too abstracted to attend to concerns as light as love, and the youthful affections. Ghita was not surprised, either at the reproaches of her suitor, or at his perseverance; and her conscience told her he uttered but the truth, in attributing to her the motives he had, in urging her uncle to make their recent change of residence; for, while a sense of duty had induced her to quit the towers, her art was not sufficient to suggest the expediency of going to any other abode than that which she was accustomed to inhabit periodically, and about which Raoul knew, from her own innocent narrations, nearly as much as she knew herself.

"I can say no more than I have said, already," the thoughtful girl answered, after Raoul had begun again to row. "It is better, on every account, that we should part. I cannot change my country; nor can you desert that glorious republic, of which you feel so proud. I am an Italian, and you are French; while, more than all, I worship my God, while you believe in the new opinions of your own nation. Here are causes enough for separation, surely, however favourably and kindly we may happen to think of each other, in general."

"Tell me not, any more, of the heart of an Italian girl,

and of her readiness to fly to the world's end, with the man of her choice!" exclaimed Raoul, bitterly. " I can find a thousand girls, in Languedoc, who would make the circuit of the earth, yearly, rather than be separated, a day, from the seamen they have chosen for their husbands."

" Then look among the girls of Languedoc, for a wife," answered Ghita, with a smile so melancholy that it contradicted her words. " Better to take one of your own nation and opinion, Raoul, than risk your happiness with a stranger; who might not answer all your hopes, when you came to know her better."

" We will not talk further of this, now, dearest Ghita, my first care must be to carry you back to the cottage of your aunt—unless, indeed, you will at once embark in le Feu-Follet, and return to the towers?"

" Le Feu-Follet!—she is hardly here, in the midst of a fleet of her enemies!—Remember, Raoul, that your men will begin to complain, if you place them too often in such risks, to gratify your own wishes."

" Peste!—I keep them in good-humour, by rich prizes. They have been successful; and that which makes yonder Nelson popular, and a great man, makes Raoul Yvard popular, and a great man, also, in his little way. My crew is like its captain—it loves adventures, and it loves success."

" I do not see the lugger—among a-hundred ships, there is no sign of yours?"

" The Bay of Napoli is large, Ghita," returned Raoul, laughing; " and le Feu-Follet takes but little room. See— yonder vaisseaux-de-ligne appear trifling among these noble mountains, and on this wide gulf; you cannot expect my little lugger to make much show. We are small, Ghita mia, if not insignificant!"

" Still, where there are so many vigilant eyes, there is always danger, Raoul! Besides, a lugger is an unusual rig, as you have owned to me, yourself."

" Not here, among all these eastern craft. I have always found, if I wished to be unnoticed, it was best to get into a crowd; whereas, he who lives in a village, lives in open day-light. But we will talk of these things, when alone, Ghita—yonder fisherman is getting ready to receive us."

By this time the skiff was near the shore, where a little

yawl was anchored, containing a solitary fisherman.   Thi
man was examining them, as they approached ; and, recog-
nising Raoul, he was gathering in his lines, and preparing
to raise his grapnel.   In a few minutes the two craft lay
side by side ; and then, though not without difficulty, owing
to a very elaborate disguise, Ghita recognised Ithuel Bolt.
A very few words sufficed to let the American into all that
it was necessary he should know, 'when the whole party
made its arrangements to depart.   The skiff which Raoul,
having found it lying on the beach, had made free with,
without leave, he anchored, in the full expectation that its
right owner might find it, some day or other ; while its cargo
was transferred to the yawl, which was one of the lugger's
own attendants.   The latter was a light, swift pulling little
boat, admirably constructed, and fit to live in a sea-way ;
requiring, moreover, but two good oars, one of which Raoul
undertook to pull, himself, while Ithuel managed the other.
In five minutes after the junction was made, the party was
moving again from the land, in a straight line across the bay,
steering in the direction of its southern cape, and proceeding
with the steady, swift movement of men accustomed to the
toil.

There are few portions of the sea in which a single ship
or boat is an object of so little notice, as the Bay of Naples.
This is true of all times and seasons ; the magnificent scale
on which nature has created her panorama, rendering ordinary objects of comparative insignificance ; while the constant movement, the fruit of a million of souls thronging
around its teeming shores, covers it, in all directions, with
boats, almost as the streets of a town are crowded with
pedestrians.   The present occasion, too, was one likely to
set everything in motion ; and Raoul judged rightly, when
he thought himself less likely to be observed in such a scene,
than on a smaller and less-frequented water. · As a matter
of course, while near the mole, or the common anchorage,
it was necessary to pass amid a floating throng ; but, once
beyond the limits of this crowd, the size of the bay rendered
it quite easy to avoid unpleasant collisions, without any apparent effort ; while the passage of a boat, in any direction,
was an occurrence too common to awaken distrust.   One
would think no more of questioning a craft that was encoun-

tered, even in the centre of that spacious bay, than he would think of inquiring about the stranger, met in a market-place. All this both Raoul and Ithuel knew and felt ; and, once in motion, in their yawl, they experienced a sense of security, that, for the four or five previous hours, had not always existed.

By this time, the sun was low, though it was possible, as Raoul perceived, to detect the speck that was still swinging at the Minerva's fore-yard-arm; a circumstance to which the young man, with considerate feeling, refrained from adverting. The Proserpine had been some time in motion, standing out of the fleet under a cloud of canvass, but with an air so light as to permit the yawl to gain on her, though the heads of both were turned in the same direction. In this manner, mile after mile was passed, until darkness came. Then the moon arose, rendering the bay less distinct, it is true, but scarcely more mysterious, or more lovely, than in the hours of stronger light. The gulf, indeed, forms an exception, in this particular, to the general rule, by the extent of its shores, the elevation of its mountains, the beauty of its water—which has the deep tint of the ocean off soundings—and the softness of the atmosphere ; lending to it, by day, all the mellowed and dreamy charms that other scenes borrow from the illusions of night, and the milder brilliance of the secondary planets. Raoul did not exert himself, at the oar ; and, as he sat aft, his companion was obliged to take the stroke from his movement. It was so pleasant to have Ghita with him, on his own element, that he never hurried himself, while in the enjoyment of her society. The conversation, it will readily be imagined, was not lively ; but the saddened melancholy of Ghita's voice, as she occasionally hazarded a remark of her own, or answered one of his questions, sounded sweeter, in his ears, than the music of the ships' bands, that was now wafted to them across the water.

As the evening advanced, the land-breeze increased, and the Proserpine gradually gained upon the boat. When the latter was about two-thirds of the distance across the bay the frigate caught the stronger current, that came down athwart the campagna, between Vesuvius and the mountains behind Castel à Mare, when she drove ahead fast. Her

15

sails, as seamen express it, were all asleep; or swelled outward without collapsing; and her rate of sailing was between
five and six miles in the hour. This brought them up with
the boat, hand-over-hand, as it is called; and Ghita, at Raoul's
request, put the helm aside, in order that they might get
out of the way of the huge body that was approaching. I
would seem that there was some design, on the part of the
ship, in coming so near, for she made a sheer towards the
yawl, in a way to frighten the timid helmswoman, and to
induce her to relinquish her hold of the tiller.

"Fear nothing," called out Griffin, in Italian—"we intend to offer you a tow. Stand by, and catch the line—
Heave—"

A small rope was thrown; and, falling directly across
Ithuel's head, that person could do no less than seize it.
With all his detestation of the English in general, and of this
vessel in particular, the man-of-all-work had the labour-
saving propensity of his countrymen; and it struck him as
a good thing, to make a "king's ship" aid an enemy's privateer, by accepting the offer. As he used the line with proper
dexterity, the yawl was soon towing on the quarter of the
frigate; Raoul taking the helm, and giving the boat the
sheer necessary to prevent her dragging in, alongside. This
was a change so sudden, and so totally unexpected, that
Ghita murmured her disapprobation, lest it should lead to a
discovery of the true character of her companions.

"Fear nothing, dearest," answered Raoul, "they cannot
suspect us; and we may learn something useful by being
here. At all events, le Feu-Follet is safe from their designs,
just at this moment."

"Are you boatmen of Capri?" called out Griffin, who
stood on the taffrail of the ship, with Cuffe and the two
Italians near by; the first dictating the questions his lieutenant put.

"S'nore, si;" answered Raoul, adopting the patois of the
country, as well as he could, and disguising his deep mellow
voice, by speaking on a high shrill key. "Boatmen of
Capri, that have been to Napoli with wine, and have been
kept out later than we intended by the spectacle at the yard-
arm of the Minerva. Cospetto! them signori make no more
of a prince, than we do of a quail, in the season, on our

little island. Pardon me, dearest Ghita; but we *must* throw dust into their eyes."

"Has any strange sail been seen about your island, within the last twenty-four hours?"

"The bay is full of strange sail, S'nore; even the Turks coming to see us, since the last trouble with the French."

"Ay—but the Turks are now your allies, like us English.—Have you seen any other strangers?"

"They tell me, there are ships from the far north, too, S'nore, off the town. Russians, I believe, they call them."

"They, too, are allies; but, I mean, enemies. Has there not been a lugger seen off your island, within the last day or two—a lugger of the French?"

"Si—si—I know what you mean, now, S'nore; there *has* been a vessel like that you mention, off the island; for I saw her with my own eyes—si—si. It was about the twenty-third hour, last evening—a lugger, and we all said she must be French, by her wicked looks."

"Raoul!" said Ghita, as if reproaching him for an indiscretion.

"This is the true way to befog them," answered the young man; "they have certainly heard of us; and by seeming to tell a little truth, frankly, it will give me an opportunity of telling more untruth."

"Ah, Raoul, it is a sad life, that renders untruths necessary!"

"It is the art of war, dearest; without it, we should soon be outwitted, by these knaves of English.—Si—si, S'nori, we all said just that, concerning her looks and rig."

"Will you sheer your boat alongside, friend!" inquired Griffin, "and come on board of us? We have a ducat, here, that wants an owner; I fancy it will fit your pocket, as well as another's. We will haul you ahead, abreast of the gangway."

"Oh! Raoul, do not think of this rash act," whispered Ghita; "the vice-governatore, or the podestà, will recollect you; and then all will be lost!"

"Fear nothing, Ghita—a good cause, and a keen wit, will carry me through; while the least hesitation might, indeed, ruin us. These English first ask, and then take,

without asking, if you tell them no.   Corpo di Bacco! who
ever heard, either, of a lazzarone's refusing a ducat!"

Raoul then whispered a few words to Ithuel, when, the
boat being, by this time, far enough ahead, he gave it a
sheer alongside of the ship, seized a man-rope, and went up
the cleets as actively as a cat.   It is certain, not a soul on
board that fine frigate had the least suspicion of the true character of the individual who now confidently trod her quarter-deck.   The young man, himself, loved the excitement of
such an adventure, and he felt the greater confidence in his
impunity, from the circumstance that there was no other
light than that of the moon.   The sails, too, cast their shadows upon deck ; and then, neither of the two Italians was
a wizard, at detecting impostors, as he knew by experience.

The watch was set for the night, and Winchester, who
had returned to duty, held the trumpet, while Griffin had no
other immediate office, but to interpret.   Two or three midshipmen were lounging about the quarter-deck ; here and
there a seaman was on the look-out, at the halyards, or on
a cat-head ; some twenty or thirty old sea-dogs were pacing
the gangways or the forecastle, with their arms crossed, and
hands stuck in their jackets ; and a quick-eyed, active
quarter-master stood near the man at the wheel, conning
the ship.   The remainder of the watch had stowed themselves between the guns, or among the booms, in readiness
to act, but, in truth, dozing.   Cuffe, Griffin, and the two
Italians, descended from the taffrail, and awaited the approach of the supposed lazzarone, or boatman of Capri, as he
was now believed to be, near the stern of the vessel.   By an
arrangement among themselves, Vito Viti became the spokesman ; Griffin translating to the captain, all that passed, in
an under-tone, as soon as it was uttered.

"Come hither, friend," commenced the podestà, in a
patronizing, but somewhat lofty manner ; "this generous and
noble English captain, Sir Kooffe, desires me to present you
with a ducat, by way of showing that he asks no more of
you than he is willing to pay for.   A ducat* is a great deal

---

* The silver ducat of Naples is worth 80 grani, or rather less than
80 cents ; the golden ducat, or sequin of Italy, Holland, Turkey, &c.
is worth a trifle more than two American dollars.   Raoul was offered
the former

of money, as you know; and good pay merits good services."

"S'nore, si; your eccellenza says the truth; a good ducat, certainly, deserves good services."

"Bene. Now, tell these signori all you know about that said lugger; where you saw her; when you saw her; and what she was about. Keep your mind clear, and tell us one thing at a time."

"S'nore, si. I will keep my mind clear, and tell you no more than one thing at a time. I believe, eccellenza, I am to begin with *where* I saw her; then I'm to tell you *when* I saw her; after which, you wish to know what she was about. I believe, this is the way you put it, S'nore?"

"Excellently well; answer in that order, and you will make yourself understood. But, first, tell me;—do all the natives of Capri speak the same sort of Italian as you do yourself, friend?"

"S'nore, si—though my mother having been a French woman, they tell me that I have caught a little from her. We all get something from our mothers, eccellenza; and its a pity we could not keep more of it."

"True, friend; but now for the lugger. Remember that honourable signori will hear what you say; therefore, for your own credit, speak to the point; and speak nothing but truth, for the love of God."

"Then, S'nore, first, as to *where* I saw her—does your eccellenza mean, where I was at the time, or where the lugger was?"

"Where the lugger was, fellow. Dost think Sir Kooffe cares where thou spent thy day!"

"Well, then, eccellenza, the lugger was near the Island of Capri, on the side next the Mediterranean, which, you know, S'nore, is on the side opposite to the bay, and near, as might be, abreast of the house of Giacomo Alberti—does your eccellenza know anything of the house I mean?"

"Not I; but tell your story, as if I knew all about it. It is these particulars which give value to a tale. How far from the nearest land?—Mention that fact, by all means, if you happen to remember."

"Well, eccellenza, could the distance be measured, now, I think it would prove to be about as far—not quite, S'nore;

20

but, I say, *about*—about as far as from the said Giacomo's largest fig-tree, to the vines of Giovanni, his wife's cousin. Si—I think, just about that distance."

"And how far may that be, friend.   Be precise, as much may depend on your answers."

"S'nore, that may be a trifle farther than it is from the church to the top of the stairs that lead to Ana Capri."

"Cospetto!—Thou wilt earn thy ducat speedily, at this rate!   Tell us, at once, in miles; was the lugger one, two, six, or twenty miles from your island, at the time thou speak'st of?"

"Eccellenza, you bid me speak of the *time*, in the second place; after I had told you of the *where*, in the first place. I wish to do whatever will give you pleasure, S'nore."

"Neighbour Vito Viti," put in the vice-governatore, "it may be well to remember that this matter is not to be recorded, as you would put on file the confessions of a thief; it may be better to let the honest boatman tell his story in his own way."

"Ay, now the veechy has set to work, I hope we shall get the worth of our ducat," observed Cuffe, in English.

"S'nori," rejoined Raoul, "it shall be just as your eccellenzi say.   The lugger you speak of was off the island, last evening, steering towards Ischia; which place she must have reached, in the course of the night, as there was a good land-wind, from the twenty-third to the fifth hour."

"This agrees with our account, as to the time and place," said Griffin; "but not at all, as to the direction the corsair was steering.   We hear, she was rather rounding the southern cape, for the Gulf of Salerno."

Raoul started, and gave thanks, mentally, that he had come on board, as this statement showed that his enemies had received only too accurate information of his recent movements.   He had hopes, however, of being able, yet, to change their intentions, and to put them on a wrong scent.

"S'nori," he said, "I should like to know who it is that mistakes south-east for north-west.   None of our pilots or boatmen, I should think, could ever make so great a blunder. S'nore, you are an officer, and understand such things; and I will just ask you, if Ischia does not lie north-west of Capri?"

"Of that fact, there can be no manner of doubt," returned Griffin; "it is equally true, that the Gulf of Salerno lies south-east of both—"

"There, now!" interrupted Raoul, with a well-acted assumption of vulgar triumph, "I knew, your eccellenza, when you came to look into it, would see the folly of saying that a vessel, which was standing from Capri towards Ischia, was going on any other course than north-west!"

"But this is not the question, amico. We all understand the bearings of these islands, which are the bearings of the whole coast, down here-away; but the question is, which way the lugger was steering?"

"I thought I had said, eccellenza, that she was heading across towards Ischia," answered Raoul, with an air of obtuse innocence.

"If you do, you give an account exactly different from that which has been sent to the admiral, by the good bishop of your own island. May I never eat another of his own quails, if I think *he* would deceive us; and it is not easy to suppose, a man like him, does not know north from south."

Raoul inwardly muttered a malediction on all priests; a class of men, which, rightly enough, he believed to be united in their hostility to France. But, it would not do to express this, in his assumed character; and he affected to listen, as one of his class ought to give ear, to a fact that came from his spiritual father.

"North from south, eccellenza!—Monsignore knows a great deal more than that, if the truth were said; though, I suppose, these noble signori are acquainted with the right reverend father's great infirmity?"

"Not we—none of us, I fancy, ever had the honour to be in his company. Surely, fellow, your bishop is a man of truth?"

"Truth!—Yes, eccellenza, so true is he, that if he were to tell me that the thing I saw myself, had not, and could not happen, I should rather believe Monsignore, than believe my own eyes. Still, signori, eyes are *something;* and as the right reverend father has *none,* or, what are as bad as none, for any use they can be in looking at a vessel half-a-mile off, he may not always see what he thinks he sees. When Monsignore tells us that so and so is Gospel, we all believe it; for we know the time has been when he *could* read; but we never think of going to his door to ask which way a ship is steering, having the use of our own senses."

"Can this fellow tell us the truth, Griffin?" asked Cuffe, a good deal mystified by Raoul's artifice, and his assumed simplicity. "If so, we shall be going exactly on the wrong scent, by hauling round Campanella, and running into the Gulf of Salerno. The French hold Gaeta, yet, and it is quite likely that Master Yvard may wish to keep a friendly port open under his lee!"

"You forget, Captain Cuffe, that his lordship has sent a light cruiser, already, up that way; and le Feu-Follet would hardly dare to show herself near one of our regular fellows—"

"Umph!—I don't know that, Mr. Griffin;—I don't exactly know that. The Proserpine is a 'regular fellow,' after a fashion, at least; and the Few-Folly has dared to show herself to *her*. Jack-o'-Lantern!—D——n-me, Griffin, but I think she is well named, now. I'd rather chase a jack-o'-lantern, in the Island of Sicily, than be hunting after such a chap;—first, he's here; then, he's there; and, presently, he's nowhere. As for the sloop, she's gone south, at my suggestion, to look into the bays along the Calabrian coast. I told Nelson I wanted another ship; for, just so certain as this Rule—Raw-owl—what the d——l do you call the pirate, Griffin?—"

"Raoul, Captain Cuffe; Raoul Yvard is his name. 'Tis thoroughly French.—Raoul, means Rodolph."

"Well, I told Nelson, if this lad should get to dodging round one of the islands, we might as well set about playing puss in the corner,' by the week, as to think of driving him off the land, for a fair chase. He works his boat like a stage-coach, turning in to an inn-yard!"

"I wonder my lord did not think of this, and give us a sloop or two, to help us."

"Catch Nel. at that!—He might send one Englishman to look after two Frenchmen; but he'd never dream of sending two Englishmen to look after one Frenchman."

"But this is not a fighting matter, sir; only a chase—and one Frenchman will run faster than two Englishmen any day of the week."

"Sa-c-r-r-r-e," muttered Raoul, in a tone that he endeavoured to suppress, and which was inaudible, to all ears, but those of Andrea Barrofaldi; the vice-governatore happening to stand nearer his person, just at that moment, than any other of the party.

"Very true," answered Cuffe; "but so it is. We are sent alone; and if this Few-Folly get in between Ischia and Procida, it will be easier to unearth a fox, than to drive her out, single-handed. As for any more boat-service against her, I suppose, you 've all had enough of *that?*"

"Why, sir, I rather think the people would be shy," answered Griffin, with a little hesitation of manner, and yet with the directness and simplicity of a truly brave man. "We must let them get over the last brush, before they are depended on much, for any new set-to, of that sort."

"*Bon!*" muttered Raoul, quite unconscious he was overheard.

"Nevertheless, we **must catch** this fellow if we wear out our shoes, in the chase."

All this time Andrea Barrofaldi and Vito Viti were profoundly ignorant of what was passing between the two officers, though Raoul listened eagerly, and so well understood every syllable they uttered. Until this moment, the vice-governatore had been rather indifferent and inattentive, as to what occurred; but the two exclamations of Raoul, awakened a vague distrust in his mind, which, while it had no direct object, was certainly pregnant with serious consequences to the Frenchman himself. Deep mortification at the manner in which they had been duped by this celebrated privateersman with a desire to absent themselves from the island, until the edge was a little taken off the ridicule they both felt they merited, blended with certain longings to redeem their characters, by assisting in capturing the corsair, were the reasons why these two worthies, the deputy-governor and the podestà were now on board the Proserpine. Cuffe had offered them cots in his cabin, and seats at his table, in a moment of confidence; and the offer was gladly accepted. Andrea had not been on board the ship a day, however, before he became thoroughly convinced of his utter uselessness; a circumstance that added materially to the awkwardness of his situation. Like all well-meaning and simple-minded men,

20 *

he had a strong wish to be doing; and day and night he ruminated on the means, by himself, or discussed them in private dialogues with his friend, the podestà. Vito Viti frankly admonished him to put his faith in heaven; affirm ing that something worth while, would yet turn up, in the cruise, to render the enterprise memorable; it being a habit, with the magistrate, to say an ave or two, on all trying occasions, and then trust to God.

"You never knew a miracle, vice-governatore," said Vito Viti, one day, when they were discussing the matter by themselves; "you never knew a miracle come to pass, that another was not close on its heels; the first being a mere preparation for the last, and the last always proving to be the most remarkable. Now, when Anina Gotti fell off the cliffs, it was a miracle she didn't break her neck, but, when she rolled over into the sea, it was a much greater she wasn't drowned!"

"It is better to leave these things to the church, neighbour Vito," was the vice-governatore's answer; "nor do I see that there has been any miracle in the affair, to start with."

"How!—Do you not call it a miracle, Signor Andrea, that two such men as you and I, should be deceived, as we were, beyond all doubt, by this knave of a French corsair? —I look upon it as so great a miracle, myself, that it ought to follow, instead of going before its companion."

To this Andrea made an answer suitable to his greater information, and the discourse took its usual direction, towards the means of doing something to relieve the two functionaries from the stigma, that they mutually felt now rested on their sagacity; and that, too, as this sagacity might be considered conjointly or individually.

It was probably owing to this fever of the mind, that the vice-governatore, a man usually so simple and confiding, was now so suspicious and keen-sighted. The presence of Carlo Giuntotardi and Ghita had, at first, struck him as a little out of the common way; and, though he could not distinguish their faces by the light of the moon, and at the distance at which they were placed in the yawl, he fancied, from the first, that his old acquaintances were in the boat the ship was towing. Now Andrea Barrofaldi, certainly, and never, before that day, connected Ghita, or her uncle, in any manner with Raoul Yvard; but, it was beyond dispute, that the mysterious manner in which they disappeared from the island, had excited some remarks; and, in his present state of mind, it was not an extraordinary circumstance that he had some distant and vague glimmerings of the truth. But for Raoul's indiscreet exclamations, however, nothing probably would have come of these indistinct fancies; and we are to refer all that followed to those unguarded outbreakings of the Frenchman's humour, rather than to any very clear process of ratiocination on the part of the vice-governatore.

Just as Cuffe made the declaration last recorded, Andrea stepped up to the spot where he and Griffin were conversing apart, and whispered a few words in the ear of the latter.

"The d——l!" exclaimed the lieutenant, in English. "If what the vice-governatore tells me, be true, Captain Cuffe, the work is half done to our hands!"

"Ay, the veechy is a good fellow, at the bottom, Griffin though he 'll never burn the bay of Naples. What has he to say, now?"

Griffin led his captain a little aside, and conferred a moment with him, alone. Orders were then passed to the officer of the deck, when Cuffe and his companion went below, like men in a hurry.

CHAPTER XVI.

"What countryman, I pray?"
"Of Mantua."
"Of Mantua, sir?— marry, God forbid!
And come to Padua, careless of your life?"
Taming of the Shrew.

DURING the momentous five minutes occupied in these private movements, Raoul affected to be gaping about in vulgar astonishment, examining the guns, rigging, ornaments of the quarter-deck, &c.; though, in truth, nothing that passed among those near him, escaped his vigilant attention. He was uneasy at the signs of the times, and now regretted his own temerity; but still he thought his incognito must be impenetrable. Like most persons, who fancy they speak a foreign language well, he was ignorant, too, in how many little things he betrayed himself; the Englishman, cæteris paribus, usually pronouncing the Italian better than the Frenchman, on account of the greater affinity between his native language and that of Italy, in what relates to emphasis and sounds. Such was the state of mind of our hero, then, as he got an intimation that the captain of the ship wished to see him below. Raoul observed, as he descended the ladder, to comply with what sounded very much like an order, that he was followed by the two Elban functionaries.

The cabin-lamp was trimmed, and the privateersman found himself under a strong light, as soon as he had crossed the threshold of the apartment. Cuffe and Griffin were standing near the table, where the vice-governatore and the podestâ took their stations, also; giving the whole arrangement a most uncomfortable air of investigation and 'ustice. For an instant, Raoul wished that it was a portion of the Holy Inquisition, rather than the tribunal before which he now found himself so unexpectedly arraigned.

"You must be cool," said Griffin, as the other moved slowly up to the table, maintaining the outward signs of steadiness, but cursing, in his heart, the severe ordeal which he felt he was undergoing; "do me the favour to put this silk handkerchief about your neck."

"S'nore, your eccellenza is pleased to joke; we men of Capri think little of the nights, at this season of the year—still, as it seems to be your wish, I will honour myself so much."

In that age, a black silk kerchief was the certain mark of a military man. The old-fashioned stock had gone out, with all but old-fashioned people, and the new-fashioned substitute did not make its appearance until many years later; the present usage, indeed, having come in from an imitation of the military mania which pervaded Christendom at the close of the last general war. Black around the neck, properly relieved by the white of the linen, was then deemed particularly military; and even in the ordinary dress, such a peculiarity was as certain a sign, as the cockade, that the wearer bore arms. Raoul knew this, and he felt he was aiding in unmasking himself, by complying; but he thought there might be greater danger, should he refuse to assume the kerchief.

"Your eccellenza is making a prince, of a very humble boatman," he said, when his neck was fairly enveloped; "and my wife will think some great general is coming, when I enter the door."

"To help the delusion, friend, wear this, also," continued Griffin, throwing the other one of his own undress uniform coats, his stature and that of Raoul being very nearly the same.

The true state of the case was now getting to be somewhat unequivocal; nevertheless, as steadiness and compliance were his only hopes, Raoul did as desired, and stood

with all his upper man decorated in an English naval undress uniform, while the nether remained à la lazzarone.

"What say you, now, vice-governatore," resumed Griffin,
"here are lights, and the dress?"

"I say that this gentleman has done me the honour of
several visits, in my poor residence, at Porto Ferrajo,"
returned Andrea; "and that never has he been more welcome, than he is at this moment. Signor Smees, you are a
great lover of masquerades, and make a carnival of the
whole year. I trust, your distinguished countryman, Sir
Cicero, will have it in his power to convince these brave
Inglese, that all is done in pure pleasantry, and without a
crime."

"Messieurs," said Raoul, stripping himself of his bor-
rowed plumes, "it is too late to feign, any longer. If I ar
Raoul Yvard, as you say, I am certainly *not* le Feu-Follet"

"Of course, you are aware, Monsieur," observed Griffin,
in French, "that you are a prisoner to His Britannic Majesty?"

"Sa Majesté Britannique has not made a conquest equal
to his success at the Nile," returned Raoul, ironically;
"but he has me in his hands. It is not the first time that I
have had the honour to be a prisoner of war, and that, too,
in one of his own ships."

"You are not to suppose that such will be your situation,
now, Monsieur Yvard. We arrest you in a totally different
character."

"Not as a friend, I trust, Monsieur; for, I protest, I have
not the smallest claim to the character; as witness a short
interview off Porto Ferrajo, and an interesting incident at
the mouth of the Golo."

"Your taunts may be spared, sir; fortune favoured you,
then, we allow; but, now, we arrest you as a spy."

"Espion!" repeated Raoul, starting; "that is an office
I never contemplated, Monsieur, on coming on board your
ship. You will do me the justice to acknowledge, that it
was only at your own invitation, that I came on deck.
'T would be an infamy to pretend differently!"

"We will endure the infamy of our acts, Monsieur Yvard.
No one accuses you of having come on board the Proserpine
as a spy; but, when an enemy is found rowing about our

fleet, which is anchored in a hostile bay, and this in a disguise like yours, it must be a very scrupulous conscience, that hesitates to pronounce him a spy, and liable to the punishment of one."

This was so true, that the unfortunate young man now felt the exceeding delicacy of his situation. In coming into the bay, he had certainly been led by no other intention than to find Ghita; and yet he could not but confess, to himself, that he should not have hesitated about profiting, in his public character, by any information incidentally obtained. He had subjected himself to the severest penalties of military law, by yielding to his passion for Ghita; and he could not discover a single available excuse, to plead in mitigation.

"What does the poor devil say, Griffin," asked Cuffe, who felt regret that so brave an enemy should be reduced to so desperate a strait, notwithstanding his determined hostility to all Frenchmen; "do not bear too hard upon him, at the first go off. Has he any excuse for his disguise?"

"The usual apology, no doubt, sir—a desire to serve his one and undivided republic! If we should believe all such chaps tell us, Captain Cuffe, we might go home, and send deputies to the National Convention; if, indeed, they would do us the favour to admit them to seats."

"Gentlemen," said Raoul, in English, "there is no longer any occasion for an interpreter between us; I speak your language sufficiently well to make myself understood."

"I am sorry for your situation, Mr. Yvard," said Cuffe, "and wish, with all my heart, you had fallen into our hand in open battle, instead of in this irregular way."

"In which case, Monsieur le Capitaine, le Feu-Follet would have been in your power, also!" returned Raoul, smiling ironically; "but, messieurs, words are idle, now; I am your prisoner, and must take my chance with you. There is no necessity, however, for causing others to suffer for my indiscretion. I shall esteem it a favour, messieurs, if you will let the good people, in the boat alongside, pull ashore, without molestation. It is getting late, and we must now, be nearly, or quite abeam of the place where they wish to land; which is the marina grande of Sorrento."

"Do you wish us to understand that your companions are not French, Monsieur Yvard?"

"Oui, Monsieur le Capitaine; there is not a Frenchman among them, I give you my parole d'honneur."

"Of that fact, it may be well to satisfy ourselves by an examination, Captain Cuffe," put in Griffin, drily.

"I have sent up to beg Mr. Winchester would get these people on board—"

"There is a young woman, in the boat, who is unaccustomed to entering ships," interrupted Raoul, hastily, "and I implore your tenderness, in her behalf. Let the men come on board, if you think it necessary; but the signorina can never climb this frigate's sides!"

"We will see to that; more especially, Monsieur Yvard, as you appear to be so much interested in the lady's comfort. At present, it will be my duty to put you under a sentry's charge; and that it may be done in a way the least offensive to yourself, your prison, for the night at least, shall be this cabin. Mr. Griffin, give orders to the marine officer, accordingly."

In a few minutes, a soldier was introduced into the forward cabin, and Raoul was regularly placed under his charge. Not till then did the officers return to the quarter-deck. All this time, Ithuel, and his companions in the yawl, were left to their own reflections, which were anything but agreeable. Matters had been conducted so quietly, in-board, however, that they possessed no clue to what had actually occurred; though Ghita, in particular, was full of forebodings and apprehensions. The frigate had towed them along at a rate, which, as Raoul had said, had brought them quite abreast of their landing, and within a league of it; and yet she showed no signs of an intention to abate her speed, nor did any one appear at the gangway, to speak to them. At length a hoarse call was heard on deck, and the ship began to shorten sail. Her fore-course was hauled up, and the spanker was brailed; then the royals were clewed up, and furled; the top-gallant-sails followed; and presently the Proserpine was reduced to her three topsails and jib. All this, finished just as Cuffe reappeared on deck, was done by the watch, and in about five minutes. As soon as sail was thus taken in, the helm was put to port, the ship came up to the wind, on the starboard tack, and the main-topsail was laid to the mast, bringing the yawl under her lee, and close

alongside of the ship. This manœuvre was no sooner executed, than a seaman ran lightly down the vessel's side, and
entered the yawl. After examining forward and aft, he
called out, "all right, sir," and shoved the boat off to a
little distance from the frigate. The yard and stay-tackles
fell, at the next instant, were overhauled down, and hooked
by the man in the boat. The boatswain's mate, in the gangway, piped, "haul-taut," and the slack of the tackle was
pulled in; then followed a long, steady blow of the call,
piping, "sway-away," and the boat, with all in her, rose
from the water, and ascended as high as the hammock-
cloths in the waist, when the stay-tackles took the strain,
the yard-tackles "eased-off," and the boat was landed in the
waist of the ship, as gingerly as if it were made of glass,
and as steadily as if it had no more weight than a seaman's
hammock. Ghita uttered a faint scream, when she found
herself rising into the air, and then she hid her face, awaiting the result with dread. As for Carlo Giuntotardi, the
movement aroused him a little from his customary apathy,
and that was all; whereas, Ithuel bethought him seriously
of leaping into the water, and striking out for the land. He
could swim a league, he thought; but there was the certainty
of being followed by boats, and overtaken; a consideration
that effectually curbed his impatience. It is not easy to
describe the sensation with which this man found himself,
once more, standing on the deck of his old prison, with the
additional danger of being detected and treated as a deserter.
It may sound revolting, at the present day, to suppose a case
in which a foreigner was thrown by violence, into the military
service of a nation, and then was put in jeopardy of his life,
because he used a privilege of nature, to fly from such persecution, as soon as circumstances placed the means in his
power. The last age, however, witnessed many scenes of
similar wrongs; and, it is to be feared, in despite of all
the mawkish philanthropy, and unmeaning professions of
eternal peace, that it is now the fashion to array against the
experience of mankind, that the next age will present their
parallels, unless the good sense of this nation infuse into the
federal legislative bodies juster notions of policy, more extended views of their own duties, and more accurate opinions
of the conditions of the several communities of Christendom,

than has marked their laws and reasoning for the few past months. In a word, the subject of all these tribulations felt an intimate conviction, that his rights, legal and moral, would avail him but little, on the present occasion. Then a man never does wrong, even in defence of that which is inherently his due, without the secret consciousness that "evil may not be done, that good may come of it;" and Ithuel ad a certain inward monitor to remind him, that, much as e had in the way of justifiable complaint, he had carried the war into the enemy's country.

The boat had no sooner touched the deck, than its cargo was handed out by the boatswain, who, keeping no watch, had not yet turned in; and who was almost as important a functionary, on board the Proserpine, as was Vito Viti, in the town of Porto Ferrajo. He examined each individual, as he or she landed, as he called it; Ghita attracting so much of his attention, as completely to eclipse her companions. The soft air and manner of the girl appeared so winning, indeed, by the light of the moon, which now fell clear upon the decks, that all near her, including the officers, submitted to very much the same influence.

"So, so, Master Yvard," said Cuffe, in English, "if you do come into an enemy's camp, incog., it is in reasonably good company. That girl is Italian, Winchester; and she even seems modest!"

"Little Ghita!" exclaimed Vito Viti, "as I hope, one day, to lie in the bosom of Father Abraham! Belissima Ghita, what has brought thee here, and in such evil company?"

Ghita was in tears; but, uncertain how far Raoul was committed, she struggled for self-command, and did succeed in suppressing emotions that might, otherwise, have rendered his situation more dangerous. Drying her eyes, she curtsied to the vice-governatore and the podestà, and then answered the question.

"Signori," she said, "it is a relief to meet countrymen and old acquaintances, on board this strange ship; and I look to you for protection. I do not call it strange, or evil company, for an orphan niece to be on the water with her uncle, and one that has ever been a father to her."

"Ah—sure enough, vice-governatore, this is Carlo Giun-

.ctardi, the uncle; and the man who dwells so much with the saints, even on earth, that he seldom speaks to a sinner. But thou knowest, little Ghita, that one of thy watermen is no less a person than Raoul Yvard, the wickedest corsair that sails out of France, and the pest and persecution of the whole Italian coast? Did the church condescend to notice such an unbelieving republican, it would be to command all its faithful to unite in their prayers for his destruction."

"Raoul Yvard!" repeated Ghita, with sufficient astonishment in her manner to satisfy any reasonable amount of wonder, on the part of the other. "Are you certain, Signor Podestâ, of the truth of what you say?"

"As certain as the confession of the party, himself, can make us."

"Confession, Signore!"

"Si, bella Ghita confession—your boatman—your man of Capri—your lazzarone, confesses himself to be neither more nor less than the commander of that worker of iniquity, le Feu-Follet."

"Does le Feu-Follet do more than other cruisers of the enemy?"—but Ghita felt she was getting to be indiscreet, and she ceased.

"I do believe, Winchester," said Cuffe, "that this is the very girl, and yonder is the very old man, who came into Nelson's cabin, to-day, with something to say about the poor prince who was executed this afternoon!"

"What could such people have in common with the unfortunate Caraccioli!"

"Sure enough—yet, these are the people. The Queen of the Fleet — our Lady Admiraless, had it all to herself; and what passed between them, in Italian, I know no more than if it had been in Greek. She never told me, you may rest assured; and, from the look of her eye, I question a good deal if she ever told Nelson."

"I wish to heaven his lordship would cut adrift from his moorings alongside of that craft, Captain Cuffe. I do assure you, sir, the fleet begins to talk loudly on the subject;—was t any other man, there'd be the devil to pay about it—but, we can all stand a good deal from Nelson and Bronté."

"Well—well—let every man father his own children: you ought to be quiet, Winchester, for he asked very kindly about your hurt, to-day, and would have sent you aboard some knick-knack or other, for the stomach, but I told him you were all a-tanto again, and at duty. What between his head, and his arm, and his eye, he's got to be such a hulk, himself, that he thinks every wounded man a sort of a relation. I should not complain, however, if the small-pox could lay hold of that beauty."

"This has been a bad day's work, for England, depend n it, Captain Cuffe!"

"Well, if it has, St. Vincent, and the Nile, were *good* days' works; and we'll let one balance the other. Inquire of this young woman, Mr. Griffin, if I had not the pleasure of seeing her, to-day, on board the Foudroyant?"

The question was put, as desired, and Ghita quietly, but unhesitatingly, answered in the affirmative.

"Then ask her to explain how she happened to fall into the company of Raoul Yvard?"

"Signori," said Ghita, naturally, for she had nothing to conceal on this point, "we live on Monte Argentaro, where my uncle is the keeper of the Prince's towers. You know, we have much to fear from the barbarians along all that coast; and last season, when the peace with France kept the Inglesi at a distance—I know not how it is, signori, but they say, the barbarians are always hardest on the enemies of Inghilterra—but, the past season a boat from a rover had seized upon my uncle and myself, and were carrying us off into captivity, when a Frenchman, and his lugger, rescued us. From that time we became friends; and our friend has often stopped near our towers, to visit us. To-day, we found him in a boat, by the side of the English admiral's ship; and, as an old acquaintance, he undertook to bring us to the Sorrentine shore, where we are, at present, staying with my mother's sister."

This was told so naturally, as to carry with it the conviction of its truth; and, when Griffin had translated it, he did not fail to assure his superior that he would pledge himself for the accuracy of the statement.

"Ay, you young luffs, Griffin, are never backward with your vows *for* or *to* pretty girls," answered Cuffe. "The girl does seem honest, however; and, what is more extra-ordinary, for the company she is in, she seems modest, too

Tell her she shall not be harmed, though we cannot deprive ourselves of the pleasure of her company immediately. She shall have the larboard state-room in my cabin, until morning, where she and her uncle may live a great deal more comfortably than in one of their out-of-door Neapolitan rookeries. Monte Argentaro, ha!—That's a bluff just beyond the Roman coast, and it is famously besprinkled with towers—half a dozen of them, at least, within as many miles, and who knows but this Jack-o'-Lantern may be extinguished some fine morning, should we fail of laying our hands on it, now?"

"We can hardly fail of the last, Captain Cuffe, having her commander in our possession."

Orders were then given to dispose of the prisoners, leaving the boat on deck. Raoul was sent below, and put in a canvass state-room, the arms having been removed, even to the razors, and a sentinel placed at the door. Escape from such a situation was impossible; and as for self-violence, when *that* point was considered, Cuffe had coolly remarked —"Poor devil; hanged he must be, and if he should be his own executioner, it will save us the discomfort of having a scene on board. I suppose Nelson will order him to our fore-yard-arm, as a jewel-block. I don't see, why he cannot use a Neapolitan frigate, for this job, too; they are good for nothing else."

"I rather think, Captain Cuffe, he will swing on board his own lugger, should we succeed in catching her," answered the lieutenant.

"By George, you're right, Griffin; and that's another inducement for looking out sharp for the Few-Folly. How much better it would have been, had we burnt them all, in a bunch, off the Golo!"

Then followed the arrangement by which the prisoner was put into the gun-room, as mentioned. Ghita and her uncle were shown into the empty cabin state-room, and mattresses were provided on which they might repose. Then the captain and his two guests retired to the after-cabin, whither Griffin was invited to accompany them. Here the captain recollected that there had been a fourth individual in the boat, and he sent an order on deck for him to come down for examination. Ithuel observing the atten tion of the officers occupied by Ghita and her uncle, had stolen back towards his own yawl, of which he had taken possession, stretching himself out at length, with the apparent design to sleep, but, in reality, to keep himself " out of mind," by remaining " out of sight ;" reserving, in petto, an intention to jump overboard, should the ship go near enough to the land to give him a chance for his life, after the moon set. In this situation he was found, aroused from his lair, and led into the cabin.

It has been mentioned that Ithuel would not consent to trust himself near the Proserpine, without disguising his person. Raoul being well provided with all the materials for a masquerade, this had been effected by putting a black curling wig over his own lank, sandy hair, colouring his whiskers and eye-brows, and trusting the remainder to the transformation which might be produced by the dress, or rather undress, of a Neapolitan waterman. The greatest obstacle to this arrangement had been a certain queue, which Ithuel habitually wore in a cured eel-skin that he had brought with him from America, eight years before, and both of which, " queue and eel-skin," he cherished as relics of better days. Once a week this queue was unbound and combed, but all the remainder of its existence it continued in a solid mass quite two feet in length, being as hard, and about as thick as a rope an inch in diameter. Now, the queue had undergone its hebdomadal combing just an hour before Raoul announced his intention to proceed to Naples in the yawl, and it would have been innovating on the only thing that Ithuel treated with reverence, to undo the work until another week had completed its round. The queue, therefore, was disposed of, under the wig, in the best manner that its shape and solidity would allow.

Ithuel was left in the fore-cabin, and his presence was announced to Cuffe.

" It's no doubt some poor devil belonging to the Few-Folly's crew," observed the English captain, in a rather compassionate manner, " and we can hardly think of stringing *him* up, most probably for obeying an order. That would never do, Griffin ; so we'll just step out and overhaul his log, in French, and send him off to England to a prison-ship, by the first return vessel."

As this was said, the four in the after-cabin left it toge
ther, and stood before this new prisoner. Of course Ithuel
understood all that was said in English, while the very idea
of being catechised in French threw him into a cold sweat.
In this strait, the idea suddenly crossed his mind, that his
greatest security would be in feigning dumbness.

"Ecoutez, mon ami," commenced Griffin, in very respectable English-French, "you are to tell me nothing but
the truth, and it may be all the better for you. You belong
to the Feu-Follet, of course?"

Ithuel shook his head in strong disgust, and endeavoured
to make a sound that he intended to represent a dumb man
struggling to utter the word "Napoli."

"What is the fellow after, Griffin?" said Cuffe. "Can
it be he doesn't understand French! Try him a touch in
Italian, and let us see what he will say to that."

Griffin repeated very much what he had said before,
merely changing the language, and received the same gag-
ging sounds for an answer. The gentlemen looked at each
other, as much as to express their surprise. But, unluckily
for Ithuel's plan, he had brought with him from the granite
state, a certain propensity to pass all the modulations of his
voice through his nose; and the effort to make a suppressed
sound brought that member more than usually into requisi-
tion, thereby producing a certain disagreeable combination
that destroyed everything like music that commonly charac-
terizes the Italian words. Now, Andrea had been struck
with this peculiarity about the tones of the American's voice,
in the interview at Benedetta's wine-house; and the whole
connection between Raoul and this singular person being
associated in his mind, the truth flashed on him, as it might
be, at a glance. His previous success that night had em-
boldened the worthy vice-governatore, and, without any
remark, he walked steadily up to Ithuel, removed the wig,
and permitted the eel-skin queue to resume its natural position down the back of its owner.

"Ha! — What, veechy," exclaimed Cuffe, laughing —
'you unearth them like so many foxes, to-night. Now,
Griffin, hang me if I do not think I've seen that chap before! Isn't he the very man we found at the wheel of la
Voltigeuse, when we boarded her?"

"Lord bless me, Captain Cuffe — no sir. This fellow is as long as two of that chap—and yet I know the face, too— I wish you'd let me send for one of the young gentlemen, sir; they're worth all the rest of the ship at remembering faces."

The permission was given, and the cabin steward was sent on deck to desire Mr. Roller, one of the oldest midshipmen, and who was known to have the watch, to come below.

"Look at this fellow, Mr. Roller," said Griffin, as soon as the youngster had taken his place in the group, "and tell us if you can make anything of him?"

"It's the lazy-rony, sir, we hoisted in, a bit ago, when we struck the boat on deck."

"Ay, no doubt of that — but we think we have seen his face before; — can *you* make that out."

Roller now walked round the immovable subject of all these remarks: and he, too, began to think the singular-looking object was no stranger to him. As soon, however, as he got a sight of the queue, he struck Ithuel a smart slap on the shoulder, and exclaimed—

"You're welcome back, my lad; I hope you'll find your berth aloft, as much to your mind as it used to be. This is Bolt, Captain Cuffe, the fore-top-man, who ran from us when last in England, was caught and put in a guard-ship, from which they sent us word he stole a boat, and got off with two or three French prisoners, who happened to be there at the moment, on some inquiry or other. Don't you remember it all, Mr. Griffin—you may remember the fellow pretended to be an American."

Ithuel was now completely exposed, and he at once perceived that his wisest way was to submit. Cuffe's countenance darkened, for he regarded a deserter with a species of professional horror, and the impressed deserter to whose services England had no other right than that of might, with an additional degree of resentment, that was very fairly proportioned to the inward consciousness he felt that a great wrong was done in detaining the man at all. There is nothing extraordinary in these feelings; a very common resource, under such circumstances, being to imagine delinquencies that justify us to ourselves, by endeavouring to believe that the subject of any act of our oppression at least merits the infliction.

"Do you dare to deny what this young gentleman has just said, sirrah?" demanded the captain. "I now remember you, myself; you are Bolt, the fore-top-man, that ran at Plymouth."

"You'd 'a run, too, Captain Cuffe, had you been in my place, had the ship been at Jericho."

"Enough—no impudence, sir. Send for the master-at-arms, Mr. Griffin, and have the fellow ironed: to-morrow we'll look into the affair."

These orders were obeyed, and Ithuel was removed to the place where the master-at-arms usually reigns on board ship. Cuffe now gave the lieutenant his congé, and then withdrew to the inner-cabin, to prepare a despatch for the rear-admiral. He was near an hour writing a letter to his mind, but finally succeeded. Its purport was as follows. He reported the capture of Raoul, explaining the mode, and the circumstances under which that celebrated privateersman had fallen into his hands. He then asked for instructions as to the manner in which he was to dispose of his prisoner. Having communicated this important fact, he ventured some suggestions as to the probable vicinity of the lugger, and the hopes he entertained of being able to find out her precise situation, through the agency of Bolt, whose condition he also explained, hinting at the same time the expediency of bringing both delinquents to as speedy trials as possible, as the most certain manner of using their apprehensions in seizing le Feu-Follet. The letter concluded with an earnest request that another frigate, which was mentioned, her captain being junior to Cuffe, and a fast-sailing sloop that was lying off Naples, might be sent down to assist him in "heading off" the lugger, as he feared the latter was too swift to be overtaken by the Proserpine alone more especially in the light winds which prevailed.

When this letter was written, addressed and sealed, Cuffe went on deck, again. It was now nine o'clock, or two bells and Winchester had the quarter-deck nearly to himself. All was as tranquil and calm on the deck of that fine frigate, as a moonlight night, a drowsy watch, a light wind, and smooth water could render things, in a bay like that of Na

ples.   Gleamings of fire were occasionally seen over Vesuvius, but things in that direction looked misty and mysterious,
though Capri loomed up, dark and grand, a few miles to-
leeward, and Ischia was visible, a confused but distant pile
on the lee-bow.   An order from Cuffe, however, set everybody in motion.   Yard and stay-tackles were overhauled,
and hooked on, the boatswain's-mate piped the orders, and
the first-cutter was hoisted over the waist-cloths, and lowered into the water.   "Away, there, you first-cutters," had
been hoarsely called on the berth-deck, and the crew were
ready to enter the boat, by the time the latter was lowered.
The masts were stepped, Roller appeared, in a pee-jacket,
to guard against the night air, and Cuffe gave him his instructions.

"Set your sails, and stretch over under the north shore,
Mr. Roller," said the captain, who stood in the lee-gangway,
to give a last word.   "You will fetch in about Queen Joan's
Palace.   There, you had better take to your oars, and pull
up along the land.   Remember, sir, to join us by the first
ship that comes out; and, if none is sent, to come down with
the morning breeze, in the boat."

Roller gave the customary "ay, ay, sir;" the boat shoved
off; as soon as from under the lee of the ship, the luggs
were set, and half an hour later, the night had swallowed
up her form.   Cuffe remained an hour longer, walking the
deck with his first-lieutenant, and then, satisfied that the
night would prove propitious, he went below, leaving orders
to keep the ship lying-to, until morning.

As for Roller, he pulled alongside of the Foudroyant, just
as the bells of the fleet were striking eight, or at midnight.
Nelson was still up, writing in his cabin.   The despatch
was delivered, and then the secretary of the admiral, with
a clerk or two, were called from their berths, for nothing
lagged that this active-minded man had in charge.   Orders
were written, copied, signed, and sent to different ships, by
two o'clock, in order that the morning breeze might not be
lost; and then, and not till then, did the employés think of
best.

Roller left the flag-ship at two, having eaten a hearty supper in Nelson's own cabin, and repaired on board the Terpsichore, a smart little frigate of thirty-two guns, twelve-

pounders, with instructions to her captain to receive him. Two hours later, this ship, in company with another still smaller, the Ringdove, 18, left her anchorage, under a cloud of canvass, and stood down the bay, carrying studding-sails on both sides, with a light wind at north-west, heading to wards Capri.

CHAPTER XVII.

"Speak to the business, Master Secretary:
Why are we met in council?"
King Henry VIII.

WHEN the idlers of the Proserpine appeared on deck the following morning, the ship was about a league to-windward of Capri, having forged well over towards the north side of the bay, during the night, wore round, and got thus far back on the other tack. From the moment light returned, look-outs had been aloft with glasses, examining every nook and corner of the bay, in order to ascertain whether any signs of the lugger were to be seen, under its bold and picturesque shore. So great is the extent of this beautiful basin, so grand the natural objects which surround it, and so clear the atmosphere, that even the largest ships loom less than usual on its waters; and it would have been a very possible thing for le Feu-Follet to anchor near some of the landings, and lie there unnoticed for a week, by the fleet above, un-less tidings were carried to the latter by observers on the shore.

Cuffe was the last to come on deck, six bells, or seven o'clock, striking, as the occupants of the quarter-deck first lifted their hats to him. He glanced around him, and then turned towards Griffin, who was now officer of the watch.

"I see two ships coming down the bay, Mr. Griffin," he said—"no signals yet, I suppose, sir?"

"Certainly not, sir, or they would have been reported

We make out the frigate to be the Terpsichore, and the sloop, I know by her new royals, is the Ringdove. The first ship, Captain Cuffe, brags of being able to travel faster than anything within the Straits!"

"I 'll bet a month's pay the Few-Folly walks away from her, on a bow-line, ten knots to her nine. If she can do that with the Proserpine, she 'll at least do that with Mistress Terpsichore. There goes a signal from the frigate now, Mr. Griffin, though a conjuror could hardly read it, tailing directly on as it does. Well, quarter-master, what do you make it out to be?"

"It's the Terpsichore's number, sir; and the other ship has just made the Ringdove's."

"Show ours, and keep a sharp look-out; there 'll be something else to tell us presently."

In a few minutes, the Terpsichore expressed a wish to speak the Proserpine, when Cuffe filled his main-top-sail, and hauled close upon a wind. An hour later, the three ships passed within hail of each other, when both the junior commanders lowered their gigs and came on board the Proserpine to report. Roller followed in the first-cutter, which had been towed down by the Terpsichore.

The Terpsichore was commanded by Captain Sir Frederick Dashwood, a lively young baronet, who preferred the active life of a sailor, to indolence and six thousand a year on shore; and who had been rewarded for his enterprise by promotion and a fast frigate, at the early age of two-and-wenty. The Ringdove was under a master-commandant, of the name of Lyon, who was just sixty years old, having worked his way up to his present rank by dint of long and arduous services, owing his last commission and his command to the accident of having been a first-lieutenant at the battle of Cape St. Vincent. Both these gentlemen appeared simultaneously on the quarter-deck of the Proserpine, where they were duly received by the captain and all the assembled officers.

"Good morrow to you, Cuffe," said Dashwood, giving the other the tip of his fingers, as soon as the ceremonious part of the reception was over; and casting a glance, half-admiring, half-critical, at the appearance of things on deck —

' What has Nelson sent us down here about, this fine morn. ing, and — ha ! — how long have you had those brass orna- ments on your capstan ?

" They were only put there yesterday, Sir Frederick ; a little slush-money did it all."

" Has Nelson seen them ? I rather fancy not—they tell me he's as savage as an Arab about knick-knackery, now- a-days. What an awkward job that was yesterday after- noon, by the way, Cuffe !"

" It has been a bad business, and, as an old Agamemnon, I would give a year's rank that it never had taken place."

" A year's rank !—that's a great deal ; a year would set me back, hard aground alongside of old Lyon, here. I was a lieutenant less than three years since, and couldn't afford half a year. But all you old Agamemnons think as much of your little Nel. as if he were a pretty girl ; isn't it true, Lyon ?"

" I dare say it may be, Sir Frederick," answered Lyon ; " and if you had been the first-lieutenant of a two-decker, off Cape St. Vincent, on the 14th February, 1797, you would have thought as much of him, too. Here we were, only fifteen sail in all, — that is, of vessels of the line — with the wind at—"

" Oh, hang your battle, Lyon, I've heard all that, at least seventeen times !"

" Well, if ye haave, Sir Frederick," returned Lyon, who was a Scotchman, " it 'll be just once a year since ye war' born, leaving out the time ye war' in the nursery. But we've not come here to enlighten Captain Cuffe in these particulars, so much as in obedience to an order of the rear- admiral's — little Nel. as ye 'll be calling him, I suppose, Sir Frederick Dashwood ?"

" Nay, it 's you old Agamemnons, or old fellows, who gave him that name —"

" Ye 'll please to excuse me, sir," interrupted Lyon, a lit- tle dogmatically—" ye 've never heard me call him anything but my lord, since His Majesty, God bless him ! was gra- ciously pleased to elevate him to the peerage — nothing but ' my lord,' and the ' rear-admiral;' naval rank being entitled to its privileges even on the throne. Many a king has been a colonel, and I see no disparagement in one's being av

22

admiral. Won't ye be thinking, Captain Cuffe, that since my lord is made Duke of Bronté, he is entitled to be called ' Your Grace'—all the Scottish dukes are so designated, and I see no reason why the rear-admiral should not have his just dues, as well as the best of them."

" Let him alone for that," said Cuffe, laughing; " Nel. will look out for himself, as well as for the king. But, gentlemen, I suppose you have not come down here merely for a morning walk — have I any reports to hear ?"

" I beg your pardon, Captain Cuffe, but I was really forgetting my errand," answered Dashwood. " Here are your orders for you, 'and we are both directed to report to you. The lieutenant who brought the package aboard *me*, said there would be a spy to try, and a lugger to catch. Did they tell you anything of this matter, Lyon ?"

" No, Sir Frederick ; not being inquisitive, I hear but little of what is going on in the fleet. My orders are to report myself and ship to Captain Cuffe, for service, which I have the honour now to do."

" Well, gentlemen, here are further instructions for you. This is an order to hold a court, composed of Captain Richard Cuffe, of the Proserpine, president ; Captain Sir Frederick Dashwood, Bart., of the Terpsichore, &c. &c. ; and Lyon, Winchester, and Spriggs, your first-lieutenant, Sir Frederick, for the trials of Raoul Yvard, a French citizen, on the charge of being a spy, and Ithuel Bolt, seaman, &c., on the charge of being a deserter. Here is everything in rule, and there are your respective orders, gentlemen."

" Bless me, I'd no notion of this !" exclaimed Lyon, who was greatly averse to this part of an officer's duty. " I'd thought it altogither a trial of speed after a Frenchman, for which purpose, the rear-admiral, or my lord, or his grace, whichever it may be right to call him, had seen fit to bring three of his fastest ships together."

" I wish it was nothing but the last, Captain Lyon ; but we have the disagreeable duty of trying a spy and a deserter, before us. You will return to your ships, gentlemen, and follow us in to an anchorage. I intend to bring up, at a single anchor, under the shore at Capri, where we can lie during the calm, and get through with our courts. The cases will be clear, and not detain us long, and we can send

ook-outs up on the heights to examine the sea and the coast
outside. In the meantime, we must be busy lest we lose the
breeze. You will attend to the signal for the court."

At this order the two visiters got into their boats, and the
Proserpine again filled. The three vessels now made the
best of their way towards the point of destination, anchoring
off the town, or village, in the island of Capri, just as two
bells struck. Ten minutes later, the Proserpine fired a gun
and ran up the flag which denotes the sitting of a court-
martial.

Although it has not been deemed necessary to relate them,
the reader will understand that all the details required by
the law, had been observed, as regards these trials; the
promptitude of the proceedings being partly characteristic
of the decision of the admiral, but more in consequence of a
wish to use the charges against the delinquents, as a means
of seizing the true hero of our tale, the little Feu-Follet.
While a mistaken, not to say a mawkish philanthropy,
is unsettling so many of the ancient land-marks of society,
and, among other heresies, is preaching the doctrine that
" the object of punishment is the reformation of the criminal," it is a truth which all experience confirms that nothing
renders justice so terrible, and consequently so efficient, as
its promptitude and certainty. When all its requirements
are observed, the speediest exercise of its functions is the
most conducive to the protection of society, the real motive
for the existence of all human regulations of this nature;
and it is a great merit of the much-abused English ordi-
nances, that the laws are rarely made stalking-horses for the
benefit of the murderer or the forger; but, that once fairly
tried and convicted, the expiation of their crimes awaits the
offenders with a certainty and energy that leave the impression on the community that punishments were intended to
produce. That this people has done well in liberating itself
from many of their inherited usages and laws, is as certain
as that one age has interests different from another; one set
of circumstances, governing principles at variance with those
which preceded them; but, it would be well, also, to remember, that, while moral changes are as necessary as physical
exercise, there are truths that are eternal, and rules of right

and prudence, which can never be departed from with im punity.

When the members of the court mentioned, assembled in the cabin of the Proserpine, it was with all the forms and exterior observances that were necessary to command respect. The officers were in full dress, the oaths were administered with solemnity, the table was arranged with taste, and an air of decent gravity reigned over all. Little time, however, was lost unnecessarily, and the officer to whom had been assigned the duty of prevôt-marshal, was directed to produce his prisoners.

Raoul Yvard and Ithuel Bolt were brought into the cabin at the same moment, though they came from different parts of the ship, and were allowed to hold no communication with each other. When both were present, they were arraigned, and the accusations were read to them. Raoul having admitted his knowledge of English, no interpreter was sworn, but the proceedings were had in the usual manner. As it was intended to try the Frenchman first, and Ithuel might be wanted as a witness, the latter was taken out of the cabin again, courts-martial never permitting one witness to hear what another has testified, although an ingenious substitute for ears has been adopted of late, by publishing in the journals, from day to day, whatever passes, when the length of the proceedings will admit of such a device.

"We will now swear the Signor Andrea Barrofaldi," commenced the Judge Advocate, as soon as the preliminaries were observed. "This is a Catholic bible, sir, and I will put the oaths in Italian, if you will have the goodness first to swear me in as an interpreter."

This was done, when the oath was duly administered to the vice-governatore. Then came a few questions as to the station, country, &c., of the witness, after which more material matter was inquired into.

"Signor Vice-Governatore, do you know the prisoner by sight?" demanded the Judge Advocate.

"Si; I have had the honour to receive him in my residence in the island of Elba."

"Under what name and circumstances was he known to you, Signore?"

" Eh—he called himself Sir Smees, a capitano in thé service of the English king."

" What vessel did he pretend to command ?"

" Ze Ving-y-Ving—a lugger, which I have since had reason to think is le Feu-Follet, a corsair under the French flag. Monsieur did me the favour to make two visits to Porto Ferrajo, in the character of Sir Smees."

" And you now know that this is Raoul Yvard, the French privateersman you have mentioned ?"

" Eh—*know?*—I know they *say* this is the Signor Yvard, and that ze Ving-y-Ving is le Feu-Follet."

" They *say*, will not do, Signor Barrofaldi. Can you no say this much of your own knowledge ?"

" Non, Signore."

The court was now cleared ; when it re-opened, Vito Viti was sent for, and properly sworn, his attention being particularly directed to the cross on the back of the book.

" Did you ever see the prisoner, before this occasion, Signor Viti," demanded the Judge Advocate, after the preliminary questions had been put.

" Signore, oftener than it is agreeable to remember. I do not think that two grave magistrates were ever more mystified, than were the vice-governatore and myself! Eh—h—h—. Signori, the wisest sometimes become like sucking children, when there passes a mist before the understanding."

" Relate the circumstances under which this occurred, to the court, Signor Podestâ."

" Why, Signori, the facts were just these. Andrea Barrofaldi, as you know, is the vice-governatore of Porto Ferrajo, and I am its unworthy podestâ. Of course, it is our duty to look into all matters affecting the public weal, and more especially into the business and occupations of strangers who come into our island. Well, it is now three weeks or more since a lugger, or felucca, was seen —"

" Which was it, a felucca, or a lugger ?" demanded the Judge Advocate, holding his pen ready to write the answer.

" Both, Signore ; a felucca and a lugger."

" Ah—there were two ; a felucca and a lugger."

" No, Signore—but this felucca was a lugger. Tommaso Tonti wished to mystify me about that, too ; but I have not been podestâ in a sea-port, so many years, for nothing. No,

22 *   17

Signori, there are all sorts of feluccas — ship-feluccas, brig-feluccas, and lugger-feluccas."

When this answer was translated, the members of the court smiled, while Raoul Yvard fairly laughed.

"Well, Signor Podestà," resumed the Judge Advocate — "the prisoner came into Porto Ferrajo in a lugger?"

"So it was said, Signore. I did not see him actually on board of her, but he professed to be the commander of a certain vessel, in the service of the King of Inghilterra, called ze Ving-y-Ving, and said that his own name was Smees—si—il capitano, or Sir Smees."

"Professed?—Do you not know that this lugger was the notorious French privateer, le Feu-Follet?"

I know they say so, now, Signori; but the vice-governatore and I supposed her to be ze Ving-y-Ving."

"And do you not know that the prisoner is actually Raoul Yvard; of your own knowledge, I mean?"

"Corpo di Bacco!—How should I know any such thing, Signor Guideca-Avvocato," exclaimed Vito Viti, who literally translated what he understood to be the title of his interrogator, thereby converting him into a sort of ship-felucca — "how should I know any such thing! I do not keep company with corsairs, except when they come upon our island and call themselves 'Sir Smees.'"

The Judge Advocate and the members of the court looked gravely at each other. No one in the least doubted that the prisoner was Raoul Yvard, but it was necessary legally to prove it, before he could be condemned. Cuffe was now asked if the prisoner had not confessed his own identity, but no one could say he had done so in terms, although much of his conversation would seem to imply as much. In a word, justice was like to be in what is by no means an unusual dilemma for that upright functionary; viz.—unable to show a fact that no one doubted. At length Cuffe recollected Ghita and Ithuel, and he wrote their names on a piece of paper, and passed them down the table to the Judge Advocate. The latter nodded his head, as much as to say he understood the president's meaning; and then he told the prisoner he might cross-examine the witness, if he saw fit.

Raoul fully understood his situation. Although he cer

tainly had not entered the Bay of Naples with any of the ordinary views of a spy, he was aware how far he had committed himself, and foresaw the readiness with which his enemies would destroy him, could they find the legal means of so doing. He also comprehended the dilemma in which his accusers were placed for the want of testimony, and, at once, resolved to turn the circumstance as much as possible to his advantage. Until that moment, the idea of denying his own identity had never crossed his mind; but perceiving what he fancied an opening for escape, it was but natural to avail himself of its protection. Turning, then, to the podestâ, he put his questions in English, that they might go fairly through the same process of interpretation as the rest of the examination.

"You say, Signor Podestâ," he commenced, "that you saw me in the town of Porto Ferrajo, and in the island of Elba?"

"Si—in which town I have the honour to be one of the authorities."

"You say I professed to command a vessel in the service of the King of England; a felucca, called ze Ving-and-Ving?"

"Si—ze Ving-y-Ving—the commander of that felucca."

"I understood you to say, Mr. Podestâ," put in Lyon, "that the craft was a lugger?"

"A felucca-lugger, Signor Capitano — nothing more nor less than that, on my honour."

"And all these honourable officers well know," observed Raoul, ironically, "that a felucca-lugger, and a lugger, such as le Feu-Follet is understood to be, are very different things. Now, Signore, you have never heard me say that I am a Frenchman?"

"Non—you have not been so weak as to confess that to one who hates the name of the Françese. Cospetto! — If all the Grand Duke's subjects detested his enemies as I do, he would be the most powerful prince in Italy!"

"No doubt, Signore; and, now, suffer me to inquire if you heard any other name for that felucca, than ze Ving-and-Ving. Did I ever call her le Feu-Follet?"

"Non — always ze Ving-y-Ving; never anything else; i it—"

"Your pardon, Signore; have the goodness to answer my questions. I called the felucca ze Ving-and-Ving; and I called myself le capitaine Smeet; is it not true?"

"Si—Ving-y-Ving and il capitano Smees—Sir Smees; a signore of an illustrious English family of that name, if I remember right."

Raoul smiled, for he was confident this notion proceeded principally from the self-illusion of the two Italians, themselves; the little he had said on the subject, having been drawn out more by their suggestions than by any design on his part. Still, he did not deem it prudent to contradict the podestà, who, as yet, had testified to nothing that could possibly criminate him.

"If a young man has the vanity to wish to be thought noble," answered Raoul, calmly, "it may prove his folly, but it does not prove him a spy. You did not hear me confess myself a Frenchman, you say: now did you not hear me say I was born in Guernsey?"

"Si—the Signore did say that the family of Smees came from that island—as the vice-governatore calls it, though I acknowledge I never heard of such an island. There are Sicilia, Sardegna, Elba, Caprea, Ischia, Irlanda, Inghilterra, Scozia, Malta, Capraya, Pianosa, Gorgona, and America, with several more in the east; but I never heard of such an island as Guernsey. Si, Signore; we are humble people, and I hope modest people in the island of Elba, but we do know something of the rest of the world, notwithstanding. If you wish to hear these matters touched on ingeniously, however, you will do well to call in the vice-governatore, for half an hour, and invite him to open his stores of knowledge. San Antonio!—I doubt if Italy has his equal—at islands, in particular."

"Good," continued Raoul; "and now tell these officers, Signore Podestà, if you can say, on your oath, that I had anything to do with that felucca, ze Ving-and-Ving, at all."

"I cannot, Signore, except from your own words. You were dressed like one of these officers, here, in an English uniform, and said you commanded ze Ving-y-Ving. While speaking of islands, Signori, I forgot Palmavola ana Ponza, both of which we passed in this ship, on our voyage from Elba."

' Good — it is always well to be particular under oath. Now, Signor Podestà, the result of all your evidence is, that you do not know that the felucca you mention was lo Feu-Follet, that I am a Frenchman even, much less that I am Raoul Yvard, and that I told you I was from Guernsey, and that my name was Jaques Smeet — is it not so ?"

" Si — you did say your name was Giac Smees, and you did not say you were Raoul Yvard. But, Signore, I saw you firing your cannon at the boats of this frigate, with French colours flying, and that is some signs of an enemy, as we understand these matters, in Porto Ferrajo."

Raoul felt that this was a direct blow ; still, it wanted the connecting link to make it testimony.

" But you did not see *me* doing this ? — You mean you saw ze Ving-and-Ving in a combat with the frigate's boats."

" Si—that was it—but you told me you were commander of ze Ving-y-Ving."

" Let us understand you," put in the Judge Advocate — " is it the intention of the prisoner to deny his being a Frenchman and an enemy ?"

" It is my intention, sir, to deny everything that is not proved."

" But your accent—your English—nay, your appearance, show that you are a Frenchman."

" Your pardon, sir. There are many nations that speak French, which are not French, to-day. All along the north frontier of France, is French spoken by foreigners—Savoy, and Geneva, and Vaud — also, the English have French subjects in the Canadas, besides Guernsey and Jersey. You will not hang a man because his accent is not from London ?"

" We shall do you justice, prisoner," observed Cuffe, " and you shall have the benefit of every doubt that makes in your favour. Still, it may be well to inform you that the impression of your being a Frenchman and Raoul Yvard, is very strong ; and if you can show the contrary, you would do well to prove it, by direct testimony."

" How will this honourable court expect that to be done ? I was taken in a boat, last night, and am tried, this morning, at a notice as short as that which was given to Caracrioli. Give me time to send for witnesses, and I will prove who and what I am."

This was said coolly, and with the air of a man assured of his own innocence, and it produced a slight effect on his judges; for an appeal to the unvarying principles of right, seldom falls unheeded on the ear. Nevertheless, there could be no doubt in the minds of the officers of the Proserpine, in particular, either as to the character of the lugger, or as to that of the prisoner; and men, under such circumstances, were not likely to allow an enemy who had done them so much injury to escape. The appeal only rendered them more cautious, and more determined to protect themselves against any charge of unfair proceedings.

"Have you any further questions to put to the witness, prisoner?" inquired the president of the court.

"None, at present, sir — we will go on, if you please, gentlemen."

"Call Ithuel Bolt," said the Judge Advocate, reading the new witness's name from a list before him.

Raoul started, for the idea of the American's being brought forward in this capacity, had never occurred to him. In a minute Ithuel appeared, was sworn, and took his place at the foot of the table.

"Your name is Ithuel Bolt?" observed the Judge Advocate, holding his pen in readiness to record the answer.

"So they say aboard here," answered the witness, coolly — "though, for my part, I 've no answer to give to such a question."

"Do you deny your name, sir?"

"I deny nothing — want to say nothing, or to have anything to do with this trial, or this ship."

Raoul breathed easier; for, to own the truth, he had not much confidence in Ithuel's constancy, or disinterestedness; and he apprehended that he had been purchased, with the promise of a pardon for himself.

"You will remember that you are under oath, and may be punished for contumacy, on refusing to answer."

"I 've some gineral idees of law," answered Ithuel, passing his hand over his queue, to make sure it was right, "for we all do a little at that in Ameriky. I practised some myself, when a young man, though it was only afore a justice-peace. We used to hold that a witness needn't answer ag'in himself."

" Is it, then, on account of criminating yourself, that you answer thus vaguely ?"

" I decline answering that question," answered Ithuel, with an air of dignity.

" Witness have you any personal knowledge of the prisoner ?"

" I decline answering that question, too."

" Do you know anything of such a person as Raou, Yvard ?"

" What if I do ? — I 'm a native American, and have a right to form acquaintances, in foreign lands, if I see it 's to my interest, or it 's agreeable to my feelin's."

" Have you never served on board His Majesty's ships ?"

" What majesty ?—There 's no majesty in Ameriky, as I know, but the majesty of heaven."

" Remember that your answers are all recorded, and may tell against you, on some other occasion."

" Not lawfully ; a witness can't be made to give answers that tell ag'in himself."

" Certainly not *made* to do it ; still he may *do* it, of his own accord."

" Then it 's the duty of the court to put him on his guard. I 've heerd that, ag'in and ag'in, in Ameriky."

" Did you ever see a vessel called le Feu-Follet ?"

" How, in natur', is a mariner to tell all the vessels he may happen to see on the wide ocean !"

" Did you ever serve under the French flag ?"

" I decline entering at all into my private affairs. Being free, I 'm free to sarve where I please."

" It is useless to ask this witness any further questions, Cuffe quietly observed. " The man is well known in this ship, and his own trial will most probably take place as soon as this is ended."

The Judge Advocate assented, and Ithuel was permitted to withdraw, his contumacy being treated with the indifference that power is apt to exhibit towards weakness. Still there was no legal proof on which to convict the prisoner. No one doubted his guilt, and there were the strongest reasons, short of a downright certainty, for supposing that he commanded the lugger which had so recently fought the boats of the very ship in which the court was sitting ; but notwithstanding, supposition was not the evidence the laws required; and the recent execution of Caraccioli had made so much conversation, that few would condemn without seeing their justification before them. Things were really getting to be seriously awkward, and the court was again cleared for the purpose of consultation. In the private discourse that followed, Cuffe stated all that had occurred, the manner in which Raoul had been identified, and the probabilities — nay, moral certainties of the case. At the same time, he was forced to allow, that he possessed no direct evidence that the lugger he had chased was a Frenchman at all, and least of all le Feu-Follet. It is true, she had worn the French flag, but she had also worn the English, and the Proserpine had done the same thing. To be sure, the lugger had *fought* under the *drapeau tricolor*, which might be taken as a strong circumstance against her; but it was not absolutely conclusive, for the circumstances might possibly justify deception to the last moment; and he admitted that the frigate, herself, had *appeared* to fire at tne batteries, under the same ensign. The case was allowed to be embarrassing; and, while no one really doubted the identity of Raoul, those who were behind the curtains greatly feared they might be compelled to adjourn the trial for want of evidence, instead of making an immediate sentence the means of getting possession of the lugger, as had been hoped. When all these points had been sufficiently discussed, and Cuffe had let his brethren into his view of the real state of the case, he pointed out a course that he still trusted would prove effectual. After a few minutes of further deliberation on this information, the doors were opened. and the court resumed its public sitting, as before.

"Let a young woman who is known by the name of Ghita, be brought in, next," said the Judge Advocate, consulting his notes.

Raoul started, and a shade of deep concern passed over his face; but he soon recovered, and seemed unmoved. Ghita and her uncle had been taken from the cabin stateroom, and placed below, in order that the private consultations might be perfectly secret, and it was necessary to wait a few minutes, until she could be summoned. These past the door opened and the girl entered the room. She cast a glance of tender concern at Raoul ; but the novelty of her situation, and the awful character of an oath to one of her sensitive conscience and utter inexperience, soon drew her attention entirely to the scene more immediately before her. The Judge Advocate explained the nature of the oath she was required to take, and then he administered it. Had Ghita been taken less by surprise, or had she, in the least, foreseen the consequences, no human power could have induced her to submit to be sworn ; but, ignorant of all this, she submitted passively, kissing the cross with reverence, and even offering to kneel as she made the solemn protestation. All this was painful to the prisoner, who distinctly foresaw the consequences. Still, so profound was his reverence for Ghita's singleness of heart and mind, that he would not by look or gesture, in any manner endeavour to undermine that sacred love of truth, which he knew formed the very foundations of her character. She was accordingly sworn, without anything occurring to alarm her affections, or to apprise her of what might be the sad result of the act.

CHAPTER XVIII.

"Hic et ubique ? Then we 'll shift our ground :—
Come hither, gentlemen,
And lay your hands upon my sword :
Swear by my sword."

Hamlet.

"Your name is Ghita," commenced the Judge Advocate, examining his memoranda—" Ghita what ?"

"Ghita Caraccioli, Signore," answered the girl, in a voice so gentle and sweet, as to make a friend of every listener.

The name, however, was not heard, without producing a general start, and looks of surprise were exchanged among all in the room ; most of the officers of the ship who were not on duty being present as spectators.

23

"Caraccioli," repeated the Judge Advocate, with empha
sis. "That is a great name in Italy. Do you assume to
belong to the illustrious house which bears this appellation?"

"Signore, I assume to own nothing that is illustrious,
being merely an humble girl who lives with her uncle, in
the prince's towers, on Monte Argentaro."

"How happens it, then, that you bear the distinguished
name of Caraccioli, signorina?"

"I dare say, Mr. Medford," observed Cuffe, in English,
of course, "that the young woman doesn't know herself,
whence she got the name. These matters are managed
very loosely in Italy."

"Signore," resumed Ghita, earnestly, after waiting respectfully for the captain to get through, "I bear the name of my
father, as is usual with children; but, it is a name on which
a heavy disgrace has fallen, so lately as yesterday; *his* father
having been a sight for the thousands of Naples to gaze on,
as his aged body hung at the yard of one of your ships."

"And do you claim to be the grand-daughter of that un
fortunate admiral?"

"So I have been taught to consider myself; may his sou
rest in a peace that his foes would not grant to his body
That criminal, as you doubtless believe him, was my father'
father, though few knew it when he was honoured as *r*
prince and a high officer of the king's."

A deep silence followed; the singularity of the circum
stance, and the air of truth which pervaded the manner o
the girl, uniting to produce a profound sensation.

"The admiral had the reputation of being childless," ob
served Cuffe, in an under tone. "Doubtless this girl's fathe
has been the consequence of some irregular connection."

"If there has been a promise, or any words of recogni
tion uttered before witnesses," muttered Lyon, "accordin'
to the laws of Scotland, issue, and a few pairtenant expressions, will splice a couple as strongly as ye 'll be doing it in
England, before either of the archbishops."

"As this is Italy, it is not probable that the same law
rules here. Proceed, Mr. Judge Advocate."

"Well, Ghita Caraccioli—if that be your name—I wish
to know if you have any acquaintance with a certain Raoul
Yvard: a Frenchman, and the commander of a private

lugger-of-war, called le Feu-Follet?—Remember. you are sworn to tell the truth, the *whole* truth, and nothing but the truth."

Ghita's heart beat violently, and the colour came into her face with the impetuosity of sensitive alarm. She had no knowledge of courts, and the object of the inquiry was unknown to her. Then followed the triumph of innocence; the purity of her mind, and the quiet of her conscience reassuring her, by bringing the strong conviction that she had no reason to blush for any sentiment she might happen to entertain.

"Signore," she said, dropping her eyes to the floor, for the gaze of all the court was fastened on her face—"I *am* acquainted with Raoul Yvard, the person you mention; this is he, who sits between those two cannon. He *is* a Frenchman, and he *does* command the lugger called the Feu-Follet."

"I knew we should get it all by this witness!" exclaimed Cuffe, unable to suppress the relief he felt at obtaining the required testimony.

"You say that you know this, of your own knowledge," resumed the Judge Advocate—

"Messieurs," said Raoul, rising, "will you grant me leave to speak? This is a cruel scene; and, rather than endure it—rather than give this dear girl the cause for future pain, that I know her answers will bring, I ask that you permit her to retire, when I promise to admit all that you can possibly prove by her means."

A short consultation followed; then Ghita was told to withdraw. But the girl had taken the alarm, from the countenance of Raoul, although she did not understand what had passed in English; and she was reluctant to quit the place in ignorance.

"Have I said aught to injure thee, Raoul?" she anxiously asked—"I was sworn on the Word of God, and by the sacred cross—had I foreseen any harm to thee, the power of England would not have made me take so solemn an oath, and then I might have been silent."

"It matters not, dearest—the fact must come out, in some way or other, and, in due time, you shall know all. And now, Messieurs,"—the door closing on Ghita—"there need be no further concealment between us. I am Raoul Yvard—the person you take me for, and the person that some of you must well know me to be. I fought your boats, Monsieur Cuffe—avoided your *brulòt*, and led you a merry chase round Elba. I deceived the Signor Barrofaldi, and his friend the podestà, and all for the love of this beautiful and modest girl, who has just left the cabin; no other motive having carried me into Porto Ferrajo, or into this Bay of Naples, on he honour of a Frenchman."

"Umph!" muttered Lyon—"it must be admitted, Sir Frederick, that the prisoner appeals to a most eligible standard!"

On another occasion, national antipathy and national prejudice might have caused the rest of the court to smile at this sally; but there was an earnestness and sincerity in the manner and countenance of Raoul, which, if they did not command entire belief, at least, commanded respect. It was impossible to deride such a man; and long-cherished antipathies were rebuked by his spirited and manly declarations.

"There will be no further occasion for witnesses, Mr. Judge Advocate, if the prisoner be disposed to acknowledge the whole truth," observed Cuffe. "It is proper, however, Monsieur Yvard, to apprise you of the possible consequences. You are on trial for your life; the charge being that of coming on board an English ship in disguise, or rather, into the centre of an English fleet, you being an alien enemy, engaged in carrying on open warfare against His Majesty."

"I am a Frenchman, Monsieur, and I serve my country," answered Raoul, with dignity.

"Your right to serve your country, no one will dispute, but you must know it is against the laws of civilized warfare to act the part of a spy. You are now on your guard, and will decide for yourself. If you have anything to say, we will hear it."

"Messieurs, there is little more to be said," answered Raoul. "That I am *your* enemy, as I am of all those who seek the downfall of France, I do not deny. You know *who* I am, and *what* I am, and I have no excuses to make for being either. As brave Englishmen, you will know how to allow for the love a Frenchman bears his country. As for roming on board this ship, you cannot bring that as a charge against me, since it was at your own invitation I did it. The rights of hospitality are as sacred as they are general."

The members of the court exchanged significant glances with each other, and there was a pause of more than a minute. Then the Judge Advocate resumed his duties, by saying—

"I wish you to understand, prisoner, the precise legal effect of your admissions; then I wish them to be made formally and deliberately; else we must proceed to the examination of other witnesses. You are said to be Raoul Yvard an alien enemy, in arms against the king."

"Monsieur, this I have already admitted; it cannot honourably be denied."

"You are accused of coming on board His Majesty's ship Proserpine disguised, and of calling yourself a boatman of Capri, when you were Raoul Yvard, an alien enemy, bearing arms against the king."

"This is all true; but I was invited on board the ship, as I have just stated."

"You are furthermore accused of rowing in among the ships of His Majesty, now lying in the Bay of Naples, and which ships are under the orders of Rear-Admiral Lord Nelson, Duke of Bronté, in Sicily, you being in the same disguise, though an alien enemy, with the intent to make your observations as a spy, and, doubtless, to avail yourself of information thus obtained, to the injury of His Majesty's subjects, and to your own advantage, and that of the nation you serve."

"Monsieur, this is not so—*parole d'honneur*, I went into the bay in search of Ghita Caraccioli, who has my whole heart, and whom I would persuade to become my wife. Nothing else carried me into the bay; and I wore this dress, because I might otherwise have been known and arrested."

"This is an important fact, if you can prove it; for, though it might not technically acquit you, it would have its effect on the commander-in-chief, when he comes to decide on the sentence of this court."

Raoul hesitated. He did not doubt that Ghita, she whose testimony had just proved so serious a matter against him would testify that she *believed* such was alone his motive; and this, too, in a way, and with corroborative circum-

23 *

stances, that would carry weight with them, more particularly as she could testify that he had done the same thing
before, in the Island of Elba, and was even in the practice
of paying her flying visits at Monte Argentaro. Nevertheless, Raoul felt a strong reluctance to have Ghita again
brought before the court. With the jealous sensitiveness of
true love, he was averse to subjecting its object to the gaze
and comments of the rude of his own sex; then he knew his
power over the feelings of the girl, and had too much sensibility not to enter into all the considerations that might
influence a man on a point so delicate; and he could not
relish the idea of publicly laying bare feelings that he wished
to be as sacred to others, as they were to himself.

"Can you prove what you have just averred, Raoul
Yvard?" demanded the Judge Advocate.

"Monsieur—I fear it will not be in my power. There is
one—but—I much fear it will not be in my power—unless,
indeed, I am permitted to examine my companion; he who
has already been before you."

"You mean Ithuel Bolt, I presume. He has not yet been
regularly before us, but you can produce him, or any other
witness; the court reserving to itself the right to decide,
afterwards, on the merits of the testimony."

"Then, Monsieur, I could wish to have Etoo-ell here."

The necessary directions were given, and Ithuel soon
stood in the presence of his judges. The oath was tendered,
and Ithuel took it like a man who had done such things
before.

"Your name is Ithuel Bolt?" commenced the Judge Advocate.

"So they call me on board this ship—but if I am to be
a witness, let me swear freely; I don't wish to have words
put into my mouth, or idees chained to me with iron."

As this was said, Ithuel raised his arms, and exhibited
his hand-cuffs, which the master-at-arms had refused to
remove, and the officers of the court had overlooked. A
reproachful glance from Cuffe, and a whisper from Yelver
.on, disposed of the difficulty—Ithuel was released.

"Now I can answer more conscientiously," continued
the witness, grinning sardonically; "when iron is eating
into the flesh, a man is apt to swear to what he thinks will

be most agreeable to his masters. Go on 'squire, if you have anything to say."

'You appear to be an Englishman."

"Do I? Then I appear to be what I am not. I'm a native of the Granite state, in North America. My fathers went to that region, in times long gone by, to uphold their religious idees. The whole country, thereabouts, sets onaccountable store by their privileges."

"Do you know the prisoner, Ithuel Bolt, the person who is called Raoul Yvard ?"

Ithuel was a little at a loss exactly how to answer this question. Notwithstanding the high motive which had led his fathers into the wilderness, and his own peculiar estimate of his religious advantages, an oath had got to be a sort of convertible obligation with him, ever since the day he had his first connection with a custom-house. A man who had sworn to so many false invoices, was not likely to stick at a trifle in order to serve a friend ; still, by denying the acquaintance, he might bring discredit on himself, and thus put it out of his power to be of use to Raoul on some more material point. As between himself and the Frenchman, there existed a remarkable moral discrepancy ; for, while he who prided himself on his religious ancestry and pious education, had a singularly pliable conscience, Raoul, almost an Atheist in opinion, would have scorned a simple lie, when placed in a situation that touched his honour. In the way of warlike artifices, few men were more subtle, or loved to practise them oftener, that Raoul Yvard ; but the mask aside, or when he fell back on his own native dignity of mind, death itself could not have extorted an equivocation from him. On the other hand, Ithuel had an affection for a lie ; more especially if it served himself, or injured his enemy—finding a mode of reconciling all this to his spirituality, that is somewhat peculiar to fanaticism, as it begins to grow threadbare. On the present occasion, he was ready to say whatever he thought would most conform to his shipmate's wishes, and luckily he construed the expression of the other's countenance aright.

"I *do* know the prisoner, as you call him, 'squire," Ithuel answered, after the pause that was necessary to come to his conclusion—"I *do* know him *well ;* and a master-crittur he is, when he fairly gets into a current of your English trade. Had there been a Rule Yvard, on board each of the French. men, at the Nile, over here, in Egypt, Nelson would have found that his letter stood in need of some post-cripts, I guess."

"Confine your answers, witness, to the purport of the question," put in Cuffe, with dignity.

Ithuel stood too much in habitual awe of the captain of his old ship, to venture on an answer; but if looks could have done harm, that important functionary would not have escaped altogether uninjured. As he said nothing, the exa-mination proceeded.

"You know him to be Raoul Yvard, the commander of the French privateer lugger, le Feu-Follet?" continued the Judge Advocate, deeming it prudent to fortify his record of the prisoner's confession of identity, with a little collateral evidence.

"Why—I *some* think—" answered Ithuel, with a peculiar provincialism, that had a good deal of granite in it—"that is, I kind o' conclude—" catching an assent from Raoul's eye—"oh! yes—of *that*, there is n't the smallest mite of doubt in the world. He's the captain of the lugger, and a right down good one he is!"

"You were with him, in disguise, when he came into the Bay of Naples yesterday?"

"I in disguise, 'squire!—What have I got to disguise? 1 am an American of different callings, all of which I prac-tyse, as convenience demands; being a neutral, I've no need of disguises to go anywhere. I am never disguised, except when my jib is a little bowsed up; and that, you know, is a come-over that befals most seafaring men, at times."

"You need answer nothing concerning yourself, that will tend to criminate you. Do you know with what induce-ment, or on what business, Raoul Yvard came into the Bay of Naples yesterday?"

"To own to you the candid truth, 'squire, I do not," answered Ithuel, simply; for the nature of the tie which bound the young Frenchman so closely to Ghita, was a pro found mystery, in all that related to its more sacred feelings, to a being generally so obtuse on matters of pure sentiment.

"Captain Rule is a good deal given to prying about on the coast; and what particular eend he had in view, in this expedition, I cannot tell you. His a'r'n'ds inshore, I must own, be sometimes onaccountable!—Witness the island of Elby, gentlemen."

Ithuel indulged in a small laugh, as he made this allusion; for, in his own way, he had a humour in which he occasionally indulged, after a manner that belonged to the class of which he was a conspicuous member.

"Never mind what occurred at Elba. Prisoner, do you wish to question the witness?"

"Etuelle," asked Raoul, "do you not know that I love Ghita Caraccioli?"

"Why, Captain Rule, I know you *think* so, and *say* so—but I set down all these matters as somewhat various and onaccountable."

"Have I not often landed on the enemy's coast, solely to see her, and to be near her?"

By this time, Ithuel, who was a little puzzled at first to understand what it all meant, had got his cue, and no witness could have acquitted himself better than he did from that moment.

"That you have," he answered; "a hundred times, at least; and right in the teeth of my advice."

"Was not my sole object in coming into the Bay yesterday, to find Ghita, and Ghita only?"

"Just so. Of that, gentlemen, there can be no more question, than there is about Vesuvius standing up at the head of the Bay, smoking like a brick-kiln. That *was* Captain Rule's sole a'r'n'd."

"I just understood ye to say, witness," put in Lyon, "and that only a bit since, that ye did not know the prisoner's motive in coming into the Bay of Naples. Ye called his behaviour unaccountable."

"Very true, sir, and so it is to *me*. I know'd all along, that *love* was at the bottom of it; but *I* don't call love a *motive*, while I do call it *onaccountable*. That's the explanation on 't. Yes, I know'd it was *love* for Miss Gyty, but hen that's not a motive in law."

"Answer to the facts. The court will judge of the motive for itself. How do you know that love for the young
18

woman you mention, was Raoul Yvard's only object in coming into the Bay ?"

" One finds out such things by keeping company with a man. Captain Rule went first to look for the young woman up on the mountain yonder, where her aunt lives, and I went with him to talk English, if it got to be necessary ; and not finding Gyty at home, we got a boat and followed her over to Naples. Thus, you see, sir, that I have reason to know what craft he was in chase of the whole time."

As all this was strictly true, Ithuel related it naturally, and in a way to gain some credit.

" You say you accompanied Raoul Yvard, witness, in a visit to the aunt of the young woman, called Ghita Carac-cioli," observed Cuffe, in a careless way, that was intended to entrap Ithuel into an unwary answer—" where did you go from, when you set out on your journey ?"

" That would depend on the place one kept his reckoning from, and the time of starting. Now, *I* might say I started from Ameriky, which part of the world I left some years since ; or I might say from Nantes, the port in which we fitted for sea. As for Captain Rule, he would probably say Nantes."

" In what manner did you come from Nantes ?" continued Cuffe, without betraying resentment at an answer that might be deemed impertinent ; or surprise, as if he found it diffi-cult to comprehend. " You did not make the journey on horseback, I should think ?"

" Oh, I begin to understand you, Captain Cuffe. Why, if the truth must be said, we came in the lugger, the Few-Folly."

" I supposed as much. And when you went to visit this aunt, where did you leave the lugger ?"

" We did n't leave her at all, sir ; being under her can-vass, our feet were no sooner in the boat, and the line cast off, than she left us as if we had been stuck up, like a tree, on dry ground."

" Where did this happen ?"

" Afloat, of course, Captain Cuffe ; such a thing would hardly come to pass, ashore."

" All that, I understand ; but you say the prisoner left his vessel, in order to visit an aunt of the young woman's thence he went into the Bay, for the sole purpose of finding the young woman herself. Now, this is an important fact, as it concerns the prisoner's motives, and may affect his life. The court must act with all the facts before it; as a commencement, tell us where Raoul Yvard left his lugger, to go on yonder head-land."

"I do not think, Captain Cuffe, you've got the story exactly right. Captain Rule did n't go on the mountain, after all, so much to see the aunt, as to see the niece at the aunt's dwelling; if one would end right in a story, he must begin right."

"I left le Feu-Follet, Monsieur le Capitaine," Raoul calmly observed, "not two cables' length from the very spot where your own ship is now lying; but it was at an hour of the night when the good people of Capri were asleep, and they knew nothing of our visit. You see the lugger is no longer here."

"And do you confirm this story, under the solemnity of your oath?" demanded Cuffe of Ithuel, little imagining how easy it was to the witness to confirm anything he saw fit, in the way he mentioned.

"Sartain; every word is true, gentlemen," answered Ithuel. "It was not more than a cable's length from this very spot, according to my judgment."

"And where is the lugger, now?" asked Cuffe, betraying the drift of all his questions, in his eagerness to learn more.

Ithuel was not to be led on so hurriedly, or so blindly. Affecting a girlish sort of coyness, he answered, simpering, "Why, Captain Cuffe, I cannot think of answering a question like that, under the solemnity of an oath, as you call it. No one can know where the little Folly is, but them hat's in her."

Cuffe was a little disconcerted at the answer, while Lyon smiled ironically; the latter then took upon himself the office of cross-examining, with an opinion of his own penetration and shrewdness, that, at least, ought to have made him quite equal to encountering one of Ithuel's readiness in subterfuges.

"We do not expect you to tell us, of your own knowledge, witness," he said, "precisely the position, by latitude and longitude, or by the points of the compass, at this identical instant, of the craft called by some the le Few-Folly, by others, the Few-Follay, and, as it would now seem, by yourself, the Little Folly ; for that, as ye 've well obsairved, can be known only to those who are actually on board her ; but ye 'll be remembering, perhaps, the place it was agreed on between you, where ye were to find the lugger at your return from this hazardous expedition that ye 've been making amang ye, into the Bay of Naples ?"

" I object to that question, as contrary to law," put in Ithuel, with a spirit and promptitude that caused the Judge Advocate to start, and the members of the court to look at each other in surprise.

" Nay, if ye object to the question on the ground that a true ainswer will be criminating yersel', ye 'll be justified in so doing, by reason and propriety ; but then ye 'll consider well the consequences it may have on your own case, when that comes to be investigated."

" I object on gin'ral principles," said Ithuel. " Whatever Captain Rule may have said on the subject, admitting that he said anything, just to bear out the argument, (by the way, Ithuel called this word argooment, a pronunciation against which we enter our solemn protest;) admitting, *I* say, that *he* said anything on the subject, it cannot be testimony, as *hear*say evidence is ag'in law, all the world over."

The members of the court looked at the Judge Advocate, who returned the glance with an air of suitable gravity ; then, on a motion of Sir Frederick's, the court was cleared, to discuss the point in private.

" How 's this, Mr. Judge Advocate," demanded Cuffe, as soon as the coast was clear ; " it is of the last importance to find where that lugger is—do you hold that the question is contrary to law ?"

" Its importance makes it pertinent, I think, sir ; as for the legality, I do not see how it can be affected by the circumstance that the fact came up in discourse."

" D'ye think so ?" observed Sir Frederick, looking much more profound than was his wont. " Legality is the boast of English law, and I should dislike excessively to fail in that great essential. What is *said*, must be *heard*, to be *repeated;* and this seems very like *hearsay* testimony. I believe it's admitted all round, we must reject *that.*"

"What is your opinion, Captain Lyon?" demanded the president.

"The case is somewhat knotty, but it may be untied," returned the Scot, with a sneer on his hard features. "No need of Alexander and his sword to cut the rope, I'm thinking, when we bring common sense to bear on the point. What is the matter to be ascertained?—Why, the place which was agreed on as the point of rendezvous between this Rawl Eevart and his people. Now, this arrangement must have been made orally, or in writing; if orally, testimony to the words uttered will not be hearsay, farther than testimony to what a man has seen will be eyesight."

"Quite true, Mr. President and gentlemen!" exclaimed the Judge Advocate, who was not a little relieved at finding a clue to lead him out of the difficulty. "If the agreement had been made in writing, then that writing would have to be produced, if possible, as the best evidence the case affords; but, being made in words, those words can be sworn to."

Cuffe was much relieved by this opinion, and, as Sir Frederick did not seem disposed to push his dissent very far the matter would have been determined on the spot, but for a love of disputation that formed part and parcel, to speak legally on a legal subject, of Lyon's moral temperament.

"I'm agreeing with the Judge Advocate, as to his distinction about the admissibility of the testimony on the ground of its not being technically what is called hearsay evidence," he observed; "but a difficulty suggests itself to my mind touching the pairtenency. A witness is sworn to speak to the point before the court; but he is not sworn to discuss all things in heaven and airth. Now, 's it pairtenent to the fact of Rawl Eevart's being a spy, that he made sairtain agreements to meet this or that fellow-creature, in this or that place. Now, as I comprehend the law, it divides all questions into two great classes—the pairtinent, and the impairtinent, of which the first are legal, and the second illegal."

"I think it would be a great piece of audacity," said Sir

24

Frederick, disdainfully, " for such a fellow as this Bolt, to
pretend to call any question we can put him, impertinent!"

" That's no just the p'int, Sir Frederick ; this being altogether a matter of law, while ye'll be thinking of station
and etiquette.   Then, there's two classes of the pairtinent,
and two of the impairtenent ; one being legal and logical, as
it might be, and the other conventional and civil, as one
may say.   There's a nice distinction, latent, between the
two."

" I believe the court is of opinion that the question may
be put," observed Cuffe, who was impatient of the Scotchman's subtleties, bowing to Sir Frederick, to ask an acquiescence which he immediately received.   " We will re-open
the doors, and proceed in the examination."

" The court is of opinion, witness," resumed the Judge
Advocate, when every one was in his place again, " that
you must answer the question.   In order that you may
understand it, I will now repeat it.   Where was it agreed
between Raoul Yvard and his people, that they should meet
again ?"

" I do not think the people of the lugger had anything to
say in the matter," answered Ithuel, in the most unmoved
manner.   " If they had, I knew nothing on 't."

The court felt embarrassed ; but as it would never do to
be thwarted in this manner, a look of determination was
exchanged between the members, and the examination proceeded.

" If not the people, the officers, then.   Where was it
agreed between the prisoner and his *officers*, that the former
should find the lugger, when he returned from his expedition
into the Bay ?"

" Well, now, gentlemen," answered Ithuel, turning his
quid from one cheek into the other, " I *some* conclude,
you've no great acquaintance with Captain Rule, a'ter all !
He is not apt to enter into any agreements, at all.   What
he wants done, he orders ; and what he orders, must be
done."

" What did he *order*, then, as respects the place where
the lugger was to wait for his return ?"

" I'm sorry to be troublesome, please the court," returned
the witness, with admirable self-possession ; " but law is

law, all over the world, and I rather guess this question is ag'in it. In the Granite state, it is always held that when a thing can be proved by the person who said any particular words, that the question must be put to him, and not to a bystander."

"Not if that person is a prisoner, and on his trial," answered the Judge Advocate, staring to hear such a distinction from such a source; "though the remark is a good one, in the cases of witnesses, purely. You must answer, therefore."

"It is unnecessary," again interposed Raoul. "I left my vessel here, where I have told you, and had I made a certain signal, the last night, from the heights of St. Agata, le Feu-Follet would have stood in, near to the rocks of the Sirens, and taken me off again. As the hour is passed, and the signal is not likely to be made, it is probable my lieutenant has gone to another rendezvous, of which the witness knows nothing, and which, certainly, I shall never betray."

There was so much manliness and quiet dignity in Raoul's deportment, that, whatever he said made an impression. His answer disposed of the matter, for the moment at least. The Judge Advocate, accordingly, turned to other inquiries. Little remained, however, to be done. The prisoner had admitted his identity; his capture, with all the attendant circumstances, were in proof, and his defence came next.

When Raoul rose to speak, he felt a choking emotion; but it soon left him, and he commenced in a steady, calm tone, his accent giving point and interest to many of his expressions.

"Messieurs," said he, "I will not deny my name, my character, or my manner of life. I am a Frenchman, and the enemy of your country. I am, also, the enemy of the King of Naples, in whose territories you found me. I have destroyed his and your ships. Put me on board my lugger, and I should do both again. Whoever is the enemy of la France, is the enemy of Raoul Yvard. Honourable seamen, like yourselves, Messieurs, can understand this. I am young. My heart is not made of rock; evil as it may be, it can love beauty, and modesty, and virtue, in the other sex. Such has been my fate—I love Ghita Caraccioli; have endeavoured to make her my wife for more than a year. She has not authorized me to say that my suit was favoured—this I must acknowledge; but she is not the less admirable for that. We differ in our opinions of religion, and I fear she left Monte Argantaro, because, refusing my hand, she thought it better, perhaps, that we should not meet again. It is so with maidens, as you must know, Messieurs. But it is not usual for us, who are less refined, to submit to such self-denial. I learned whither Ghita had come, and followed; my heart was a magnet, that her beauty drew after it, as our needles are drawn towards the pole. It was necessary to go into the Bay of Naples, among the vessels of enemies, to find her I loved; and this is a very different thing, from engaging in the pitiful attempts of a spy. Which of you would not have done the same, Messieurs? You are braves Anglais, and I know you would not hesitate. Two of you are still youthful, like myself, and must still feel the power of beauty; even the Monsieur that is no longer a young man, has had his moments of passion, like all that are born of woman. Messieurs, I have no more to say: you know the rest. If you condemn me, let it be as an unfortunate Frenchman, whose heart had its weaknesses—not as an ignominious and treacherous spy."

The earnestness and nature with which Raoul spoke, were not without effect. Could Sir Frederick have had his way, the prisoner would have been acquitted on the spot. But, Lyon was sceptical, as to the story of love, a sentiment about which he knew very little; and there was a spirit of opposition in him, too, that generally induced him to take the converse of most propositions that were started. The prisoner was dismissed, and the court closed its doors, to make up its decision, by itself, in the usual form.

We should do injustice to Cuffe, if we did not say that he had some feeling in favour of the gallant foe, who had so often foiled him. Could he have had his will at that moment, he would have given Raoul his lugger, allowed the latter a sufficient start, and then gladly have commenced a chase round the Mediterranean, to settle all questions between them. But it was too much to give up the lugger, as well as the prisoner. Then his oath, as a judge, had its obligations also, and he felt himself bound to yield to the arguments of the Judge Advocate, who was a man of technicalities, and thought no more of sentiment than Lyon, himself.

The result of the deliberation, which lasted an hour, was a finding against the prisoner. The court was opened, the record made up and read, the offender introduced, and the judgment delivered. The finding was "that Raoul Yvard had been caught in disguise, in the midst of the allied fleets, and that he was guilty as a spy." The sentence was to suffer death the succeeding day, by hanging at the yardarm of such ship, as the commander-in-chief might select, on approving of the sentence.

As Raoul expected little else, he heard his doom with steadiness, bowing with dignity and courtesy to the court, as he was led away, to be placed in irons, as befitted one condemned.

CHAPTER XIX.

"The world's all title-page; there's no contents;
The world's all face; the man who shows his heart
Is hooted for his nudities, and scorned."
Night Thoughts.

BOLT had not been tried. His case had several serious difficulties, and the orders allowed of a discretion. The punishment could scarcely be less than death, and, in addition to the loss of a stout, sinewy man, it involved questions of natural right, that were not always pleasant to be considered. Although the impressment of American seamen into the British ships of war was probably one of the most serious moral, as well as political wrongs, that one independent nation ever received at the hands of another, viewed as a practice of a generation's continuance, it was not wholly without some relieving points. There was a portion of the British marine that disdained to practise it at all; leaving it to the coarser spirits of the profession to discharge a duty

24 *

that they, themselves, found repugnant to their feelings and thei: habits. Thus, we remember to have heard an American seaman say, one who had been present on many occasions when his countrymen were torn from under their flag, that in no instance he ever witnessed, was the officer who committed the wrong of an air and manner that he should describe as belonging to the class of gentlemen, on shore. Whenever one of the latter boarded his vessel, the crew was permitted to pass unquestioned.

. Let this be as it might, there is no question that a strong and generous feeling existed in the breasts of hundreds in the British navy, concerning the nature of the wrong that was done a foreign people, by the practice of impressing men from under their flag. Although Cuffe was too much of a martinet to carry his notions on the subject to a very refined point, he was too much of a man not to be reluctant to punish another for doing what he felt he would have done himself, under similar circumstances, and what he could not but know he would have had a perfect right to do. It was impossible to mistake one like Ithuel, who had so many of the Granite peculiarities about him, for anything but what he was; and so well was his national character established in the ship, that the *sobriquet* of The Yankee had been applied to him, by his shipmates, from the very first. The fact, therefore, stood him so far in hand, that Cuffe, after a consultation with Winchester, determined not to put the alleged deserter on trial; but, after letting him remain a short time in irons, to turn him to duty, again, under a pretence that was often used on such occasions, viz., to give the man an opportunity of proving his American birth, if he were really what he so strenuously professed to be. Poor Ithuel was not the only one who was condemned to this equivocal servitude, hundreds passing weary years of probation, with the same dim ray of hope, for ever deferred, gleaming in the distance. It was determined, however, not to put Ithuel on his trial, until the captain had conversed with the admiral on the subject, at least; and Nelson, removed from the influence of the siren by whom he was enthralled, was a man inclined to leniency, and of even chivalrous notions of justice. To such contradictions is even a great mind subject, when it loses sight of the polar star of its duties!

When the sentence on Raoul was pronounced, therefore, and the prisoner was removed, the court adjourned; a boat being immediately despatched to the Foudroyant with a copy of the proceedings, for the rear-admiral's approbation. Then followed a discussion on much the most interesting topic for them all; the probable position of, and the means of capturing the lugger. That le Feu-Follet was near, all were convinced; but where she was to be found, it was hard to tell. Officers had been sent on the heights of Capri, one of which towers more than a thousand feet above the sea; but they returned from a bootless errand. Nothing resembling the lugger was visible in the offing, among the islands, or in the bays. A cutter had been sent to look round Campanella, and another crossed the mouth of the bay, to take a look to the northward of Ischia, in order to make certain that the treacherous craft had not gone behind the mountains of that island, for a refuge. In short, no expedient, likely to discover the fugitive, was neglected. All failed, however; boat after boat came back, without success, and officer after officer returned wearied and disappointed.

Much of the day was passed in this manner, for it was a calm, and moving either of the ships was out of the question. In the full expectation of discovering the lugger somewhere in striking distance, Cuffe had even gone so far as to detail a party from each vessel, with a view to attack her in boats, again; feeling no doubt of success, now that he had the disposable force of three vessels to send against his enemy. Winchester was to have commanded, as a right purchased by his blood; nor was the hope of succeeding, in this way abandoned, until the last boat, that which had been sent round Ischia, returned, and reported its total want of success.

"I have heard it said," observed Cuffe, as he and hi brother captains stood conversing together on the quarter deck of the Proserpine, just after this last report had been made—"I have heard it said, that this Raoul Yvard has actually gone boldly into several of our ports, under English or neutral colours, and lain there a day or two at a time, unsuspected; until it has suited him to go out again. Can it be possible he is up, off the town?—There is such a fleet

of craft, in and about the mole, that a little lugger, with her
paint and marks altered, *might* be among them.——What
think you, Lyon?"

" It is sairtainly a law of nature, Captain Cuffe, that
smaller objects should be overlooked, in the presence of
greater ; and such a thing *might* happen, therefore ; though
I should place it among the improbables, if not absolutely
among the impossibles.   'T would be far safer, nevertheless,
to run in, in the manner you designate, among a hundred or
two of ships, than to venture alone into a haven or a roadstead.   If you wish for retirement, Sir Frederick, plunge at
once into the Strand, or take lodgings on Ludgate Hill ; but
if you wish to be noticed, and chased, go into a highland
village, and just conceal your name for a bit !   Ah——he
knows the difference, well, who has tried both modes of
life !"

" This is true, Cuffe," observed the Baronet, " and yet I
hardly think a Frenchman, big or little, would be apt to
come and anchor under Nelson's nose."

" 'T would be something like the lion's lying down with
the lamb, certainly, and ought not to be counted on as very
likely.   Mr. Winchester, is not that our boat coming round
the sloop's quarter ?"

" Yes, sir—she has got back from Naples—quarter-
master——"

" Ay, quarter-master" —— interrupted Cuffe, sternly —— " a
pretty look-out is this !   Here is our own boat close in upon
us, and not a word from your lips on the interesting subject,
sir !"

This word, *sir*, is much used on board a man-of-war, and
in all its convertible significations.   From the inferior to the
superior, it comes as natural, as if it were a gift from above ;
from equal to equal, it has a ceremonious and be-on-your-
guard air, that sometimes means respect, sometimes disrespect ; while, from a captain to a quarter-master, it always
means reproof, if it do not mean menace.   In discussions of
this sort, it is wisest for the weaker party to be silent ; and
nowhere is this truth sooner learned, than on ship-board.
The quarter-master, consequently, made no answer, and the
gig came alongside, bringing back the officer who had car
ried the proceedings of the court up to Naples.

" Here we have it," said Cuffe, opening the important document, as soon as he and his brother captains were again in the cabin. ' Approved—ordered that the sentence be carried into execution on board his Majesty's ship, the Proserpine, Captain Cuffe, to-morrow, between the hours of sunrise and sun-set.' "

Then followed the date, and the well-known signature of " Nelson and Bronté." All this was what Cuffe both wished and expected, though he would have preferred a little more grace in carrying out the orders. The reader is not to suppose from this, that our captain was either vengeful or bloody-minded ; or that he really desired to inflict on Raoul any penalty for the manner in which he had baffled his own designs and caused his crew to suffer. So far from this, his intention was to use the sentence to extort from the prisoner a confession of the orders he had given to those left in the lugger, and then to use this confession as a means of obtaining his pardon, with a transfer to a prison-ship. Cuffe had no great veneration for privateersmen, nor was his estimate of their morality at all unreasonable, when he inferred that one, who served with gain for his principal object, would not long hesitate about purchasing his own life, by the betrayal of a secret like that he now asked. Had Raoul belonged even to a republican navy, the English man-of-war's-man might have hesitated about carrying out his plan ; but, with the master of a corsair, it appeared to be the most natural thing imaginable to attempt its execution. Both Sir Frederick and Lyon viewed the matter in the same light ; and, now that everything was legally done that was necessary to the design, the capture of the lugger was deemed more than half accomplished.

" It is somewhat afflicting, too, Cuffe," observed Sir Frederick, in his drawling, indolent way ; " it is somewhat afflicting, too, Cuffe, to be compelled to betray one's friends, or to be hanged ! In parliament, now, we say we 'll be hanged if we do, and here you say you 'll be hanged if you don't."

" Poh, poh, Dashwood ; no one expects this Raoul Yvard will come to that fate, for no one thinks he will hold out. We shall get the lugger, and that will be the end of it. I 'd give a thousand pounds to see that d———d Few-Folly at

anchor, within pistol-shot of my stern, at this blessed moment. My feelings are in the matter."

"Five hundred would be a high price," observed Lyon
drily. "I much doubt if the shares of us three come to as
much as a hundred apiece, even should the craft fall into
our hands."

"By the way, gents," put in Sir Frederick, gaping—
"suppose we toss up, or throw the dice, to see which shall
have all, on the supposition we get her within the next
twenty-four hours, timing the affair by this ship's chrono-
meters. You've dice on board, I dare say, Cuffe, and we
can make a regular time of it, here, for half an hour, and
no one the wiser."

"Your pardon, Captain Dashwood; I can suffer no such
amusement. It is unmilitary, and contrary to regulations;
and, then, hundreds are not as plenty with Lyon and myself, as they are with you. I like to pocket my prize-
money first, and sport on it, afterwards."

"You're right, Captain Cuffe," said Lyon; "though
there can be no great innovation in sporting on Sir Frederick's portion, if he see fit to indulge us. Money is an
agreeable acquisition beyond a doubt, and life is sweet to
saint and sinner alike; but I much question your facility in
persuading this Monshure Rawl to tell you his secret con-
sairning the lugger, in the manner ye anticipate."

This opinion met with no favour; and after discussing the
point among themselves a little longer, the three captains
were on the point of separating, when Griffin burst into the
cabin, without even knocking, and altogether regardless of
the usual observances.

"One would think it blew a typhoon, Mr. Griffin," said
Cuffe, coldly, "by the rate at which you run before it."

"It's an ill wind that blows no luck, sir," answered the
lieutenant, actually panting for breath, so great had been
his haste to communicate what he had to say. "Our look-
out, on the heights above Campanella, has just signalled us
that he sees the lugger to the southward and eastward—
somewhere near the point of Piane, I suppose, sir; and what
is better, the wind is coming off-shore earlier than common
this evening."

"That *is* news!" exclaimed Cuffe, rubbing his hands with

delight. " Go on deck, Griffin, and tell Winchester to un-
moor; then make a signal to the other ships to do the same.
Now, gentlemen, we have the game in our own hands, and
let us see and play it skilfully. In a couple of hours it will
be dark, and our movements can all be made without being
seen. As the Proserpine is, perhaps, the fastest ship,"—at
this remark, Sir Frederick smiled ironically, while Lyon
raised his eyebrows like one who saw a marvel—" As the
Proserpine is, perhaps, the fastest ship, she ought to go the
farthest to leeward; and I will get under way, and stand
off to sea, keeping well to the northward and eastward, as
if I were running for the straits of Bonifacio, for instance,
until it gets to be dark, when I will haul up south, for a
couple of hours or so; then come up as high as south-east,
until we are to the southward of the gulf of Salerno. This
will be before daylight, if the wind stand. At daylight,
then, you may look out for me, off Piane, say two leagues
and to seaward, I hope, of the lugger. You shall follow,
Sir Frederick, just as the sun sets, and keep in my wake, as
near as possible; heaving-to, however, at midnight. This
will bring you fairly abreast of the gulf, and about midway
between the two capes, a little west of south from Campanella. Lyon, you can lie here until the night has fairly set
in, when you can pass between Capri and the cape, and run
down south two hours, and heave-to. This will place you
in a position to watch the passage to and from the gulf,
under the northern shore."

" And this arrangement completed to your satisfaction
Captain Cuffe," asked Lyon, deliberately helping himself to
an enormous pinch of snuff, " what will be your pleasure in
the posterior evolutions?"

" Each ship must keep her station until the day has fairly
dawned. Should it turn out, as I trust it may, that we've
got the le Few-Folly in-shore of us, all we'll have to do,
will be to close in upon her, and drive her up, higher and
higher, into the Bay. She will naturally run into shallow
water; when we must anchor off, man the boats, send them
north and south of her, and let them board her, under cover
of our fire. If we find the lugger embayed, we'll have her,
as sure as fate."

" Very prettily conceived, Captain Cuffe; and in a way

to be handsomely executed. But if we should happen to find the heathen outside of us?"

" Then make sail in chase to seaward, each ship acting for the best. Come, gentlemen, I do not wish to be inhospitable, but the Proserpine must be off. She has a long road before her; and the winds of this season of the year can barely be counted on for an hour at a time."

Cuffe being in such a hurry, his guests departed without further ceremony. As for Sir Frederick, the first thing he did, was to order dinner an hour earlier than he had intended, and then to invite his surgeon and marine-officer, two capital pairs of knives and forks, to come and share it with him; after which, he sat down to play somewhat villanously on a flute. Two hours later, he gave the necessary orders to his first-lieutenant; after which, he troubled himself very little about the frigate he commanded. Lyon, on the other hand, sat down to a very frugal meal alone, as soon as he found himself again in his sloop; first ordering certain old sails to be got on deck, and to be mended for the eighth or ninth time.

With the Proserpine it was different. Her capstan-bars flew round, and one anchor was actually catted, by the time her captain appeared on deck. The other soon followed, the three topsails fell, were sheeted-home and hoisted, and then sail was set after sail, until the ship went steadily past the low promontory of Ana Capri, a cloud of canvass. Her head was to the westward, inclining a little north; and had there been any one to the southward, to watch her movements, as there was not, so far as the eye could see, it would have been supposed that she was standing over towards the coast of Sardinia, most probably with an intention of passing, by the Straits of Bonifacio, between that island and Corsica. The wind being nearly east, and it blowing a good breeze, the progress of the ship was such as promised to fulfil all the expectations of her commander.

As the sun set, and darkness diffused itself over the Mediterranean, the lighter steering-sails were taken in, and the Proserpine brought the wind abeam, standing south. One of the last things visible from the decks, besides the mountains of the islands and of the main, the curling smoke of Vesuvius, the blue void above and the bluer sea below, was the speck of the Terpsichore, as that ship followed, as near as might be, in her wake; Sir Frederick and his friends still at table, but with a vigilant and industrious first-lieutenant on deck, who was sufficient in himself for all that was required of the vessel, in any emergency. The latter had his orders, and he executed them with a precision and attention that promised to leave nothing to be wished for. On the other hand, the people of the Ringdove were kept at work mending old sails until the hour to " knock-off work" arrived; then the ship unmoored. At the proper time, the remaining anchor was lifted, and the sloop went through the pass, between Capri and Campanella, as directed, when Lyon sent for the first-lieutenant to join him in his cabin.

"Look you here, McBean," said Lyon, pointing to the chart which lay on the table; " Captain Cuffe has just run down off Piane, and will find himself well to leeward, when the west wind comes to-morrow; Sir Frederick has followed, famously clear of the land, and won't be in a much better box. Now, this lugger must be pretty picking, if all they say of her be true. Ten to one, but she has gold in her. These corsairs are desperate rogues after the siller, and, taking hull, sails, armament, head-money, and the scrapings of the lockers together, I shouldn't marvel, if she come to something as good as 8 or £10,000. This would be fair dividing for a sloop, but would amount to a painfully small trifle, as between the officers of three ships, after deducting the admiral's share. What are you thinking of, Airchy?"

"Of just that, Captain Lyon. It would be dividing every lieutenant's share by three, as well as every captain's."

"That 's it, Airchy, and so ye 'll have a shairp look out, on deck. There 'll be no occasion to run down quite as far as Captain Cuffe suggested, ye 'll obsairve; for, if in the bay, the lugger will work her way up towards this headland, and we 'll be all the more likely to fall in with her, by keeping near it ourselves. Ye 'll take the idea?"

"It 's plain enou', Captain Lyon; and I 'll be obsairving it. How is the law understood as respects dairkness?—I understand that none share but such as are in *sight;* but is dairkness deemed a legal impediment?"

"To be sure it is; the idea being that all who can see may act. Now, if we catch the lugger before Captain Cuffe

19

and Sir Frederick even know where she is, on what principle can they aid and sustain us in the capture?"

" And you wish a shairp look-out, the night, Captain Lyon?"

" That's just it, Airchy. Ye'll all be doing your best, in the way of eyes, and we may get the lugger alone. 'T would be such a pity, Mr. McBean, to divide by three, when the sums might be kept entire!"

Such was the state of feeling with which each of these three officers entered on his present duty. Cuffe was earnest in the wish to catch his enemy, and this principally for the credit of the thing, though a little out of a desire to revenge his own losses; Sir Frederick Dashwood, indifferent to all but his own pleasures; and Lyon, closely attentive to the main chance. An hour or two later, or just before Cuffe turned in, he sent a message to request the presence of his first-lieutenant, if the latter were still up. Winchester was writing up his private journal; closing the book, he obeyed the order, in that quiet, submissive manner, which a first-lieutenant is more apt to use towards his captain, than towards any one else.

" Good-evening, Winchester," said Cuffe, in a familiar, friendly way, which satisfied the subordinate that he was not sent for to be " rattled-down"; " draw a chair, and try a glass of this Capri wine, with some water. It's not carrying sail hard to drink a gallon of it; yet I rather think it fills up the chinks better than nothing."

" Thank'ee, Captain Cuffe; we like it in the gun-room, and got off a fresh cask or two, this morning, while the cour. was sitting. So they tell me, sir, his lordship has put his name to it, and that this Frenchman is to swing from our fore-yard-arm, sometime to-morrow?"

" It stands so on *paper*, Winchester; but if he confess where his lugger lies, all will go smoothly enough with him. However, as things look, *now*, we'll have her, and thanks only to ourselves."

" Well, sir, that will be best, on the whole. I do not like to see a man selling his own people."

" There you are right enough, Winchester, and I trust we shall get along without it; though the lugger must be ouis. I sent for you, by the way, about this Bolt—something must be done with that fellow."

"It's a clear case of desertion, Captain Cuffe; and, as it would now seem, of treason, in the bargain. I would rather hang ten such chaps, than one man like the Frenchman."

"Well, it's clear, Mr. Winchester, *you* do not bear malice! Have you forgotten Porto Ferrajo, and the boats, already? or do you love them that despitefully use you?"

"'T was all fair service, sir, and one never thinks anything of that. I owe this Monsieur Yvard no grudge for what he did; but, now it's all fairly over, I rather like him the better for it. But it's a very different matter as to this Bolt; a skulking scoundrel, who would let other men fight his country's battles, while he goes a-privateering against British commerce."

"Ay, there's the rub, Winchester! *Are* they *his* country's battles?"

"Why we took him for an Englishman, sir, and we must act up to our own professions, in order to be consistent."

"And so hang an innocent man for a treason that he *could* not commit?"

"Why, Captain Cuffe, do you believe the fellow's whining story about his being a Yankee? If that be true, we have done him so much injustice already, as to make his case a very hard one. For my part, I look upon all these fellows as only so many disaffected Englishmen, and treat them accordingly."

"That is a sure way to quiet one's feelings, Winchester, but it's most too serious when it comes to hanging. If Bolt deserve any punishment, he deserves death; and that is a matter about which one ought to be tolerably certain, before he pushes things too far. I've sometimes had my doubts about three or four of our people's being Englishmen, after all."

"There can be no certainty in these matters, unless one could carry a parish register for the whole kingdom, in his ship, Captain Cuffe. If they are not Englishmen, why do they not produce satisfactory proofs to show it? That is but reasonable, you must allow, sir?"

"I don't know, Winchester; there are two sides to that question, too. Suppose the King of Naples should seize you here, ashore, and call on you to prove that you are not one of his subjects?—How would you go to work to make it out—no parish register being at hand?"

"Well, then, Captain Cuffe, if we are so very wrong, we had better give all these men up, at once—though one of them is the very best hand in the ship; I think it right to tell you that, sir."

"There is a wide difference, sir, between giving a man up, and hanging him. We are short-handed as it is, and cannot spare a single man. I've been looking over your station bills, and they never appeared so feeble before. We want eighteen or nineteen good seamen to make them respectable again; and, though this Bolt is no great matter, as a seaman, he can turn his hand to so many things, that he was as useful as the boatswain. In a word, we cannot spare him; either to let him go, or to hang him; even were the latter just."

"I'm sure, sir, I desire to do nothing unjust, and so act your pleasure in the affair."

"My pleasure is just this then, Winchester. We must turn Bolt to duty. If the fellow is really an American, it would be a wretched business even to flog him for desertion; and as to treason, you know, there can be none without allegiance. Nelson gives me a discretion, and so we'll act on the safe side, and just turn him over to duty again. When there comes an opportunity, I'll inquire into the facts of his case, and if he can make out that he is not an Englishman, why he must be discharged. The ship will be going home in a year or two, when everything can be settled fairly and deliberately. I dare say, Bolt will not object to the terms."

"Perhaps not, sir. Then there's the crew, Captain Cuffe.—They may think it strange, treason and desertion go unpunished! These fellows talk and reason more than is always known, aft."

I've thought of all that, Winchester. I dare say you have heard of such a thing as a King's evidence?—Well, here has Raoul Yvard been tried and found guilty as a spy; Bolt having been a witness. A few remarks judiciously made, may throw everything off on that tack; and appearances will be preserved, so far as discipline is concerned."

"Yes, sir, that might be done, it's true; but an uneasy berth will the poor devil have of it, if the people fancy he has been a King's evidence! Men of that class hate a traitor worse than they do crime, Captain Cuffe, and they'll ride Bolt down like the main tack."

"Perhaps not; and if they do, 'twill not be as bad as hanging. The fellow must think himself luckily out of a bad scrape, and thank God for all his mercies. You can see that he suffers nothing unreasonable, or greatly out of the way. So send an order to the master-at-arms to knock the irons off the chap, and send him to duty, before you turn in, Winchester."

This settled the matter as to Ithuel, for the moment, at least. Cuffe was one of those men who was indisposed to push things too far, while he found it difficult to do his whole duty. There was not an officer in the Proserpine who had any serious doubts about the true country of Bolt, though there was not one officer, among them all, who would openly avow it. There was too much "granite" about Ithuel to permit Englishmen long to be deceived, and that very language on which the impressed man so much prided himself, would have betrayed his origin, had other evidence been wanting. Still there was a tenacity about an English ship of war, in that day, that did not easily permit an athletic hand to escape its grasp, when it had once closed upon him. In a great and enterprising service, like that of Great Britain, an *esprit de corps* existed in the respective ships, which made them the rivals of each other, and men being the great essentials of efficiency, a single seaman was relinquished with a reluctance that must have been witnessed, fully to be understood. Cuffe, consequently could not make up his mind to do full justice to Ithuel, while he could not make up his mind to push injustice so far as trial and punishment. Nelson had left him a discretion, as has been said, and this he chose to use in the manner just mentioned.

Had the case of the New Hampshire man been fairly brought before the British Admiral, his discharge would have been ordered without hesitation. Nelson was too far removed from the competition of the separate ships, and ordinarily under the control of too high motives, to be

25 *

necessary to the injustice of forcibly detaining a foreigner in his country's service; for it was only while under the malign influence to which there has already been allusion, that he ceased to be high-minded and just. Prejudiced he was, and in some cases, exceedingly so; America standing but little better in his eyes than France herself. For the first of these antipathies he had some apology; since in addition to the aversion that was naturally produced by the history of the cis-atlantic Republic, accident had thrown him in the way, in the West Indies, of ascertaining the frauds, deceptions, and cupidities of a class of men that never exhibit national character in its brightest and most alluring colours. Still, he was too upright of mind, willingly to countenance injustice, and too chivalrous to oppress. But Ithuel had fallen into the hands of one who fell far short of the high qualities of the Admiral, while, at the same time, he kept clear of his more prominent weaknesses, and who *was* brought within the sphere of the competition between the respective ships and their crews.

Winchester, of course, obeyed his orders. He roused the master-at-arms from his hammock, and directed him to bring Ithuel Bolt to the quarter-deck.

" In consequence of what took place this morning," said the first-lieutenant, in a voice loud enough to be heard by all near him, " Captain Cuffe has seen fit to order you to be released, Bolt, and turned to duty again. You will know how to appreciate this leniency, and will serve with greater zeal than ever, I make no doubt. Never forget that you have been with a yard-rope, as it might be, round your neck. In the morning you will be stationed and berthed anew."

Ithuel was too shrewd to answer. He fully understood the reason why he escaped punishment, and it increased his hopes of eventually escaping from the service itself. Still he gagged a little at the idea of passing for one who peached —or for a " *State's*-evidence" as he called it; that character involving more of sin, in vulgar eyes, than the commission of a thousand legal crimes. This gave Winchester no concern. After dismissing his man, he gossiped a minute or two with Yelverton, who had the watch, gaped once or twice somewhat provokingly, and going below, was in a deep sleep in ten minutes.

CHAPTER XX.

"White as a white sail on a dusky sea,
When half the horizon's clouded and half free,
Fluttering between the dun wave and the sky,
Is hope's last gleam in man's extremity."
The Island.

THE dawning of day, on the morning which succeeded, was a moment of great interest, on board the different English ships which then lay off the Gulf of Salerno. Cuffe and Lyon were called, according to especial orders left by themselves, while even Sir Frederick Dashwood allowed himself to be awakened, to hear the report of the officer of the deck. The first was up quite half-an-hour before the light appeared. He even went into the main-top, again, in order to get as early and as wide a survey of the horizon as he wished. Griffin went aloft with him, and, together they stood leaning against the top-mast rigging, watching the slow approach of those rays which gradually diffused themselves over the whole of a panorama that was as bewitching as the hour and the lovely accessories of an Italian landscape could render it.

"I see nothing, *in-shore*," exclaimed Cuffe, in a tone of disappointment, when the light permitted a tolerable view of the coast. "If she should be *outside* of us, our work will be only half done!"

"There is a white speck close in with the land, sir," returned Griffin; "here, in the direction of those ruins, of which our gentlemen that have been round in the boats to look at, tell such marvels; I believe, however, it is only a felucca or a sparanara. There is a peak to the sail that does not look lugger-fashion."

"What is this, off here at the north-west, Griffin?—Is it too large for the le Few-Folly?"

"That must be the Terpsichore, sir. It's just where she *ought* to be, as I understand the orders; and, I suppose, Sir Frederick has carried her there. But yonder's a sail, in the northern board, which may turn out to be the lugger; she's fairly within Campanella, and is not far from the north shore of the bay."

"By George!"—that *must* be she; Monsieur Yvard has kept her skulking round and about Amalfi, all this time! Let us go down, and set everything that will draw, at once, sir."

In two minutes Griffin was on deck, hauling the yards, and clearing away to make sail. As usual, the wind was light at the southward, again, and the course would be nearly before it. Studding-sail booms were to be run out, the sails set, and the ship's head laid to the northward, keeping a little to seaward of the chase. At this moment the Proserpine had the Point of Piane, and the little village of Abate, nearly abeam. The ship might have been going four knots through the water, and the distance across the mouth of the bay was something like thirty miles. Of course, eight hours would be necessary to carry the frigate over the intervening space, should the wind stand, as it probably would not, at that season of the year. A week later, and strong southerly winds might be expected, but that week was as interminable as an age, for any present purpose.

Half-an-hour's trial satisfied all on the deck of the Proserpine, that the chase was keeping off, like themselves, and that she was standing towards the mountains of Amalfi. Her progress, too, was about equal to that of the frigate, for, dead before the wind, the latter ship was merely a good sailer; her great superiority commencing only when she brought the breeze forward of the beam. It had been supposed that the stranger, when first seen, was about fifteen miles distant, his canvass appearing both small and shapeless; but some doubts now began to be entertained, equally as to his rig, his size, and his distance. If a large or a lofty vessel, of course he must be materially farther off, and if a large or lofty vessel it could not be le Feu-Follet.

The other frigate took her cue from the Proserpine, and stood across for the northern side of the gulf; a certain proof that nothing was visible, from her mast-heads, to lead her in any other direction. Two hours, however, satisfied all on board the latter ship, that they were on a wrong scent, and that the vessel to-leeward was their own consort, the sloop; Lyon having, in his eagerness to get the prize before she could be seen from the other ships, carried the Ringdove quite within the bay, and thus misled Cuffe and Sir Frederick.

"There can no longer be any doubt!" exclaimed the captain of the Proserpine, dropping his glass, with vexation too strongly painted in his manner to be mistaken; ".that is a ship; and, as you say, Winchester, it must be the Ringdove; though what the devil Lyon is doing away in there with her, unless he sees something close under the land, is more than I can tell. As there is clearly nothing in this quarter, we will stand on, and take a look for ourselves."

This nearly destroyed the hope of success. The officers began to suspect that their look-out on Campanella had been deceived, and that what he had supposed to be a lugger, was, in truth, a felucca, or perhaps a xebec; a craft which might well be mistaken for a lugger, at the distance of a few leagues. The error, however, was with those in the ship. The officer sent upon the heights was a shrewd, practised master's-mate, who knew everything about his profession, that properly came within his line, and knew little else. But for a habit of drinking, he would long since have been a lieutenant, being, in truth, an older sailor than Winchester; but, satisfied of his own infirmity, and coming from a class in life in which preferment was viewed as a God-send, rather than as a right, he had long settled down into the belief that he was to live and die in his present station, thereby losing most of the desire to rise. The name of this man was Clinch. In consequence of his long experience, within the circle of his duties, his opinion was greatly respected by his superiors, when he was sober; and, as he had the precaution not to be otherwise, when engaged on service, his weakness seldom brought him into any serious difficulties. Cuffe, as a last hope, had sent him up on the heights of Campanella, with a perfect conviction that, if anything were really in sight, he would not fail to see it. All this confidence, however, had now ended in disappointment; and, half-an-hour later, when it was announced to Cuffe, that "the cutter, with Mr. Clinch, was coming down the bay towards them," the former even heard the name of his drunken favourite with disgust. As was usual with him, when out of humour, he went below, as the boat drew near, leaving orders for her officer to be sent down to him, the instant the latter got on board. Five minutes later, Clinch thrust his hard-looking, weather-beaten, but handsome red countenance in at the cabin-door.

"Well, sir," commenced the captain, on a tolerably high key—"a d——d pretty wild goose chase you've sent us all on, down here, into this bay! The southerly wind is failing already, and, in half-an-hour, the ships will be frying the pitch off their decks, without a breath of air : when the wind does come, it will come out at west, and bring us all four or five leagues dead to leeward !"

Clinch's experience had taught him the useful man-of-war lesson, to bow to the tempest, and not to attempt to brave it. Whenever he was "rattled-down," as he called it, he had the habit of throwing an expression of surprise, comically blended with contrition, into his countenance that seemed to say, "what have I done, now?"—or, "if I have done anything amiss, you see how sorry I am for it." He met his irritated commander, on the present occasion, with this expression, and it produced the usual effect of mollifying him, a little.

"Well, sir — explain this matter, if you please." continued Cuffe, after a moment's hesitation.

"Will you please to tell me, sir, what you wish explained?" inquired Clinch, throwing more surprise than common, even, into his countenance.

"That is an extraordinary question, Mr. Clinch! I wish the signal you made from yonder head-land explained, sir. Did you not signal the ship, to say that you saw the le Few-Folly down here, at the southward?"

"Well, sir, I'm glad there was no mistake in the matter,' answered Clinch, in a confident and a relieved manner. "I was afraid, at first, Captain Cuffe, my signal had not been understood."

"Understood!—How could it be mistaken? You showed a black ball, for 'the lugger's in sight.' You'll not deny that, I trust?"

"No, sir — one black ball, for 'the lugger's in sight.' That's just what I did show Captain Cuffe."

' And *three* black balls together, for 'she bears due south from Capri.' What do you say to *that?*"

"All right, sir. Three black balls together, for 'she bears due south from Capri.' I didn't tell the distance, Captain Cuffe, because Mr. Winchester gave me no signals for that."

"And these signals you kept showing every half-hour, as long as it was light; even until the Proserpine was off."

"All according to orders, Captain Cuffe, as Mr. Winchester will tell you. I was to repeat every half-hour, as long as the lugger was in sight, and the day lasted."

"Ay, sir; but you were not ordered to send us after a jack-o'-lantern, or to mistake some xebec or other, from one of the Greek islands, for a light, handy French lugger."

"Nor did I, Captain Cuffe, begging your pardon, sir. I signalled the Few-Folly, and nothing else, I give you my word for it."

Cuffe looked hard at the master's-mate for half a minute, and his ire insensibly lessened as he gazed.

"You are too old a seaman, Clinch, not to know what you were about! If you saw the privateer, be good enough to tell us what has become of her?"

"That is more than I can say, Captain Cuffe, though *see* her I did; and that so plainly, as to be able to make out her jigger, even. You know, sir, we shot away her jigger-mast in the chase off Elba, and she got a new one that steves for'rard uncommonly. I noticed *that* when we fell in with her in the canal of Piombino; and seeing it again, could not but know it. But there's no mistaking the saucy Folly, for them that has once seen her; and I am certain we made her out, about four leagues to the southward of the cape, at the time I first signalled."

"Four leagues!—I had thought she must be at least eight or ten, and kept off that distance, to get her in the net. Why did you not let us know her distance?"

"Had no signals for that, Captain Cuffe."

"Well, then, why not send a boat to tell us the fact?"

"Had no orders, sir. Was told by Mr. Winchester just to signal the lugger and her bearings; and this, you must own, Captain Cuffe, we did plain enough. Besides, sir—"

"Well; besides *what?*" demanded the captain, observing that the master's-mate hesitated.

"Why, sir, how wa' I to know that any one in the ship would think a lugger *could* be seen eight or ten leagues? That's a long bit of water, sir; and it would take a heavy ship's spars to rise high enough for such a sight."

"The land you were on, Clinch, was much loftier than any vessel's spars."

"Quite true, sir; but not lofty enough for that, Captain Cuffe. That I saw the Folly, I'm as certain as I am of being in this cabin."

"What has become of her, then? — You perceive she is not in the bay now."

"I suppose, Captain Cuffe, that she stood in until near enough for her purpose, and that she must have hauled off the land, after night set in. There was plenty of room for her to pass out to sea again between the two frigates, and not be seen in the dark."

This conjecture was so plausible, as to satisfy Cuffe; and yet it was not the fact. Clinch had made le Feu-Follet, from his elevated post, to the southward, as his signal had said; and he was right in all his statements about her, until darkness concealed her movements. Instead of passing out of the Bay, as he imagined, however, she had hauled up within a quarter of a league of Campanella, doubled that point, brushed along the coast to the northward of it, fairly within the Bay of Naples, and pushed out to sea, between Capri and Ischia; going directly athwart the anchorage the men-of-war had so recently quitted, in order to do so.

When Raoul quitted his vessel, he ordered her to stand directly off the land, just keeping Ischia and Capri in view, lying-to under her jigger. As this was low sail, and a lugger shows so little aloft, it was a common expedient with cruisers of that rig, when they wished to escape observation. Monsieur Pintard, Raoul's first-lieutenant, had expected a signal from his commander at the very spot where Clinch had taken his station; but seeing none, he had swept along the coast, after dark, in the hope of discovering his position by the burning of a blue-light. Failing of this, however, he went off the land again, in time to get an offing before the return of day, and to save the wind. It was the boldness of the manœuvre, that saved the lugger; Lyon going out through the pass between Capri and Campanella, about twenty minutes before Pintard brushed close round the rocks, under his jigger and jib only, anxiously looking out for a signal from his captain. The Frenchmen saw the sloop-of-war quite plainly, and, by the aid of their night-glasses, ascertained her character; mistaking her, however, for another ship, bound to Sicily or Malta; while their own vessel escaped observation, owing to the little sail she carried, the want of hamper, and her situation so near the land, which gave her a back-ground of rocks. Clinch had not seen the movements of the lugger after dark, in consequence of his retiring to the village of St. Agata to seek lodgings, as soon as he perceived that his own ship had gone to sea, and left him and his boat's crew behind. The following morning, when he made the ship to the southward, he pushed off, and pulled towards his proper vessel, as related.

"Where did you pass the night, Clinch?" demanded the captain, after they had discussed the probabilities of the lugger's escape. "Not on the heights, under the canopy of heaven?"

"On the heights, and under the great canopy that has covered us both so often, Captain Cuffe; but with a good Neapolitan mud-roof between it and my head. As soon as it was dark, and I saw that the ship was off, I found a village named St. Agata, that stands on the heights, just abeam of those rocks they call the Sirens, and there we were well berthed until morning."

"You are lucky in bringing back all the boat's crew, Clinch. You know it's low-water with us as to men, just now; and our fellows are not all to be trusted ashore, in a country that is full of stone walls, good wine, and pretty girls."

"I always take a set of regular steady-ones with me, Captain Cuffe; I haven't lost a man from a boat, these five years."

"You must have some secret, then, worth knowing; for even the admirals sometimes lose their barge-men. I dare say, now, yours are all married chaps, that hold on to their wives, as so many sheet-anchors; they say that is often a good expedient."

26

"Not at all, sir. I did try that, till I found that half the fellows would run to get rid of their wives. The Portsmouth and Plymouth marriages don't always bring large estates with them, sir, and the bridegrooms like to cut adrift at the end of the honey-moon. Don't you remember when we were in the Blenheim together, sir, we lost eleven of the launch's crew at one time; and nine of them turned out to be vagabonds, sir, that deserted their weeping wives and suffering families at home!"

"Now you mention it, I do remember something of the sort; draw a chair, Clinch, and take a glass of grog. Tim, put a bottle of Jamaica before Mr. Clinch. I have heard it said that you are married yourself, my gallant master's-mate?"

"Lord, Captain Cuffe, that's one of the young gentlemen's stories! If a body believed all they say, the Christian religion would soon get athwart-hawse, and mankind be all adrift in their morals," answered Clinch, smacking his lips, after a very grateful draught. "We've a regular set of high-flyers, aboard this ship, at this blessed minute, Captain Cuffe, sir, and Mr. Winchester has his hands full of them! I often wonder at his patience, sir."

"We were young once ourselves, Clinch, and ought to be indulgent to the follies of youth. But, what sort of a berth did you find last night, upon the rocks yonder?"

"Why, sir, as good as one can expect out of Old England. I fell in with an elderly woman calling herself Giuntotardi—which is regular-built Italian, isn't it, sir?"

"That it is—but, you speak the language, I believe, Clinch?"

"Why, sir, I've been drifting about the world so long, that I speak a little of everything, finding it convenient when I stand in need of victuals and drink. The old lady on the hill and I overhauled a famous yarn between us, sir. It seems she has a niece and a brother at Naples, who ought to have been back night before last; and she was in lots of tribulation about them, wanting to know if our ship had seen anything of the rovers?"

"By George, Clinch, you were on soundings, there, had you but known it! Our prisoner has been in that part of the world, and we might get some clue to his manœuvres by questioning the old woman closely. I hope you parted good friends?"

"The best in the world, Captain Cuffe. No one that feeds and lodges *me* well, need dread me as an enemy."

"I 'll warrant it! That 's the reason you are so loyal, Clinch."

The hard, red face of the master's-mate worked a little, and, though he could not well look all sorts of colours, he looked all ways, but in his captain's eye. It was now ten years since he ought to have been a lieutenant, having once actually outranked Cuffe, in the way of date of service at least; and his conscience told him two things, quite distinctly; first, the fact of his long and weary probation; and second, that it was, in a great degree, his own fault.

"I love His Majesty, sir," Clinch observed, after giving a gulp," and I never lay anything that goes hard with myself to his account. Still, memory will be memory; and spite of all I can do, sir, I sometimes remember what I *might* have been, as well as what I *am*. If His Majesty *does* feed me, it is with the spoon of a master's-mate; and if he *does* lodge me, it is in the cockpit."

"I have been your shipmate, often, and for years at a time," answered Cuffe, good-naturedly, though a little in the manner of a superior; "and no one knows your history better. It is not your friends who have failed you, at need, so much as a certain enemy, with whom you will insist on associating, though he harms them most, who love him best."

"Ay, ay, sir—that can't be denied, Captain Cuffe; yet it 's a hard life that passes altogether without hope."

This was uttered with an expression of melancholy that said more for Clinch's character than Cuffe had witnessed in the man for years, and it revived many early impressions in his favour. Clinch and he had once been messmates, even; and, though years of a decided disparity in rank had since interposed their barrier of etiquette and feeling, Cuffe never could entirely forget the circumstance.

"It is hard, indeed, to live as you say, without hope," returned the captain; "but hope *ought* to be the last thing to die. You should make one more rally, Clinch, before you throw up, in despair."

"It's not so much for myself, Captain Cuffe, that I mind it, as for some that live ashore. My father was as reputable a tradesman as there was in Plymouth, and when he got me on the quarter-deck, he thought he was about to make a gentleman of me, instead of leaving me to pass a life, in a situation that may be said to be even beneath what his own was."

"Now you undervalue your station, Clinch. The berth of a master's-mate, in one of His Majesty's finest frigates, is something to be proud of; I was once a master's-mate — nay, Nelson has doubtless filled the same station. For that matter, one of His Majesty's own sons may have gone through the rank."

"Ay, gone *through* it, as you say, sir," returned Clinch, with a husky voice. "It does well enough for them that go *through* it, but it's death to them that *stick*. It's a feather in a midshipman's cap to be rated a mate; but 'it's no honour to be a mate, at my time of life, Captain Cuffe."

"What is your age, Clinch?—You are not much my senior."

"Your senior, sir!—The difference in our years is not as great as in our rank, certainly, though I never shall see thirty-two, again. But it's not so much *that*, after all, as the thoughts of my poor mother, who set her heart on seeing me with His Majesty's commission in my pocket; and of another, who set her heart on one that I'm afraid was never worthy her affection."

"This is new to me, Clinch," returned the captain, with interest. "One so seldom thinks of a master's-mate marrying, that the idea of your being in that way has never crossed my mind, except in the manner of a joke."

"Master's-mates *have* married, Captain Cuffe, and they have ended in being very miserable. But Jane, as well as myself, has made up her mind to live single, unless we can see brighter prospects before us than what my present hopes afford."

"Is it quite right, Jack, to keep a poor young woman, towing along in this uncertainty, during the period of life when her chances for making a good connection are the best?"

Clinch stared at his commander, until his eyes filled with

tears. The glass had not touched his lips since the conversation took its present direction; and the usual, hard, settled character of his face was becoming expressive, once more, with human emotions.

"It's not my fault, Captain Cuffe," he answered, in a low voice; "it's now quite six years, since I insisted on her giving me up; but she wouldn't hear of the thing. A very respectable attorney wished to have her, and I even prayed her to accept his offer; and the only unkind glance I ever got from her eye, was when she heard me make a request that she told me sounded impiously, almost, to her ears. She would be a sailor's wife, or die a maid."

"The girl has unfortunately got some romantic notions concerning the profession, Clinch, and they are ever the hardest to be convinced of what is for their own good."

"Jane Weston!—Not she, sir—There is not as much romance about her, as in the fly-leaves of a prayer-book. She is all *heart*, poor Jane; and how I came to get such a hold of it, Captain Cuffe, is a great mystery to myself. I certainly do not *deserve* half her affection, and I now begin to despair of ever being able to repay her for it."

Clinch was still a handsome man, though exposure and his habits had made some inroads on a countenance, that by nature was frank, open, and prepossessing. It now expressed the anguish that occasionally came over his heart, as the helplessness of his situation presented itself fully to his mind. Cuffe's feelings were touched, for he remembered the time when they were messmates, with a future before them, that promised no more to the one than to the other, the difference in the chances which birth afforded the captain, alone excepted. Clinch was a prime seaman, and as brave as a lion, too; qualities that secured to him a degree of respect, that his occasional self-forgetfulness had never entirely forfeited. Some persons thought him the most skilful mariner the Proserpine contained; and, perhaps, this was true, if the professional skill were confined strictly to the handling of a ship, or to taking care of her on critical occasions. All these circumstances induced Cuffe to enter more closely into the master-mate's present distress than he might otherwise have done. Instead of showing the bottle to him, however, as if conscious how much disappointed

26 * 20

hope had already driven the other to its indiscreet use, he pushed it gently aside, and taking his old messmate's hand, with a momentary forgetfulness of the difference in rank, he said in a tone of kindness and confidence, that had long been strangers to Clinch's ears—

"Jack, my honest fellow, there is good stuff in you yet, if you will only give it fair play. Make a manly rally, respect yourself for a few months, and something will turn up, that will yet give you your Jane, and gladden your old mother's heart."

There are periods in the lives of men, when a few kind words, backed by a friendly act or two, might save thousands of human beings from destruction. Such was the crisis in the fate of Clinch. He had almost given up hope, though it did occasionally revive in him, whenever he got a cheering letter from the constant Jane, who pertinaciously refused to believe anything to his prejudice, and religiously abstained from all reproaches. But, it is necessary to understand the influence of rank, on board a man-of-war, fully to comprehend the effect, which was now produced on the master's-mate, by the captain's language and manner. Tears streamed out of the eyes of Clinch, and he grasped the hand of his commander, almost convulsively.

"What can I do, sir?—Captain Cuffe, what can I do?" he exclaimed. "My duty is never neglected; but there *are* moments of despair, when I find the burthen too hard to be borne, without calling upon the bottle for support."

"Whenever a man drinks with such a motive, Clinch, I would advise him to abstain altogether. He cannot trust himself; and that which he terms his friend, is, in truth, his direst enemy. Refuse your rations, even; determine to be free. One week, nay, one day, may give a strength that will enable you to conquer, by leaving your reason unimpaired. Absence from the ship has accidentally befriended you, for the little you have taken here, has not been sufficient to do any harm. We are now engaged on a most interesting duty, and I will throw service into your way, that may be of importance to you. Get your name once fairly in a despatch, and your commission is safe. Nelson loves to prefer old tars: and nothing would make him happier, than to be able to serve *you* Put it in my power to ask it of him, and I'll answer for the result. Something may yet come out of your visit to the cottage of this woman, and do you be mindful to keep yourself in fortune's way."

"God bless you, Captain Cuffe — God bless you, sir,"— answered Clinch, nearly choked,—"I'll endeavour to do as you wish."

"Remember Jane and your mother. With such a woman dependent for her happiness on his existence, a man must be a brute, not to struggle hard."

Clinch groaned, for Cuffe probed his wound deep ; though it was done with an honest desire to cure. After wiping the perspiration from his face, and writhing on his chair, however, he recovered a little of his self-command, and became comparatively composed.

"If a friend could only point out the way by which I might recover some of the lost ground," he said, "my gratitude to him would last as long as life, Captain Cuffe."

"Here is an opening then, Clinch. Nelson attaches as much importance to our catching this lugger as he ever did to falling in with a fleet. The officer who is serviceable on this occasion may be sure of being remembered, and I will give you every chance in my power. Go, dress yourself in your best ; make yourself look as you know you can ; then be ready for boat service. I have some duty for you now, which will be but the beginning of good luck, if you only remain true to your mother, to Jane, and to yourself."

A new life was infused into Clinch. For years he had been overlooked ; apparently forgotten, except when thorough seamanship was required ; and even his experiment of getting transferred to a vessel commanded by an old messmate had seemingly failed. Here was a change, however, and a ray, brighter than common, shone athwart the darkness of his future. Even Cuffe was struck with the cheerfulness of his countenance, and the alacrity of the master's-mate's movements, and he reproached himself with having so long been indifferent to the best interests of one who certainly had some claims on his friendship. Still, there was nothing unusual in the present relations between these old messmates. Favoured by family and friends, Cuffe had never been permitted to fall into despondency, and had pursued his career successfully and with spirit ; while the other, unsupported, and failing of any immediate opportunity for getting ahead, had fallen into evil ways, and come to be, by slow degrees, the man he was.   Such instances as the latter, are of not unfrequent occurrence even in a marine in which promotion is as regular as our own, though it is rare indeed that a man recovers his lost ground, when placed in circumstances so trying.

In half an hour Clinch was ready, dressed in his best. The gentlemen of the quarter-deck saw all these preparations with surprise ; for, of late, the master's-mate had seldom been seen in that part of the ship at all. But, in a man-of-war, discipline is a matter of faith, and no one presumed to ask questions.   Clinch was closeted with the Captain for a few minutes, received his orders, and went over the ship's side with a cheerful countenance, actually entering the Captain's gig, the fastest rowing boat of the ship.   As soon as seated, he shoved off, and held his way towards the point of Campanella, then distant about three leagues.   No one knew whither he was bound, though all believed it was on duty that related to the lugger, and duty that required a seaman's judgment.   As for Cuffe, his manner, which had begun to be uneasy and wandering, became more composed when he saw his old messmate fairly off, and that too, at a rate which would carry him even to Naples, in the course of a few hours should his voyage happen to be so long.

CHAPTER XXI.

"His honour's link'd
Unto his life; he that will seek the one
Must venture for the other, or lose both."
                                        TATHAM.

It was now certain that the Feu-Follet was not in the Bay of Salerno. By means of the lofty spars of the ship, and the aid of glasses, the whole coast had been effectually surveyed, and no signs of such a craft were visible. Even Lyon had given it up, had wore round, and was standing along the land again, towards Campanella, a disappointed man. As Cuffe expected the next wind from the westward, he continued on to the northward, however, intending to go off Amalfi, and question any fisherman he might fall in with. Leaving the ship slowly pursuing her course in that direction, then, we will turn our attention to the state of the prisoners.

Ghita and her uncle had been properly cared for, all this time. The gunner's wife lived on board, and, being a respectable woman, Cuffe had the delicacy to send the poor girl forward to the state-room and mess of this woman. Her uncle was provided for near by, and, as neither was considered in any degree criminal, it was the intention to put them ashore, as soon as it was certain that no information concerning the lugger was to be obtained from them. Ithuel was at duty again, having passed half the morning in the fore-top. The shore-boat, which was in the way on deck, was now struck into the water, and was towing astern, in waiting for the moment when Carlo Giuntotardi and his niece were to be put in possession of it again, and permitted to depart. This moment was delayed, however, until the ship should again double Campanella, and be once more in the Bay of Naples, as it would have been cruel to send two such persons as the uncle and niece adrift, at any material distance from their proper place of landing.

It was very different with Raoul Yvard, however. He was under the charge of a sentry on the berth-deck, in waiting for the fearful moment when he should be brought forth for execution. His sentence was generally known in the ship, and with a few he was an object of interest; though punishment, deaths in battle, and all the other casualties of nautical life, were much too familiar in such a war to awaken anything like a sensation in an active cruising frigate. Still, some had a thought for the prisoner's situation. Winchester was a humane man, and, to his credit, he bore no malice for his own defeat and sufferings; while in his capacity of first-lieutenant, it was in his power to do much towards adding to the comfort of the condemned. He had placed the prisoner between two open ports, where

the air circulated freely, no trifling consideration in so warm
a climate, and had ordered a canvass bulk-head to be placed
around him, giving Raoul the benefit of a state-room for his
meditations at so awful a moment. His irons, too, had
been removed as useless; though care had been had to take
away from the prisoner everything by which he might
attempt his own life. The probability of his jumping
through a port had been discussed between the first and
second lieutenants; but the sentry was admonished to be on
his guard against any such attempt, and little apprehension
was felt, Raoul being so composed and so unlikely to do
anything precipitately. Then it would be easy to pick him
up, while the vessel moved so slowly. To own the truth
too, many would prefer his drowning himself, to seeing him
swinging at a yard-arm.

In this narrow prison, then, Raoul passed the night and
morning. It would be representing him as more stoical
than the truth, if we said he was unmoved. So far from this,
his moments were bitter, and his anguish would have been
extreme, were it not for a high resolution which prompted
him to die, as he fancied it, like *un Français*. The numerous executions by the guillotine, had brought fortitude
under such circumstances, into a sort of fashion, and there
were few who did not meet death with decorum. With our
prisoner, however, it was still different; for, sustained by a
dauntless spirit, he would have faced the great tyrant of the
race, even in his most ruthless mood, with firmness, if not
with disdain. But, to a young man and a lover, the last
great change could not well approach without bringing with
it a feeling of hopelessness, that, in the case of Raoul, was
unrelieved by any cheering expectations for the future. He
fully believed his doom to be sealed, and that, less on
account of his imaginary offence as a spy, than on account
of the known and extensive injuries he had done to the English commerce. Raoul was a good hater; and, according
to the fashion of past times, which we apprehend, in spite of
a vast deal of equivocal philanthropy that now circulates
freely from mouth to mouth, and from pen to pen, will continue to be the fashion of times to come, he heartily disliked
the people with whom he was at war, and consequently, was
ready to believe anything to their prejudice that political

rivalry might invent; a frame of mind that led him to think his life would be viewed as a trifle, when put in the scales against English ascendency, or English profit. He was accustomed to think of the people of Great Britain as a "nation of shop-keepers," and, while engaged himself in a calling that bears the brand of rapacity on its very brow, he looked upon his own pursuit as comparatively martial and honourable; qualities, in sooth, it was far from being without, as he himself had exercised its functions. In a word, Raoul understood Cuffe, as little as Cuffe understood him; facts that will sufficiently appear in the interview which it has now become our office to relate.

The prisoner received one or two friendly visits in the course of the morning; Griffin, in particular, conceiving it to be his duty to try to cheer the condemned man, on account of his own knowledge of foreign tongues. On these occasions, the conversation was prevented from falling into anything like the sombre, by the firmness of the prisoner's manner. With a view to do the thing handsomely, Winchester had caused the canvass bulk-head to include the guns on each side, which of course gave more air and light within the narrow apartment, as it brought both ports into the little room. Raoul adverted to this circumstance, as, seated on one stool, he invited Griffin, in the last of his visits, to take another.

" You find me, here, supported by a piece of eighteen on each side," observed the prisoner, smiling, " as becomes a seaman who is about to die. Were my death to come from the mouths of your cannon, Monsieur Lieutenant, it would only meet me a few months or perhaps a few days sooner than it might happen by the same mode, in the ordinary course of events."

" We know how to feel for a brave man in your situation," answered Griffin, with emotion ; " and nothing would make us all happier than to have it as you say ; you in a good warm frigate, on our broadside, and we in this of our own, contending fairly for the honour of our respective countries."

" Monsieur, the fortune of war has ordered it otherwise—but, you are not seated, Monsieur Lieutenant."

" *Mon pardon*—Captain Cuffe has sent me to request you

will favour him with your company, in his cabin, as soon as
it may be agreeable to yourself, Monsieur Yvard."

There is something in the polished expressions of the
French language, that would have rendered it difficult for
Griffin to have been other than delicate in his communications with the prisoner, had he been so disposed ; but, such
was not his inclination ; for, now that their gallant adversary was at their mercy, all the brave men in the Proserpine
felt a disposition to deal tenderly with him. Raoul was
touched with these indications of generosity, and, as he had
witnessed Griffin's spirit in the different attempts made on
his lugger, it inclined him to think better of his foes. Rising,
he professed his readiness to attend the captain, at that very
moment.

Cuffe was waiting in the after-cabin. When Griffin and
the prisoner entered, he courteously requested both to be
seated, the former being invited to remain, not only as a
witness of what might occur, but to act as interpreter in
case of need. A short pause succeeded, and then the captain opened the dialogue, which was carried on in English,
with occasional assistance from Griffin, whenever it became
necessary.

" I greatly regret, Monsieur Yvard, to see a brave man
in your situation," commenced Cuffe, who, sooth to say,
apart from the particular object he had in view, uttered no
more than the truth. " We have done full justice to your
spirit and judgment, while we have tried the hardest to get
you into our power. But the laws of war are severe, necessarily, and we English have a commander-in-chief who is
not disposed to trifle in matters of duty."

This was said, partly in policy, and partly from a habit
of standing in awe of the character of Nelson. Raoul
received it, however, in the most favourable light ; though
the politic portion of the motive was altogether thrown away,
as will be seen in the sequel.

" Monsieur, un Français knows how to die in the cause
of liberty and his country," answered Raoul, courteously,
yet with emphasis.

" I do not doubt it, Monsieur ; still, I see no necessity of
things being pushed to that extremity. England is as liberal
of her rewards, as she is powerful to resent injuries. Per-

haps some plan may be adopted which will avert the necessity of sacrificing the life of a brave man, in so cruel a
mode."

" I shall not affect to play the hero, Monsieur le Capitaine.
If any proper mode of relieving me, in my present crisis,
can be discovered, my gratitude will be in proportion to the
service rendered."

" This is talking sensibly, and to the purpose : I make no
doubt, when we come to a right understanding, everything
will be amicably arranged between us. Griffin, do me the
favour to help yourself to a glass of wine and water, which
you will find refreshing this warm day. Monsieur Yvard
will join us ; the wine coming from Capri, and being far
from bad ; though some do prefer the Lachrymæ Christi
that grows about the foot of Vesuvius, I believe."

Griffin did as desired, though his own countenance was
far from expressing all the satisfaction that was obvious in
the face of Cuffe. Raoul declined the offer ; waiting for the
forthcoming explanation with an interest he did not affect to
conceal. Cuffe seemed disappointed and reluctant to proceed ; but, finding his two companions silent, he was obliged
to make his proposal.

" Oui, Monsieur," he added, " England is powerful to
resent, but ready to forgive. You are very fortunate in
having it in your power, at so serious a moment, to secure
her pardon for an offence that is always visited in war with
a punishment graver than any other."

" In what way can this be done, Monsieur le Capitaine ?
I am not one who despises life ; more especially when it is
in danger of being lost by a disgraceful death."

" I am rejoiced, Monsieur Yvard, to find you in this frame
of mind ; it will relieve me from the discharge of a most
painful duty, and be the means of smoothing over many
difficulties. Without doubt, you have heard of the character
of our celebrated admiral, Nelson ?"

" His name is known to every seaman, Monsieur,"
answered Raoul, stiffly ; his natural antipathies being far
from cured by the extremity of his situation. " He has
written it on the waters of the Nile, in letters of blood !"

" Ay, his deeds, *there*, or elsewhere, will not soon be forgotten. He is a man of an iron will ; when his heart is set
27

on a thing, he sticks at no risk to obtain it, especially if the means be lawful, and the end is glory.   To be frank, Monsieur, he wishes much for your lugger, the le Few-Folly."

"Ah!" exclaimed Raoul, smiling ironically—" Nelson is not the only English admiral who has had the same desire. Le Feu-Follet, Monsieur le Capitaine, is so charming, that she has many admirers!"

" Among whom Nelson is one of the warmest.   Now, this makes your case so much the easier to be disposed of.   You have nothing to do but put the lugger into our hands, when you will be pardoned, and be treated as a prisoner of war."

" Does Monsieur Nelson authorize you to make this proposal to me?" asked Raoul, gravely.

" He does.   Intrusted with the care of his country's interests, he is willing to overlook the offence against her, under the law of nations, to deprive the enemy of the means of doing so much harm.   Put the lugger into our hands, and you shall be sent to an ordinary prison-ship.   Nay, merely let us into the secret of her position, and *we* will see to her capture."

" Monsieur Nelson doubtless does no more than his duty," answered Raoul, quietly, but with an air of severe self-respect.   " It is his business to have a care for English commerce, and he has every right to make this bargain. But the treaty will not be conducted on equal terms; while he is doing no more than his duty, I have no powers."

" How?—You have the power of speech; that will suffice to let us into the secret of the orders you have given the lugger, and where she is probably to be found, at this moment."

" Non, Monsieur; I have not even *that* power.   I can do nothing that must cover me with so much infamy.   My tongue is under laws that I never made, when treachery is in question."

Had Raoul assumed a theatrical tone and manner, as might have been expected, probably it would have made very little impression on Cuffe; but his quiet simplicity and steadiness carried conviction with them.   To say the truth the captain was disappointed.   He would have hesitated about making his proposition to an officer of the regular French marine, low as even these stood, at that day, in the

estimation of Nelson's fleet, in particular; but from a privateersman, he expected a greedy acquiescence, in á plan that
offered life as a reward, in exchange for a treachery like
that he proposed. At first he felt disposed to taunt Raoul
with the contradiction between what he, Cuffe, conceived to
be his general pursuits, and his present assumption of principles; but, the unpretending calmness of the other's manner,
and the truth of his feelings, prevented it. Then, to do
Cuffe, himself, justice, he was too generous to abuse the
power he had over his prisoner.

"You may do well to think of this, Monsieur Yvard"—
observed the captain, after a pause of quite a minute. "The
interest at stake is so heavy, that reflection may yet induce
you to change your mind."

"Monsieur Cuffe, I pardon you, if you can pardon yourself," answered Raoul, with severe dignity in his manner,
rising as he spoke, as if disdaining civilities which came
from his tempter. "I know what you think of us corsairs—
but an officer in an honourable service, should hesitate long,
before he tempts a man to do an act like this. The fact that
the life of your prisoner is at stake, ought to make a brave
seaman still more delicate how he tries to work on his ter-
rors or his principles. But, I repeat, I forgive you, Monsieur,
if you can forgive yourself."

Cuffe stood confounded. The blood rushed to his heart;
after which, it appeared as if about to gush through the pores
of his face. A feeling of fierce resentment almost consumed
him; then he became himself again, and began to see things,
as was his wont, in cooler moments. Still he could not
speak, pacing the cabin to recover his self-command.

"Monsieur Yvard," he at length said, "I ask your for-
giveness, sincerely, and from the bottom of my heart. I
did not know you, or such a proposal would never have
insulted you, or disgraced a British officer, in my person.
Nelson, too, is the last man living, to wound the feelings of
an honourable enemy; but we did not know you. All privateersmen are not of your way of thinking, and it was
there we fell into our mistake."

"*Touchez-la*," said Raoul, frankly extending his hand.
"Monsieur le Captiaine, you and I ought to meet in two
fine frigates, each for his country's honour; let what would

be the result, it would lay the foundations of an eternal
friendship. I have lived long enough in *votre Angleterre,*
to understand how little you know *notre France ; mais
n'importe.* Brave men can understand one another, all over
the world ; for the little time which is left me, we shall be
friends."

Cuffe seized Raoul's hand, and even a tear escaped him,
as he squeezed it warmly.

" This has been a d——d miserable business, Griffin," said
the captain, as soon as he could speak without betraying
weakness, " and one no man will ever find me employed in
again, though a fleet as large as that up in the Bay yonder
were the price."

" I never thought it would succeed, sir ; and, to say the
truth, I never hoped it would. You'll excuse me, Captain
Cuffe, but we English don't give the continentals exactly
the credit they deserve ; and particularly the French. I
thought it wouldn't do, from the first."

Cuffe now repeated his apologies ; and after a few expressions of friendly esteem on both sides, Raoul returned to his
little room, declining the captain's offer to occupy one of the
cabin state-rooms. Griffin was soon back again, and then
the conversation was resumed between the two officers.

" This is altogether a most painful business, Griffin,"
observed Cuffe. " There is no doubt that Monsieur Yvard
is technically a spy, and guilty, according to the forms of
law ; but I entertain not the smallest doubt of the truth of
his whole story. This Ghita Caraccioli, as the girl calls
herself, is the very picture of truth ; and was actually in
Nelson's cabin the day before yesterday, under circumstances that leave no doubt of the simplicity and truth of
her character, while every part of the tale corresponds with
the other. Even the veechy, and this pursy old podestâ,
confirm the account ; for they have seen Ghita in Porto
Ferrajo, and begin to think the Frenchman came in there
solely on her account."

" I make no doubt, Captain Cuffe, that Lord Nelson will
give a respite, or even a pardon, were the facts fairly laid
before him," observed Griffin, who felt a generous interest
in preserving the life of Raoul, the very man he had endeavoured to destroy by fire only a few weeks before : but such

is the waywardness of man, and such are the mixed feelings generated by war.

"This is the most serious part of the affair, Griffin. The sentence is approved; with an order that it shall be carried into effect this very day, between the hours of sunrise and sunset; while here it is already noon, and we are to the southward of Campanella, and so distant from the flag-ship, as to put signals out of the question."

Griffin started; all the grave difficulties of the case glancing upon his mind in a moment. An order, according to the habits of the service, and more especially an order of this serious character, was not to be questioned; yet here was a dilemma in which there appeared no means of relief.

"Good God, Captain Cuffe, how unlucky! Cannot an express be sent across by land, so as yet to reach the flag-ship in time?"

"I have thought of that, Griffin, and Clinch has gone precisely on that errand."

"Clinch!—Pardon me, sir; but such a duty requires a very active and *sober* officer!"

"Clinch is active enough, and I *know* his besetting weakness will have no power over him to-day. I have opened the way for a commission to him, and no one in the ship can go to Naples in a boat sooner than Clinch, if he really try. He will make the most of the afternoon's breeze, should there be any, and I have arranged a signal with him, by which he may let us know the result even at the distance of eight or ten miles."

"Has Lord Nelson left no discretion in the orders, sir?"

"None; unless Raoul Yvard distinctly consent to give up the lugger. In that case, I have a letter, which authorizes me to delay the execution, until I can communicate directly with the commander-in-chief."

"How very unlucky it has been, all round! Is there no possibility, sir, of making up a case that might render this discretion available?"

"That might do among you irresponsibles, Mr. Griffin," answered Cuffe, a little sharply; "but I would rather hang forty Frenchmen than be Bronted by Nelson, for neglect of duty.'

27 *

Cuffe spoke more strongly than he intended, perhaps ; but, the commander of a ship-of-war does not always stop to weigh his words, when he condescends to discuss a point with an inferior. The reply put a check upon Griffin's zeal, however, though the discourse did not the less proceed.

"Well, sir," the lieutenant answered, "I'm sure we are all as anxious as you can be, to avert this affair from our ship. 'T was but the other day, we were boasting in the gun-room, to some of the Lapwing's officers that were on a visit here, that the Proserpine never had an execution or a court-martial flogging on board her, though she had now been under the British ensign near four years, and had been seven times under fire !"

"God send, Griffin, that Clinch find the admiral, and get back in time !"

"How would it do, sir, to send the vice-governatore to try the prisoner ; perhaps *he* might persuade him to *seem* to consent—or, some such thing, you know, sir, as might justify a delay. They say the Corsicans are the keenest-witted fellows in all these seas ; and Elba is so near to Corsica, that one cannot fancy there is much difference between their people."

"Ay, your veechy is a regular witch !—He made out so well in his first interview with Yvard, that no one can doubt his ability to overlay him, in another !"

"One never knows, Captain Cuffe. The Italian has more resources than most men ; and the Signor Barrofaldi is a discreet, sensible man, when he acts with his eyes open. Le Feu-Follet has cheated others besides the vice-governatore, and the podestâ !"

"Ay, these d——d Jack-o'-Lanterns are never to be trusted. It would hardly surprise me to see the Folly coming down, wing-and-wing, from under the land, and passing out to sea, with a six-knot breeze, while we lay as still as a cathedral, with not air enough to turn the smoke of the galley-fire from the perpendicular."

"She's not inside of us, Captain Cuffe ; of that we may be certain. I have been on the main-top-gallant-yard, with the best glass in the ship, and have swept the whole coast, from the ruins over against us, here to the eastward, up to the town of Salerno; there is nothing to be seen, as large as a sparanara."

"One would think, too, this Monsieur Yvard might give up, to save his own life, after all!"

"*We* should hardly do it, I hope, Captain Cuffe?"

"I believe you are right, Griffin; one feels forced to respect the privateersman, in spite of his trade. Who knows but something might be got out of that Bolt? He must know as much about the lugger as Yvard himself."

"Quite true, sir; I was thinking of proposing something of the sort, not a minute since. Now, that's a fellow one may take pleasure in riding down, as one would ride down the main tack. Shall I have him sent for, Captain Cuffe?"

The captain hesitated; for the previous experiments on Ithuel's selfishness had failed. Still, the preservation of Raoul's life, and the capture of the lugger, were now objects of nearly equal interest with Cuffe, and he felt disposed to neglect no plausible means of effecting either. A sign of approbation was all the lieutenant needed; and, in a few minutes, Ithuel stood, again, in the presence of his captain.

"Here is an opportunity for you to fetch up a good deal of lee-way, Master Bolt," commenced the captain; "and I am willing to give you a chance to help yourself. You know where you last left the Few-Folly, I suppose?"

"I don't know but I might, sir," answered Ithuel, rolling his eyes around him, curious to ascertain what the other would be at. "I don't know but I might remember, on a pinch, sir; though, to own the truth, my memory is none of the most desperate best."

"Well, then, where was it? Recollect that the life of your late friend, Raoul Yvard, may depend on your answer."

"I want to know!—Well, this Europe *is* a curious part of the world, as all must admit, that come from Ameriky. What has Captain Rule done now, sir, that he stands in such jeopardy?"

"You know that he is convicted as a spy; and my orders are to have him executed, unless we can get his lugger. *Then*, indeed, we may possibly show him a little favour; as we do not make war so much on individuals, as on nations."

Cuffe would probably have been puzzled to explain the application of his own sentiment to the case before him ; but, presuming on his having to deal with one who was neither very philosophical nor logical himself, he was somewhat indifferent to his own mode of proceeding, so that it effected the object. Ithuel, however, was not understood. Love for Raoul, or the lugger, or, indeed, for anything else, himself excepted, formed no part of his character ; while hatred of England had got to be incorporated with the whole of his moral system ; if such a man could be said to have a moral system at all. He saw nothing to be gained by serving Raoul, in particular ; though this he might have done did nothing interfere to prevent it ; while he had so strong an aversion to suffering the English to get le Feu-Follet, as to be willing even to risk his own life, in order to prevent it. His care, therefore, was to accomplish his purpose, with the least hazard to himself.

" And, if the lugger can be had, sir, you intend to let Captain Rule go ?" he asked, with an air of interest.

" Ay, we *may* do that ; though it will depend on the admiral. Can you tell us where you left her, and where she probably now is ?"

" Captain Rule has said the first, already, sir. He told the truth, about that, before the court. But, as to telling where the lugger is now, I'll defy any man to do it ! Why, sir, I've turned in, at eight bells, and left her, say ten or fifteen leagues dead to leeward of an island, or a light-house, perhaps ; and on turning out at eight bells, in the morning, found her, just as far to windward of the same object. She's as oncalculating craft as I ever put foot aboard of."

" Indeed !" said Cuffe, ironically ; " I do not wonder that her captain's in a scrape."

" Scrape, sir !—The Folly is nothing *but* a scrape. I've tried my hand at keeping her reck'nin'."

" You !"

" Yes, sir, I ; Ithuel Bolt, that's my name, at hum' or abroad, and I've tried to keep the Folly's reck'nin', with all the advantage of thermometer, and lead-lines, and logarithms, and such necessaries, you know, Captain Cuffe ; and *I* never yet could place her within a hundred miles of the spot where she was actually seen to be."

"I am not at all surprised to hear this, Bolt; but what I want at present, is to know what you think may be the precise position of the lugger, without the aid of the thermometer, and of logarithms; I 've a notion you would make out better, by letting such things alone?"

"Well, who knows but I might, sir! My idee of the Folly, just now, sir, is that she is somewhere off Capri, under short canvass, waiting for Captain Rule and I to join her, and keeping a sharp look-out after the inimies' cruisers."

Now, this was not only precisely the position of the lugger at that very moment, but it was what Ithuel actually believed to be her position. Still, nothing was farther from this man's intention than to betray his former messmates. He was so very cunning, as to have detected how little Cuffe was disposed to believe him; and he told the truth, as the most certain means of averting mischief from the lugger. Nor did his *ruse* fail of its object. His whole manner had so much deceit and low cunning about it, that neither Cuffe nor Griffin believed a word he said; and after a little more pumping, the fellow was dismissed in disgust, with a sharp intimation that it would be singularly for his interest to look out how he discharged his general duties in the ship.

"This will never do, Griffin," exclaimed the captain, vexed and disappointed. "Should anything occur to Clinch, or should the admiral happen to be off, with the king, on one of his shooting excursions, we shall be in a most serious dilemma. Would to God, we had not left the anchorage, at Capri! *Then*, one might communicate with the flag, with some certainty. I shall never forgive myself, if anything fatal actually take place!"

"When one does all for the best, Captain Cuffe, his mind ought to be at ease, and you could not possibly foresee what has happened. Might not—one wouldn't like either—but—necessity is a hard master—"

"Out with it, Griffin—anything is better than suspense.'

"Well, sir, I was just thinking that possibly this young Italian girl might know something about the lugger, and, as she clearly loves the Frenchman, we should get a strong purchase on her tongue, by means of her heart."

Cuffe looked intently at his lieutenant, for half a minute; then he shook his head in disapprobation.

21

" No, Griffin, no," he said, " to this I never can consent. As for this quibbling, equivocating Yankee, if Yankee he be, one wouldn't feel many scruples of delicacy ; but to probe the affections of a poor, innocent girl, in this way, would be going too far. The heart of a young girl should be sacred, under every circumstance."

Griffin coloured, and he bit his lip. No one likes to be outdone, in the appearance of. generosity, at least ; and he felt vexed that he should have ventured on a proposition that his superior treated as unbecoming.

" Nevertheless, sir, she might think the lugger cheaply sold," he said, with emphasis, " provided her lover's life was what she got in exchange. It would be a very different thing were we to ask her to sell her admirer, instead of a mere privateer."

" No matter, Griffin. We will not meddle with the private feelings of a young female, that chance has thrown into our hands. As soon as we get near enough in with the land, I intend to let the old man take his boat, and carry his niece ashore. That will be getting rid of *them*, at least, honourably and fairly. God knows what is to become of the Frenchman."

.This terminated the conference. Griffin went on deck, where duty now called him ; and Cuffe sat down to re-peruse, for the ninth or tenth time, the instructions of the admiral.

CHAPTER XXII.

" I have no dread,
And feel the curse to have no natural fear,
Nor fluttering throb, that beats with hopes or wishes,
Or lurking love of something on the earth."
Manfred.

By this time, the day had materially advanced, and there were grave grounds for the uneasiness which Cuffe began so seriously to feel. All three of the ships were still in the Bay
8 *

of Salerno, gathering in towards its northern shore, however. The Proserpine, the deepest embayed, the Terpsichore, and the Ringdove, having hauled out towards Campanella, as soon as satisfied nothing was to be seen in-shore of them. The heights, which line the coast, from the immediate vicinity of the town of Salerno, to the head-land that ends near Capri, have long been celebrated, not only for their beauty and grandeur, but in connection with the lore of the middle ages. As the Proserpine had never been in this bay before, or never so near its head, her officers found some temporary relief from the very general uneasiness that was felt on account of their prisoner, in viewing scenery that is remarkable even in that remarkable section of the globe. The ship had gone up abreast of Amalfi, and so close in, as to be less than a mile from the shore. The object was to communicate with some fishermen, which had been done; the information received going to establish the fact, that no craft resembling the lugger had been in that part of the Bay. The vessel's head was now laid to the southward and westward, in waiting for the zephyr, which might soon be expected. The gallant frigate, seen from the impending rocks, looked like a light merchantman, in all but her symmetry and warlike guise; nature being moulded on so grand a scale all along that coast, as to render objects of human art, unusually diminutive to the eye. On the other hand, the country-houses, churches, hermitages, convents, and villages, clustered all along the mountain sides, presented equally delusive forms, though they gave an affluence to the views, that left the spectator in a strange doubt, which most to admire, their wildness, or their picturesque beauty. The little air that remained, was still at the southward, and as the ship moved slowly along this scene of singular attraction, each ravine seemed to give up a town, each shelf of rock, a human habitation, and each natural terrace, a villa and a garden.

Of all men, sailors get to be the most *blazés* in the way of the sensations produced by novelties, and fine scenery. It appears to be a part of their calling, to suppress the emotions of a greenhorn; and, generally, they look upon anything that is a little out of the ordinary track, with the coolness of those who feel it is an admission of inferiority to betray surprise. 't seldom happens with them, that anything occurs, or any-

thing is seen to which the last cruise, or, if the vessel be engaged in trade, the last voyage, did not at least furnish a
parallel; usually the past event, or the more distant object, has the advantage. He who has a sufficient store of
this reserved knowledge and experience, it will at once be
seen, enjoys a great superiority over him who has not, and
is placed above the necessity of avowing a sensation as humiliating as wonder. On the present occasion, however,
but few held out against the novelty of the actual situation
of the ship; most on board being willing enough to allow
that they had never before been beneath cliffs that had such
a union of the magnificent, the picturesque, and the soft;
though a few continued firm, acting up to the old characters,
with the consistency of settled obstinacy.

Strand, the boatswain, was one of those who, on all such
occasions, " died hard." He was the last man in the ship
who ever gave up a prejudice; and this for three several
reasons : he was a cockney, and believed himself born in
the centre of human knowledge; he was a seaman, and understood the world; he was a boatswain, and stood upon his
dignity.

As the Proserpine fanned slowly along the land, this personage took a position between the knight-heads, on the
bowsprit, where he could overlook the scene, and at the
same time hear the dialogue of the forecastle; and both with
suitable decorum. Strand was as much of a monarch forward, as Cuffe was aft; though the appearance of a lieutenant, or of the master, now and then, a little dimmed the
lustre of his reign. Still, Strand succumbed completely to
only two of the officers—the captain and the first-lieutenant;
and not always to these, in what he conceived to be purely
matters of sentiment. In the way of duty, he understood
himself too well, ever to hesitate about obeying an order;
but when it came to opinions, he was a man who could
maintain his own, even in the presence of Nelson.

The first captain of the forecastle, was an old seaman of
the name of Catfall. At the precise moment when Strand
occupied the position named, between the knight-heads, this
personage was holding a discourse with three or four of the
forecastle-men, who stood on the heel of the bowsprit,
inboard — the etiquette of the ship not permitting these wor-

thies to show their heads above the rettings. Each of the party had his arms folded ; each chewed tobacco ; each had his hair in a queue ; and each occasionally hitched up his trousers, in a way to prove that he did not require the aid of suspenders in keeping his nether garments in their proper place. It may be mentioned, indeed, that the point of division between the jacket and the trousers, was marked in each by a bellying line of a clean white shirt, that served to relieve the blue of the dress, as a species of marine facing. As was due to his greater experience and his rank, Catfall was the principal speaker among those who lined the heel of the bowsprit.

"This here coast is moun*tain*ious, as one may own," observed the captain of the forecastle ; " but what I say is, that it 's not *as* moun*tain*ious as some I 've seen. Now, when I went round the 'arth with Captain Cook, we fell in with islands that were so topped off with rocks, and the like o' that, that these here affairs, alongside on 'em, wouldn't pass for anything more than a sort of jury mountains."

" There you 're right, Catfall," said Strand, in a patronizing way ; " as anybody knows as has been round the Horn. I didn't sail with Captain Cook, seeing that I was then the boatswain of the Hussar, and she couldn't have made one of Cook's squadron, being a post-ship, and commanded by a full-built captain ; but I *was* in them seas when a younker, and can back Catfall's account of the matter by my largest anchor, in the way of history. D——e, if I think these hillocks would be called even jury mountains, in that quarter of the world. They tell me there 's several noblemen's and gentlemen's parks near Lunnun, where they make mountains just to look at ; that must be much of a muchness with these here chaps. I never drift far from Wappin', when I 'm at home, and so I can't say I 've seen these artifice hills, as they calls them, myself ; but there 's one Joseph Shirk, that lives near St. Katharine's Lane, that makes trips regularly into the neighbourhood, who gives quite a particular account of the matter."

" I dare to say it 's all true, Mr. Strand," answered the captain of the forecastle, " for I 've know'd some of them travelling chaps who have seen stranger sights than that. No, sir, I calls these mountains no great matter ; and as to

28

the houses and villages on 'em, where you see one, here, you might say you could see two on some of the desert islands—"

A very marvellous account of Cook's Discoveries was suddenly checked by the appearance of Cuffe on the forecastle. It was not often the captain visited that part of the ship; but he was considered a privileged person, let him go where he would. At his appearance, all the "old salts" quitted the heel of the spar, tarpaulins came fairly down to a level with the bag-reefs of the shirts, and even Strand stepped into the nettings, leaving the place between the knight-heads clear. To this spot Cuffe ascended with a light, steady step, for he was but six-and-twenty, just touching his hat, in return to the boatswain's bow.

A boatswain, on board an English ship-of-war, is a more important personage than he is apt to be on board an American. Neither the captain nor the first-lieutenant disdains conversing with him, on occasions; and he is sometimes seen promenading the starboard side of the quarter-deck, in deep discourse with one or the other of those high functionaries. It has been said that Cuffe and Strand were old shipmates, the latter having actually been boatswain of the ship in which the former first sailed. This circumstance was constantly borne in mind by both parties, the captain seldom coming near his inferior, in moments of relaxation, without having something to say to him.

" Rather a remarkable coast, this, Strand," he commenced, on the present occasion, as soon as fairly placed between the knight-heads; " something one might look for a week, in England, without finding it."

" I beg your pardon, sir, but I'm not of the same way of thinking. I was just telling the forecastle lads, down there, that there's many a nobleman and gentleman, at home, as has finer hills than these, made by hand, in his parks and gardens, just to look at."

" The d——l you have!—And what did the forecastle lads, down there, say to that?"

" What could they, sir? It just showed the superiority of an Englishman to an Italian; and that ended the matter. Don't you remember the Injees, sir?—" -

"'The Indies!—Why the coast between Bombay and Calcutta is as flat as a pancake, most of the distance."

"Not them Injees, sir, but t' other—the West, I mean. The islands and mountains we passed and went into in the Rattler; your honour was only a young gentleman, then, but was too much aloft to miss the sight of anything—and all along America, too."

As Strand was speaking, he glanced complacently round, as if to intimate to the listeners what an old friend of the captain's they enjoyed in the person of their boatswain.

"Oh! the West-Indies—you're nearer right there, Strand; and yet they have nothing to compare to this. Why, here are mountains, alive with habitations, that fairly come up to the sea!"

"Well, sir, as to habitations, what's these to a street in Lunnun? Begin on the starboard hand, for instance, as you walk down Cheapside, and count as you go; my life for it, you'll reel off more houses, in half an hour's walk, than are to be found in all that there village yonder. Then you'll remember, sir, that the starboard hand only has half, every Jack having his Jenny. I look upon Lunnun as the finest sight in nature, Captain Cuffe, after all I have seen in many cruises!"

"I don't know, Mr. Strand.—In the way of coast, one may very well be satisfied with this. Yonder town, now, is called Amalfi; it was once a place of great commerce they say."

"Of commerce, sir!—why it's nothing but a bit of a village, or at most, of a borough, built in a hollow.—No haven, no docks, no comfortable place, even, for setting up the frame of a ship on the beach. The commerce of such a town must have been mainly carried on by means of mules and jackasses, as one reads of in the trade of the Bible."

"Carried on as it might be, trade it once had.—There does not seem to be any hiding-place, along this shore, for a lugger like the Folly, after all, Strand."

The boatswain smiled, with a knowing look, while, at the same time, the expression of his countenance was like that of a man who did not choose to let others into all his secrets.

" The Folly is a craft we are not likely to seé, again, Captain Cuffe," he then answered, if it were only out of respect to his superior.

" Why so ?—The Proserpine generally takes a good look at everything she chases."

" Ay, ay, sir ; that may be true, as a rule, but I never knew a craft found, after a third look for her. Everything seems to go by thirds, in this world, sir ; and I always look upon a third chase as final. Now, sir, there are three classes of admirals, and three sets of flags ; a ship has three masts ; the biggest ships are three deckers ; then there are three planets—"

" The d——l there are !—How do you make *that* out, Strand ?"

" Why, sir, there 's the sun, moon and stars ; that makes just three, by my count."

" Ay, but what do you say to Jupiter, Saturn, Venus, and all the rest of them, the earth included ?"

" Why, sir, they 're all the rest of the stars, and not planets, at all. Then, sir, look around you, and you 'll find everything going by threes. There are three topsails, three jibs, and three top-gallant-sails—"

" And two courses," said the captain, gravely, to whom this theory of the threes was new.

" Quite true, sir, in name, but your honour will recollect the spanker is nothing but a fore-and-aft course, rigged to a mast, instead of to a jack-yard, as it used to be."

" There are neither three captains nor three boatswains, to a ship, Master Strand."

" Certainly not, sir ; that would be oppressive, and they would stand in each other's way ; still, Captain Cuffe, the thirds hold out wonderfully, even in all these little matters. There 's the three lieutenants ; and there 's the boatswain, gunner and carpenter—and—"

" Sail-maker, armourer, and captain of the mast," interrupted Cuffe, laughing.

" Well, sir, you may make anything seem doubtful, by bringing forward a plenty of reasons ; but all my experience says, a third chase never comes to anything, unless it turns out successful ; but that *after* a third chase, all may as well be given up."

"I fancy, Lord Nelson holds a different doctrine, Strand. He tells us to follow a Frenchman round the earth, rather than let him escape."

"No doubt, sir. Follow him round three earths, if you can keep him in sight; but not round *four*. That is all I contend for, Captain Cuffe. Even women, they tell me, take what is called their thirds, in a fellow's forti'n."

"Well, well, Strand, I suppose there must be some truth in your doctrine, or you wouldn't hold out for it so strenuously; and, as for this coast, I must give it up, too, for I never expect to see another like it; much less a third."

"It's my duty to give up to your honour; but I ask permission to think a third chase should always be the last one. That's a melancholy sight to a man of feelin', Captain Cuffe, the object between the two midship-guns, on the starboard side of the main-deck, sir?"

"You mean the prisoner?—I wish, with all my heart, he was not there, Strand. I think I would rather he were in his lugger again, to run the chances of that fourth chase of which you seem to think so lightly."

"Your hanging ships are not often lucky ships, Captain Cuffe. In my judgment, asking your pardon, sir, there ought to be a floating gaol in every fleet, where all the courts and all the executions should be held."

"It would be robbing the boatswains of no small part of their duty, were the punishments to be sent out of the different vessels," answered Cuffe, smiling.

"Ay, ay, sir—the punishments, I grant, your honour; but hanging is an *execution*, and not a punishment. God forbid that, at my time of life, I should be ordered to sail in a ship that has no punishment on board; but I'm really getting to be too old to look at executions with any sort of pleasure. Duty that isn't done with pleasure, is but poor duty, at the best, sir."

"There are many disagreeable, and some painful duties to be performed, Strand; this of executing a man, let the offence be what it may, is among the most painful."

"For my part, Captain Cuffe, I do not mind hanging a mutineer so very much, for he is a being that the world ought not to harbour; but it is a different thing with an enemy, and a spy. It's our duty to spy as much as we

28 *

can for our king and country, and one ought never to bear
too hard on such as does their duty.   With a fellow that
can't obey orders, and who puts his own will above the
pleasure of his superiors, I have no patience; but I do not
so much understand why the gentlemen of the courts are so
hard on such as do a little more reconn'itrin' than common."

"That is because ships are less exposed to the attempts
of spies than armies, Strand.   A soldier hates a spy, as
much as you do a mutineer.   The reason is, that he may
be surprised by an enemy through his means, and butchered
in his sleep.   Nothing is so unpleasant to a soldier as a
surprise; and the law against spies, though a general law of
war, originated with soldiers, rather than with us sailors, I
should think."

"Yes, sir, — I dare say your honour is right. He's a
rum 'un a soldier, at the best; and this opinion proves it.
Now, sir, Captain Cuffe, just suppose a Frenchman of about
our own metal, took it into his head to surprise the Proserpine, some dark night: what would come of it, after all?
There's the guns, and it's only to turn the hands up, to set
'em at work, just the same as if there wasn't a spy in the
world.   And should they prefer to come on board us, and
to try their luck at close quarters, I rather think, sir, the
surprise would meet 'em face to face.   No—no—sir; spies
is nothing to us, though it might teach 'em manners to keel-
haul one, once-and-a-while."

Cuffe now became thoughtful and silent, and even Strand
did not presume to speak, when the Captain was in this
humour. The latter descended to the forecastle, and walked
aft, his hands behind his back, and his head inclining
downward.   Every one he met made way for him, as a
matter of course; in that mood, he moved among the throng
of a ship of war, as a man tabooed.   Even Winchester respected his commander's abstraction, although he had a
serious request to make, which it is time to explain.

Andrea Barrofaldi and Vito Viti remained on board the
frigate, inmates of the cabin, and gradually becoming more
accustomed to their novel situation.   They did not escape
the jokes of a man-of-war, but, on the whole, they were well
treated, and were tolerably satisfied; more especially as the

hope of capturing le Feu-Follet began to revive. As a matter of course, they were apprised of the condition of Raoul, and, both kind and benevolent men in the main, they were desirous of conversing with the prisoner, and of proving to him that they bore no malice. Winchester was spoken to on the subject, but before he granted the permission, he thought it safest to consult the Captain in the matter. At length an opportunity offered, Cuffe suddenly rousing himself, and giving an order in relation to the canvass the ship was under.

"Here are the two Italian gentlemen, Captain Cuffe," observed Winchester, "desirous of speaking to the prisoner. I did not think it right, sir, to let him have communication with any one, without first ascertaining your pleasure."

"Poor fellow!—His time is getting very short, unless we hear from Clinch; and there can be no harm in granting him every indulgence. I have been thinking of this matter, and do not possibly see how I can escape ordering the execution, unless it be countermanded from Nelson himself."

"Certainly not, sir. But Mr. Clinch is an active and experienced seaman, when he is in earnest; we may still hope something from him. What is to be done with the Italians, sir?"

"Let them, or any one else that poor Yvard is willing to see, go below."

"Do you mean to include old Giuntotardi and his niece, Captain Cuffe?— and this deserter of our own, Bolt, — he, too, has had something to say of a wish to take leave of his late shipmate?"

"We might be justified in denying the request of the last, Mr. Winchester, but hardly of the others. Still, if Raoul Yvard wishes to see even him, his desire may as well be granted."

Thus authorized, Winchester no longer hesitated about granting the several permissions. An order was sent to the sentinel, through the corporal of the guard, to allow any one to enter the prisoner's room, whom the latter might wish to receive. A ship was not like a prison on shore, escape being next to impossible, more especially from a vessel at sea. The parties accordingly received intimation that they

might visit the condemned man, should the latter be disposed
to receive them.

By this time, something like a general gloom had settled
on the ship.   The actual state of things was known to all
on board, and few believed it possible that Clinch could reach
the Foudroyant, receive his orders, and be back in time to
prevent the execution.   It wanted now but three hours of
sunset, and the minutes appeared to fly, instead of dragging.
The human mind is so constituted, that uncertainty increases
most of its sensations;—the apprehension of death even,
very usually exciting a livelier emotion than its positive
approach.   Thus it was with the officers and people of the
Proserpine: had there been no hope of escaping the execution, they would have made up their minds to submit to the
evil, as unavoidable; but the slight chance which did actually exist, created a feverish excitement that soon extended
to all hands; and this as completely as if a chase were in
sight, and each individual was bent on overtaking her.   As
minute after minute flew by, the feeling increased, until it
would not much exceed the bounds of truth to say, that,
under none of the vicissitudes of war, did there ever exist so
feverish an hour, on board his Britannic Majesty's ship, the
Proserpine, as the very period of which we are now writing.
Eyes were constantly turned towards the sun, and several
of the young gentlemen collected on the forecastle, with no
other view than to be as near as possible to the head-land,
around which the boat of Clinch was expected to make her
re-appearance, as behind it she had last been seen.

The zephyr had come at the usual hour, but it was light,
and the ship was so close to the mountains, as to feel very
little of its force.   It was different with the two other
vessels.   Lyon had gone about in time, to get clear of the
highest mountains, and his lofty sails took enough of the
breeze, to carry him out to sea, three or four hours before;
while the Terpsichore, under Sir Frederick Dashwood, had
never got near enough in with the land, to be becalmed at
all.   Her head had been laid to the south-west, at the first
appearance of the afternoon wind; and that frigate was now
hull-down to sea-ward—actually making a free wind of it,
as she shaped her course up between Ischia and Capri.   As
for the Proserpine, when the bell struck three, in the first

dog-watch, she was just abeam of the celebrated little islets of the Sirens, the western breeze now beginning, to die away, though, getting more of it, the ship was drawing ahead, faster than she had been since the turn of the day.

Three bells, in the first dog-watch, indicate the hour of half-past five. At that season of the year, the sun sets a few minutes past six. Of course, there remained but little more than half-an-hour, in which to execute the sentence of the law. Cuffe had never quitted the deck, and he actually started, when he heard the first sound of the clapper. Winchester turned. towards him, with an inquiring look; for every thing had been previously arranged between them; he received merely a significant gesture in return. This, however, was sufficient. Certain orders were privately issued. Then there appeared a stir among the fore-topmen, and on the forecastle, where a rope was rove at the fore-yard-arm, and a grating was rigged for a platform—unerring signs of the approaching execution.

Accustomed as these hardy mariners were to brave dangers of all sorts, and to witness human suffering of nearly every degree, a feeling of singular humanity had come over the whole crew. Raoul was their enemy, it is true, and he had been sincerely detested by all hands, eight-and-forty hours before; but circumstances had entirely changed the ancient animosity into a more generous and manly sentiment. In the first place, a successful and a triumphant enemy was an object very different from a man in their own power, and who lay entirely at their mercy. Then, the personal appearance of the young privateersman was unusually attractive, and altogether different from what it had been previously represented, and that, too, by an active rivalry, that was not altogether free from bitterness. But chiefly, was the generous sentiment awakened by the conviction that the master-passion, and none of the usual inducements of a spy, had brought their enemy into this strait; and though clearly guilty, in a technical point of view, that he was influenced by no pitiful wages, even allowing that he blended with the pursuit of his love, some of he motives of his ordinary warfare. All these considerations, coupled with the reluctance that seamen ever feel to having an execution in their ship, had entirely turned the tables ; and there, where Raoul would have found so lately, between two and three hundred active and formidable enemies, he might almost be said now to have as many sympathizing friends.

No wonder, then, that the preparations of the fire topmen were regarded with unfavourable eyes. The unseen hand of authority, nevertheless, held all in restraint. Cuffe himself did not dare to hesitate any longer. The necessary orders were given, though with deep reluctance, and then the captain went below, as if to hide himself from human eyes.

The ten minutes that succeeded were minutes of intense concern. All hands were called, the preparations had been completed, and Winchester waited only for the re-appearance of Cuffe, to issue the order to have the prisoner placed on the grating. A midshipman was sent into the cabin, after which, the commanding officer came slowly, and with a lingering step, upon the quarter-deck. The crew was assembled on the forecastle and in the waists ; the marine guard was under arms ; the officers clustered around the capstan ; and a solemn, uneasy expectation, pervaded the whole ship. The lightest foot-fall was audible. Andrea and his friend stood apart, near the taffrail, but no one saw Carlo Giuntotardi, or his niece.

"There is yet some five-and-twenty minutes of sun, I should think, Mr. Winchester," observed Cuffe, feverishly glancing his eye at the western margin of the sea, towards which the orb of day was slowly settling, gilding all that side of the vault of heaven with the mellow lustre of the hour and the latitude.

"Not more than twenty, I fear, sir," was the reluctant answer.

"I should think five might suffice, at the worst ; especially, if the men made a swift run." This was said in a half whisper, and thick, husky, tones, the Captain looking anxiously at the lieutenant the while.

Winchester shrugged his shoulders, and turned away unwilling to reply.

Cuffe now had a short consultation with the surgeon, the object of which was to ascertain the minimum of time a man might live suspended by the neck at the yard-arm of a frigate. The result was not favourable; for a sign followed to bring forth the prisoner.

Raoul came on deck, in charge of the master-at-arms, and the officer who had acted as prevost-martial. He was clad in his clean white lazzarone garb, wearing the red Phrygian cap already mentioned. Though his face was pale, no man could detect any tremor in the well-turned muscles that his loose attire exposed to view. He raised his cap courteously to the group of officers, and threw an understanding glance forward, at the fearful arrangement on the fore-yard. That he was shocked, when the grating and the rope met his eye, is unquestionable; but, rallying in an instant, he smiled, bowed to Cuffe, and moved towards the scene of his contemplated execution, firmly, but without the smallest signs of bravado in his manner.

A death-like stillness prevailed, while the subordinates adjusted the rope, and placed the condemned man on the grating. Then the slack of the rope was drawn in, by hand, and the men were ordered to lay hold of the instrument of death, and to stretch it along the deck.

" Stand by, my lads, to make a swift run, and a strong jerk, at your first pull," said Winchester in a low voice, as he passed down the line. " Rapidity is mercy, at such a moment."

" Good God !" muttered Cuffe, " can the man die in this manner, without a prayer ; without even a glance towards heaven, as if asking for mercy ?"

" He is an unbeliever, I hear, sir," returned Griffin. " We have offered him all the religious consolation we could ; but he seems to wish for none."

" Hail the top-gallant yards once more, Mr. Winchester," said Cuffe, huskily.

"Fore-top-gallant yard, there !"

" Sir ?"

" Any signs of the boat—look well into the bay of Naples —we are opening Campanella now sufficiently to give you a good look up towards the head."

A pause of a minute succeeded. Then the look-out aloft shook his head in the negative, as if unwilling to speak. Winchester glanced at Cuffe, who turned anxiously, mounted a gun, and strained his eyes in a gaze to the northward.

"All ready, sir," said the first-lieutenant, when another minute elapsed.

Cuffe was in the act of raising his hand, which would have been the signal of death, when the dull, heavy report of a distant gun, came booming down from the direction of the town of Naples.

"Stand fast!" shouted Cuffe, fearful the men might get the start of him. "Make your mates take their calls from their mouths, sir. Two more guns, Winchester, and I am the happiest man in Nelson's fleet!"

A second gun *did* come, just as these words were uttered: then followed a breathless pause of half a minute, when a third, smothered, but unequivocal report succeeded.

"It must be a salute, sir," Griffin uttered, inquiringly.

"The interval is too long. Listen! I hope to God, we have had the last!"

Every ear in the ship listened intently, Cuffe holding his watch in his hand. Two entire minutes passed, and no fourth gun was heard. As second after second went by, the expression of the captain's countenance changed, and then he waved his hand in triumph.

"It's as it should be, gentlemen," he said. "Take the prisoner below, Mr. Winchester. Unreeve the rope, and send that d———d grating off the gun. Mr. Strand, pipe down the people."

Raoul was immediately led below. As he passed through the after-hatch, all the officers on the quarter-deck bowed to him; and not a man was there in the ship, who did not feel he happier for the reprieve.

CHAPTER XXIII.

" He saw with his own eyes the moon was round,
Was also certain that the earth was square,
Because he 'd journey'd fifty miles, and found
No sign that it was circular anywhere."

Don Juan.

RAOUL YVARD was indebted to a piece of forethought in Clinch, for his life. But for the three guns, fired so opportunely from the Foudroyant, the execution could not have been stayed; and but for a prudent care on the part of the master's-mate, the guns would never have been fired. The explanation is this : When Cuffe was giving his subordinate instructions how to proceed, the possibility of detention struck him, and he bethought him of some expedient by which such an evil might be remedied. At his suggestion, then, the signal of the guns was mentioned by the captain, in his letter to the commander-in-chief, and its importance pointed out. When Clinch reached the fleet, Nelson was at Castel a Mare, and it became necessary to follow him to that place by land. Here Clinch found him in the palace of Qui-Si-Sane, in attendance on the court, and delivered his despatches. Nothing gave the British admiral greater pleasure, than to be able to show mercy ; the instance to the contrary already introduced, existing as an exception in his private character and his public career; and it is possible that an occurrence so recent, and so opposed to his habits, may have induced him the more willingly now to submit to his ordinary impulses, and to grant the respite asked, with the greater promptitude.

" Your captain tells me, here, sir," observed Nelson, after he had read Cuffe's letter a second time, " little doubt exists that Yvard was in the Bay on a love affair, and that his purposes were not those of a spy, after all ?"

" Such is the opinion aboard us, my lord," answered the master's-mate. " There are an old man and a very charming young woman in his company, whom Captain Cuffe

29   22

says were in the cabin of this ship, on a visit to your lordship, only a few days since."

Nelson started, and his face flushed. Then he seized a
pen, and, with the only hand he had, scratched a letter,
directing a reprieve until further orders. This he signed,
and handed to Clinch, saying, as he did so—

" Get into your boat, sir, and pull back to the frigate as
fast as possible; God forbid that any man suffer wrong-
fully!"

" I beg your pardon, my lord—but there is not time,
now, for me to reach the ship before the sun set. I have
a signal prepared in the boat, it is true ; but the frigate may
not come round Campanella before the last moment, and
then all these pains will be lost. Does not Captain Cuffe
speak of some guns to be fired from the flag-ship, my lord?"

" He does, sir ; and this may be the safest mode of communicating, after all. With this light westerly air, a gun
will be heard a long distance at sea. Take the pen
write as I dictate, sir."

Clinch seized the pen, which the admiral, who had lost
his right arm only a few years before, really felt unable to
use, and wrote as follows—

" Sir—Immediately on receipt of this, you will fire three
heavy guns, at intervals of half-a-minute, as a signal to the
Proserpine to suspend an execution.

" To the Commanding Officer of His Majesty's Ship
Foudroyant."

As soon as the magical words of " Nelson and Bronté"
were affixed to this order, with a date, Clinch rose to depart.
After he had made his bows, he stood with his hand on the
lock of the door, as if uncertain whether to prefer a request
or not.

" This is a matter of moment, sir, and no time is to be
lost," added Nelson. " I feel great anxiety about it, and
wish you to desire Captain Cuffe to send you back with a
report of all that has passed, as soon as convenient."

" I will report your wishes, my lord," answered Clinch,
brightening up ; for he only wanted an opportunity to speak
of his own promotion, and this was now offered in per-

spective. "May I tell the commanding officer of the flag-
ship to use the lower-deck guns, my lord?"

"He will do that of his own accord, after reading those
orders — heavy guns, mean the heaviest. Good-afternoon,
sir; for God's sake, lose no time."

Clinch obeyed this injunction to the letter. He reached
the Foudroyant, some time before sunset, and immediately
placed the order in her captain's hands. A few words of
explanation set everything in motion, and the three guns
were fired on the side of the ship towards Capri, most
opportunely for our hero.

The half-hour that succeeded, on board the Proserpine,
was one of gaiety and merriment. Every person was glad
that the ship had escaped an execution; and then, it was
the hour for piping down the hammocks, and for shifting
the dog-watches. Cuffe recovered all his animation, and
conversed cheerfully, having Griffin for an interpreter, with
his two Italian guests. These last had been prevented from
paying their visit to the prisoner, on account of the latter's
wish to be alone; but the intention was now renewed; and
sending below, to ascertain if it would be agreeable, they
proceeded together on their friendly mission. As the two
worthies, who had not altogether got their sea-legs, slowly
descended the ladder, and threaded their way among the
throng of a ship, the discourse did not flag between them.

"Cospetto!" exclaimed the podestà; "Signor Andrea,
we live in a world of wonders! A man can hardly say
whether he is actually alive, or not. To think how near
this false Sir Smees was to death, half an hour since; and,
now, doubtless he is as much alive, and as merry as any
of us!"

"It would be more useful, friend Vito Viti," answered the
philosophical vice-governatore, "to remember how near
those who live are always to death, who has only to open
his gates, to cause the strongest and fairest to pass at once
nto the tombs."

"By San Stefano, but you have a way with you, vice-
governatore, that would become a cardinal! It's a thou
sand pities the church was robbed of such a support; though
I do think, Signor Andrea, if your mind would dwell less on
another state of being, it would be more cheerful; and I

may say more cheering to those with whom you discourse. There are evils enough, in this life, without thinking so much of death."

"There are philosophers who pretend, good Vito, that nothing that we see around us actually has an existence. That we *fancy* everything : fancy that this is a sea called the Mediterranean ; fancy this is a ship — yonder is the and ; fancy that we live ; and even fancy death."

"Corpo di Bacco ! Signor Andrea," exclaimed the other, stopping short at the foot of the ladder, and seizing his companion by a button, afraid he would desert him in the midst of a strange delusion, " you would not trifle in such a matter with an old friend — one who has known you from childhood ? *Fancy* that I am alive !"

"*Si* — I have told you only the truth. The imagination is very strong, and may easily give the semblance of reality to unreal things."

"And that I am not a podestâ in fact, but one only in fancy !"

"Just so, friend Vito ; and that I am only a vice-governatore, too, in the imagination."

"And that Elba is not a real island, or Porto Ferrajo a real town , and that even all our iron, of which we *seem* to send so much about the world, in good, wholesome ships, is only a sort of ghost of solid substantial metal !"

"*Si—si*—that everything which appears to be material, is, in fact, imaginary ; iron, gold, or flesh."

"And then I am not Vito Viti, but an impostor ? What a rascally philosophy is this ! Why, both of us are as bad as this Sir Smees, if what you say be true, vice-governatore —or make-believe vice-governatore."

"Not an impostor, friend Vito ; for there is no real being of thy name, if thou art not he."

"Diavolo ! A pretty theory this, which would teach the young people of Elba that there is no actual podestâ in the island, but only a poor miserable sham one ; and no Vito Viti on earth. If they get to think this, God help the place as to order and sobriety."

"I do not think, neighbour, that you fully understand the matter, which may be owing to a want of clearness on my part ; but as we are now on our way to visit an unfortunate prisoner, we may as well postpone the discussion to another time. There are many leisure moments on board a ship, to the language of which one is a stranger, that might be usefully and agreeably relieved by going into the subject more at large."

"Your pardon, Signor Andrea;—but there is no time like the present. Then, if the theory be true, there is no prisoner at all—or, at the most, an imaginary one—and it can do Sir Smees no harm to wait; while, on the other hand, I shall not have a moment's peace, until I learn whether there is such a man as Vito Viti, or not, and whether I am he."

"Brother Vito, thou art impatient; these things are not learned in a moment; moreover, every system has a beginning and an end, like a book; and who would ever become learned, that should attempt to read a treatise backward?"

"I know what is due to you, Signor Andrea, both on account of your higher rank, and on account of your greater wisdom, and will say no more at present; though to keep from *thinking* on a philosophy that teaches I am not a podestà, or you a vice-governatore, is more than flesh and blood can bear."

Andrea Barrofaldi, glad that his companion was momentarily appeased, now proceeded towards Raoul's little prison, and was immediately admitted by the sentry, who had his orders to that effect. The prisoner received his guests courteously and cheerfully; for we are far from wishing to represent him as so heroic as not to rejoice exceedingly at having escaped death by hanging, even though it might prove to be a respite, rather than a pardon. At such a moment, the young man could have excused a much more offensive intrusion, and the sudden change in his prospects disposed him a little to be jocular; for truth compels us to add, that gratitude to God entered but little into his emotions. The escape from death, like his capture, and the other incidents of his cruise, were viewed simply as the results of the fortune of war.

Winchester had directed that Raoul's state-room should be supplied with every little convenience that his situation required, and, among other things, it had two common ship's stools. One of these was given to each of the Italians, while the prisoner took a seat on the gun-tackle of one of the two guns that formed the sides of his apartment. It was now night, and a mist had gathered over the arch above, which hid the stars, and rendered it quite dark. Still, Raoul had neither lamp, nor candles; and, though they had been offered him, he declined their use, as he had found stranger eyes occasionally peeping through the openings in the canvass, with the idle curiosity of the vulgar, to ascertain the appearance and employments of one condemned to die. He had experienced a good deal of annoyance from this feeling, the previous night; and the same desire existing to see how a criminal could bear a respite, he had determined to pass his evening in obscurity. There was a lantern, or two, however, on the gun-deck, which threw a dim light, even beyond the limits of the canvass bulk-heads. As has been said already, these bulk-heads extended from gun to gun, so as to admit light and air from the ports. This brought the tackles, on one side, into the room; and on one of these Raoul now took his seat.

Andrea Barrofaldi, from his superior condition in life, as well as from his better education, and nicer natural tact, far surpassed his companion in courtesy of demeanour. The latter would have plunged in *medias res* at once,-but the vice-governatore commenced a conversation on general matters, intending to offer his congratulations for the recent respite, when he conceived that a suitable occasion should offer. This was an unfortunate delay in one respect; for Vito Viti no sooner found that the main object of the visit was to be postponed, than he turned with eagerness to the subject in discussion, which had been interrupted in order to enter the state-room.

"Here has the vice-governatore come forward with a theory, Sir Smees," he commenced, the moment a pause in the discourse left him an opening—"here has the vice-governatore come forward with a theory, that I insist the church would call damnable, and at which human nature revolts—"

"Nay, good Vito, thou dost not state the case fairly," interrupted Andrea, whose spirit was a little aroused at so abrupt an assault. "The theory is not mine; it is that of a certain English philosopher, in particular who, let it be said, too, was a bishop."

"A Lutheran!—was it not so, honourable Signor An
drea?—a bishop so called?"

"Why, to confess the truth, he *was* a heretic, and not
to be considered as an apostle of the true church."

"Ay—I would have sworn to that. No true son of
the church would ever broach such a doctrine. Only
fancy, signori, the number of imaginary fires, tongues, and
other instruments of torture that would become necessary
to carry on punishment under such a system! To be consistent, even the devils ought to be imaginary."

"Comment, signori!" exclaimed Raoul, smiling, and
arousing to a sudden interest in the discourse; "did any
English bishop ever broach such a doctrine? Imaginary
devils, and imaginary places of punishment, are coming near
to our revolutionary France! After this, I hope our much
abused philosophy will meet with more respect."

"My neighbour has not understood the theory of which
he speaks," answered Andrea, too good a churchman not to
feel uneasiness at the direction things were taking; "and so,
worthy Vito Viti, I feel the necessity of explaining the whole
matter, at some length. Sir Smees," so the Italians called
Raoul, out of courtesy, still, it being awkward for them,
after all that had passed, to address him by his real name—
"Sir Smees will excuse us, for a few minutes; perhaps it
may serve to amuse him, to hear to what a flight the imagination of a subtle-minded man can soar."

Raoul civilly expressed the satisfaction it would give him
to listen, and stretching himself on the gun-tackle, in order
to be more at ease, he leaned back with his head fairly within
the port, while his feet were braced against the inner truck
of the gun-carriage. This threw him into a somewhat re-
cumbent attitude, but it being understood as intended to
render what was but an inconvenient seat at the best, tolerably comfortable, no one thought it improper.

It is unnecessary for us to repeat, here, all that Andrea
Barrofaldi thought proper to say, in his own justification, and
in explanation of the celebrated theory of Bishop Berkely.
Such a task was not performed in a minute; and, in truth,
prolixity, whenever he got upon a favourite theme, was apt
to be one of the vice-governatore's weaknesses. He was far
from acquiescing in the doctrine, though he annoyed his old

neighbour exceedingly, by presenting the subject in such a way as to render it respectable in appearance, if not conclusive in argument. To the latter, it was peculiarly unpleasant to imagine, even for the sake of argument, that there was no such island as Elba, and that he was not its podestâ; and all his personal and egotistical propensities came in aid of his official reluctance, to disgust him thoroughly with a theory that he did not hesitate to say, "was an outrage on every honest man's nature."

"There are fellows in the world, Signor Andrea," the straight-forward podestâ urged, in continuation of his objections, "who might be glad enough to find everything imaginary, as you say—chaps that cannot sleep of nights, for bad consciences, and to whom it would be a great blessing if the earth would throw them overboard, as they say in this ship, and let them fall into the great ocean of oblivion. But they are baroni in grain, and ought not to pass for anything material, among honest people. I 've known several of those rogues at Livorno, and, I dare say, Napoli is not altogether without them; but that is a very different matter from telling a handsome and virtuous young maiden, that her beauty and modesty are both seeming; and respectable magistrates, that they are as great impostors as the very rogues they send to the prisons; or, perhaps, to the galleys."

To speeches like these, Andrea opposed his explanations and his philosophy, until the discussion became animated, and the dialogue loud. It is rather a peculiarity of Italy, that one of the softest languages of Christendom is frequently rendered harsh and unpleasant, by the mode of using it. On this occasion, certainly, the animation of the disputants did not mitigate the evil. Griffin happened to pass the spot, on the outside of the canvass, just at this moment, and, catching some of the words, he stopped to listen. His smiles and translations soon collected a group of officers, and the sentry respectfully dropping a little on one side, the deck around the state-room of the prisoner became a sort of parquet to a very amusing representation. Several of the young gen lemen understood a little Italian, and Griffin translating rapidly, though in an under-tone, the whole affair was deemed to be particularly diverting.

"This is a rum way of consoling a man who is con

demned to die," muttered the master; " I wonder the French man stands all their nonsense."

" O !" rejoined the marine officer, " drill will do anything. These Revolutionists are so drilled into hypocrisy, that, I dare say, the fellow is grinning, the whole time, as if perfectly delighted."

Raoul, in fact, listened with no little amusement. At first, his voice was occasionally heard in the discussion, evidently aiming at exciting the disputants ; but the warmth of the latter soon silenced him, and he was fain to do nothing but listen. Shortly after the discussion got to be warm, and just as Griffin was collecting his group, the prisoner stretched himself still further into the port, to enjoy the coolness of the evening breeze, when, to his surprise, a hand was laid gently on his forehead.

" Hush !" whispered a voice close to his ear, " it is the American—Ithuel—be cool ;—now is the moment to pull for life."

Raoul had too much self-command to betray his astonishment, but, in an instant, every faculty he possessed was on the alert. Ithuel, he knew, was a man for exigencies. Experience had taught him a profound respect for his enterprise and daring, when it became necessary to act. Something must certainly be in the wind, worthy of his attention, or this cautious person would not have exposed himself in a situation which would be sure to lead to punishment, if detected. Ithuel was seated astride of one of the chains, beneath the main-channel of the ship, a position which might be maintained without detection, possibly, so long as it continued dark ; but which, in itself, if seen, would have been taken as a proof of an evil intention.

" What would you have, Etooelle?" whispered Raoul, who perceived that his companions were too much occupied to observe his movements, or to hear his words.

" The *Eye*talian, and his niece, are about to go ashore. Everything is ready and understood. I 've consaited you might pass out of the port, in the dark, and escape in the boat. Keep quiet—we shall see."

Raoul understood his respite to be a thing of doubtful ermination. Under the most favourable results, an English orison remained in perspective, and then the other side of the picture offered the image of Ghita to his eye! He was in a tumult of feeling, but, accustomed to self-command, still no exclamation escaped him.

"When—cher Etooelle? *when?*" he asked, his whisper being tremulous, in spite of every effort to command himself.

"Now—*too-der-sweet*—(*tout-de-suite*)—the boat is at the gangway, and old Giuntotardi is in her—they are rigging a chair for the gal.—Ay—there she swings off!—don't you hear the call?"

Raoul did hear the whistle of the boatswain, which was piping "lower away," at that very moment. He listened intently, as he lay stretched upon the gun-tackles; and then he heard the splash in the water, as the boat was hauled closer to, in order to be brought beneath the chair. The rattling of oars, too, was audible, as Ghita left the seat, and moved aft. "Round in," called out the officer of the deck; after which Carlo Giuntotardi was left in quiet possession of his own boat.

The moment was exceedingly critical. Some one, in all probability, was watching the boat from the deck; and, though the night was dark, it required the utmost caution to proceed with any hopes of success. At this instant, Ithuel again whispered—

"The time's near. Old Carlo has his orders, and little Ghita is alive to see them obeyed. All now depends on silence and activity. In less than five minutes, the boat will be under the port."

Raoul understood the plan; but, it struck him as hopeless. It seemed impossible that Ghita could be permitted to quit the ship, without a hundred eyes watching her movements; and though it was dark, it was far from being sufficiently so, to suppose it practicable for any one to join her and not be seen. Yet this risk must be taken, or escape was out of the question. An order given through the trumpet, was encouraging; it announced that the officer of the watch was employed at some duty that must draw his attention another way. This was a great deal; few presuming to look aside, while this functionary was inviting their attention in another direction.

Raoul's brain was in a whirl. The two Italians were at

the height of their discussion ; and fortunately, the clamour they made was at the loudest. Even the suppressed laughter of the officers on the outside of the canvass, was audible to *him ;* though the disputants could hear nothing but their own voices. Every knock of the boat against the ship's side, every sound of the oars, as Carlo's foot rattled them about, and the wash of the water, were audible. It seemed as if all the interests of life—the future, the past, and the present, together with the emotions of his whole heart, were compressed into that single instant. Ignorant of what was expected, he asked Ithuel, in French, the course he ought to take.

" Am I to fall, head-foremost, into the water ? What would you have of me ?" he whispered.

" Lie quiet, till I tell you to move. I 'll make the signal, Captain Rule ; let the Eyetalians blaze away."

Raoul could not see the water, as he lay with his head fairly in the port ; and he had to trust entirely to the single sense of hearing. Knock, knock, knock ; the boat dropped slowly along the ship's side, as if preparing to shove off. All this, Carlo Giuntotardi managed exceedingly well. When he lay immediately beneath the main-channels, it would not have been an easy thing to see his boat, even had there been any one on the look-out. Here he held on ; for he was not so lost to external things, as not fully to understand what was expected of him. Perhaps he was less attended to, by those on deck, from the circumstance that no one believed him capable of so much worldly care.

" Is everything safe for a movement, inboard ?" whispered Ithuel.

Raoul raised his head and looked about him. That a group was collected around the state-room, he understood by the movements, the low conversation, and the suppressed laughter ; still, no one seemed to be paying any attention to himself. As he had not spoken for some time, however, he thought it might be well to let his voice be heard ; and, taking care that it should sound well within the port, he made one of the light objections to the vice-governatore's theory, that he had urged at the commencement of the controversy. This was little heeded, as he expected ; but it served to make those without know that he was in his prison, and might prevent an untimely discovery. Everything else seemed propitious; and laying down again, at his length, his face came within a few inches of Ithuel's.

"All safe," he whispered, "what would you have me do?"

"Nothing, but shove yourself ahead carefully, by means of your feet."

This Raoul did; at first, as it might be, inch by inch, until Ithuel put the end of a rope into his hands, telling him it was well fast to the channel above. The rope rendered the rest easy; the only danger now being of too much precipitation. Nothing would have been easier, than for Raoul to drag his body out at the port, and to drop into the boat; but, to escape, it was still necessary to avoid observation. The ship was quite half-a-league from the point of Campanella, and directly abreast of it; and there was no security to the fugitives unless they got some distance the start of any pursuers. This consideration induced the utmost caution on the part of Ithuel; nor was it entirely lost on his friend. By this time, however, Raoul found he was so completely master of his movements, as to be able to swing his legs out of the port, by a very trifling effort; then the descent into the boat would be the easiest thing imaginable. But a pressure from the hand of Ithuel checked him.

"Wait a little," whispered the latter, "till the Eyetalians are at it, cat and dog fashion."

The discussion was now so loud and warm, that it was not necessary to lose much time. Ithuel gave the signal, and Raoul dragged his head and shoulders up by his arms, while he placed his feet against the gun; the next moment he was hanging perpendicularly, beneath the main-chains. To drop lightly and noiselessly into the boat, took but a second. When his feet touched a thwart, he found that the American was there before him. The latter dragged him down to his side, and the two lay concealed in the bottom of the yawl, with a cloak of Ghita's thrown over their persons. Carlo Giuntotardi was accustomed to the management of a craft like that in which he now found himself; simply releasing his boat-hook from one of the chains, the ship passed slowly ahead, leaving him, in about a minute fairly in her wake, a hundred feet astern.

So far, everything had succeeded surprisingly. The night was so dark, as to embolden the two fugitives now to rise, and to take their seats on the thwarts; though all this was done with exceeding caution, and without the least noise. The oars were soon out, Carlo took the tiller, and a feeling of exultation glowed at the heart of Raoul, as he bent to his ashen implement, and felt the boat quiver with the impulse.

"Take it coolly, Captain Rule," said Ithuel, in a low voice; "it's a long pull, and we are still within ear-shot of the frigate. In five minutes more we shall be dropped so far, as to be beyond sight; then we may pull directly out to sea, if we wish."

Just then the bell of the Proserpine struck four; the signal it was eight o'clock. Immediately after, the watch was called, and a stir succeeded in the ship.

"They only turn the hands up," said Raoul, who perceived that his companion paused, like one uneasy.

"That is an uncommon movement for shifting the watch! What is *that?*"

It was clearly the overhauling of tackles; the plash of a boat, as it struck the water, followed.

CHAPTER XXIV.

"Our dangers, and delights, are near allies
"From the same stem the rose and prickle rise."
ALLEYN.

It has been seen that a generous sympathy had taken place of hostile feeling, as respects Raoul, in the minds or most on board the Proserpine. Under the influence of this sentiment, an order had been passed through the sentries not to molest their prisoner, by too frequent or unnecessary an examination of the state-room. With a view to a proper regard to both delicacy and watchfulness, however, Winchester had directed that the angle of the canvass nearest the cabin-door lantern, should be opened a few inches, and that the sentinel should look in, every half-hour; or as often

30

as the ship's bell told the progress of time. The object was simply to be certain that the prisoner was in his room, and that he was making no attempt on his own life; a step that had been particularly apprehended previously to the respite. Now, the whole of the dispute between the two Italians, and that which had passed beneath the ship's channels, did not occupy but six or seven minutes; and the little cluster of officers was still gaining recruits, when Raoul was fairly in the yawl of his own lugger. At this moment the ship's bell struck the hour of half-past seven. The marine advanced, with the respect of a subordinate, but with the steadiness of a man on post, to examine the state-room. Although the gentlemen believed this caution unnecessary, the loud voices of Andrea and Vito Viti being of themselves a sort of guarantee that the prisoner was in his cage, they gave way to a man, fully understanding that a sentinel was never to be resisted. The canvass was opened a few inches, the light of the lantern at the cabin-door shot in, and there sat the vice-governatore and the podestà, gesticulating, and staring into each other's face, still in hot dispute;—but the place of Raoul Yvard was empty!

Yelverton happened to look into the room with the sentinel. He was a young man of strong powers of perception, with all the phrenological bumps that are necessary to the character, and he saw, at a glance, that the bird had flown. The first impression was, that the prisoner had thrown himself into the sea, and he rushed on deck, without speaking to those around him, made a hurried statement to the officer of the deck, and had a quarter-boat in the water in a surprisingly short time. His astonished companions below, were less precipitate, though the material fact was soon known to them. Griffin gave a hasty order, and the canvass bulk-head came down, as it might be, at a single jerk, leaving the two disputants in full view, utterly unconscious of the escape of their late companion, sputtering and gesticulating, furiously.

"Halloo! vice-governatore," cried Griffin, abruptly, for he saw that the moment was not one for ceremony; "what have you done with the Frenchman?—where is Raoul Yvard?"

"Il Signor, Sir Smees? Monsieur Yvard, if you will?

Neighbour Vito, what, indeed, has become of the man who so lately sat *there* ?"

" Cospetto !—according to your doctrine, Signor Andrea, there never was a man there at all—only the imagination of one ; it is not surprising that such a being should be missed. But, I protest against any inferences being drawn from this accident. All Frenchmen are flighty and easily carried away, and now that they are no longer ballasted by religion, they are so many moral feathers. No, no — let a man of respectable information, of sound principles, and a love for the saints, with a good, substantial body, like myself, vanish only once, and then I may confess, it will tell in favour of your- logic, vice-governatore."

" An obstinate man, neighbour Vito, is a type of the imperfections that a—"

" Your pardon, Signor Barrofaldi,"—interrupted Griffin— " this is not a moment for philosophical theories, but for us seamen to do our duty. What has become of Raoul Yvard —your Sir Smees ?"

" Signor Tenente, as I hope to be saved, I have not the smallest idea! There he was, a minute or two since, seated by that cannon, apparently an attentive and much edified auditor of a discussion we were holding on the celebrated theory of a certain bishop of your own country ; which theory, rightly considered—mind I say *rightly considered*, neighbour Vito ; for the view you have taken of this matter is—"

" Enough of this, for the present, Signori"—added Griffin. " The Frenchman was in this place when you came here ?"

" He was, Signor Tenente, and seemed greatly to enjoy the discussion in which—"

" And you have not seen him quit you—through the canvass, or the port ?"

" Not I, on my honour,— I did suppose him too much entertained to leave us."

" Ah ! Sir Smees has just vanished into the imagination," growled the podestà, " which is going home to the great 'ogical family of which he is an ideal member! There being no lugger, no corsair, no sea, and no frigate, it seems to me that we are all making a stir about nothing."

Griffin did not stop to question farther. He was quickly

on deck, where he found Cuffe, who had just been brought out of his cabin by a hurried report.

"What the d——l is the meaning of all this, gentlemen?" demanded the latter, in that tone which a commander so naturally assumes when things go wrong. "Whoever has suffered the prisoner to escape may expect to hear from the Admiral directly, on the subject."

"He is not in his state-room, sir," answered Griffin, "and I directed the boatswain to pipe away all the boats'-crews as I came up the ladder."

As this was said, boat after boat was falling, and, in two or three minutes, no less than five were in the water, including that in which Yelverton was already rowing round the ship to catch the presumed swimmer, or drowning man.

"The Frenchman is gone, sir," said Winchester, "and he must have passed out of the port. I have sent one of the gentlemen to examine if he is not stowed away about the chains."

"Where is the boat of the old Italian and his niece?"

A pause succeeded this question, and light broke in upon all at the same instant.

"That yawl *was* alongside," cried Griffin,—"no one was in her, however, but Giuntotardi and the girl"

"Beg your pardon, sir," said a young fore-top-man, who had just descended the rigging,—"I saw the boat from aloft sir, and it hung some time, sir, under the starboard main-chains.—It is so dark I couldn't fairly make it out; but summat seemed to be passed into it, from a port. I didn't like the look of the thing, and so our captain just told me to come on deck and report it, sir."

"Send Ithuel Bolt here, Mr. Winchester—bear a hand. sir, and let us have a look at that gentleman."

It is needless to say that the call was unanswered; and then all on board began to understand the mode of the escape. Officers rushed into the several boats, and no less than five different parties commenced the pursuit. At the same time the ship hoisted a lantern, as a signal for the boats to rally to.

It has been said that the Proserpine, when this incident occurred, was off the point of the Campanella, distant about half a marine league. The wind was light at east, or was what is called the land breeze, and the vessel had about three knots way on her. The head-land was nearly abeam, and she was looking up through the pass which separates Capri from the main, hauling round into the Bay of Naples; intending to anchor in the berth she had left the previous day. The night was too dark to permit an object small as a boat to be seen at any distance, but the black mass of Capri was plainly visible in its outlines, towering into the air near two thousand feet; while the formation of the coast on the other side, might be traced with tolerable certainty and distinctness. Such was the state of things when the five boats mentioned quitted the ship.

Yelverton had acted as if a man were overboard; or, he had not waited for orders. While pulling round the ship alone, he caught sight, though very dimly, of the yawl, as it moved in towards the land, and without communicating with any on board, the truth flashed on his mind also, and he gave chase. When the other boats were ready, the two that were on the outside of the ship pulled off to seaward a short distance, to look about them in that direction; while the two others, hearing the oars of the light gig, in which Yelverton was glancing ahead, followed the sound, under the impression that they were in pursuit of the yawl. Such was the state of things at the commencement of an exceedingly vigorous and hot pursuit.

As Raoul and Ithuel had been at work, while time was lost in doubt in and around the ship, they had got about three hundred yards the start of even Yelverton. Their boat pulled unusually well, and being intended for only two oars, it might be deemed full manned, with two as vigorous hands in it as those it had. Still it was not a match for the second gig, and the four chosen men who composed its crew, which was the boat taken by Yelverton, in the hurry of the moment. In a pull of a mile and a half, the yawl was certain to be overtaken, and the practised ears of Raoul soon assured him of the fact. His own oars were muffled. He determined to profit by the circumstance, and turn aside, in the hope that his fleet pursuers would pass him unseen. A sheer was accordingly given to the boat, and instead of pulling directly towards the land, the fugitives inclined to the westward; the sea appearing the most obscure in that

30 *　　　　23

direction, on account of the proximity of Capri. This arti
fice was completely successful. Yelverton was so eager in
the chase, that he kept his eyes riveted before him, fancying, from time to time, that he saw the boat ahead, and he
passed within a hundred and fifty yards of the yawl, without
in the least suspecting her vicinity. Raoul and Ithuel ceased
rowing, to permit this exchange of position, and the former
had a few sarcastic remarks on the stupidity of his enemies,
as some relief to the feelings of the moment. None of the
English had muffled oars. On the contrary, the sounds of the
regular man-of-war jerks were quite audible in every direction ; but so familiar were they to the ears of the Proserpines,
that the crews of the two boats that came next after Yelverton, actually followed the sounds of his oars, under the
belief that they were in the wake of the fugitives. In this
manner, then, Raoul suffered three of the five boats to pass
ahead of him. The remaining two were so distant as not
to be heard, and when those in advance were sufficiently in
advance, he and Ithuel followed them, with a leisurely stroke,
reserving themselves for any emergency that might occur.

It was a fair race between the gig and the two cutters
that pursued her. The last had the sounds of the former's
oars in the ears of their crews to urge them to exertion ; it
being supposed they came from the strokes of the pursued,
while Yelverton was burning with the desire to outstrip
those who followed, and to secure the prize for himself.
This made easy work for those in the yawl, which was soon
left more than a cable's-length astern.

"One would think, Ghita," said Raoul, laughing, though
he had the precaution to speak in an under-tone——" one
would think that your old friends, the vice-governatore and
the podestâ, commanded the boats in-shore of us, were it not
known that they are this very moment quarrelling about the
fact, whether there is such a place as Elba on this great
planet of ours, or not."

"Ah ! Raoul, remember the last dreadful eight-and-forty
hours ! do not stop to trifle, until we are once more fairly
beyond the power of your enemies."

"Peste!——I shall be obliged to own, hereafter, that there
is some generosity in an Englishman. I cannot deny their
treatment, and yet I had rather it had been more ferocious."

" This is an unkind feeling; you should strive to tear ii from your heart."

" It's a great deal to allow to an Englishman, Captain Rule, to allow him gineros'ty," interrupted Ithuel. " They're a fierce race, and fatten on mortal misery."

" Mais, bon Etouelle, your back has escaped this time; you ought to be thankful."

" They're short-handed, and didn't like to cripple a top-man," answered he of the Granite state, unwilling to con cede anything to liberal or just sentiments. " Had the ship's complement been full, they wouldn't have left as much skin on my back as would cover the smallest-sized pin-cushion. I owe 'em no thanks, therefore."

" Bien; quant à moi, I shall speak well of the bridge which carries me over," said Raoul. " Monsieur Cuffe has given me good food, good wine, good words, a good state-room, a good bed, and a most timely reprieve."

" Is not your heart grateful to God for the last, dear Raoul?" asked Ghita, in a voice so gentle and tender, that the young man could have bowed down and worshipped her.

After a pause, however, he answered, as if intentionally to avoid the question by levity.

" I forgot the philosophy, too," he said. *That* was no small part of the good cheer. Ciel! it was worth some risk to have the advantage of attending such a school. Did you understand the matter in dispute between the two Italians, brave Etooelle?"

" I heerd their *Eye*-talian jabber," answered Ithuel; " but supposed it was all about saints' days, and eating fish. No reasonable man makes so much noise when he is talking senso."

" Pardie—it was *philosophy!* They laugh at us French for living by the rules of reason, rather than those of preju-dice; and then to hear what *they* call philosophy! You would scarce think it, Ghita," continued Raoul, who was now light of heart, and full of the scene he had so recently witnessed—" you would hardly think it, Ghita, but Signor Andrea, sensible and learned as he is, maintained that it was not folly to believe in a philosophy which teaches that nothing we see or do actually exists, but that everything was mere seeming. In short, that we live in an imaginary world, with imaginary people in it; float on an imaginary sea, and cruise in imaginary ships."

" And was all that noise about an idee, Captain Rule?"

" Si—but men will quarrel about an idea—an imaginary thing, Etooelle, as stoutly as about substantials. Hist! They will chase imaginary things, too, as are the boats ahead of us at this moment."

" There are others following us," observed Carlo Giunto tardi, who was more alive to surrounding objects than common; and who, from his habitual silence, often heard that which escaped the senses of others. " I have noticed the sound of their oars some time."

This produced a pause, and even a cessation in the rowing, in order that the two seamen might listen. Sure enough, the sound of oars was audible outside, as well as in-shore, leaving no doubt that some pursuers were still behind them. This was bringing the fugitives between two fires, as it might be; and Ithuel proposed pulling off at right angles to the course again, in order to get into the rear of the whole party. But to this, Raoul objected. He thought the boats astern were still so distant as to enable them to reach the shore in time to escape. Once on the rocks, there could be little danger of being overtaken in the darkness. Still, as it was a first object with Raoul to rejoin his lugger as soon as possible, after landing Ghita, he did not wish to place his boat in any situation of much risk. This induced some deliberation; and it was finally determined to take a middle course, by steering into the pass between Capri and Campanella, in the expectation that, when the leading English boats reached the point of the latter, they would abandon the pursuit as hopeless, and return to the ship.

" We can land you, dearest Ghita, at the Marina Grande of Sorrento; then your walk to St. Agata will be neither ong nor painful."

" Do not mind me, Raoul; put me on the land at the nearest place, and go you to your vessel. God has relieved you from this great jeopardy, and your duty is to strive to act as it is evident he intends you to do. As for me, leagues will be light, if I can only be satisfied that thou art in safety."

"Angel!— Thou never thinkest of self! But not a foot this side of Sorrento will I quit thee. We can pull thither in an hour or two; then I shall feel that I have done a duty. Once ashore, Etooelie and I can set our little sail, and will run out to sea between the two islands. No fear but what we can do that, with this land breeze; after which, a few rockets burned, will tell us where to find le Feu-Follet."

Ghita again remonstrated, but in vain. Raoul persisted and she was obliged to submit. The conversation now ceased; the two men plying the oars diligently, and to good effect. Occasionally they ceased, and listened to the sounds of the oars in the frigate's boats, all which were evidently collecting in the vicinity of the point or cape. By this time, the yawl had the extremity of the land abeam, and it soon passed so far into the Bay, as to bring most, if not all, of the pursuers astern. In the darkness, with no other guide than the sounds mentioned, and with so many pursuers, there was some uncertainty, of course, as to the position of all the boats; but there was little doubt that most of them were now somewhere in the immediate vicinity of Campanella. As Raoul gave this point a good berth, and his own progress was noiseless, this was bringing himself and companions, after their recent dangers, into comparative security.

More than an hour of steady rowing followed, during which time the yawl was making swift way towards the Marina Grande of Sorrento. After passing Massa, Raoul felt no further uneasiness, and he requested Carlo Giuntotardi to sheer in towards the land, where less resistance from the breeze was met with, and where it was also easier to know the precise position. Apprehension of the boats now ceased, though Ithuel fancied, from time to time, that he heard smothered sounds, like those of oars imperfectly muffled. Raoul laughed at his conceits and apprehensions, and, to confess the truth, he became negligent of his duty, again, in the soothing delight of finding himself, once more, free, in all but heart, in the company of Ghita. In this manner the yawl moved ahead, though with materially diminished speed, until, by the formation of the heights, and the appearance of the lamps and candles on the piano, Ghita knew

that they were drawing quite near to the indentation of the
coast on which is situate the town of Sorrento.

"As soon as my uncle and myself have landed at the
Marina Grande, Raoul," said Ghita, "thou and the American will be certain to seek thy lugger; then thou promisest
to quit the coast?"

"Why ask promises of one that thou dost not sufficiently
respect to think he will keep them?"

"I do not deserve this, Raoul; between thee and me, no
promise has ever been broken."

"It is not easy to break vows with one who will neither
give nor accept them. I cannot boast of keeping such idle
faith as this! Go with me before some priest, Ghita, ask
all that man ever has or can swear to, and then thou shalt
see how a sailor can be true to his vow."

"And why before a priest? Thou know'st, Raoul, that,
in thine eyes, all the offices of the church are mummery;
that nothing is more sacred, with thee, for being sworn to at
the altar of God, and with one of his holy ministers for a
witness!"

"Every oath or promise made to *thee*, Ghita, is sacred,
in my eyes. It wanteth not any witness, or any consecrated
place, to make it more binding than thy truth and tenderness
can insure. Thou art my *priest*—my *altar*—my—"

"Forbear!" exclaimed Ghita, in alarm, lest he should
utter the name of that holy Being towards whom her heart
was even at that moment swelling with gratitude for his own
recent escape from death. "Thou know'st not the meaning
of thine own words, and mightst add that which would give
me more pain than I can express."

"Boat, ahoy!" cried a deep, nautical voice, within twenty
yards of them, and in-shore; the hail coming in the sudden,
quick demand that distinguishes the call of a man-of-war's-
man.

A pause of half a minute succeeded, for they in the yawl
were completely taken by surprise.

At length Ithuel, who felt the necessity of saying something, if he would not bring the stranger close alongside of
them, answered in the customary manner of the Italians.

Clinch, for it was he, scouring the shore in quest of the
lugger, on his way back to the Proserpine, gave a growl,

when he found that he must speak in a foreign tongue, if he would continue the discourse; then he mustered all the Italian of which he was master for the occasion. Having cruised long on the station, this was sufficient, however, for his present purpose.

"Is that a boat from Massa or from Capri?" he inquired

"Neither, S'nore," answered Raoul, afraid to trust Carlo's conscience with the management of such a dialogue. "We come round the cape, from St. Agata, and carry figs to Napoli."

"St. Agata! ay, that is the village on the heights; I passed a night there, myself, in the house of one Maria Giuntotardi—"

"Who can this be?" murmured Ghita—"my aunt knows no forestieri!"

"An Inglese, by his thick speech and accent. I hope he will not ask for figs for his supper!"

Clinch was thinking of other things, at that moment; and when he continued, it was to follow the train of his own thoughts.

"Have you seen anything of a barone-looking lugger," he asked, "French-rigged, and French manned, skulking anywhere about this coast?"

"Si—she went north, into the Gulf of Gaeta, just as the sun was setting, and is, no doubt, gone to anchor under the cannon of her countrymen."

"If she has, she'll find herself in hot water," answered Clinch, in English. "We've craft enough, up there, to hoist her in and dub her down to a jolly-boat's size, in a single watch. Did you see anything of a frigate, this evening, near the Point of Campanella?—An Inglese, I mean; a tight six-and-thirty, with three new topsails."

"Si—the light you see, here, just in a range with Capri, is at her gaff; we have seen her the whole afternoon and evening. In fact, she towed us kindly round the cape, until we got fairly into this Bay."

"Then you are the people for me!—Was there a man hanged on board her or not, about sunset?"

This question was put with so much interest, that Raoul cursed his interrogator, in his heart; imagining that he was burning with the wish to learn his own execution. He was also now aware that this was the boat which had left the Proserpine about noon.

" I can tell you there was not, s'nore—if that will gladden your heart. A man was all *ready* to be hanged, when Capitaine Cuffe was pleased to order him taken down."

" Just as three heavy guns were fired up at town—was it not so?" Clinch eagerly inquired.

" Diable! this man may have been my preserver, after all!—You say true, s'nore; it *was* just as three guns were fired up at Naples, though I did not know those guns had anything to do with the intended execution. Can you tell me if they had?"

" If they had!—Why I touched them off with my own hands; they were signals made by the admiral to spare poor Raoul Yvard, for a few days, at least. I am rejoiced to hear that all my great efforts to reach the fleet were not in vain. I don't like this hanging, Mr. Italian."

" S'nore, you show a kind heart, and will one day reap the reward of such generous feelings. I wish I knew the name of so humane a gentleman, that I might mention him in my prayers."

" They 'll never fancy that Captain Rule said *that*," muttered Ithuel, grinning.

" As for my name, friend, it 's no great matter. They call me Clinch, which is a good fast word to sail under, too; but it has no handle to it, other than of a poor devil of a master's-mate; and that, too, at an age when some men carry broad-pennants."

This was said bitterly, and in English; when uttered, the supposed Italian was wished a " buona sera," and the gig proceeded.

" That is *un brave*," said Raoul, with emphasis, as they parted. " If ever I meet with Monsieur Cleench, he will learn that I do not forget his good wishes. *Peste!* if there were a hundred such men in the British marine, Etooelle, we might love it."

" They 're fiery sarpents, Captain Rule, and not to be trusted, any on 'em. As for fine words, I might have fancied myself a cousin of the king's, if I 'd only put my name to their shipping articles. This Mr. Clinch is well enough, in the main ; being his own worst inimy, in the way of the grog pitcher "

" Boat, ahoy !" shouted Clinch again, now about a hundred yards distant, having passed towards the cape. Raoul and Ithuel mechanically ceased rowing, under the impression that the master's-mate had still something to communicate.

" Boat, ahoy !—Answer at once, or you'll hear from me," repeated Clinch.

" Ay, ay," answered another voice, which, in fact, was Yelverton's ; " Clinch, is that you ?"

" Ay, ay, sir—Mr. Yelverton, is it not ?—I think I know the voice, sir."

" You are quite right ; but make less noise—who was that you hailed, a minute or two since ?"

Clinch began to answer ; but, as the two gigs were approaching each other all the time, they were soon so near as to render it unnecessary to speak loud enough to be heard at any distance. All this time, Raoul and Ithuel lay on their oars, almost afraid to stir the water, and listening with an attention that was nearly breathless. They were satisfied that the oars of the English were now muffled ; a sign that they were in earnest in the pursuit, and bent on making a thorough search. The two gigs could not be more than a hundred yards from the yawl, and Ithuel knew that they were the two fastest-rowing boats of the English fleet— so fast, indeed, that Cuffe and his lieutenants had made several successful matches with them, against the officers of different vessels.

" Hist !" said Ghita, whose heart was in her mouth. " Oh ! Raoul, they come !"

Coming, indeed, were they ; and that with vast velocity. So careful, however, was the stroke, that they were within two hundred feet of the yawl, before Raoul and his companion took the alarm, and plunged their own oars again into the water. Then, indeed, the gigs might be dimly seen ; though the shadows of the land deepened the obscurity of night so far, as to render objects at even a less distance quite indistinct. The suddenness and imminency of the danger appeared to arouse all there was of life in Carlo Giuntotardi. He steered, and steered well, being accustomed to the office, by living so long on the coast ; and he

sheered in for the rocks, with the double view of landing, if
necessary, and of getting still deeper within the shadows.

It was soon evident the English gained. Four oars
against two were fearful odds; and it was plainly apparent
the yawl must be overtaken.

"Oh! uncle, towards the arch and water-cavern of the
point," whispered Ghita, whose hands were clasped on her
breast, as if to keep down her emotions. "*That* may yet
save him!"

The yawl was in the act of whirling round the rocks,
which form the deep cove, on which the Marina Grande of
Sorrento lies. Carlo caught his niece's idea, and he kept
his tiller hard a-port; telling Raoul and Ithuel, at the same
time, to take in their oars, as quick as possible. The men
obeyed, supposing it was the intention to land, and take to
the heights for shelter. But just as they supposed the boat
was about to strike against some perpendicular rocks, and
Raoul was muttering his surprise that such a spot should be
chosen to land at, it glided through a low natural arch, and
entered a little basin, as noiselessly as a bubble floating in a
current. The next minute, the two gigs came whirling
round the rocks; one following the shore, close in, to prevent
the fugitives from landing, and the other steering more
obliquely athwart the bay. In still another minute, they
had passed a hundred yards ahead, and the sound of their
movements was lost

CHAPTER XXV.

"And chiefly thou, O spirit, that dost prefer,
  Before all temples, the upright heart and pure,
  Instruct me; for thou know'st."

                              MILTON.

THE spot in which Carlo Giuntotardi had taken refuge,
✔ well known on the Sorrentine shore, as the water-cavern,
at the ruins of Queen Joan's country-house. Cavern it is

not, though the entrance is beneath a low, natural arch; the basin within being open to the heavens, and the place resembling an artificial excavation, made to shelter boats in; profiting by the natural passage to obtain an entrance. Let the origin of this little haven be what it may, art could not have devised a more convenient, or a more perfect refuge than it afforded to our fugitives at a most critical moment. Once through the arch, the boat would have been effectually concealed from her pursuers, under a noon-day sun; nor would any, who were unacquainted with the peculiarities of the entrance, dream of a boat's lying, as it might be, buried in the rocks of the little promontory. Neither Ghita nor her uncle any longer felt concern; but, the former announced her intention to land here, assuring Raoul that she could easily find her way into the bridle-path which leads to St. Agata.

The desperate character of the recent chase, aided by his late almost miraculous escape from death, joined to the necessity of parting from his mistress, rendered our hero melancholy, if not moody. He could not ask Ghita to share his dangers any longer; and yet he felt, if he permitted her now to quit him, the separation might be for ever. Still he made no objection; but, leaving Ithuel in charge of the boat, he assisted Ghita up the funnel-like sides of the basin, and prepared to accompany her on her way to the road. Carlo preceded the pair; telling his niece that she would find him at a cottage on the way, that was well known to both.

The obscurity was not so great as to render the walking very difficult; and Raoul and Ghita pursued their course slowly along the rocks, each oppressed with the same sensation of regret at parting, though influenced by nearly opposing views for the future. The girl took the young man's arm without hesitation; and there was a tenderness in the tones of her voice, as well as in her general manner, that betrayed how nearly her heart was interested in what was passing. Still, principle was ever uppermost in her thoughts; and she determined, now, to speak plainly, and to the purpose.

"Raoul," she said, after listening to some one of those fervent declarations of love that were peculiarly agreeable to one of her affectionate and sincere nature, even when she most felt the necessity of repelling the insinuating suit ; " there must be an end of this. I can never go through, again, the scenes I have lately witnessed, nor allow you to run such fearful risks. The sooner we understand each other, and I may say, the sooner we part, it will be the wiser, and the better for the interests of both. I blame myself, for suffering the intimacy to last so long, and for proceeding so far."

" And this is said by a fervent-souled Italian girl !—One f eighteen years ;—who comes of a region in which it is the boast, that the heart is even warmer than the sun ; of a race, among whom it is hard to find *one—oui*, even a poor *one* — who is not ready to sacrifice home, country, hopes, fortune, nay, life itself, to give happiness to the man who has chosen her from all the rest of her sex."

" It *would* seem to *me* easy to do all this, Raoul. *Si*—I think I could sacrifice everything you have named, to make *you* happy ! Home I have not, unless the Prince's Towers can thus be called ; country, since the sad event of this week, I feel as if I had altogether lost ; of hopes, I have few in this world, with which your image has not been connected ; but, those which were once so precious to me, are now, I fear, lost ; you know I have no fortune, to tempt me to stay, or you to follow ; as for my life, I fear it will soon be very valueless—am sure it will be miserable."

" Then why not decide at once, dearest Ghita, to throw the weight of your sorrows on the shoulders of one strong enough to bear them ? You care not for dress, or gay appearances, and can take a bridegroom even with the miserable aspect of a lazzarone, when you know the heart is right. You will not despise me because I am not decked as I might be for the bridal. Nothing is easier than to find an altar and a priest among these monasteries ; and the hour for saying mass is not very distant. Give me a right to claim you, and I will appoint a place of rendezvous, bring in the lugger to-morrow night, and carry you off in triumph to our gay Provence ; where you will find hearts gentle as your own, to welcome you with joy, and call you sister."

Raoul was earnest in his manner, and it was not possible to doubt his sincerity Though an air of self-satisfaction gleamed in his face, when he alluded to his present personal appearance, for he well knew all his advantages in that way, in spite of the dress of a lazzarone.

"Urge me not, dear Raoul," Ghita answered, though, unconsciously to herself, she pressed closer to his side, and both sadness and love were in the very tones of her voice.; "urge me not, dear Raoul; this can never be. I have already told you the gulf that lies between us; you *will* not cross it, to join *me*, and I *cannot* cross it, to join *you*. Nothing but *that* could separate us; but that, to my eyes, grows broader and deeper every hour."

"Ah, Ghita, thou deceivest me, and thyself. Were thy feelings as thou fanciest, no human inducement could lead thee to reject me."

"It is not a human inducement, Raoul; it is one above earth, and all it holds."

"Peste!—These priests are scourges sent to torment men in every shape! They inflict hard lessons in childhood, teach asperity in youth, and make us superstitious and silly in age. I do not wonder that my brave compatriots drove them from France; they did nothing but devour like locusts, and deface the beauties of providence."

"Raoul, thou art speaking of the ministers of God!" Ghita observed meekly, but in sorrow.

"Pardon me, dearest Ghita; I have no patience when I remember what a trifle, after all, threatens to tear us asunder. Thou pretendest to love me?"

"It is not pretence, Raoul, but a deep, and I fear, a painful reality."

"To think that a girl so frank, with a heart so tender, and a soul so true, will allow any secondary thing to divide her from the man of her choice!"

"It is not a secondary, but a primary thing, Raoul; oh! that I could make thee think so. The question is between thee and God—were it aught else, thou might'st indeed prevail."

"Why trouble thyself about my religion, at all? Are there not thousands of wives who tell their beads, and repeat their aves, while their husbands think of anything but heaven? Thou and I can overlook this difference; others overlook them, and keep but one heart between them still. I never would molest thee, Ghita, in thy gentle worship."

31 *

"It is not thou that I dread, Raoul, but myself;" answered the girl, with streaming eyes, though she succeeded in suppressing the sobs that struggled for utterance. "'A house divided against itself cannot stand,' they say; how could a heart that was filled with thee, find place for the love it ought to bear the author of its being. When the husband lives only for the world, it is hard for the wife to think of heaven as she ought."

Raoul was deeply touched with the feeling Ghita betrayed, while he was ready to adore her for the confiding sincerity with which she confessed his power over her heart. His answer was given with seductive tenderness of manner, which proved that he was not altogether unworthy of the strange conflict he had created in so gentle a breast.

"Thy God will never desert *thee*, Ghita," he said; "thou hast nothing to fear as my wife, or that of any other man. None but a brute could ever think of molesting thee in thy worship, or in doing aught that thy opinions render necessary, or proper. I would tear the tongue from my mouth, before reproach, sneer, or argument, should be used to bring thee pain, after I once felt that thou leanedst on me for support. All that I *have* said has come from the wish that thou would'st not misunderstand me, in a matter that I know thou think'st important."

"Ah! Raoul, little dost thou understand the hearts of women. If thy power is so great over me to-day, as almost to incline me from the most solemn of all my duties, what would it become when the love of a girl should turn into the absorbing affection of a wife! I find it hard, even now, to reconcile the love I bear to God, with the strong feeling thou hast created in my heart. A year of wedded life would endanger more than I can express to you in words."

"And, then, the fear of losing *thy* salvation, is stronger than thy earthly attachments?"

"Nay, Raoul, it is not *that*. I am not selfish, or cowardly as respects myself, I hope; nor do I think, at all, of any *punishment* that might follow from a marriage with an unbeliever; what I most apprehend is being taught to love my God less than I feel I now do, or than, as the creature of his mercy, I ought."

"Thou speakest as if man could rival the being whom

thou worshippest. I have always understood, that the love
we bear the Deity, and that we bear each other, are of a
very different quality. I can see no necessity for their in-
terfering with each other."

"Nothing can be less alike, Raoul; yet one may impair,
if not destroy the other. Oh! if thou would'st but believe
that thy Saviour was thy God, if thou could'st but be dead
to his love, and not active against him, I might hope for
better things; but I *dare* not pledge all my earthly duties
to one who is openly an enemy of my own great Master and
Redeemer."

"I will not, cannot deceive thee, Ghita—*that* I leave to
the priests. Thou know'st my opinions, and must take me
as I am, or wholly reject me. This I say, though I feel
that disappointment, if you persist in your cruelty, will drive
me to some desperate act, by means of which I shall yet
taste of the mercies of these English."

"Say not so, Raoul; be prudent for the sake of your
country—"

"But not for thine, Ghita?"

"Yes, Raoul, and for mine also. I wish not to conceal
how much happier I shall be in hearing of your welfare and
peace of mind. I fear, though an enemy, it will ever give
me pleasure to learn that thou art victorious. But, here is
the road, yonder the cottage where my uncle waits for me,
and we must part. Heaven bless thee, Raoul; my prayers
will be full of thee. Do not—do not, risk more to see me,
but, if—" The heart of the girl was so full, that emotion
choked her. Raoul listened intently for the next word, but
he listened in vain.

"If what, dear Ghita? Thou wert about to utter something that I feel is encouraging."

"Oh! how I hope it may be so, my poor Raoul! I was
going to add, if God ever touches thy heart, and thou
would'st stand before his altar, a believer, with one at thy
side who is ready and anxious to devote all to thee, but her
love of the Being who created her, and her treasures of
future happiness, seek Ghita; thou wilt find *her* thou
would'st have."

Raoul stretched forth his arms to clasp the tender girl to
his bosom; but, fearful of herself, she avoided him, and fled

along the path like one terrified with the apprehension of pursuit. The young man paused a moment, half inclined to follow; then prudence regained its influence, and he bethought him of the necessity of getting to a place of safety while it was yet night. The future was still before him, in hope, and that hope led him to look forward to other occasions to press his suit.

Little, however, did Raoul Yvard, much as he prized her, know Ghita Caraccioli. Her nature was full of womanly sensibilities, it is true, and her heart replete with tenderness for him in particular; but the adoration she paid to God, was of that lasting character which endures to the end. In all she said and felt, she was truth itself; and while no false shame interposed to cause her to conceal her attachment, there was a moral armour thrown about her purposes, that rendered them impregnable to the assaults of the world.

Our hero found Ithuel sleeping in the boat, in perfect security. The graniteman thoroughly understood his situation, and foreseeing a long row before him, he had quietly lain down in the stern-sheet of the yawl, and was taking his rest, as tranquilly as he had ever done in his berth on board le Feu-Follet. He was even aroused with difficulty, and he resumed the oar with reluctance. Before descending the funnel, Raoul had taken a survey of the water from the rocks above. He listened intently, to catch any sounds that might arise from the English boats. But nothing was visible in the obscurity, while distance, or caution, prevented anything from being audible. Satisfied that all was safe outside, he determined to row out into the Bay, and, making a circuit to avoid his enemies, push to the westward, in the expectation of finding his lugger in the offing. As there was now a considerable land-breeze, and the yawl was lightened of so much of her freight, there was little doubt of his being able to effect his purpose, so far as getting out of sight was concerned, at least, long ere the return of light.

"*Pardie*, Etooelle?" Raoul exclaimed, after he had given the American, jog the third, "you sleep like a friar who is paid for saying masses at midnight. Come, ami; now is our time to move, for all is clear outside."

"Well, natur', they say is a good workman, Captain Rule," answered Ithuel, gaping and rubbing his eyes; "and never did she turn off a prettier hiding-place than this. One sleeps so quietly in it! Heigho! I suppose the ash must be kept moving, or we may yet miss our passage back to France. Shove her bows round, Captain Rule; here is the hole, which is almost as hard to find, as it is to thread a needle with a cable. A good shove, and she will shoot out into the open water."

Raoul did as desired. Ithuel touching the tiller, the yawl glided through the opening, and felt the long ground-swel of the glorious Bay. The two adventurers looked about them with some concern, as they issued from their-hiding place, but the obscurity was too deep to bring anything in view on the face of the waters. The flashing that occasionally illuminated the summit of Vesuvius, resembled heat-lightning, and would have plainly indicated the position of that celebrated mountain, had not its dark outlines been visible, exposing a black mass at the head of the Bay. The ragged mountain-tops, behind and above Castel a Mare, were also to be traced, as was the whole range of the nearer coast, though that opposite was only discoverable by the faint glimmerings of a thousand lights, that were appearing and disappearing, like stars eclipsed, on the other side of the broad sheet of placid water. On the Bay itself little could be discerned; under the near coast, nothing, the shadows of the rocks obscuring its borders with a wide belt of darkness.

After looking around them quite a minute in silence, the men dropped their oars, and began to pull from under the point, with the intention of making an offing before they set their little luggs. As they came out, the heavy flap of canvass, quite near, startled their ears, and both turned instinctively to look ahead. There, indeed, was a vessel, standing directly in, threatening even to cross their very track. She was close on a wind, with her larboard tacks aboard, and had evidently just shaken everything, in the expectation of luffing past the point without tacking. Could she succeed in this, it would be in her power to stand on, until compelled to go about beneath the very cliffs of the town of Sorrento. This was, in truth, her aim; for again she shook all her sails.

"Peste!" muttered Raoul; "this is a bold pilot—he loves

24

the rocks, as if they were his mistress! We must lie quiet, Etooelle, and let him pass; else he may trouble us."

" 'Twill be the wisest, Captain Rule; though I do not think him an Englishman. Hark! The ripple under his bow is like that of a knife going through a ripe water-melon."

" Mon Feu-Follet!" exclaimed Raoul, rising and actually extending his arms, as if to embrace the beloved craft. " Etooelle, they seek us, for we are much behind our time!"

The stranger drew near fast; when his outlines became visible, there was no mistaking them. The two enormous luggs, the little jigger, the hull, almost awash, and the whole of the fairy form, came mistily into view, as the swift bird assumes colour and proportion, while it advances out of the depth of the void. The vessel was but a hundred yards distant; in another minute, she would be past.

"*Vive la Republique!*" said Raoul, distinctly, though he feared to trust his voice with a loud hail.

Again the canvass flapped, and the trampling of feet was heard on the lugger's deck; then she came sweeping into the wind, within fifty feet of the yawl. Raoul watched the movement; and by the time her way was nearly lost, he was alongside, and had caught a rope. At the next instant, he was on board her.

Raoul trod the deck of his lugger, again, with the pride of a monarch, as he ascends his throne. Certain of her sailing qualities, and confident of his own skill, this gallant seaman was perfectly indifferent to the circumstance that he was environed by powerful enemies. The wind and the hour were propitious, and no sensation of alarm disturbed the exultation of that happy moment. The explanations that passed between him and his first-lieutenant, Pintard, were brief but distinct. Le Feu-Follet had kept off the land, with her sails lowered, a trim in which a vessel of her rig and lowness in the water would not be visible more than five or six miles, until sufficient time had elapsed, when she was taken into the Gulf of Salerno, to look for signals from the heights of St. Agata. Finding none, she went to sea again, as has been stated, sweeping along the coast, in the hope of falling in with intelligence. Although she could not be seen by her enemies, she saw the three cruisers who were on the

ook-out, and great uneasiness prevailed on board, concern
ing the fates of the absentees. On the afternoon of that
day, the lugger was carried close in with the north-west side
of Ischia, which island she rounded at dusk, seemingly
intending to anchor at Baiæ, a harbour seldom without allied
cruisers. As the wind came off the land, however, she kept
away, and passing between Procida and Mysenum, she came
out into the Bay of Naples, about three hours before meeting
with Raoul, with the intention of examining the whole of the
opposite coast, in search of the yawl. She had seen the
light at the gaff of the Proserpine, and, at first, supposed it
might be a signal from the missing boat. With a view to
make sure of it, the lugger had been kept away, until the
night-glasses announced a ship; when she was hauled up on
a wind, and had made two or three successive half-boards,
to weather the point where her captain lay concealed; the
Marina Grande of Sorrento being one of the places of rendez
vous mentioned by our hero, in his last instructions.

There was a scene of lively congratulation, and of even
pleasing emotion, on the deck of the lugger, when Raoul so
unexpectedly appeared. He had every quality to make
himself beloved by his men. Brave, adventurous, active,
generous and kind-hearted, his qualities rendered him a
favourite to a degree that was not common even among the
people of that chivalrous nation. The French mariner will
bear familiarity better than his great rival and neighbour,
the Englishman; and it was natural with our hero to be
frank and free with all; whether above him or below him in
condition. The temperaments to be brought into subjection
were not as rude and intractable as those of the Anglo-Saxon;
and the off-hand, dashing character of Raoul was admirably
adapted to win both the admiration and the affections of his
people. They now thronged about him, without hesitation
or reserve, each man anxious to make his good wishes
known, his felicitations heard.

"I have kept you playing about the fire, *camarades,*"
said Raoul, affected by the proofs of attachment he received,
' but, we will now take our revenge. There are English
boats in chase of me, at this moment, under the land; we
will try to pick up one or two of them, by way of letting
hem know there is still such a vessel as Le Feu-Follet."

An exclamation of pleasure followed; then an old quarter-master, who had actually taught his commander his first lessons in seamanship, shoved through the crowd, and put his questions with a sort of authority.

"*Mon capitaine*," he said, "have you been near these English?"

"Ay, Benoit; somewhat nearer than I could wish. To own the truth, the reason you have not sooner seen me, was, that I was passing my time on board our old friend, La Proserpine. Her officers and crew would not lose my company, when they had once begun to enjoy it."

"*Peste!—mon cher capitaine*—were you a prisoner?"

"Something of that sort, Benoit. At least, they had me on a grating, with a rope round the neck, and were about to make me swing off, as a spy, when a happy gun or two, from Nelson, up above there, at the town, ordered them to let me go below. As I had no taste for such amusements, and wanted to see mon cher Feu-Follet, Etooelle and I got into the yawl, and left them; intending to return and be hanged, when we can find nothing better to do."

This account required an explanation, which Raoul gave in a very few words, and then the crew were directed to go to their stations, in order that the lugger might be properly worked. The next minute the sails were filled, on the larboard-tack, as before, and le Feu-Follet again drew ahead, standing in for the cliffs.

"There is a light in motion, near Capri, mon capitaine," observed the first-lieutenant; "I suppose it to be on board some enemy. They are plenty as gulls, about this bay."

"You are very right, Monsieur. 'Tis la Prosperine; she shows the light for her boats. She is too far to leeward to meddle with us, however, and we are pretty certain there is nothing between her and the ships off the town, that can do us any harm. Are all our lights concealed? Let them be well looked to, monsieur."

"All safe, mon capitaine. Le Feu-Follet never shows her lantern, until she wishes to lead an enemy into the mire!"

"Raoul laughed, and pronounced the word "*bon*" in the emphatic manner peculiar to a Frenchman. Then, as the lugger was drawing swiftly in towards the rocks, he went on the forecastle himself, to keep a proper look-out ahead; Ithuel, as usual, standing at his side.

The piano, or plain, of Sorrento terminates, on the side of the bay, in perpendicular cliffs of tufa, that vary from one to near two hundred feet in height. Those near the town are among the highest, and are lined with villas, convents, and other dwellings, of which the foundations are frequently placed upon shelves of rock, fifty feet below the adjacent streets. Raoul had been often here, during the short reign of the Rufo faction, and was familiar with most of the coast. He knew that his little lugger might brush against the very rocks, in most places, and was satisfied that if he fell in with the Prosperine's boats at all, it must be quite near the land. As the night wind blew directly down the bay, sighing across the campagna between Vesuvius and Castel a Mare, it became necessary to tack off-shore, as soon as le Feu-Follet got close to the cliffs, where the obscurity was greatest, and her proportions and rig were not discernible at any distance. While in the very act of going round, and before the head-sheets were drawn, Raoul was startled by a sudden hail.

"Felucca, ahoy!" cried one, in English, from a boat that was close on the lugger's bow.

"Halloo!" answered Ithuel, raising an arm, for all near him to be quiet.

"What craft's that?" resumed he in the boat.

"A felucca sent down by the admiral, to look for the Proserpine—not finding her at Capri, we are turning up to the anchorage of the fleet again."

"Hold on a moment, sir, if you please; I'll come on board you. Perhaps, I can help you out of your difficulty; for I happen to know something of that ship."

"Ay, ay—bear a hand, if you please; for we want to make the most of this wind while it stands."

It is singular how easily we are deceived, when the mind commences by taking a wrong direction. Such was now he fact, with him in the boat, for he had imbibed the notion that he could trace the outlines of a felucca, o. which so many navigate those waters, and the idea that it was the very lugger he had been seeking, never crossed his mind.

32

Acting under the delusion, he was soon alongside, and on the deck of his enemy.

"Do you know this gentleman, Etooelle?" demanded Raoul, who had gone to the gangway to receive his visiter."

"It is Mr. Clinch, the master's-mate of the accursed Proserpine; he who spoke us in the yawl, off the point yonder."

"How!" exclaimed Clinch, his alarm being sufficiently apparent in his voice; "have I fallen into the hands of Frenchmen?"

"You have, Monsieur," answered Raoul, courteously, "but not into the hands of enemies.   This is le Feu-Follet, and I am Raoul Yvard."

"Then all hope for Jane is gone, for ever!—I have passed a happy day, though a busy one, for I did begin to think there was some chance for me.   A man cannot see Nelson without pulling up, and wishing to be something like him, but, a prison is no place for promotion."

"Let us go into my cabin, Monsieur.   There we can converse more at our ease; and we shall have a light."

Clinch was in despair; it mattered not to him, whither he was taken.   In the cabin he sat the picture of a helpless man, and a bottle of brandy happening to stand on the table, he eyed it with something like the ferocity with which the hungry wolf may be supposed to gaze at the lamb ere he leaps the fold.

"Is this the gentleman you mean, Etooelle?" demanded Raoul, when the cabin-lamp shone on the prisoner's face; "he who was so much rejoiced to hear that his enemy was not hanged?"

"'Tis the same, Captain Rule; in the main, he is a good-natured officer—one that does more harm to himself than to any one else.   They said, in the ship, that he went up to Naples to do you some good turn or other."

"Bon!—You have been long in your boat, Mr. Clinch—we will give you a warm supper and a glass of wine—after which, you are at liberty to seek your frigate, and to return to your own flag."

Clinch stared as if he did not, or could not, believe what he heard—then the truth flashed on his mind, and he burst into tears.   Throughout that day his feelings had been in extremes, hope once more opening a long vista of happiness for the future, through the renewed confidence and advice of his captain. Thus far he had done well, and it was by striving to do still better that he had fallen into the hands of the enemy. For a single moment the beautiful fabric which revived hopes had been industriously weaving throughout the day, was torn into tatters. The kindness of Raoul's manner, however, his words, and the explanations of Ithuel, removed a mountain from his breast, and he became quite unmanned. There is none so debased as not to retain glimmerings of the bright spirit that is associated with the grosser particles of their material nature. Clinch had in him the living consciousness that he was capable of better things, and he endured moments of deep anguish, as the image of the patient, self-devoting, and constant Jane rose before his mind's eye to reproach him with his weaknesses.

It is true that she never made these reproaches in terms; so far from that, she would not even believe the slanders of those she mistook for his enemies; but Clinch could not always quiet the spirit within him, and he often felt degraded as he remembered with how much more firmness Jane supported the load of hope deferred, than he did himself. The recent interview with Cuffe had aroused all that was left of ambition and self-respect, and he had left the ship that morning with a full and manly determination to reform, and to make one continued and persevering effort to obtain a commission, and with it Jane. Then followed capture and the moment of deep despair. But Raoul's generosity removed the load, and again the prospect brightened.

CHAPTER XXVI.

"Oh! many a dream was in the ship
An hour before her death;
And sight of home, with sighs disturb'd
The sleeper's long-drawn breath."

WILSON.

RAOUL soon decided on his course. While he was consoling Clinch, orders had been sent to Pintard to look for the other gig; but a few minutes' search, under the cliffs, satisfied those on deck that she was not to be found; and the fact was so reported below. Nor could all Ithuel's ingenuity extract from the captured boat's crew, any available information on the subject. There was an *esprit de corps* among the Proserpines, as between their own ship and le Feu-Follet, which would have withstood, on an occasion like this, both threats and bribes; and he of the Granite state was compelled to give the matter up as hopeless; though, in so doing, he did not fail to ascribe the refusal to betray their shipmates, on the part of these men, to English obstinacy, rather than to any creditable feeling. The disposition to impute the worst, to those he hated, however, was not peculiar to Ithuel or his country; it being pretty certain he would have fared no better on board the English frigate, under circumstances at all analogous.

Satisfied, at length, that the other boat had escaped him, and feeling the necessity of getting out of the Bay while it was still dark, Raoul reluctantly gave the order to bear up, and put the lugger dead before the wind, wing-and-wing. By the time this was done, the light craft had turned so far o windward, as to be under the noble rocks that separate the piano of Sorrento from the shores of Vico; a bold promontory, that buttresses the sea, with a wall of near or quite a thousand feet in perpendicular height. Here she felt the full force of the land-wind; and when her helm was put up, and her sheets eased off, a bird turning on the wing would not have come round more gracefully, and scarcely with greater velocity. The course now lay from point to point, in order to avoid being becalmed within the indentations of the coast. This carried the lugger athwart the cove of Sorrento, rather than into it, and, of course, left Yelverton, who had landed at the smaller marina, quite out of the line of her course.

So swift was the progress of the little craft, that within fifteen minutes after bearing up, Raoul and Ithuel, who again occupied their stations on the forecastle, saw the head-land where they had so lately been concealed, and ordered the helm a-port, in order to sheer out and give it a berth. Then rock was passed after rock, cove after cove, and village after village, until the entrance between Capri and Campanella was again reached. In sweeping down the shore, in this manner, the intention was to pick up any boat that might happen to be in the lugger's track; for, while Raoul was disposed to let his prisoner go, he had a strong desire to seize any other officers of the frigate that might fall in his way. The search was ineffectual, however; and when the lugger came out into the open sea, all expectation of further success, of this nature, was reluctantly abandoned.

As le Feu-Follet was now in dangerous proximity to three cruisers of the enemy, the moment was one that called for decision. Fortunately, the positions of the English vessels were known to Raoul, a circumstance that lessened the danger, certainly; but it would not do to continue long within a league of their anchorage, with the risk of the land breezes failing. As yet the darkness, and the shadows of the land, concealed the privateer, and her commander determined, if not literally to make hay while the sun shone, at least to profit by its absence. With this view, then, he ordered the lugger hove-to, the boat of Clinch hauled to the lee gangway, and the prisoners to be all brought on deck; the common men, in the waist, and the master's-mate, aft.

"Here I must lose the pleasure of your company, Monsieur Clinch," said Raoul, with a courtesy that may almost be termed national. "We are quite as near *votre belle Proserpine* as is safe, and *I* long for *notre belle France*. The wind is fair to take us off the coast, and two hours will carry us out of sight, even were it noon-day. You will have the complaisance to make my duty to Monsieur Cuffe—oui-

32 *

pardie ! and to *ces braves Italiens,* who are so much ze amis of Sir Smees !　*Touchez-la.*"

Raoul laughed, for his heart was light, and sundry droll conceits danced through his brain. As for Clinch, the whole was Greek to him, with the exception that he understood it was the intention of the French to take their vessel off the coast, a circumstance that he was not sorry to learn, though he would have given so much, a few hours earlier, to have known where to find her. Raoul's generosity had worked a revolution in his feelings, however, and nothing was farther from his wishes, now, than to be employed against the celebrated privateersman. Still, he had a duty to perform to the service of which he was a member, another to Jane, and a last to himself.

"Captain Yvard," said the master's-mate, taking the other's offered hand, " I shall never forget this kindness on your part ; it comes at a most fortunate moment for me. My happiness in this world, and perhaps in the world to come,"—an ejaculation of " bah !" involuntarily escaped the listener—" depended on my being at liberty. I hold it to be fair, however, to tell you the whole truth. I must do all I can to capture or destroy this very lugger, as well as any other of the king's enemies, as soon as I am my own master again."

" *Bon !*— I like your frankness, Monsieur Clinch, as much as I like your humanity. I always look for a brave enemy when *un Anglais* comes against me ; if you are ever in the number, I shall expect nothing worse."

" It will be my duty, Captain Yvard, to report to Captain Cuffe, where I found the Folly, where I left her, and where I think she is steering ! Even your armament, crew, and all such little particulars, I shall be questioned on ; I must answer honestly."

" *Mon cher,* you are ' honest fellow,' as you Anglais say. I wish it was noon-day, that you might better see our deck —Le Feu-Follet is not ugly, that she should wish to wear a veil. Tell everything, Clinch, mon brave ; if Monsieur Cuffe wish to send another party against our lugger, come in the first boat *en personne.* We shall always be happy to see Monsieur Clinch. As for where we steer, you see our

head is toward la belle France; and there is plenty of room
for a long chase. *Adieu, mon ami—au revoir.*"

Clinch now shook hands, heartily, with all the officers;
again expressed his sense of the liberality with which he
was treated, and this, too, with emotion; then he followed
his people into the boat, and pulled away from the lugger's
side, holding his course toward the light which was still
burning on board the Proserpine. At the same time le Feu-
Follet filled, and soon disappeared from his eyes, in the
darkness, running off, wing-and-wing, and steering west, as
if really making the best of her way towards the Straits of
Bonifacio, on her road to France.

But, in fact, Raoul had no such intention. His cruise
was not up, and his present position, surrounded as he was
with enemies, was full of attraction to one of his temperament.
Only the day before he appeared in the disguise of a lazzarone, he had captured, manned, and sent to Marseilles a
valuable store-ship; and he knew that another was hourly
expected in the bay. This was an excuse to his people for
remaining where they were. But the excitement of constantly running the gauntlet, the pleasure of demonstrating
the superior sailing of his lugger, the opportunities for distinction, and every other professional motive, was trifling, as
compared with the tie which bound him to, the feeling that
unceasingly attracted him towards Ghita. With his love,
also, there began to mingle a sensation approaching to
despair. While Ghita was so gentle, and even tender, with
him, he had ever found her consistent, and singularly firm
in her principles. In their recent dialogues, some that we
have forborne to relate on account of their peculiar character, Ghita had expressed her reluctance to trust her fate with
one whose God was not her God, with a distinctness and
force that left no doubt of the seriousness of her views, or
of her ability to sustain them in acts. What rendered her
resolution more impressive, was the ingenuous manner
with which she never hesitated to admit Raoul's power over
her affections, leaving no pretext for the common-place supposition that the girl was acting. The conversation of that
night, weighed heavily on the heart of the lover, and he could
not summon sufficient resolution to part — perhaps for
months — with such an apparent breach between him and
his hopes.

As soon as it was known, therefore, that the lugge . . .
far enough at sea, to be out of sight from the boat of Clinch,
she came by the wind on the larboard tack, again, heading
up towards the celebrated ruins of Pæstum, on the eastern
shore of the Bay of Salerno. To one accustomed to the
sea, there would not have seemed sufficient wind to urge
even that light craft along, at the rate with which she glided
through the water. But the land breeze was charged with
the damps of midnight; the canvass was thickened from the
same cause; and the propelling power had nearly double its
apparent force. In an hour after hauling up, le Feu-Follet
tacked, quite eight miles distant from the spot where she
altered her direction, and far enough to windward to lay her
course in, directly for the cliffs beneath the village of St.
Agata; or the present residence of Ghita. In proceeding
thus, Raoul had a double intention before him. English
ships were constantly passing between Sicily, Malta, and
Naples; and, as those bound north would naturally draw in
with the land at this point, his position might enable him to
strike a sudden blow, with the return of day, should any
suitable vessel be in the offing next morning. Then he hoped
for a signal from Ghita, at least—and such things were very
dear to his heart; or, possibly, anxiety and affection might
bring her down to the water-side, when another interview
would be possible. This was the weakness of passion; and
Raoul submitted to its power, like feebler-minded and less
resolute men; the hero becoming little better than the vulgar
herd, under its influence.

The two or three last days and nights had been hours of
extreme anxiety and care to the officers and crew of the
lugger, as well as to their commander, and all on board
began to feel the necessity of sleep. As for Ithuel, he had
been in his hammock an hour; and Raoul now thought
seriously of following his example. Giving his instructions
to the young lieutenant who was in charge of the deck, our
hero went below, and, in a few minutes, he was also lost to
present hopes and fears.

Everything seemed propitious to the lugger, and the intentions of her commander. The wind went down, gradually,
until there was little more than air enough to keep steerage-
way on the vessel, while the ripple on the water disappeared,

leaving nothing behind it but the long, heavy, ground-swell, that always stirs the bosom of the ocean, like the heaving respiration of some gigantic animal. The morning grew darker, but the surface of the gulf was glassy and tranquil, leaving no immediate motive for watchfulness, or care.

These are the lethargic moments of a seaman's life. Days of toil bring nights of drowsiness; and the repose of nature presents a constant temptation to imitate her example. The reaction of excitement destroys the disposition to indulge in the song, the jest, or the tale; and the mind, like the body, is disposed to rest from its labours. Even the murmuring wash of the water, as it rises and falls against the vessel's sides, sounds like a lullaby, and sleep seems to be the one great blessing of existence. Under such circumstances, therefore, it is not surprising that the watch on the deck of the lugger, indulged this necessary want. It is permitted to the common men to doze at such moments, while a few are on the alert; but, even duty, in the absence of necessity, feels its task to be irksome, and difficult of performance. Look-out after look-out lowered his head; the young man who was seated on the arm-chest aft began to lose his consciousness of present things, in dreamy recollections of Provence, his home, and the girl of his youthful admiration. The seaman at the helm alone kept his eyes open, and all his faculties on the alert. This is a station in which vigilance is ever required; and it sometimes happens, in vessels where the rigid discipline of a regular service does not exist, that others rely so much on the circumstance, that they forget their own duties, in depending on the due discharge of his, by the man at the wheel.

Such, to a certain degree, was now the fact on board le Feu-Follet. One of the best seamen in the lugger was at the helm, and each individual felt satisfied that no shift of wind could occur, no change of sails become necessary, that Antoine would not be there to admonish them of the circumstance. One day was so much like another, too, in that tranquil season of the year, and in that luxurious sea, that all on board knew the regular mutations that the hours produced. The southerly air in the morning; the zephyr in the afternoon; and the land wind at night, were as much matters of course, as the rising and setting of the sun. No one felt apprehension, while all submitted to the influence of a want of rest, and of the drowsiness of the climate.

Not so with Antoine. His hairs were grey. Sleep was no longer so necessary to him. He had much pride of calling, too; was long experienced, and possessed senses sharpened and rendered critical by practice, and many dangers. Time and again, did he turn his eyes towards Campanella, to ascertain if any signs of the enemy were in sight; the obscurity prevented anything from being visible, but the dark outline of the high and rock-bound coast. Then he glanced his eyes over the deck, and felt how completely everything depended on his own vigilance and faithfulness. The look at the sails and to windward brought no cause for uneasiness, however, and presuming on his isolation, he began to sing, in suppressed tones, an air of the Troubadours; one that he had learned in childhood, in his native *langue du midi.* Thus passed the minutes, until Antoine saw the first glimmerings of morning, peeping out of the darkness, that came above the mountain-tops, that lay in the vicinity of Eboli. Antoine felt solitary; he was not sorry to greet these symptoms of a return to the animation and communion of a new day.

"Hist! *mon lieutenant!*" whispered the old mariner, unwilling to expose the drowsiness of his young superior to the gaze of the common men; " *mon lieutenant*—'tis I, Antoine.'

" Eh!—*bah!*—Oh, *Antoine est-ce-que toi? Bon*—what would you have, *mon ami.*"

" I hear the surf, I think, *mon lieutenant.* Listen—is not that the water striking on the rocks of the shore?"

" *Jamais!* You see the land is a mile from us; this coast has no shoals. The captain told us to stand close in, before we hove-to, or called him. *Pardie!*—Antoine, how the little witch has travelled in my watch! Here we are, within a musket's range from the heights, yet there has been no wind."

" *Pardon, mon lieutenant*—I do not like that sound of the surf; it is too near for the shore. Will you have the kindness to step on the forecastle and look ahead, monsieur? the light is beginning to be of use."

The young man yawned, stretched his arms, and walked forward; the first to indulge himself, the first, also, to relieve the uneasiness of an old shipmate, whose experience he respected. Still his step was not as quick as common, and it was near a minute ere he reached the bows, or before he gained the knight-heads. But his form was no sooner visible there, than he waved his arms frantically, and shouted in a voice that reached the recesses of the vessel—

"Hard up — hard up with the helm, Antoine — ease off the sheets, *mes enfans !*"

Le Feu-Follet rose on a heavy ground-swell, at that moment; in the next she settled down with a shock resembling that which we experience when we leap and alight sooner than was expected; there she lay cradled in a bed of rocks, as immoveable as one of the stones around her;— stones that had mocked the billows of the Mediterranean, within the known annals of man, more than three thousand years. In a word, the lugger had struck on one of those celebrated islets, under the heights of St. Agata, known as the Islands of the Sirens, and which are believed to have been commemorated by the oldest of all the living profane writers, Homer himself. The blow was hardly given, before Raoul appeared on deck. The vessel gave up all that had life in her, and she was, at once, a scene of alarm, activity, and exertion.

It is at such a moment as this, that the most useful qualities of a naval captain render themselves apparent. Of all around him, Raoul was the calmest, the most collected, and the best qualified to issue the orders that had become necessary. He made no exclamations — uttered not a word of reproach — cast not even a glance of disapprobation on any near him. The mischief was done; the one thing needful was to repair it, if possible, leaving to the future the cares of discipline and the distribution of rewards and punishments.

"She is as fast anchored as a cathedral, mon lieutenant," he quietly observed to the very officer through whose remissness the accident had occurred; "I see no use in these sails. Take them in, at once; they may set her further on the rocks, should she happen to lift."

The young man obeyed; every nerve in his body agitated by the sense of delinquency. Then he walked aft, cast one look around him at the desperate condition of the lugger and, with the impetuosity of character that belongs to his country, he plunged into the sea, from which his body never re-appeared. The melancholy suicide was immediately reported to Raoul.

"*Bon*"—was the answer. "Had he done it an hour earlier, le Feu-Follet would not have been set up on these rocks, like a vessel in a ship-yard—*mais, mes enfans, courage!*—We'll yet see if our beautiful lugger cannot be saved."

If there were stoicism and bitterness in this answer, there was not deliberate cruelty. Raoul loved his lugger, next to Ghita, before all things on earth, and, in his eyes, the fault of wrecking her in a calm, was to be classed among the unpardonable sins. Still, it was by no means a rare occurrence. Ships, like men, are often cast away by an excess of confidence; and our own coast, one of the safest in the known world for the prudent mariner to approach, on account of the regularity of its soundings, has many a tale to tell of disasters similar to this, which have occurred, simply because no signs of danger were apparent. Our hero would not have excused himself for such negligence, and that which self-love will not induce us to pardon, will hardly be conceded to philanthropy.

The pumps were sounded, and it was ascertained that the lugger had come down so easily into her bed, and lay there with so little straining of her seams, that she continued tight as a bottle. This left all the hope which circumstances would allow, of still saving the vessel. Raoul neglected no useful precaution. By this time the light was strong enough to enable him to see a felucca coming slowly down from Salerno, before the wind, or all that was still left of the night air, and he despatched Ithuel with an armed boat to seize her, and bring her alongside of the rocks. He took this course with the double purpose of using the prize, if practicable, in getting his own vessel off, or, in the last resort, of making his own escape, and that of his people, in her to France. He did not condescend to explain his motives, however; nor did any one presume to inquire into them. Raoul was now strictly a commander, acting in a desperate emergency. He even succeeded in suppressing the constitutional volubility of his countrymen, and in substituting for it the deep, attentive silence of thorough discipline; one of the great causes of his own unusual success in maritime enterprises. To the want of this very silence and attention may be ascribed so many of those naval disasters which have undeniably befallen a people of singular enterprise and courage. Those who wish them well, will be glad to learn that the evil has been, in a great measure, repaired.

As soon as the boat was sent to seize the felucca, the yawl was put into the water, and Raoul, himself, began to sound around the lugger. The rocks of the Sirens, as the islets are called to this day, are sufficiently elevated above the surface of the sea to be visible at some distance; though, lying in a line with the coast, it would not have been easy for the look-outs of le Feu-Follet to discern them at the hour when she struck, ever had they been on the alert. The increasing light, however, enabled the French fully to ascertain their position, and to learn the extent of the evil. The lugger had been lifted into a crevice between two of the rocks, by a ground-swell heavier than common; and though there was deep water all round her, it would be impossible to get her afloat again without lightening. So long as the wind did not blow, and the sea did not rise, she was safe enough; but a swell that should force the hull to rise and fall, would inevitably cause her to bilge. These facts were learned in five minutes after the yawl was in the water, and much did Raoul rejoice at having so promptly sent Ithuel in quest of the felucca. The rocks were next reconnoitred, in order to ascertain what facilities they offered to favour the discharging of the vessel's stores. Some of them were high enough to protect articles from the wash of the water, but it is at all times difficult to lie alongside of rocks that are exposed to the open sea; the heaving and setting of the element, even in calms, causing the elevation of its surface so much to vary. On the present occasion, however, the French found less swell than common, and that it was possible to get their stores ashore at two or three different points.

Raoul now directed the work to commence in earnest. The lugger carried four boats; viz—a launch, a cutter, the yawl, and a jolly-boat. The second had been sent after the felucca, with a strong crew in her; but the three others were employed in discharging stores. Raoul perceived at once that the moment was not one for half-way measures,

and that large sacrifices must be made, to save the hull of
the vessel. This, and the safety of his crew, were the two
great objects he kept before him. All his measures were
directed to that end. The water was started, in the lugger's hold, by staving the casks, and the pumps were set in
motion, as soon as possible. Provisions, of all sorts, were
cast into the sea, for le Feu-Follet had recently supplied
herself, from a prize, and was a little deeper than her best
trim allowed. In short, everything that could be spared, was
thrown overboard, barely a sufficiency of food and water
being retained, to last the people, until they could reach
Corcica ; whither it was their captain's intention to proceed,
the moment he got his vessel afloat.

The Mediterranean has no regular tides, though the water
rises and falls materially, at irregular intervals ; either the
effect of gales, or of the influence of the adjacent seas. This
circumstance prevented the calamity of having gone ashore,
at high water, while it also prevented the mariners from
profiting by any flood. It left them, as they had been placed
by the accident, itself, mainly dependent on their own exertions.

Under such circumstances, then, our hero set about the
discharge of his responsible duties. An hour of active toil,
well directed, and perseveringly continued, wrought a material
change. The vessel was small, while the number of hands
was relatively large. At the end of the time mentioned, the
officer charged with the duty, reported that the hull moved
under the power of the heaving sea, and that it might soon
be expected to strike, with a force to endanger its planks
and ribs. This was the sign to cease discharging, and to
complete the preparations that had been making, for heaving the lugger off; it being unsafe to delay that process,
after the weight was sufficiently lessened, to allow it. The
launch had carried out an anchor, and was already returning towards the rocks, paying out cable, as it came in
But the depth of the water rendered this an anxious service
since there was the danger of dragging the ground-tackle
home, as it is termed, on account of the angle at which it
lay.

At this moment, with the exception of the difficulty last
named, everything seemed propitious. The wind had gone

down entirely, the southerly air having lasted but a short time, and no other succeeding it. The sea was, certainly, not more disturbed than it had been all the morning, which was at its minimum of motion, while the day promised to be calm and clear. Nothing was in sight but the felucca, and she was not only in Ithuel's possession, but she had drawn within half-a-mile of the rocks, and was sweeping still nearer at each instant. In ten minutes she must come alongside. Raoul had ascertained that there was water enough, where le Feu-Follet lay, to permit a vessel like his prize, to touch her; and many things lay on deck, in readiness to be transferred to this tender, previously to beginning to heave. The rocks, too, were well garnished with casks, cordage, shot, ballast, and such other articles as could be come at—the armament and amunition excepted. These last our hero always treated with religious care, for, in all he did, there was a latent determination resolutely to defend himself. But, there were no signs of any such necessity's being likely to occur, and the officers began to flatter themselves, with their ability to get their lugger afloat, and in sailing trim, before the usual afternoon's breeze should set in. In waiting, therefore, for the arrival of the felucca, and, in order that the work might meet with no interruption, when the men once began to heave, the people were ordered to get their breakfasts.

This pause in the proceedings gave Raoul an opportunity to look about him, and to reflect. Twenty times did he turn his eyes, anxiously, towards the heights of St. Agata, where there existed subjects equally of attraction and apprehension. It is scarcely necessary to say that the first was Ghita; while the last arose from the fear that some curious eye might recognise the lugger, and report her condition to the enemies known to be lying at Capri; only a league or two on the other side of the hills. But all was seemingly tranquil there, at that early hour; and the lugger making very little show when her canvass was not spread, there was reason to hope that the accident was as yet unseen. The approach of the felucca would probably betray it; though the precaution had been taken to order Ithuel to show no signs of national character.

Raoul Yvard was a very different man, at this moment of leisure and idleness, from what he had been a few hours earlier. Then he trod the deck of his little cruiser with some such feelings as the man who exults in his strength, and rejoices in his youth. Now he felt as all are apt to feel who are rebuked by misfortunes and disease. Nevertheless, his character had lost none of its high chivalry; and even here, as he sat on the taffrail of the stranded Feu-Follet, he meditated carrying some stout Englishman by surprise and boarding, in the event of his not succeeding in getting off the lugger. The felucca would greatly aid such an enterprise; and his crew was strong enough, as well as sufficiently trained, to promise success.

On such an expedient, even, was he ruminating, as Ithuel, in obedience to an order given through the trumpet, brought his prize alongside, and secured her to the lugger. The men who had accompanied the American were now dismissed to their morning's meal, while Raoul invited their leader to share his frugal repast, where he sat. As the two broke their fasts, questions were put and answered, concerning what had occurred, during the hour or two the parties had been separated. Raoul's tale was soon told; but the other learned with concern, that the crew of the felucca had taken to their boat, and escaped to the landing of the Scaricatojo, on finding that the capture of their vessel was inevitable. This proved that the character of the wreck was known, and left but little hope that their situation would not be reported to the English, in the course of the morning.

CHAPTER XXVII.

—————— " But now lead on ;
In me is no delay ; with thee to go,
Is to stay here ; with thee here to stay,
Is to go hence unwilling ; thou to me
Art all things under heav'n, all places thou."
                                        MILTON.

THE intelligence communicated by Ithuel essentially altered Raoul's views of his actual situation. An active man might go from the Marinella, at the foot of the Scaricatojo, or the place where the crew of the felucca had landed, to the Marina Grande of Sorrento, in an hour. At the latter beach, boats were always to be found, and two hours more would carry the messenger, by water, to the ships off Capri, even in a calm. The first of these important hours had now elapsed some time ; and he could not doubt, that vigorous arms were already employed in pulling across the few leagues of water that separated the island from the shores of Sorrento. The day was calm, it is true ; and it would be impossible to move the ships ; but two frigates and a heavy sloop-of-war, might send such a force against him in boats, as, in his present situation, would render resistance next to hopeless.

Raoul ceased eating, and, standing on the taffrail, he cast anxious looks around him. His sturdy followers, ignorant of all the dangers by which they were environed, were consuming their morning's meal, with the characteristic indifference to danger that marks the ordinary conduct of seamen. Even Ithuel, usually so sensitive on the subject of English power, and who had really so much to apprehend, should he again fall into the hands of the Proserpines, was masticating his food, with the keen relish of a man who had been hard at work the whole morning. All appeared unconscious of their critical condition ; and to Raoul it seemed as if the entire responsibility rested on his own shoulders. Fortunately, he was not a man to shrink from his present duties ; and he occupied the only leisure moment that would

33 *

he likely to offer that day, in deliberating on his resources, and in maturing his plans.

The armament still remained in the lugger, but it was doubtful if she would float without removing it; and, admitting this necessity, the question arose of, what was to be done with it, in order to render it available, in the event of an attack. Two, or even four of the light guns might be worked on the decks of the felucca; and here he determined they should be immediately placed, with a proper supply of cartridges and shot. Twenty men thrown into that light craft, which Ithuel reported as sailing and sweeping well, might prove of the last importance. Then one of the islets had a ruin on it, of what was believed to be an ancient temple. It is true, these ruins were insignificant, and scarcely visible at any distance; but, on a close examination, and by using some of the displaced stones with judgment, it was possible to entrench a party behind them, and make a stout resistance against light missiles; or such as boats would most probably use. Raoul got into the yawl, and sculled himself to this spot, examining the capabilities with care and judgment. After this, his mode of proceeding was matured to his own satisfaction.

The usual time had been consumed, and the hands were "turned to;" each officer receiving the orders necessary to the discharge of the duty confided to his particular superintendence. As Ithuel had captured the felucca, Raoul felt it right to intrust him with the command of the prize. He was directed to take on board the armament and ammunition necessary to a defence, to mount the guns in the best manner he could, and to make all the other fighting preparations; while another gang struck into the felucca's hold, such articles from the lugger, as it was desirable to save.

Another party, under the first-lieutenant, landed the remainder of the light carronades, pieces of twelve pounds only, with the proper stores, and commenced the arrangements to place them in battery among the ruins. A small supply of food and water was also transferred to this islet.

While these dispositions were in progress, Raoul himself, assisted by his sailing-master, prepared to heave the lugger off the rocks. To this, at present the most important duty, our hero gave his personal inspection; for it required skill judgment, and caution. The physical force of the crew was reserved to aid in the attempt. At length everything was ready, and the instant had arrived when the momentous trial was to be made. The lugger had now been ashore quite four hours, and the sun had been up fully three. By this time, Raoul calculated that the English, at Capri, knew of his misfortune, and little leisure remained in which to do a vast deal of work. The hands were all summoned to the bars, therefore, and the toil of heaving commenced.

As soon as the cable got the strain, Raoul felt satisfied that the anchor would hold. Fortunately, a fluke had taken a rock, a circumstance that could be known only by the result; but, so long as the iron held together, there was no danger of that material agent's failing them. The last part of the process of lightening was now performed as rapidly as possible, and then came the trial-heave at the bars. Every effort was fruitless, however, inch being gained after inch, until it seemed as if the hemp of the cable were extending its minutest fibres, without the hull's moving any more than the rocks on which it lay. Even the boys were called to the bars; but the united force of all hands, the officers included, produced no change. There was an instant when Raoul fancied his best course would be to set fire to the hulk, get on board the felucca, and sweep off to the southward, in season to avoid the expected visit from the English. He even called his officers together, and laid the proposition before them. But the project was too feebly urged, and it met with too little response in the breasts of his auditors to be successful. The idea of abandoning that beautiful and faultless little craft, was too painful, while the remotest hope of preserving it remained.

Raoul had measured his hours with the accuracy of a prudent general. It was now almost time for the English boats to appear, and he began to hope that the Neapolitans had made the great mistake of sending their information to the fleet off Naples, rather than carrying it to the ships at Capri. Should it prove so, he had still the day before him, and might retire under cover of the night. At all events, the lugger could not be abandoned without an enemy in sight, and the people were again called to the bars for a renewed effort. As water might be obtained at a hundred points on the coast, and the distance to Corsica was so small, the last gallon had been started and pumped out, during the recent pause.

Our hero felt that this was the final effort. The hold of le Feu-Follet was literally empty, and all her spare spars were floating among the rocks. If she could not be started now, he did not possess the means to get her off. The anchor held; the cable, though stretched to the utmost, stood, and every creature, but himself, was at the bars. The ground-swell had been lessening all the morning, and little aid was now to be had from the rising of the water. Still that little must be obtained; without it, the task seemed hopeless.

"Get ready, men," cried Raoul, as he paced the taffrail; "and heave at the word. We will wait for a swell, then strain every nerve till something part. *Pas encore, mes enfans—pas encore!* Stand by!—Yonder comes a fellow who will lift us—heave a strain—heave harder—heave, body and soul!—heave, altogether!"

The men obeyed. First they hove a gentle strain; then the effort was increased, and, obedient to the order, just as the ground-swell rolled under the lugger's bottom, they threw out their utmost strength, and the hull started for the first time. This was encouraging, though the movement did not exceed six inches. It was a decided movement, and was made in the right direction. This success nerved the people to an increased effort. It was probable that, at the next strain, they would throw a tenth more impetus into their muscles. Of all this, Raoul was aware, and he determined not to let the feeling flag.

"*Encore, mes enfans!*" he said. "Heave, and get ready! Be watchful—now's your time! Heave, and rip the planks off the lugger's bottom — heave, men, heave!"

This time, the effort answered to the emergency; the swell rolled in, the men threw out their strength, a surge was felt, it was followed up by a strain, and le Feu-Follet shot off her bed into deep water, rolling, for want of ballast, nearly to her hammock-cloths. She soon lay directly over her anchor.

Here was success!—Triumphant success; and that, at a moment when the most sanguine had begun to despair

The men embraced each other, showing a hundred manifestations of extravagant joy. The tears came to Raoul's eyes; but he had no opportunity of concealing them, every officer he had pressing around him to exchange felicitations. The scene was one of happy disorder. It had lasted two or three minutes, when Ithuel, always cold and calculating, edged his way through the throng to his commander's side and pointed significantly in the direction of Campanella. There, indeed, was visible, a division of the expected boats. It was pulling towards them, having that moment doubled the cape!

Ithuel's gesture was too significant to escape attention, and every eye followed its direction. The sight was of a nature not to be mistaken. It at once changed the current of feeling in all who beheld it. There was no longer a doubt concerning the manner in which the news of the accident had travelled, or of its effect on the English at Capri. In point of fact, the padrone of the captured felucca, with a sole eye to the recovery of his vessel, had ascended the Scaricatojo, after landing at the Marinella, at its foot, fast as legs could carry him; had rather run, than glided, along the narrow lanes of the piano and the hill-side to the beach of Sorrento; had thrown himself into a boat, manned by four lusty Sorrentine watermen—and Europe does not contain lustier or bolder; had gone on board the Terpsichore, and laid his case before Sir Frederick Dashwood, ignorant of the person of the real commanding officer among the three ships. The young baronet, though neither very wise, nor very much experienced in his profession, was exceedingly well disposed to seek distinction. It immediately occurred to his mind, that the present was a fitting opportunity to gain laurels. He was second in rank, present; and, in virtue of that claim, he fancied that the first could do no more than send him in command of the expedition, which he rightly foresaw Cuffe would order against the French. But there arose a difficulty. As soon as Sir Frederick reported the nature of the intelligence he had received to his senior captain, and his own wish to be employed on the occasion, the rights of Winchester interposed to raise a question. Cuffe was prompt enough in issuing an order for each ship to man and arm two boats, making six in all and

in giving the necessary details, but he lost some precious
time in deciding as to who was to command.   This was
the cause of delay, and had given rise to certain hopes in
Raoul, that facts were subsequently to destroy.   In the end,
Sir Frederick prevailed ; his rank giving him a decided advantage ; and the division of boats that was now approaching
was under his orders.

Raoul saw he had rather more than an hour to spare.
To fight the felucca, unsupported, against so many enemies,
and that in a calm, was quite out of the question.   That
small, low craft might destroy a few of her assailants, but
she would inevitably be carried at the first onset.   There
was not time to get the ballast and other equipments into
the lugger, so as to render her capable of a proper resistance ; nor did even she offer the same advantages for a
defence, unless in quick motion, as the ruins.   It was determined, therefore, to make the best disposition of the two
vessels that circumstances would allow, while the main
dependence should be placed on the solid defences of stone.
With this end, Ithuel was directed to haul his felucca to a
proper berth ; the first-lieutenant was ordered to get as
much on board le Feu-Follet as possible, in readiness to
profit by events ; while Raoul himself, selecting thirty of
his best men, commenced preparing the guns on the rocks
for active service.

A single half-hour wrought a material change in the
state of things.   Ithuel had succeeded in hauling the felucca
into a berth among the islets, where she could not easily be
approached by boats, and where her carronades might be
rendered exceedingly useful.   Much of the ballast was again
on board the lugger, and a few of her stores, sufficient to render her tolerably stiff, in the event of a breeze springing up ;
and Raoul had directed the two inside guns of the felucca
to be sent on board her and mounted, that she might assist
in the defence with a flanking fire.   The great difficulty
which exists in managing a force at anchor, is the opportunity that is given the assailant of choosing his point of
attack, and by bringing several of the vessels in a line,
cause them to intercept each other's fire.   In order to prevent this, as much as in his power, Raoul placed his two
floating-batteries out of line, though it was impossible to

make such a disposition of them as would not leave each exposed, on one point of attack, in a degree greater than any other. Nevertheless, the arrangement was so made, that either a vessel or the ruins might aid each craft respectively against the assault on her weakest point.

When his own guns were ready, and the two vessels moored, Raoul visited both the lugger and felucca, to inspect their preparations, and to say a cheerful word to their men. He found most things to his mind; where they were not, he ordered changes to be made. With the lieutenant, his conversation was brief, for that officer was one who possessed much experience in this very sort of warfare, and could be relied on. With Ithuel, he was more communicative; not that he distrusted the citizen of the Granite state, but that he knew him to be a man of unusual resources, could the proper spirit be aroused within him.

"*Bien*, Etooelle," he said, when the inspection was ended, " much will depend on the use you make of these two guns."

"I know that, as well as you do yourself, Captain Rule," answered the other, biting off at least two inches from half a yard of pig-tail; " and, what 's more, I know that I fight with a rope round my neck. The spiteful devils will hardly overlook all that 's passed; and though it will be dead ag'in all law, they 'll work out their eends on us both, if we don't work out our eends on them. To my mind, the last will be the most agreeable, as well as the most just."

" Bon !—Do not throw away your shot, Etooelle."

" I !—why, Captain Rule, I 'm nat'rally economical. That would be wasteful, and waste I set down for a sin. The only place I calculate on throwing the shot, is into the face and eyes of the English. For my part, I wish Nelson, himself, was in one of them boats—I wish the man no harm but I *do* wish he was in one of them very boats."

" And, Etooelle, I do *not*. It is bad enough as it is, *entr nous ;* and Nelson is very welcome to stay on board his Foudroyant; *voilà !*—The enemy is in council; we shall soon hear from them. Adieu, *mon ami ;* remember our two *Républiques !*"

Raoul squeezed Ithuel's hand, and entered his boat. The distance to the ruin was trifling, but it was necessary to make a small circuit in order to reach it. While doing this the young mariner discovered a boat pulling from the direction of the marinella, at the foot of the Scaricatojo, which had got so near, unseen, as, at first, to startle him by its proximity. A second look, however, satisfied him that no cause of apprehension existed, in that quarter. His eye could not be deceived. The boat contained Ghita and her uncle; the latter rowing, and the former seated in the stern, with her head bowed to her knees, apparently in tears Raoul was alone, sculling the light yawl with a single hand, and he exerted himself to meet these unexpected, and, in the circumstances, unwelcome visiters, as far as possible from the rocks. Presently the two boats lay side by side.

" What means this, Ghita !" the young man exclaimed ; " do you not see the English, yonder ; at this moment making their preparations to attack us. In a few minutes we shall be in the midst of a battle, and thou here !"

" I see it all, now, Raoul," was the answer, " though we did not on quitting the shore ; but we would not turn back, having once come upon the Bay. I was the first in St. Agata to discover the evil that had befallen thee ; from that moment I have never ceased to entreat my uncle, until he has consented to come hither."

" With what motive, Ghita ?" asked Raoul, with sparkling eyes—" at length thou relentest—wilt become my wife ! In my adversity, thou rememberest thou art a woman !"

" Not exactly that, dear Raoul ; but I cannot desert thee, altogether, in this strait. The same objection exists now, I fear, that has ever existed to our union ; but that is no reason I should not aid thee. We have many friends along the heights, here, who will consent to conceal thee ; and I have come to carry thee and the American to the shore, until an opportunity offer to get thee to thine own France."

" What! desert *ces braves,* Ghita, at a moment like this ! —Not to possess thy hand, dearest girl, could I be guilty of an act so base."

" Thy situation is not theirs. The condemnation to death hangs over thee, Raoul ; shouldst thou again fall into English hands, there will be no mercy for thee."

" *Assez*—this is no moment for argument. The English are in motion, and there is barely time for thee to get to a safe distance, ere they begin to fire. Heaven bless thee, Ghita! This care of thine draws my heart to thee closer than ever; but we must now separate. Signor Giuntotardi, pull more towards Amalfi. I see that the English mean to attack us from the side of the land—pull more towards Amalfi."

"Thou tellest us this in vain, Raoul," Ghita quietly, but firmly answered. "We have not come here on an unmeaning errand—if thou refusest to go with us, we will remain with thee. These prayers, that thou so despisest, may not prove useless."

"Ghita!—this can never be. We are without cover—almost without defences—our vessel is unfit to receive thee, and this affair will be very different from that off Elba. Thou would'st not willingly distract my mind with care for thee, at such a moment!"

"We will remain, Raoul. There may come a moment, when thou wilt be glad to have the prayers of believers. God leadeth us hither, either to take thee away, or to remain, and look to thy eternal welfare, amid the din of war."

Raoul gazed at the beautiful enthusiast, with an intensity of love and admiration, that even her truthful simplicity had never before excited. Her mild eyes were kindling with holy ardour, her cheeks were flushed, and something like the radiance of heaven seemed to beam upon her countenance. The young man felt that time pressed; he saw no hope of overcoming her resolution, in season to escape the approaching boats; and it might be, that the two would be safer in some nook of the ruins, than in attempting to return to the shore. Then, that never-dying, but latent, wish to have Ghita with him, aided his hasty reasoning and he decided to permit the girl, and her uncle, to come upon the islet, that he was to defend in person.

Some signs of impatience had begun to manifest themselves among his people, ere Raoul made up his mind to the course he would follow. But, when he landed, supporting Ghita, that chivalry of character, and homage to the sex, which distinguishes the southern Frenchman, changed the current of feeling, and their two acquaintances were received with acclamation. The acts of self-devotion seemed heroic, and that is always enough to draw applause among

34

a people so keenly alive to glory. Still, the time to make
the necessary dispositions was short. Fortunately, the
surgeon had taken his post on this islet, as the probable scene
of the warmest conflict, and he had contrived to make his
preparations to receive the hurt, in a cavity of the rock,
behind a portion of the ruin, where the person would be
reasonably safe. Raoul saw the advantages of this position, and he led Ghita and her uncle to it, without pausing
to deliberate. Here he tenderly embraced the girl, a liberty
Ghita could not repel at such a moment ; then he tore himself away, to attend to duties which had now become
urgently pressing.

In point of fact, Sir Frederick Dashwood had made his
dispositions, and was advancing to the assault, being already
within the range of grape. For the obvious reason of preventing the French from attempting to escape to the shore,
he chose to approach from that side himself, an arrangement that best suited Raoul ; who, foreseeing the probability
of the course, had made his own preparations with an eye
to such an event.

Of boats, there were eight in sight, though only seven
were drawing near, and were in line. Six had strong
crews, were armed, and were evidently fitted for action.
Of these, three had light boat-guns in their bows, while the
other three carried small-arms-men, only. The seventh
boat was the Terpsichore's gig, with its usual crew, armed ;
though it was used by the commanding officer himself, as a
sort of *cheval de bataille*, in the stricter meaning of the term.
In other words, Sir Frederick Dashwood pulled through the
line in it, to give his orders, and encourage his people.
The eighth boat, which kept aloof, quite out of the range of
grape, was a shore-craft, belonging to Capri, in which
Andrea Barrofaldi, and Vito Viti had come, expressly, to
witness the capture, or destruction, of their old enemy.
When Raoul was taken in the Bay of Naples, these two
worthies fancied that their mission was ended—that they
might return, with credit, to Porto Ferrajo, and again hold
up their heads, with dignity and self-complacency, among
the functionaries of the island. But, the recent escape, and
the manner in which they had been connected with it,
entirely altered the state of things. A new load of re

sponsibility rested on their shoulders; fresh opprobrium was to be met, and put down; and the last acquisition of ridicule, promised to throw the first proofs of their simplicity and dullness entirely into the shade. Had not Griffin and his associates been implicated in the affair, it is probable the vice-governatore and the podestà would have been still more obnoxious to censure; but, as things were, the sly looks, open jests, and oblique innuendoes of all they met in the ship, had determined the honest magistrates, to retire to their proper pursuits, on terra-firmâ, at the earliest occasion. In the mean time, to escape persecution, and to obtain a modicum of the glory that was now to be earned, they had hired a boat, and accompanied the expedition, in the character of amateurs. It formed no part of their plan, however, to share in the combat; a view of its incidents being quite as much, as Vito Viti strongly maintained, when his friend made a suggestion to the contrary, as was neces sary to vindicate their conduct and courage, in the judgment of every Elban.

"Cospetto!" he exclaimed, in the warmth of opposition— "Signor Andrea, your propositions are more in the spirit of an unreflecting boy, than in that of a discreet vice-governatore. If we take swords and muskets in the boat, as you appear to wish, the devil may tempt us to use them; and what does either of us know of such things? The pen is a more befitting weapon for a magistrate, than a keen-edged sword, or a foul-smelling piece of fire-arms. I am amazed that your native sensibilities do not teach you this. There is an indecency in men's mistaking their duties, and, of all things on earth, heaven protect me from falling into such an error! A false position is despicable."

"Thou art warm, friend Vito, and that without occasion. For my part, I think men should be prepared for any emergency that may happen. History is full of examples in which civilians and scholars, ay, even churchmen, have distinguished themselves by feats of arms, on proper occasions; and I confess to a philosophical curiosity to ascertain he sensations with which men seek and expose life."

"That's your besetting weakness, Signor Andrea, and he emergency drives me so far to lose sight of the respect that a podestà owes to a vice-governatore, as to feel constrained to tell you as much. Philosophy plays the very devil with your judgment. With about half of what you possess, the Grand Duke couldn't boast of a more sensible subject. As for history, I don't believe anything that's in it; more especially since the nations of the north have begun to write it. Italy once *had* histories; but where are they now? For my part, I never heard of a man's fighting who was not regularly bred to arms; unless it might be some fellow who had reason to wish he had never been born."

"I can name you several men of letters, in particular, whose fame as soldiers is only eclipsed by that earned by their more peaceful labours, honest Vito—Michael Angelo Buonaretti, for instance, to say nothing of various warlike popes, cardinals, and bishops. But we can discuss this matter after the battle is over. Thou seest the English are already quitting their ships, and we shall be in the rear of the combatants."

"So much the better, Corpo di Bacco!—who ever heard of an army that carries its brains in its head, like a human being? No—no—Signor Andrea; I have provided myself with a string of beads, which I intend to count over, with aves and paters, while the firing lasts, like a good Catholic; if you are so hot, and bent on making one in this battle, you may proclaim in a loud voice one of the speeches of the ancient consuls and generals, such as you will find them, in any of the old books."

Vito Viti prevailed. The vice-governatore was obliged to leave the arms behind him, and this, too, without making any great difference in the result of the day's fighting, inasmuch as the boatmen employed, in addition to asking a triple price for their time and labour, obstinately refused to go nearer to the French than half a league. Distant as this was, however, Raoul, while reconnoitring the enemy with a glass, detected the presence of the two Elbans. He laughed outright at the discovery, notwithstanding the many serious reflections that naturally pressed upon his mind at such a moment.

But this was not the time to indulge in merriment, and the countenance of our hero almost immediately resumed its look of care. Now, that he felt certain of the manner in which the English intended to assail him, he had new orders to give to all his subordinates. As has been said, the principal point was to make the different guns support each other; in order to do this effectually, it became necessary to spring the lugger's broadside round more obliquely towards the felucca; which accomplished, Raoul deemed his arrangements complete.

Then followed the pause which ordinarily prevails between preparation and the battle. This, in a vessel, is always a period of profound and solemn stillness. So important to concert, order, and intelligent obedience, in the narrow compass, and amid the active evolutions of a ship, does silence become at such moments, that one of the first duties of discipline is to inculcate its absolute necessity; and a thousand men shall be seen standing in their batteries, ready to serve the fierce engines of war, without a sound arising among them all, of sufficient force to still the washing of the gentlest waves. It is true, the French were not now strictly arrayed for a naval action; but they carried into the present conflict, the habits and discipline of the peculiar branch of service to which they belonged.

CHAPTER XXVIII.

"His back against a rock he bore,
And firmly placed his foot before:—
'Come one, come all! this rock shall fly
From its firm base as soon as I!'"
Lady of the Lake.

OUR battle will be told with greater clearness, if the read er is furnished with an outline of its order. As has been more than once intimated already, Sir Frederick Dashwood had made all his preparations to commence the assault from the side of the land, the object being to prevent a retreat to the shore. Raoul had foreseen the probability of this, and, with a special view to prevent the two vessels from being

34 *   26

easily boarded, he had caused both to be placed in such positions as left low barriers of rocks between them and that
quarter of the bay.   These rocks were portions that were
not visible at any distance, being just awash, as it is termed,
or on a level with the surface of the water; offering the
same sort of protection against an attack in boats, that ditches
afford in cases of assaults on *terra-firmâ*.   This was a material advantage to the expected defence, and our hero showed
his discrimination in adopting it.   On board the felucca,
which was named The Holy Michael, was Ithuel with fifteen
men, and two twelve-pound carronades, with a proper supply
of small-arms and ammunition.   The Granite-man was the
only officer, though he had with him three or four of the
lugger's best men.

Le Feu-Follet was confided to the care of Jules Pintard,
her first-lieutenant, who had under -his immediate orders
some five-and-twenty of the crew, to work four more of the
carronades.   The lugger had a part only of her ballast in,
and something like a third of her stores.   The remainder
of both still lay on the adjacent rocks, in waiting for the
result of the day.   She was thought, however, to be sufficiently steady for any service that might be expected of her
while moored, and might even have carried whole sail, in
light winds, with perfect safety.   All four of her guns were
brought over on one side, in readiness to use in battery in
the same direction.   By this arrangement the French essentially increased their means of defence, bringing all their
artillery into use at the same time; an expedient that could
not have been adopted had they been fought in broadside.

Raoul had planted among the ruins the remaining four
guns.   With the aid of a few planks, the breechings, tackles,
and other appliances of a vessel, this had been easily effected; and, on reviewing his work, he had great confidence in
the permanency of his pieces.   The ruins themselves were
no great matter; at a little distance they were scarcely perceptible; though, aided by the formation of the natural rock,
and by removing some of the stones to more favourable positions, they answered the purpose of the seamen sufficiently
well.   The carronades were placed *en-barbette;* but a falling of the surface of the rock enabled the men to cover

even their heads, by stepping back a few feet. The danger would be much the greatest to those whose duty it would be to reload.

The surgeon, Carlo Giuntotardi, and Ghita, were established in a cavity of the rocks, perfectly protected against missiles, so long as the enemy continued on the side next the land, and yet within fifty feet of the battery. Here the former made the usual bloody-looking if not bloody-minded preparations for applying tourniquets and for amputating, al unheeded, however, by his two companions, both of whom were lost to the scene around them, in devout prayer.

Just as these several dispositions were completed, Ithuel, who ever kept an eye to windward, called out to Raoul, and inquired if it might not be well to run the yards up to the mast-heads, as they would be more out of the way in their place aloft than littering the decks. There was no possible objection to the measure, it being a dead calm, and both the lugger and the felucca swayed their yards into their places, the sails being bent, and hanging in the brails. This is the ordinary state of craft of the latter rig, though not always that of luggers; and the Granite-man, mindful that his own gear was down, in consequence of having been lowered by her former owners previously to the capture, bethought him of the expediency of getting everything ready for a run. He wished the lugger to be in an equal state of preparation, it being plain enough that two to be pursued, would embarrass the English, in a chase, twice as much as one. This was the reason of his suggestion; and he felt happier for seeing it attended to.

On the other side, all preliminary difficulties had been disposed of. Captain Sir Frederick Dashwood was in command, and lieutenants Winchester and Griffin, after a few open protestations, certain grimaces, and divers secret curses, were fain to submit. The discussion, however, had produced one result, not altogether unfavourable to the Proserpines. Cuffe sent four of her boats against the enemy, while he restricted the Terpsichore to two, including her gig, and the Ringdove to two. Each ship sent her launch, as a matter of course, with a twelve-pound boat-gun on its grating. Griffin was in that of the Proserpine; Mr. Stothard, the second of the other frigate, was in the Terpsichore's; and

McBean, as of right, commanded the Ringdove's. Griffin was in the first cutter of his own ship, and Clinch had charge of the second. The third was headed by Strand, whose call was to have precedence on the occasion. The other boats had subordinates, from their respective ships. All were in good heart; and, while all expected a severe struggle for her, knowing the desperate character of their enemy, every man in the boats felt confident that the lugger was finally to fall into British hands. Still, a grave consideration of the possible consequences to the actors, mingled with the exultation of the more reflecting men among the assailants.

Sir Frederick Dashwood, who ought to have felt the moral responsibility of his command, of all the higher officers present, was the most indifferent to consequences. Constitutionally brave, personal considerations had little influence on him; habitually confident of English prowess, he expected victory and credit as a matter of course; and, favoured by birth, fortune and parliamentary interest, he gave himself no trouble as to the possibility of a failure, certain (though not avowing that certainty even to himself,) that any little mishap would be covered by the broad mantle of the accident, that had so early raised him to the rank he held.

In making his dispositions for the fight, however, Sir Frederick had not disdained the counsels of men older and more experienced than himself. Cuffe had given him much good advice, before they parted, and Winchester and Strand had been particularly recommended to him as seamen whose suggestions might turn out to be useful.

"I send a master's-mate named Clinch, in charge of one of our boats, too, Dashwood," added the senior captain, as he concluded his remarks; "who is one of the most experienced seamen in the Proserpine. He has seen much boat-service, and has always behaved himself well. A vile practice of drinking has kept the poor fellow under; but he is now determined to make an effort, and I beg you will put him forward to-day, that he may have a chance. Jack Clinch has the right sort of stuff in him, if opportunities offer to bring it out."

"I flatter myself, Cuffe, that all hands will meet with opportunity enough," answered Sir Frederick, in his drawling way ; " for, I intend to put 'em all in together, like a thorough pack coming in at the death. I 've seen Lord Echo's harriers so close, at the end of a long chase, that you might have covered the whole with this ship's main-course ; and I intend it shall be so with our boats, to-day. By the way, Cuffe, that would be a pretty figure for a despatch, and would make Bronté smile—ha !—wouldn't it ?"

" D———n the figure, the harriers, and the despatch, too, Dashwood ; first win the day, before you begin to write poetry about it. Bronté, as you call Nelson, has lightning in him, as well as thunder, and there isn't an admiral in the service, who cares less for blood and private rank than himself. The way to make him smile, is to do a thing neatly and well. For God's sake, now, be careful of the men ;— we are short-handed, as it is, and can't afford such another scrape, as that off Porto Ferrajo."

" Never fear for us, Cuffe ; you'll never miss the men I shall expend."

Every captain had a word to say to his officers ; but none other worth recording, with the exception of what passed between Lyon and his first-lieutenant.

" Ye'll remember, Airchy, that a ship can have a reputation for economy, as well as a man. There's several of our own countrymen about the Admiralty just now ; and next to courage and enterprise, they view the expenditures with the keenest eyes. I 've known an admiral reach a red ribbon just on that one quality ; his accounts showing cheaper ships and cheaper squadrons than any in the sairvice. Ye'll all do your duties, for the honour o' Scotland ; but there's six or seven Leith and Glasgow lads in the boats, that it may be as well not to let murder themselves, out of a' need. I 've put the whole of the last draft from the river guard-ship, into the boats, and with them there 's no great occasion to be tender. They 're the sweepings of the Thames and Wapping ; and quite half of them would have been at Botany Bay before this, had they not been sent ere."

" Does the law about being in sight, apply to the boats, or to the ships, the day, Captain Lyon ?"

" To the boats, man ; or who the de'il do you think would lrirve in them ! It's a pitiful affair, altogether, as it has

turned out ; the honour being little more than the profit, I
opine ; and yet 't will never do to let old Scotia lag astairn,
in a hand-to-hand battle.　Ye 'll remember, we have a name
for coming to the claymore ; and so do yer best, every
mither's son o' ye."

McBean grunted an assent, and went about his work as
methodically as if it were a sum in algebra.　The second-
lieutenant of the Terpsichore was a young Irishman, with a
sweet, musical voice ; and, as the boats left the ships, he was
with difficulty kept in the line, straining to move ahead, with
his face on a grin, and his cheers stimulating the men to
undue, or unreasonable efforts.　Such is an outline of the
English materials on this occasion ; both parties being now
ready for the struggle.　If we add that it was already past
two, and that all hands began to feel some anxiety on the
score of the wind, which might soon be expected, the preliminary picture is sufficiently sketched.

Sir Frederick Dashwood had formed his line about a mile
within the rocks, with one launch in the centre, and one on
each extremity.　That in the centre was commanded by
O'Leary, his own second-lieutenant ; that on the left of his
force by McBean, and the one on its right by Winchester.
O'Leary was flanked by Griffin and Clinch, in the Proserpine's cutters, while the intervals were filled by the remaining
boats.　The captain kept moving about in his own gig, giving
his directions, somewhat confusedly, beyond a question ; yet
with a cheerfulness and indifference of air that aided in keeping alive the general *gaité de cœur*.　When all was ready,
he gave the signal to advance, pulling, for the first half mile,
chivalrously in advance of the line, with his own gig.

Raoul had noted the smallest movement of the enemy
with a glass, and with grave attention.　Nothing escaped
his jealous watchfulness ; and he saw that Sir Frederick had
made a capital error in the outset.　Had he strengthened
his centre, by putting all his carronades in the same battery,
as it might be, the chances for success would have been
doubled ; but, by dividing them, he so far weakened their
effect, as to render it certain no one of the three French batteries could be wholly crippled by their fire.　This, of
course, left the difficult task to the English of pushing up to

their hand-to-hand work, under the embarrassment of receiving constant discharges of grape and canister.

The few minutes that intervened between the order to advance, and the moment when the boats got within a quarter of a mile of the rock, were passed in a profound quiet, neither side making any noise, though Raoul had no small difficulty in restraining the constitutional impatience of his own men to begin. A boat presents so small an object, however, to artillerists as little skilled as seamen generally are, who depend more on general calculations than on the direct or scientific aim, the latter being usually defeated by the motion of their vessels, that he was unwilling to throw away even his canister. A Frenchman himself, however, he could refrain no longer, and he pointed a carronade, firing it with his own hand. This was the commencement of the strife. All the other guns in the ruin followed, and the lugger kept time, as it might be by note. The English rose, gave three cheers, and each launch discharged her gun. At the same instant, the two men who held the matches in the felucca, applied them briskly to the vents of their respective pieces. To their surprise, neither exploded, and, on examination, it was discovered that the priming had vanished. To own the truth, he of the Granite state had slily brushed his hand over the guns, and robbed them of this great essential of their force. He held the priming-horns in his own hands, and resolutely refused to allow them to pass into those of any other person.

It was fortunate Ithuel was known to be such a determined hater of the English, else might his life have been the forfeit of this seeming act of treachery. But he meditated no such dereliction of duty. Perfectly aware of the impossibility of preventing his men from firing, did they possess the means, this deliberate and calculating personage had resorted to this expedient to reserve his own effort, until, in his judgment, it might prove the most available. His men murmured, but, too much excited to deliberate, they poured in a discharge of musketry, as the only means of annoying the enemy then left them. Even Raoul glanced aside, a little wondering at not hearing the felucca's carronades, but perceiving her people busy with their fire-arms, he believed all right.

The first discharge, in such an affair, is usually the most destructive. On the present occasion, the firing was not without serious effects. The English, much the most exposed, suffered in proportion. Four men were hurt in Winchester's boat; two in Griffin's.; six or eight men in the other launches and cutters, and one of Sir Frederick's gigmen was shot through the heart; a circumstance which induced that officer to drop alongside of a cutter, and exchange the dead body for a living man.

On the rocks, but one man was injured. A round-shot had hit a stone, shivered it in fragments, and struck down a valuable seaman, just as he was advancing, with a gallant mien, to spunge one of the guns.

"Poor Josef!" said Raoul, as he witnessed the man's fall; "carry him to the surgeon, *mes braves*."

"Mon Capitaine—Josef is dead."

This decided the matter, and the body was laid aside, while another stepped forward and spunged the gun. At that moment Raoul found leisure to walk a yard or two towards the rear, in order to ascertain if the cover of Ghita were sufficient. The girl was on her knees, lost to all around her, though, could he have read her heart, he would have found it divided between entreaties to the Deity and love for himself.

The lugger sustained no harm. O'Leary had overshot her, in his desire to make his missiles reach. Not even a canister had lodged in her spars, or torn her sails. The usual luck appeared to attend her, and the people on board fought with renewed confidence and zeal. Not so with the felucca, however. Here the fire of the English had been the most destructive. The wary and calculating McBean had given his attention to this portion of the French defences, and the consequences partook of the sagacity and discretion of the man. A charge of canister had swept across the felucca's decks, more than decimating Ithuel's small force; for it actually killed one, and wounded three of his party.

But, the din once commenced, there was no leisure to pause. The fire was kept up with animation, on both sides, and men fell rapidly. The boats cheered and pressed ahead, the water becoming covered with a wide sheet of smoke.

In moments like this, the safest course for the assailants

is to push on. This the English did, firing and cheering at every fathom they advanced, but suffering also. The constant discharge of the carronades, and the total absence of wind, soon caused a body of smoke to collect in front of the rock, while the English brought on with them another, trailing along the water, the effect of their own fire. The two shrouds soon united, and then there was a minute when the boats could only be seen with indistinctness. This was Ithuel's moment. Perceiving that the ten or twelve men who remained to him were engrossed with their muskets, he pointed the two carronades himself, and primed them from the horns which he had never quitted. For the felucca he felt no present concern. Winchester, and all the boats in the centre of the English line, were most in advance, the fire of the ruins urging them to the greatest exertion. Then McBean, beside being more distant, could not cross the rock in front of the felucca, without making a circuit, and he must, as yet, be ignorant of the existence of the impediment. Ithuel was cool and calculating by nature, as well as by habit; but this immunity from present risk, probably increased the immediate possession of qualities so important in battle. His carronades were loaded to their muzzles, with bags of bullets, and he beckoned to the best seaman of his party to take one of the matches, while he used the other himself, each holding a monkey's-tail in one hand, in readiness to train the light gun, as circumstances required. The pieces had been depressed by Ithuel himself, in the midst of the fray, and nothing remained but to wait the moment for using them.

This moment was now near. The object of the English was to land on the principal islet, and to carry the ruin by storm. In order to do this, all the boats of their centre converged in their courses to the same point, and the smoke being driven off, by each concussion of the guns, a dark cluster of the enemy diverged from the ragged outline of the vapour, within fifty yards of the intended point of landing. Ithuel and his companion were ready. Together they sighted, and together they fired. This unexpected discharge from a quarter that had been so comparatively silent, surprised both friends and foes, and it drove a fresh mantle of

35

smoke momentarily athwart the rock and the open space in its front.

A cry arose from the dense shroud of battle, that differed from the shouts of success and courage. Physical agony had extorted shrieks from the stoutest hearts, and even the French in the ruins paused to look for the next act of the desperate drama. Raoul seized the opportunity to prepare for the expected hand-to-hand struggle; but it was unnecessary. The cessation in the firing was common in both parties, and it gave the vapour a minute in which to lift the curtain from the water.

When the late obstacle was raised high enough to admit of a view, the result became evident. All the English boats but one had scattered, and were pulling swiftly, in different directions, from the scene of slaughter. By taking this course they diverted and divided the fire of their enemies; an expedient of which it would have been happier had they bethought them earlier. The remaining boat was a cutter of the Terpsichore. It had received the weight of canister from Ithuel's own gun, and of sixteen men it had contained when it left the frigate's side, but two escaped. These fellows had thrown themselves into the sea, and were picked up by passing boats. The cutter itself came drifting slowly in towards the rock, announcing the nature of its fearful cargo, by the groans and cries that arose from out its bosom. Raoul stopped the fire, equally from humanity and policy, after a few discharges at the retreating boats; and the first act of the battle closed.

The breathing time gave both parties a desirable opportunity for ascertaining in what positions they were left. In the whole, the French had lost the services of eleven men; all, with the exception of Ithuel's four, in the ruin. The loss of the English amounted to thirty-three, including several officers. The master's-mate, who had commanded the crippled cutter, lay over its stern, flat on his back, with no less than five musket-balls through his chest. His passage into another state of existence had been sudden as the flight of the electric spark. Of his late companions several were dead also, though most were still enduring the pain of fractured bones and bruised nerves. The boat itself slowly touched the rocks, raising fresh cries among the wounded, by the agony they endured from the shocks of rising and falling under the ground-swell.

Raoul was too deliberate, and too much collected, not to feel his advantage. Anxious to keep his means of further defence in the best condition, he directed all the guns to cease, and the damages to be repaired. Then he went with a party towards the boat that had fallen into his hands. To encumber himself with prisoners of any sort, in his actual situation, would have been a capital mistake; but to do this with wounded men, would have been an act of folly. The boat had tourniquets and other similar appliances in it, and he directed some of the French to use them on those that wanted them most. He also supplied the parched lips of the sufferers with water, when, conceiving that his duty was performed, he gave an order to haul the boat on one side, and to shove it forcibly out of the line of any coming conflict.

"Halloo, Captain Rule!" called out Ithuel, "you are wrong there. Let the boat lie where it is, and it will answer a better turn than another breastwork. The English will scarcely fire through their own wounded."

The look that Raoul cast towards his auxiliary was fierce, even indignant; but, disregarding the advice, he motioned for his own men to obey the order he had already given them. Then, as if mindful of Ithuel's importance, his late timely succour, and the necessity of not offending him. he walked to the side of the islet nearest to the felucca, and spoke courteously and cheerfully to him whose advice he had just treated with indifference, if not with disdain. This was not hypocrisy, but a prudent adaptation of his means to his circumstances.

"Bon — brave Etooelle," he said, "your bags of bullets were welcome friends, and they arrived at the righ' moment."

"Why, Captain Rule, in the Granite country we are never wasteful of our means. You can always wait for the white of Englishmen's eyes, in these affairs. They're spiteful d——ls, on the whull, and seem to be near-sighted ,o a man. They came so clus' at Bunker Hill, our folks——"

"Bon——" repeated Raoul, feeling no wish to hear a thrice-told tale gone through again, Bunker Hill invariably placing

Ithuel on a great horse in the way of bragging; for he no
only imagined that great victory a New-England triumph,
as in fact it was, but he was much disposed to encourage
the opinion that it was in a great measure "granite."
" *Bon,*" interrupted Raoul — " Bunkair was good ;—*mais,
les Rochess aux Sirens* is bettair.   If you have more *de
ces balles,* load *encore.*"

   " What think you of this, Captain Rule?" asked the
ther, pointing up at a little vane that began to flutter at the
head of one of his masts.   " Here is the west wind, and an
opportunity offers to be off.   Let us take wit, and run !"

   Raoul started, and gazed at the heavens, the vane, and
the surface of the sea ; the latter beginning to show a
slightly ruffled surface.   Then his eye wandered towards
Ghita.   The girl had risen from her knees, and her eyes
followed his every movement.   When they met his, with a
sweet, imploring smile, she pointed upward, as if beseech-
ing him to pay the debt of gratitude he owed to that dread
Being who had, as yet, borne him unharmed through the
fray.   He understood her meaning, kissed his hand in
affectionate gallantry, and turned towards Ithuel, to pursue
the discourse.

   " It is too soon," he said.   "We are impregnable here,
and the wind is still too light.   An hour hence, and we will
all go together."

   Ithuel grumbled ; but his commander heeded it not.   The
judgment of the latter had decided right.   The boats were
rallying within musket-shot, indifferent to the danger, and
it was evident the attack was to be renewed.   To have
attempted to escape at such an instant, would have been
throwing away the great advantage of the ruins, and might
have endangered all, without benefiting any one.

   In point of fact, Sir Frederick Dashwood had become
keenly alive to a sense of the disgrace he was likely to
incur, in the event of the ship's getting round, and robbing
him of the credit of capturing the lugger.   The usually
apathetic nature of this young man was thoroughly aroused,
and, like all who are difficult to excite, he became respectable
when his energies were awakened.   The boats were already
collected ; all the disabled were put into one of them, and
ordered off to the ships ; and with those that remained

ι.rangements were made to renew the attempt. It was fortunate that Cuffe had sent an expedition so strong-handed ;
for, notwithstanding the loss, the three launches and the
cutters could still muster double the number of the French.

This time, Sir Frederick was willing to listen to counsel.
Winchester, McBean, Griffin, and Strand, united in advising
that the boats should separate, and make their assaults from
different points. This would prevent the possibility of a
recurrence of so concentrated a disaster as that which had
already befallen them. To the Scotchman, was assigned
the felucca ; the Terpsichore's launch was to assail the
lugger ; while the two cutters, and the heavier boat of the
Proserpine, were to dash in at the ruins. Sir Frederick still
remained in his own gig, to push for the point that might
seem to require his presence.

McBean was the first to fire on this occasion. He threw
a round-shot from his carronade into the felucca, aimed by
himself, and directed with care. It fell upon one of Ithuel's
carronades, broke into a dozen pieces, knocked down no less
than three men, besides injuring others less severely, and
actually drove the gun it struck off its slide into the felucca's hold. This was a rough commencement, and the result being seen by all hands, it greatly encouraged the assailants. Three hearty English cheers followed, and Ithuel
was so far disconcerted as to fire the remaining gun, loaded
as before, with bullets, at least two minutes too soon. The
sea was thrown into a foam, but not a man in the boats was
hurt. Then the fire became general ; gun after gun explod-
ing ; the rattling of small-arms filling up the pauses. The
boats came on with steady, strong pulls of the oar, and this
too with an impunity that often happens, though difficult
to be explained. Several shot fell among the ruins, knocking the stones about, and for a minute or two all the injury
was on one side. But Pintard and Ithuel felt the security
conferred by the rocks in their front, and each endeavoured
to give one effective discharge. Ithuel succeeded the best.
He repaid McBean in his own coin, sending a grist of bullets
into the bows of his launch, which admonished that prudent
officer of the necessity of sheering towards the islet of the
ruins. Pintard's assailant was brought up by the barrier in
front, and turned aside also. Then, in the midst of a cloud

35 *

of smoke, shouts, curses, cries, shrieks, orders, and the roa. of guns, all the English precipitated themselves in a body on the principal post, and became the masters of the battery in the twinkling of an eye.

CHAPTER XXIX.

"Thus doth the ever-changing course of things,
Run a perpetual circle, ever turning;
And that same day, that highest glory brings,
Brings us to the point of back-returning."

DANIEL.

In scenes like that just related, it is not easy to collect details. All that was ever known beyond the impetuous manner of the assault, in which the ruins were carried, was in the dire result. Half the French on the islet were weltering in their blood, and the surface of the rocks was well sprinkled with enemies who had not been more fortunate. It had been a desperate onset, in which mortification increased natural intrepidity, which had been nobly resisted, but in which numbers had necessarily prevailed. Among the English slain was Sir Frederick Dashwood himself; he lay about a yard from his own gig, with a ball directly through his head. Griffin was seriously hurt, but Clinch was untouched, on the low rampart, waving an English Jack —after having hauled down a similar emblem of the French. His boat had first touched the rock, her crew had first reached the ruin, and of all in her, he, himself, had taken the lead. Desperately had he contended for Jane and a commission, and, this time, Providence appeared to smile on his efforts. As for Raoul, he lay in front of his own rampart, having rushed forward to meet the party of Clinch, and had actually crossed swords with his late prisoner, when a musket-ball, fired by the hands of McBean, traversed his body.

"*Courage, mes braves! en avant!*" he was heard to shout, as he leaped the low wall, to repel the invaders—and when he lay on the hard rock, his voice was still strong enough to make itself heard, crying—" *Lieutenant—nom de Dieu—sauve mon Feu-Follet !*"

It is probable that Pintard would not have stirred, even at his order, had not the English ships been seen, at that instant, coming round Campanella, with a leading westerly wind. The flap of canvass was audible near by, too, and turning, he saw the Michael falling off, under her foresail, and already gathering steerage-way. Not a soul was visible on her decks, Ithuel, who steered, lying so close, as to be hid by her waist-cloths. The hawsers of the lugger were cut, and le Feu-Follet started back like an affrighted steed. It was only to let go the brails and her foresail fell. Light, and feeling the breeze, which now came in strong puffs, she shot out of the little bay and wore short round on her keel. Two or three of the English boats attempted to follow, but it was idle. Winchester, who now commanded, recalled them, saying, that it remained for the ships to perform their task. The day had been too bloody, indeed, to think of more than securing the present success, and of attending to the hurt.

Leaving the party on the islets for a moment, we will follow the two vessels in their attempt to escape. Pintard and his companions abandoned Raoul with heavy hearts, but they plainly saw him prostrated on the rocks, and by the hand placed on his side, understood the desperate nature of his wound. Like him, they felt some such interest as one entertains for a beloved mistress in the fate of the lugger, and the words—" *sauve mon Feu-Follet !*" were ringing in their ears.

As soon as the lugger got round, she set her after-sail, and then she began to glide through the water, with the usual knife-like parting of the element under her bows. The course she steered led her directly out of the bay, seeming to lead across the fore-foots of the English ships. Ithuel did not imitate this manœuvre. He kept more away in the line for Pæstum, rightly enough believing that in the greedy desire to overtake the lugger, his own movement would pass unheeded. The owner of this craft was still on board the Terpsichore ; but every remonstrance, and all the requests he made, that his own vessel might be followed and cap·

tured, were utterly unheeded by the lieutenant now in command. To him, as to all others in authority, there seemed to be but one thing desirable, and that was to secure the lugger. Of course none yet knew of the fatal character of the struggle on the rocks, or of the death of the English leader, though the nature of the result was sufficiently understood by seeing the English Jack flying among the ruins, and the two vessels under way, endeavouring to escape.

The season was now so far advanced as to render the old stability of the breezes a little uncertain. The zephyr had come early, and it had come fresh; but there were symptoms of a sirocco, about the barometer, and in the atmosphere. This rendered all in the ships eager to secure their prize before a shift of wind should come. Now that there were three fast vessels in chase, none doubted of the final result; and Cuffe paced the quarter-deck of the Proserpine, rubbing his hands with delight, as he regarded all the propitious signs of the times.

The Ringdove was ordered, by signal, to haul up south-south-west, or close on a wind, with a view to make such an offing as would prevent the possibility of the lugger's getting outside of the ships, and gaining the wind of them; an achievement Cuffe thought she might very well be enabled to accomplish, could she once fairly come by the wind under circumstances that would prevent any of his vessels from bringing her under their guns. The Terpsichore was directed to run well into the bay, to see that a similar artifice was not practised in that direction; while the Proserpine shaped her own course at the angle that would intercept the chase, should the latter continue to stand on.

It was an easy thing for the French to set all their canvass, the hamper of a lugger being so simple. This was soon done; and Pintard watched the result, with intense interest, well knowing that everything now depended on heels, and ignorant what might be the effect of her present trim on the sailing of his beautiful craft. Luckily, some attention had been paid to her lines, in striking in the ballast again; and it was soon found that the vessel was likely to behave well. Pintard thought her so light as to be tender; but, not daring to haul up high enough to prove her, in that way, it remained a matter of opinion only. It was enough for him that she lay so far to the west of south as to promise to clear the point of Piano, and that she skimmed along the water at a rate that bade fair to distance all three of her pursuers. Anxious to get an offing, however, which would allow him to alter his course at night in more directions than one, he kept luffing, as the wind favoured, so as sensibly to edge off the land.

As the two chases commenced their flight quite a mile to the southward of the ships, having that much the start of them on account of the position of the rocks, it rendered them both tolerably free from all danger of shot, at the beginning of the race. The course steered by Ithuel, soon placed him beyond their reach, altogether; and Cuffe knew that little would be gained, while much might be lost, in making any attempt of this sort on the lugger. Consequently, not a gun was fired; but the result was thrown fairly on the canvass, and on the sailing of the respective vessels.

Such was the state of things at the beginning of this chase. The wind freshened fast, and soon blew a strong breeze; one that drove the ships ahead, under clouds of studding-sails and stay-sails, the latter being much used at that period, at the rate of quite ten knots the hour. But neither gained on le Feu-Follet. The course was by no means favourable to her, the wind being well on her quarter; still, she rather gained, than was gained on. All four vessels went off rapidly to the southward, as a matter of course; nor was it long before they were to leeward of the felucca, which had both shortened sail, and hauled up to the eastward, as soon as Ithuel felt satisfied he was not to be followed. After a sufficient time had elapsed, the Holy Michael tacked, and came out of the bay, crossing the wake of the Terpsichore, just beyond gun-shot. Of course, this manœuvre was seen from the frigate; and the padrone of the felucca tore his hair, threw himself on the quarter-deck, and played many other desperate antics, in the indulgence of his despair, or to excite sympathy: but all in vain; the lieutenant was obstinate; refusing to alter tack or sheet to chase a miserable felucca, with so glorious an object in full view before him, as the celebrated lugger of Raoul Yvard. As a matter of course, Ithuel passed out to sea unmolested; and, it may as well be said here, that, in due time, he reached Marseilles in safety

27

where the felucca was sold, and the Granite-seaman disappeared for a season. There will be occasion to speak of him only once again, in this legend.

The trial of speed must soon have satisfied Pintard that he had little to apprehend from his pursuers, even with the breeze there was. But circumstances favoured the lugger. The wind hauled materially to the northward, and before the sun set, it enabled the French to run off wing-and-wing, still edging from the land. It now began to blow so heavily as to compel the ships to reduce their light canvass. Some time before the night set in, both frigates and the sloop were under main-top-gallant-sails only, with top-mast and lower studding-sails on each side. Le Feu-Follet made no change. Her jigger had been taken in, as soon as she kept dead away, and then she dashed ahead, under her two enormous luggs, confident in their powers of endurance. The night was not very dark; but it promised to carry her beyond the vision of her pursuers, even before eight bells, did the present difference in sailing continue.

A stern chase is proverbially a long chase. For one fast vessel to outsail another a single mile in an hour, is a great superiority; and even in such circumstances, many hours must elapse ere one loses sight of the other, by day. The three English ships held way together surprisingly, the Proserpine leading a little; while le Feu-Follet might possibly have found herself, at the end of a six hours' chase, some four miles in advance of her, three of which she had gained since keeping off, wing-and-wing. The lightness of the little craft essentially aided her. The canvass had less weight to drag after it; and Pintard observed that the hull seemed to skim the waves, as soon as the sharp stem had divided them, and the water took the bearings of the vessel. Hour after hour did he sit on the bowsprit, watching her progress; a crest of foam scarce appearing ahead, before it was glittering under the lugger's bottom. Occasionally, a pursuing sea cast the stern upward, as if about to throw it in advance of the bows; but le Feu-Follet was too much accustomed to this treatment to be disturbed, and she ever rose on the billow, like a bubble, and then the glancing arrow scarce surpassed the speed with which she hastened forward, as if to recover lost time.

Cuffe did not quit the deck until the bell struck two, in the middle watch. This made it one o'clock. Yelverton and the master kept the watches between them, but the captain was always near with his advice and orders.

"That craft seems faster when she gets her sails wing-and-wing than she is even close-hauled, it seems to me, Yelverton," observed Cuffe, after taking a long look at the chase with a night-glass; "I begin to be afraid we shall lose her. Neither of the other ships does anything to help us. Here we are all three, dead in her wake, following each other like so many old maids going to church of a Sunday morning."

"It *would* have been better, Captain Cuffe, had the Ringdove kept more to the westward, and the frigate further east. Fast as the lugger is with her wings spread, she's faster with them jammed up on a wind. I expect every moment to find her sheering off to the westward, and gradually getting us in *her* wake *on* a wind. I fear we should find that worse work than even this, sir."

"I would not lose her now, for a thousand pounds! I do not see what the d——l Dashwood was about, that he did not secure her, when he got possession of the rocks. I shall rattle him down a little, as soon as we meet."

Cuffe would have been shocked had he known that the body of Sir Frederick Dashwood was, just at that moment, going through the melancholy process of being carried on board a two-decker, up at Naples, the captain of which was his kinsman. But he did not know it, nor did he learn his death, for more than a week; or after the body had been interred.

"Take the glass, Yelverton, and look at her. To me she grows very dim — she must be leaving us, fast. Be careful to note if there are any signs of an intention to sheer to the westward."

"That can hardly be done without jibing her forward lugg —— hang me, Captain Cuffe, if I can see her at all. Ah! here she is, dead ahead as before, but as dim as a ghost. I can barely make out her canvass—she is still wing-and-wing, d——n her, looking more like the spectre of a craft, than a real thing. I lost her in that yaw, sir——I wish you would try, Captain Cuffe——do my best, I cannot find her again."

Cuffe did try, but without success. Once, indeed, he fancied he saw her but further examination satisfied him it was a mistake. So long had he been gazing at the same object, that it was easy for the illusion to pass before his mind's eye, of imagining a dim outline of the little lugger flying away, like the scud of the heavens, wing-and-wing, ever seeming to elude his observation. That night he dreamed of her, and there were haply five minutes, during which his wandering thoughts actually pourtrayed the process of taking possession, and of manning the prize.

Previously to this, however, signals were made to the other ships, ordering them to alter their courses, with a view to meet anticipated changes in that of le Feu-Follet. Lyon was sent to the westward, the Terpsichore a little easterly, while the Proserpine herself ventured so far as to steer south-west, after two o'clock. But a sudden and violent shift of wind came an hour before day. It was the expected—nay, the announced sirocco, and it brought the lugger to windward beyond all dispute. The south breeze came strong from the first puff; and, while it did not amount to a gale until the afternoon of the next day, it blew heavily, in squalls, after the first hour.

When the day dawned, the three ships were out of sight of each other. The Proserpine, which we shall accompany, as our old acquaintance, and an actor in what is to succeed, was under double-reefed topsails, with her head up as high as west-south-west, labouring along through the troughs of the seas left by the late Tramontana. The weather was thick, rain and drizzle coming in the squalls, and there were moments when the water could not be seen a cable's-length from the ship; at no time was the usual horizon fairly visible. In this manner the frigate struggled ahead, Cuffe unwilling to abandon all hopes of success, and yet seeing little prospect of its accomplishment. The look-outs were aloft, as usual, but it was as much for form as for any great use they were likely to be, since it was seldom a man could see further from the cross-trees than he could from the deck.

The officers, as well as the men, had breakfasted. A species of sullen discontent pervaded the ship, and the recent kind feelings towards Raoul Yvard had nearly vanished in disappointment. Some began to grumble about the chances of the other ships falling in with the lugger, while others swore "that it mattered not who *saw* her ; *catch* her none could, who had not an illicit understanding with the Father of Lies. She was well named the Jack-o'-Lantern ; for Jack-o'-Lantern she was, and Jack-o'-Lantern would she ever prove to be. As well might a false fire be followed in a meadow, as such a craft at sea. They might think themselves fortunate, if the officers and people sent against her in the boats ever got back to their own wholesome ship again."

In the midst of such prognostics and complaints, the captain of the fore-top shouted the words ' sail ho !' The usual inquiry and answer followed, and the officers got a glimpse of the object. The stranger was distant half a league, and he was seen very indistinctly on account of the haze ; but seen he *was.*

" 'Tis a xebec," growled the master, who was one of the grumblers of the day—" a fellow with his hold crammed with a wine that would cover the handsomest woman's face in Lunnun with wrinkles."

" By Jupiter Ammon !" Cuffe exclaimed, " 'tis the le Feu-Folly, or I do not know an old acquaintance. Quarter-master hand me the glass—not that, the shorter glass is the best."

" Long or short, you 'll never make *that* out," muttered the master. " The Folly has more folly about her than I give her credit for, if *we* get another look at her this summer."

" What do you make of him, Captain Cuffe ?" Yelverton eagerly demanded.

" Just what I told you, sir—'tis the lugger—and—I cannot be mistaken.—Ay, by Jove, she is coming down before it, wing-and-wing, again ! That's her play, just now, it would seem, and she does not appear to have got enough of it yet."

An attentive look satisfied Yelverton that his commander was right. Even the master had to confess his error, though he did it ungraciously and with reluctance. It was the lugger, of a certainty, though so dimly seen as to render it difficult, at moments, to trace her outlines at all. She was running in a line that would carry her astern of the frigate

36

about a mile, and she was rather more than thrice that distance to windward.

"She cannot see us," said Cuffe, thoughtfully. "Beyond a doubt she thinks us to windward, and is endeavouring to get out of our neighbourhood. We must get round, gentlemen, and now is a favourable moment. Tack ship, at once, Mr. Yelverton—I think she'll do it."

The experiment was made, and it succeeded. The Proserpine worked beautifully, and Yelverton knew how to humour her to a nicety. In five minutes the ship was round, with everything trimmed on the other tack ;—close-reefed mizon, and double-reefed fore and main-top-sails—a reefed main-sail, with other sails to suit. As she was kept a rap full, or a little off, indeed, to prevent the lugger from slipping past, she might have gone from five to six knots.

The next five minutes were intensely interesting to the people of the Proserpine. The weather became thicker, and all traces of le Feu-Follet were lost. Still, when last seen, she was wing-and-wing, flying rather than sailing, down towards their own track. By Cuffe's calculation, the two vessels would nearly meet in less than a quarter of an hour, should neither alter her course. Several guns were got ready, in preparation for such a rencontre.

"Let the weather hold thick a few minutes longer, and we have her!" cried Cuffe. "Mr. Yelverton, you must go down and see to those guns yourself. Plump it right into her, if you're ordered to fire. The fellow has no hamper, and stripping him must be a matter of pure accident. Make it too hot for him on deck, and he'll have to give up, Raoul Yvard, or the d—l!"

"There she is, sir!" shouted a midshipman from a cat-head—for everybody who dared had crowded forward to get an early look at the chase.

There she was, sure enough, wing-and-wing, as before. The dullness of the lugger's look-outs have never been explained, as a matter of course; but it was supposed, when all the circumstances came to be known, that most of her people were asleep, to recover from the recent extraordinary fatigue, and a night in which all hands had been kept on deck, in readiness to make sail ; the vessel having but some thirty souls in her. At length the frigate was seen, the weather lighting, and it was not an instant too soon. The two vessels, at that critical instant, were about half a mile apart, le Feu-Follet bearing directly off the Proserpine's weather-bow. In the twinkling of an eye, the former jibed; then she was seen coming to the wind, losing sufficient ground in doing so, to bring her just in a range with the two weather chase-guns. Cuffe instantly gave the order to open a fire.

"What the d—l has got into her?" exclaimed the captain,—"she topples like a mock mandarin,—she used to be as stiff as a church! What can it mean, sir?"

The master did not know, but we may say that the lugger was too light for so much canvass in such heavy weather, and there was not time to shorten sail. She lurched heavily under the sea that was now getting up, and, a squall striking her, her lee guns were completely buried. Just at this moment the Proserpine belched forth her flame and smoke. The shot could not be followed, and no one knew where they struck. Four had been fired, when a squall succeeded that shut in the chase, and, of course, the firing was suspended. So severe was this momentary effort of the African gales, hot, drowsy, and deadening as they are, that the Proserpine started her mizzen-top-sail sheets, and clewed up her main-course, to save the spar. But, the tack was instantly boarded again, and the top-sail set. A gleam of sunshine succeeded, but the lugger had disappeared!

The sun did not remain visible, and that faintly, but a minute; still, the eye could range several miles, for thrice that period. After this the horizon became more limited, but no squall occurred for a quarter of an hour. When the lugger was missed, the Proserpine was heading up within half a point of the spot at which she was supposed to be. In a short time she drove past this point, perhaps a hundred fathoms to leeward of it. Here she tacked, and stretching off a sufficient distance to the southward and westward, came round again, and heading up east-south-east, was thought to sweep along over the empty track. Not a sign of the missing vessel was discovered. The sea had swallowed all, lugger, people, and hamper. It was supposed that, owing to the fact that so many light articles had been left on the rocks, nothing remained to float. All had accompanied le Feu-Follet to the bottom. Of boats there were none, these being at the islet of the ruins, and, if any seaman swam off in the desperate attempt to save his life in the midst of the cauldron of waters, he did not succeed, or was overlooked by the English in their search. The latter, indeed, may have miscalculated their distances, and not have passed within a cable's-length of the place where the victims, if any such there were, still struggled for existence.

Cuffe, and all around him, were forcibly struck with so unlooked-for and so dire a calamity. The loss of a vessel, under such circumstances, produces an effect like a sudden death among companions. It is a fate all may meet with, and it induces reflection and sadness. Still, the English did not give up the hope of rescuing some unfortunate wretch, clinging to a spar, or supporting himself by supernatural efforts, for several hours. At noon, however, the ship squared away, and ran for Naples, before the wind, being drawn aside from her course by another chase, in which she succeeded better, capturing a sloop-of-war, which she carried in, several days later.

The first act of Cuffe, on anchoring in the fleet, was to go on board the Foudroyant, and report himself and his proceedings to the rear-admiral. Nelson had heard nothing of the result, beyond what had occurred at the islets, and the separation of the ships.

" Well, Cuffe," he said, reaching out his remaining hand, kindly, to his old Agammenon, as the other entered the cabin—" the fellow has got off, after all ! It has been a bad business, altogether, but we must make the best of it. Where do you fancy the lugger to be ?"

Cuffe explained what had happened, and put into the admiral's hand an official letter, explaining his recent success. With the last, Nelson was pleased—at the first, surprised. After a long, thoughtful pause, he went into the after-cabin, and returned, throwing a small, jack-like, flag on the floor.

" As Lyon was cruising about," he said, " and his sloop was pitching her cat-heads under, this thing was washed upon a spare anchor, where it stuck. It's a queer flag. Can it have had any connection with the lugger ?"

Cuffe looked, and he immediately recognized the little

ala e ala jack, that the Italians had described to him, in their many conversations. It was the only vestige that was ever found of the Wing-and-Wing.

CHAPTER XXX.

" How beautiful is sorrow, when 'tis drest
By virgin innocence !   It makes
Felicity in others, seem deformed."

DAVENANT.

WE must return to the rocks, and the melancholy scene they offered. Our purposes will be answered, however, by advancing the time into the evening, omitting many things that the reader can imagine, without our relating them.

It is scarcely necessary to say, that Andrea Barrofaldi, and Vito Viti, took no part in the bloody transactions we have related. When all was over, however, they drew near to the rocks, and, sitting in their boat, contemplating the sad spectacle presented within the narrow compass of the islet of the ruins, the following short dialogue occurred between them :—

" Vice-governatore," demanded the podestà, pointing to the place where Sir Frederick lay, a motionless corpse, Raoul bleeding, and others were writhing under their wounds—" do you call this reality, or is it a part of that damnable doctrine, which is enough to set the whole earth by the ears, and to turn men into tigers and hawks ?"

" I fear, neighbour Vito, this will only prove too true. I see the bodies of Sir Dashwood and Sir Smees ; and God knows how many more have this day departed for the world of spirits."

" Leaving behind them only a world of shadows," muttered Vito Viti, even that melancholy spectacle failing to draw his thoughts altogether from a discussion that had now 'asted near four-and-twenty hours. But the moment was

36 *

not propitious to argument, and the two Italians landed
This was within half-an-hour after the struggle had ceased;
and our intentions are to advance the time to the moment
mentioned in the opening of this Chapter.

We must give here, however, a rapid sketch of the proceedings that narrowed down the view to that we intend
shortly to lay before the reader. As soon as there was
leisure, Winchester made a survey of the field of battle. He
found many of his own men slain, and more wounded. Of
the French on the islet, quite half were hurt; but the mortal
wound received by their leader, was the blow that all
lamented. The surgeon soon pronounced Raoul's case to
be hopeless; and this declaration was heard with regret even
by generous enemies. The defence had been desperate;
it would have succeeded, had it been within the scope
of possibility for so few courageous men to repel double
their numbers of those who were equally brave. Both sides
had fought for honour; and, when this is the case, victory
generally awaits the strongest.

As soon as it was perceived that all the ships were likely
to be led far to leeward, in chase, the English officers felt
the necessity of acting for themselves. The medical men
had been busy from the first, and in the course of a couple
of hours, all had been done for the wounded that present
circumstances would allow. The amputations were few,
and each vessel having sent a surgeon, these were all made,
while the other appliances had been successfully used in such
cases as would be benefited by them. The day was drawing near a close, and the distance from the fleet was so great
as to call for exertion.

As soon, therefore, as the uninjured men were refreshed,
and the wounded cared for, the latter were put into the
launches, in the best manner they might be, and the cutters
took them in tow. One had no sooner received its melancholy freight, than it left the islets, on its way to the hospital-
ship of the fleet. The others succeeded, in turn; the unhurt
French willingly offering to assist in the performance of this
pious duty. At length, but three boats remained. One was
Sir Frederick's gig, which Winchester had kept for his own
particular use; another was the yawl of Andrea Barrofaldi;
and the third, the little craft in which Carlo Giuntotardi had

come from the shore. Of the French, no one remained but the surgeon of the lugger, Raoul's steward and personal attendant, and Raoul himself. If to these be added the two Italians, and their oarsmen, Carlo and his niece, with Winchester and his boat's crew, we enumerate all who now remained at the rocks.

By this time the sun had sunk below the adjacent hills, and it was necessary to decide on some course. Winchester consulted the surgeon as to the expediency of removing his patient. Could it be done, it had better be done soon.

"*Mons. lieutenant*," answered this personage a little drily, "*mon brave capitaine* has but a short time to live. He has entreated to be left here, on the scene of his glory, and in the company of that female whom he so well loved—*mais*—you are the victors"— shrugging his shoulders—"and you will do your own pleasure."

Winchester coloured and bit his lips. The idea of torturing Raoul, either in body or mind, was the last intention of one so humane, but he felt indignant at the implied suspicion. Commanding himself, notwithstanding, he bowed courteously, and intimated that he would remain himself, with his prisoner, until all were over. The Frenchman was surprised, and when he read the sympathy of the other in the expression of his countenance, he felt regret for his own distrust, and still more at having expressed it.

"*Mais, Monsieur*," he answered, "night will soon come —you may have to pass it on the rocks."

"And if we do, doctor, it is no more than we seamen are used to. Boat-service is common duty with us. I have only to wrap myself in my cloak, to enjoy a seaman's comfort."

This settled the matter, and no more was said. The surgeon, a man accustomed to the exercise of such resources, soon managed to make his dispositions for the final scene. n clearing the lugger, a hundred light articles had been thrown on the islet on which she had touched, and among others were several rude mattresses of the seamen. Two or three of these were procured, placed on the smoothest surface of the rock, and a bed formed for Raoul. The medical man, and the seamen, would have erected a tent with a sail, but this the wounded man forbade.

" Let me breathe the free air," he said—" I shall use but little of it ;—let that little be free."

It was useless to oppose such a wish, nor was there any motive for it. The air was pure, and little need be apprehended from the night, in behalf of Ghita, surrounded as they were by the pure waters of the ocean. Even when the Tramontana came, although it was cool, its coolness was not unpleasant, the adjacent hill sheltering the islets from its immediate influence.

The English seamen collected some fuel from the spare spars of the lugger, and lighted a fire on the rock where they had been found. Food of all sorts was abundant, and several casks of water had been struck out whole, as provision against a siege. Here they made coffee, and cooked enough food for the wants of all the party. The distance prevented their disturbing those who remained near Raoul, while the light of the fire, which was kept in a cheerful blaze, cast a picturesque glow upon the group around the dying man, as soon as the night had fairly set in. It superseded, too, the necessity of any lamps or torches.

We pass over all the first outpourings of Ghita's anguish, when she learned the wound of Raoul, her many and fervent prayers, and the scenes that took place during the time that the islet was still crowded with the combatants. More quiet hours succeeded when these last were gone ; and as the night advanced, something like the fixed tranquillity of settled despair followed the first emotions. When ten o'clock arrived, we reach the moment at which we wish to raise the curtain once more, in order to present the principal actors in the scene.

Raoul lay on the summit of the islet, where his eye could range over the mild waters that washed the rock, and his ear listen to the murmuring of his own element. The Tramontana, as usual, had driven all perceptible vapour from the atmosphere, and the vault of heaven, in its cerulean blue, and spangled with thousands of stars, stretched itself above him, a glorious harbinger for the future, to one who died in hope. The care of Ghita and the attendants had collected around the spot, so many little comforts as to give it the air of a room suddenly divested of sides and ceiling, but habitable and useful. Winchester, fatigued with his day's work,

nd mindful of the wish that Raoul might so naturally feel
o be alone with Ghita, had lain down on a mattress, leav-
ng orders to be called should anything occur; while the
surgeon, conscious that he could do no more, had imitated
his example, making a similar request. As for Carlo Giun-
otardi, he seldom slept; he was at his prayers in the ruins.
Andrea and the podestà paced the rock to keep themselves
warm, slightly regretting the sudden burst of humanity
which had induced them to remain.

Raoul and Ghita were alone. The former lay on his
back, his head bolstered, and his face upturned towards the
vault of heaven. The pain was over, and life was ebbing
fast. Still, the mind was unshackled, and thought busy as
ever. His heart was still full of Ghita; though his extraordinary situation, and more especially, the glorious view
before his eyes, blended certain pictures of the future, with
his feelings, that were as novel as he found them powerful.

With the girl it was different. As a woman, she had felt
the force of this sudden blow in a manner that she found
difficult to bear. Still, she blessed God, that what had
occurred, happened in her presence, as it might be; leaving
her the means of acting, and the efficacy of prayer. To say
that she did not yet feel the liveliest love for Raoul, all that
tenderness which constitutes so large a portion of woman's
nature, would be untrue; but, her mind was now made up
to the worst, and her thoughts were of another state of
being.

A long pause had occurred, in which Raoul remained
steadfastly gazing at the starry canopy above.

"It is remarkable, Ghita," he said, at length, "that I—
Raoul Yvard—the corsair—the man of wars and tempests—
fierce combats and hair-breadth escapes—should be dying
here, on this rock, with all those stars looking down upon
me, as it might be, from your heaven, seeming to smile upon
me!"

"Why not *your* heaven, as well as mine, Raoul?" Ghita
answered, tremulously. "It is as vast as He who dwells in
it—whose throne it is—and can contain all who love him.
and seek his mercy."

"Dost thou think one like me would be received into his
presence, Ghita?"

" Do not doubt it — free from all error and weakness
Himself, his Holy Spirit delights in the penitent and the sorrowful.   Oh ! dearest, dearest Raoul, if thou *would'st* but
pray !"

A gleam, like that of triumph, glowed on the face of the
wounded man ; and Ghita, in the intensity of her expectation, rose, and stood over him, her own features filled with a
momentary hope.

" Mon Feu-Follet !" exclaimed Raoul, letting the tongue
reveal the transient thought which brought the gleam of
triumph to his countenance.   " Thou, at least, hast escaped !
These English will not count thee among their victims, and
glut their eyes on thy charming proportions !"

Ghita felt a chill at her heart.   She fell back on her seat,
and continued watching her lover's countenance, with a
feeling of despair, though inextinguishable tenderness was
still crowding around her soul.   Raoul heard the movement ; and turning his head, he gazed at the girl, for quite
a minute, with a portion of that intense admiration that used
to gleam from his eyes in happier moments.

" It is better as it is, Ghita," he said,   " than that I should
live without thee.   Fate has been kind, in thus ending my
misery."

" Oh ! Raoul ! there is no fate, but the holy will of God.
Deceive not thyself, at this awful moment ; but bow down
thy proud spirit, in humility, and turn to Him for succour !"

" Poor Ghita !—Well, thine is not the only innocent mind
by millions, that hath been trammelled by priests ; and, I
suppose, what hath commenced with the beginning, will last
till the end."

" The beginning and the end, are both God, Raoul.   Since
the commencement of time, hath he established laws which
have brought about the   trials of thy life——the sadness of
this very hour."

" And dost thou think he will pardon all thy care of one
so unworthy ?"

Ghita bowed her head to the mattress over which she
leaned, and buried her face in her hands.   When the minute
of prayer, that succeeded, was over, and her face was again
raised with the flush of feeling tempered by innocence on it,
Raoul was lying on his back, his eyes riveted, again, on the

vault of heaven. His professional pursuits had led him farther into the study of astronomy than comported with his general education ; and, addicted to speculation, its facts had often seized upon his fancy, though they had failed to touch his heart. Hitherto, indeed, he had fallen into the common error of limited research, and found a confirmation of his suspicions, in the assumed grasp of his own reason. The dread moment that was so near, could not fail of its influence, however ; and that unknown future over which he hung, as it might be, suspended by a hair, inevitably led his mind into an inquiry after the unknown God.

" Dost thou know, Ghita," he asked, " that the learned of France tell us that all yonder bright stars are worlds, peopled most probably like this of our own, and to which the earth appears but as a star itself, and that, too, of no great magnitude ?"

" And what is this, Raoul, to the power and majesty of Him who created the universe ? Ah ! think not of the things of his hand, but of Him who made them !"

" Hast thou ever heard, my poor Ghita, that the mind of man hath been able to invent instruments to trace the movements of all these worlds, and hath power, even, to calculate their wanderings with accuracy, for ages to come ?"

" And dost *thou* know, my poor Raoul, what this mind of man is ?"

" A part of his nature—the highest quality ; that which maketh him the lord of earth."

" His highest quality—and that which maketh him lord of earth, in one sense, truly ; but, after all, a mere fragment —a spot on the width of the heavens—of the spirit of God himself. It is, in this sense, that he hath been made in the mage of his creator."

" Thou think'st then, Ghita, that man is God, after all."

" Raoul !—Raoul ! if thou would'st not see me die with thee, interpret not my words in this manner !"

" Would it, then, be so hard to quit life in my company, Ghita ?" To me it would seem supreme felicity were our places to be changed."

" To go whither ? Hast thou bethought thee of this, my beloved ?"

Raoul answered not for some time. His eyes were fast-

ened on a bright star, and a tumult of thought began to
crowd upon his brain.   There are moments in the life of
every man, when the mental vision obtains clearer views of
remote conclusions, equally in connection with the past and
the future, as there are days, when an atmosphere purer
than common, more readily gives up its objects to the physical organs, — leaving the mind momentarily the master,
almost without control.   One of these gleams of truth passed
over the faculties of the dying man, and it could not be altogether without its fruits.   Raoul's soul was agitated by novel
sensations.

"Do thy priests fancy that they who have known and
loved each other in this life," he asked, "will know and
love each other, in that which they fancy is to come?"

"The life that is to come, Raoul, is one all love, or one
all hatred.   That we may know each other, I try to hope;
nor, do I see any reason for disbelieving it.   My uncle is
of opinion it must be so."

"Thy uncle, Ghita?   What, Carlo Giuntotardi—he who
seemeth never to think of things around him — doth a mind
like his dwell on thoughts as remote and sublime as this?"

"Little dost thou know, or understand him, Raoul.   His
mind seldom ceases to dwell on thoughts like these; this is
the reason why earth, and all it contains, seem so indifferent."

Raoul made no answer, but appearing to suffer under the
pain of his wound, the feelings of woman so far prevailed
over Ghita's tender nature, that she had not the heart to
press even his salvation on him, at such a moment.   She
offered him soothing drinks, and nursed him with unabated
care; and when there seemed to be a cessation to his sufferings, she again passed minutes on her knees, her whole soul
absorbed in his future welfare.   An hour passed in this
manner, all on, or near the rock sleeping, overcome by
fatigue, but Ghita and the dying man.

"That star haunts me, Ghita!" Raoul at length muttered.
"If it be really a world, some all-powerful hand must have
created it.   Chance never made a world, more than chance
made a ship.   Thought — mind — intelligence must have
governed at the formation of one, as well as of the other."

For months Ghita had not known an instant as happy as

that. It appeared as if the mind of Raoul were about to extricate itself from the shallow philosophy so much in fashion, and which had hitherto deadened a nature so kind, an intellect ordinarily so clear. Could his thoughts but once take the right direction, she had strong confidence in the distinctness of their views, but most of all in the goodness of the Deity.

"Raoul," she whispered, "God is there, as he is with us, on this rock. His spirit is everywhere. Bless him!—bless him in thy soul, my beloved, and be for ever happy!"

Raoul answered not. His face was upturned, and his eye still remained riveted on that particular star. Ghita would not disturb him, but taking his hand in hers, she once more knelt, and resumed her prayers. Minute passed after minute, and neither seemed disposed to speak. At length Ghita became woman again, and bethought her of her patient's bodily wants. It was time to administer the liquids of the surgeon, and she advanced to hold them to his lips. The eye was still fastened on the star, but the lips did not meet her with the customary smile of love. They were compressed, as when the body was about to mingle in the strife of a battle, a sort of stern resolution being settled on them. Raoul Yvard was dead.

The discovery of the truth was a fearful moment to Ghita. Not a living being near her had the consciousness of her situation; all being bound in the sleep of the weary. The first feeling was that which belonged to her sex. She threw herself on the body, and embraced it wildly, giving way to those pent-up emotions, of which her lover, in his moody humours, was wont to accuse her of not possessing. She kissed the forehead, the cheeks, the pallid, stern lips of the dead; and, for a time, there was the danger that her own spirit might pass away in the paroxysm of her grief. But, it was morally impossible for Ghita to remain long under the influence of despair. Her gentle spirit had communed too long and too closely with her Heavenly Father, not to resort to his support in all the critical moments of life. She prayed, for the tenth time, that night, and arose from her knees calm, if not absolutely resigned.

The situation of Ghita was now as wildly picturesque as it was moving to her inmost spirit. All around her still slept.

37   28

and that, to the eye, as profoundly as he who was only to rise again, when the sea and the land gave up their dead. The excitement and exertions of the past day produced their reaction, and seldom did sleep exercise a more profound influence. The fire was still burning bright, on the islet of the gig-men, casting its rays fairly atwhart the ruins, the different sleepers in them, and the immoveable body of the dead. At moments, gusts of the Tramontana, which was now blowing fresh, descended so low as to fan the flames, when the glare that succeeded seemed to give a startling reality to all that surrounded the place.

Still, the girl was too highly sustained, to be moved with anything but her loss, and her restless inquietude for the departed spirit. She saw that even her uncle slept, leaving her truly alone with Raoul. Once a feeling of desertion came over her, and she was inclined to arouse some of the sleepers. She did approach the spot where the surgeon lay, and her hand was raised to stir him, when a flash of light shot atwhart the pallid countenance of Raoul, and she perceived that his eyes were still open. Drawing near, she bent over the body, gazing long and wistfully into those windows of the soul, that had so often beamed on her in manly tenderness, and she felt, like a miser with his hoarded gold, unwilling to share it with any other.

Throughout the livelong night did Ghita watch by the body of her well-beloved, now hanging over it with a tenderness no change could extinguish, now besieging heaven with her prayers. Not one awoke, to interfere with the strange happiness she felt in those pious offices, or to wound her sensibilities, by the surprise or the sneers of the vulgar. Ere the day came, she closed the eyes of Raoul with her own hands, covered his body with a French ensign, that lay upon the rock, and sat, patient and resigned, awaiting the moment when some of the others might be ready to aid her in performing the last pious offices in behalf of the dead. As a Romanist, she found a holy consolation in that beautiful portion of her church's creed, that admits of unceasing petition for the souls of the departed, even to the latest hour of earthly things.

Winchester was the first to stir. Starting up, he appeared to be astonished at the situation in which he found

himself; but a glance around told the whole truth Ad
vancing towards Ghita, he was about to inquire after the
welfare of Raoul, when, struck by the expression of her
seraphic countenance, he turned to the body, and read the
truth in the appropriate pall. - It was no time for self
upbraidings, or for reproaches to others; but arousing the
sleepers, in a subdued and respectful manner, he gave to the
place the quiet and seeming sanctity of a chapel.

Carlo Giuntotardi, soon after, begged the dead body from
the conquerors. There was no motive for denying the
request, and it was placed in a boat, and towed to the shore,
accompanied by all who had remained. The heavy sirocco
that soon succeeded, drove the waves atwhart the islet of the
ruins, effectually erasing its stains of blood, and sweeping
every trace of le Feu-Follet, and of the recent events, into
the sea.

At the foot of the Scaricatojo, the seamen constructed a
rude bier, and thus they bore the dead up that wild, and yet
lovely precipice, persevering in their good work until they
reached the cottage of Carlo Giuntotardi's sister. A little
procession accompanied the body from the first; and, Ghita
being universally known and respected among the simple
inhabitants of those heights, when it entered the street of
St. Agata, it had grown into a line that included a hundred
believers.

The convent, the empty buildings of which still crown
the summit of one of the adjacent hills, was then in existence as a religious community; and the influence of Carlo
Giuntotardi was sufficient to procure its offices in behalf
of the dead. For three days and nights did the body of
Raoul Yvard, the unbeliever, lie in the chapel of that holy
fraternity, his soul receiving the benefit of masses; and then
it was committed to holy ground, to await the summons of
the last trump.

There is a strange disposition in the human breast to
withhold praise from a man when living, that is freely
accorded to him when dead. Although we believe that
envy, and its attendant evil, detraction, are peculiarly demo-
cratic vices, meaning thereby that democracy is the most
fertile field in which these human failings luxuriate, yet is
here much reason to think that our parent nation is pre-

eminent in the exhibition of the peculiarity first mentioned.
That which subsequently awaited Napoleon, after his im-
prisonment and death, was now exhibited in the case of
Raoul Yvard, on a scale suited to his condition and renown.
From being detested in the English fleet, he got to be
honoured and extolled.   Now that he was dead and harm
less, his seamanship could be praised, his chivalry emulated,
his courage glorified.   Winchester, McBean, O'Leary, an
Clinch, attended his funeral, quite as a matter of course
They had proved themselves worthy to be there; but many
others insisted on being of the party.   Some came to get a
last look of so celebrated an adventurer, even in his coffin ;
others to say they had been present; and not a few to catch
a glimpse of the girl whose romantic, but innocent passion,
had got to be the subject of much discourse in the ships.
The result was such a procession, and such funeral honours,
as threw the quiet little hamlet of St. Agata into commotion.   All noted the particulars, and all were pleased but
Ghita.   On her, these tardy compliments failed of their
effect, her soul being engrossed with the great care of
petitioning heaven in behalf of the deceased.

Andrea Barrofaldi and Vito Viti, too, figured on this
occasion ; the latter taking care to let all who would listen,
understand how closely he had been connected with "Sir
Smees;" no longer viewed as an impostor, but honoured as
a hero.   He even created a little difficulty in claiming a
precedency for the *toga* over arms on the occasion; well
knowing that if the vice-governatore got a conspicuous
place in the ceremony, that the podestâ could not fail to be
near at hand.   The matter was settled entirely to Andrea's
satisfaction, if not to that of his friend.

To confess the truth, Nelson was not sorry for what had
occurred.   When he learned the desperate nature of Raoul's
defence, and heard some traits of his liberal conduct on
various occasions, he felt a generous regret at his death,
but he thought even this preferable to escape.   When Cuffe
got in, and brought the report of the lugger's fate, though he
would have preferred her capture, the common sentiment
settled down into a feeling that both lugger and commander
had fared as well as a privateer and her people usually
merited.

As a matter of course, those concerned in the capture, and who survived the affair, reaped some advantages from their success. England seldom fails in the duty of confer ring rewards, more especially in her marine. When Cook returned from his renowned voyages, it was not to meet with persecution and neglect, but credit and justice. Nelson knew how to appreciate that spirit and enterprise, which were so often exercised by himself. As for Sir Frederick Dashwood, little could be done besides giving his name an honourable place on the list of those who had fallen in battle. His heir wore mourning, seemed filled with sorrow, and inwardly rejoiced at being a baronet with some thousands a year. Lyon got his ship, and, from that moment, he ceased to consider the chase and all connected with le Feu-Follet an unprofitable thing. Airchy followed him to the Terpsichore, with visions of prize-money before his eyes, which were tolerably realized in the course of the succeeding five years.

Winchester was promoted into the Ringdove, and Griffin became first of the Proserpine. This, of course, made Yelverton second, and left one vacancy. Thus far the orders had been made out, when Cuffe dined with the Admiral, by invitation, tête-à-tête.

" One of my objects in having you here to-day, Cuffe,' observed Nelson, as they sat together over their wine, the cabin cleared, " was to say something about the vacant berth in your gun-room, and the other was to beg a master's-mate of you, in behalf of Berry. You remember that some of your people were received on board here, before you got in, the other day ?"

" I do, my lord; and I meant to make my acknowledg. ments for the favour. The poor fellows had a warm time of it at the rocks, and deserved comfortable berths after it was over."

" I believe we gave them as much—at least, I know few suffer in this ship. Well, there was a mate among them, who is a little advanced, and who is likely to stick where he is, by what I learn. We want just such a man for the hold, and I have promised my Captain to speak to you about him. Don't let him go if there 's any reason for wishing to retain

37 *

him; but we have three seamen ready to exchange against
him; good fellows too, they tell me."

Cuffe picked some nuts, and appeared a little at a loss for
a reply. Nelson saw this, and he fancied the other reluctant to give up his mate.

"Well, I see how it is," he said, smiling. "We must do
without him, and you will keep your Mr. Clinch. A thorough
officer in a ship's hold is an advantage not to be thrown
away; and I suppose, if Hotham had asked such a thing of
old Agamemnon, he might have whistled for the favour.
The deuce is in it, if we do not get as good a mate somewhere!"

"It's not that, my lord—you're welcome to the man,
though a better, in his station, cannot be had. But, I was
in hopes his recent good conduct, and his long services, might
give him a lift into the vacant gun-room berth."

The Admiral appeared surprised, while he did not seem
to be exactly pleased.

"It has a hard look, I grant you, Cuffe, to keep a poor
devil ten or fifteen years in the same station, and this, too,
after he has served long enough for a commission. I was
a captain ten years younger than this Mr. Clinch must be
to-day, and it does *seem* hard; and yet I doubt not it is just.
I have rarely known a midshipman or a mate passed over, in
this way, that there was not some great fault at the bottom
We must think of the service, as well as of generosity."

"I confess all this, my lord—and yet I did hope poor
Clinch's delinquencies would at length be forgotten."

"If there are any particular reasons for it, I should like
to hear them."

Cuffe now related all that had passed between himself and
the master's-mate; taking care to give Jane a due place in
his history. Nelson began to twitch the stump of his arm,
and by the time the story was told, Clinch's promotion was
settled. An order was sent forthwith, to the secretary, to
make out the orders, and Cuffe carried them back with him
to the Proserpine that night, when he returned to his own
ship.

All Nelson's promotions were confirmed by the Admiralty,
pretty much as a matter of course. Among others was that
of Clinch, who now became the junior lieutenant of the Pro-

serpine. This elevation awakened new feelings within him. He dressed better; refrained from the bottle; paid more attention to his mind; improved in manners, by keeping better company; and, in the course of the next twelvemonth, had made rapid advances towards respectability. At the end of that time, the ship was sent home; and Jane, in her imagination at least, received the reward of all her virtuous constancy, by becoming his wife. Nor did Cuffe cease his friendly offices, here. He succeeded in getting Clinch put in command of a cutter; in which he captured a privateer, after a warm action, within a month. This success procured him a gun-brig, and with her he was still more fortunate; actually cutting out, with her boats, a French sloop-of-war, that was not half manned, it is true, but which was still considered a handsome prize. For this affair he got the sloop; thus demonstrating the caprice of fortune, by whose means he found himself a commander in less than three years after he had been a mate. Here he stuck, however, for a long time, until he got another sloop in fair fight, when he was posted. From that moment we have lost sight of him.

Cuffe being sent into the Gulf of Genoa, shortly after, seized the opportunity to restore the vice-governatore and his friend to their native island. The fame of their deeds had preceded them, exaggerated, as a matter of course, by the tongue of rumour. It was understood that the two Elbans were actually in the fight, in which Raoul Yvard fell; and, there being no one to deny it, many even believed that Vito Viti, in particular, had killed the corsair with his own hand. A discreet forbearance on the part of the podestà always kept the matter so completely involved in mystery that we question if any traveller who should visit the island, even at this day, would be able to learn more than we now tell the reader. In a word, the podestà, for ever after, passed for a hero, through one of those mysterious processes by which men sometimes reach fame; quite as much, perhaps, to their own astonishment, as to the surprise of everybody else.

As for Ithuel, he did not appear in America for many years. When he did return, he came back with several thousand dollars; how obtained no one knew, nor did he

choose to enter into particulars.   He now married a widow,
and settled in life.   In due time he " experienced religion,"
and, at this moment, is an active abolitionist, a patron of the
temperance cause, tee-totally, and a general terror to evil-
doers, under the appellation of Deacon Bolt.

It was very different with the meek, pious and single-
minded Ghita ; though one was e'en a Roman Catholic,
and the ‑ other a Protestant, and that, too, of the Puritan
school.   Our heroine had little of this world left to live for.
She continued, however, to reside with her uncle, until his
days were numbered ; and then she retired to a convent,
not so much to comply with any religious superstitions, as
to be able to pass her time, uninterrupted, in repeating
prayers for the soul of Raoul.   To her latest hour, and she
lived until quite recently, did this pure-minded creature
devote herself to what she believed to be the eternal welfare
of the man who had so interwoven himself with her virgin
affections, as to threaten, at one time, to disturb the just
 scendency of the dread Being who had created her.

CPSIA information can be obtained
at www.ICGtesting.com
Printed in the USA
BVHW081613220819
556561BV00018B/4012/P